Putting Health into Place

Space, Place, and Society
John Rennie Short, *Series Editor*

Putting Health into Place

Landscape, Identity, and Well-being

Edited by
Robin A. Kearns
and Wilbert M. Gesler

SU Syracuse University Press

Syracuse, New York 13244-5160

First Edition 1998
98 99 00 01 02 03 6 5 4 3 2 1

The paper used in this publication meets the minimum requirements of American National Standard for Information Sciences—Permanence of Paper for Printed Library Materials, ANSI Z39.48-1984. ∞™

Library of Congress Cataloging-in-Publication Data

Putting health into place : landscape, identity, and well-being / edited by Robin A. Kearns and Wilbert M. Gesler. — 1st ed.
p. cm. — (Space, place, and society)
Includes bibliographical references and index.
ISBN 0-8156-2767-X (cloth : alk. paper). — ISBN 0-8156-2768-8 (pbk. : alk. paper)
1. Medical geography. 2. Human geography. 3. Social medicine. I. Kearns, Robin A., 1959– . II. Gesler, Wilbert M., 1941– . III. Series.
RA792.P88 1998
614.4'2—dc21 97-36239

Manufactured in the United States of America

Contents

Illustrations vii

Preface ix

Contributors xi

1. Introduction
ROBIN A. KEARNS AND WILBERT M. GESLER 1

PART ONE
Therapeutic Landscapes

2. Bath's Reputation as a Healing Place
WILBERT M. GESLER 17

3. Surviving on Metaphor
How "Health = Hot Springs" Created and Sustained a Town
MARTHA E. GEORES 36

4. Landscapes of State Violence and the Struggle to Reclaim Community
Mental Health and Human Rights in Iquique, Chile
LESSIE JO FRAZIER AND JOSEPH L. SCARPACI 53

PART TWO
Identity, Difference, and Health

5. Place, Identity, and Disability
Narratives of Intellectually Disabled People in Toronto
GLENDA LAWS AND JOHN RADFORD 77

6. Women with Disabilities and Everyday Geographies
Home Space and the Contested Body
ISABEL DYCK 102

7. Homeless Health and Service Needs
An Urban Political Economy of Service Distribution
JONGGYU LEE, JENNIFER R. WOLCH, AND JESSICA WALSH 120

8. Concepts of Difference in Community Health
LOIS M. TAKAHASHI 143

9. The Relevance of Place in HIV Transmission and Prevention
The Commercial Sex Industry in Madras
SHEENA ASTHANA 168

PART THREE
Place, Policy, and Well-being

10. Making Connections Between Housing and Health
SOPHIE HYNDMAN 191

11. Smoking, Stigma, and the Purification of Public Space
BLAKE D. POLAND 208

12. "Going It Alone"
Place, Identity and Community Resistance to Health Reforms in Hokianga, New Zealand
ROBIN A. KEARNS 226

13. Place, Participation, and Policy
People in and for Health-Care Policy
JOHN EYLES AND ANDREÀ LITVA 248

14. Place, Space, and Health Service Reform
GRAHAM MOON AND TIM BROWN 270

15. Conclusion
ROBIN A. KEARNS AND WILBERT M. GESLER 289

References 297

Index 337

Illustrations

Tables

5.1	Intellectually Disabled Sample Characteristics	84
7.1	Homeless Service Programs, Los Angeles County, 1992	126
7.2	Subregional Distribution of Homeless Shelter/Services, Los Angeles County	129
7.3	Regression Analysis of Shelter/Service Distribution, Los Angeles County	132
7.4	Service-Rich and Service-Poor Subregions, Los Angeles County	134
8.1	Hierarchy of Acceptance, 1970	148
8.2	Hierarchy of Acceptance, 1980	149
8.3	Demographic Characteristics of National Sample Comparison with U.S. Census	152
8.4	National Hierarchy of Acceptance	153
8.5	Acceptance for Homeless Shelters by Sociodemographic and Spatial Characteristics	155
8.6	Regional Ranking by Facility Type	158
8.7	National Dimensions of Behavior Toward Facilities	159
10.1	Studies of Housing Dampness and Health	197
12.1	Aims of the Hokianga Health Enterprise Trust	240

Figures

4.1. Clandestine grave sites in Chile created during Pinochet regime, 1973–1990 55
7.1. Hierarchy of homeless shelter/services 124
7.2. Distribution of gatekeeper service programs by subregion and community, Los Angeles County 130
7.3. Adjusted distribution of gatekeeper service programs by subregion and community, Los Angeles County 135
9.1. Recorded HIV positive cases per million population, India, June 1994 174
9.2. HIV positive cases per 10,000 cases screened for HIV infection, India, June 1994 175
9.3. Distribution of commercial sex outlets in Madras 183
10.1 Definitions of housing 194
10.2. Associations between housing and health 205
12.1. Hokianga in its regional context 235

Preface

This book has its origins in a conversation between the editors at the Fifth International Symposium in Medical Geography, held in Charlotte, North Carolina, in August 1992. Wilbert Gesler had presented material on "therapeutic landscapes" and Robin Kearns had discussed space and place in medical geography. We recognized that our work was part of an expanding of the horizons of medical geography but that contributions to this expansion remained scattered in disparate journals and conference proceedings. We perceived the need for a resource for teaching and research that would add momentum to these theoretical directions and present case studies of specific instances of the links between place and health in policy and lived experience. In the years between when the idea for the book was developed and its publication, interest in health geographies has increased. The launching of the journal *Health and Place* in 1995 has added to this momentum. In this book we express the commitment of a community of scholars to extend the boundaries of medical geography, to (re)place health concerns within the broader projects of social and cultural geography, and to embrace new directions without necessarily discarding established routes.

Sadly, one of our contributors, Glenda Laws, died suddenly during the preparation of this book. Glenda was an active and enthusiastic contributor to theoretical debates that have helped reshape medical geography. She is missed by us all, and it is our hope that this book will contribute to the memory of Glenda's contribution to health geography.

Any research—even sole authored work—is, if we are honest, the product of team effort. Invariably, secretarial, cartographic, or computing staff provide advice, if not direct assistance. Given the range of chapters in this volume, we cannot recognize all by name. We record, however, collective appreciation to all who might otherwise remain unacknowledged in the process of authorship. We particularly thank Jan Kelly and Frances Fernandez of the University of Auckland Department of Geography for cartographic and secretarial assistance. We also thank Graham Moon and Michael Hayes for suggestions and encouragement, those colleagues who kindly agreed to act as anonymous reviewers of contributed chapters, and our spouses, Pat and Joyce, for forbearance amid the preoccupations of editorial work.

Contributors

Sheena Asthana is senior lecturer in social policy at the University of Plymouth, U.K. Her research interests include the role of community participation in health development, women's health and HIV/AIDS, with a focus on India.

Tim Brown is a researcher at the University of Portsmouth. He is completing a Ph.D. on official discourses concerning HIV/AIDS and has interests in poststructuralist approaches to the geography of health.

Isabel Dyck is associate professor at the School of Rehabilitation Sciences, University of British Columbia. She has a masters in social anthropology and a doctorate in geography. Her publications include a number of articles concerning women with disabilities, cultural issues in health care research, and feminist methodologies.

John Eyles holds a research chair in environmental health and is professor of geography at McMaster University. He holds concurrent appointments in clinical epidemiology and biostatistics; in sociology; and at the Centre of Health Economics and Policy Analysis. His research interests include community decision-making processes, resource allocation strategies, environmental health policy analysis, and the determinants of health.

Lessie Jo Frazier is a doctoral student in anthropology at the University of Michigan. She has undertaken research in both the United States and Chile, examining indigenous rights and the human rights movement in those places, respectively.

Martha E. Geores is assistant professor in the Department of Geography, University of Maryland, College Park. She has published on environmental issues in developing countries and has a forthcoming book, "Common Ground: Struggle for Ownership of the Black Hills."

Wilbert M. Gesler is professor in geography at the University of North Carolina, Chapel Hill. His publications include more than twenty refereed journal articles on largely health care concerns and two books, including, *The Cultural Geography of Health Care* (1991).

Sophie Hyndman is a research associate with the Health Services Research Group at the University of Cambridge. Her doctorate from the University of London examined housing dampness and health in East London, and this research was followed by a period as research officer for the Royal College of Nursing. She has published a range of papers on the housing and health theme.

Robin A. Kearns is senior lecturer in geography at the University of Auckland where he teaches and researches in social and cultural geography. He has published more than forty refereed journal articles on topics ranging across primary health care, mental health, housing policy, maternity services, and philosophical orientations to geographies of health.

Glenda Laws was associate professor of geography and women's studies at Pennsylvania State University. At the time she was preparing her chapter, her research focused on urban social geography and the construction of elderly identities.

Jonggyu Lee undertook graduate work at Seoul National University and the University of Southern California. He is currently senior researcher at the Seoul Development Institute and is investigating postmodern urbanism.

Andreà Litva undertook graduate studies at McMaster University where her research was on the impacts of space on lay perceptions of health and illness. She currently holds a research fellowship at the University of Portsmouth.

Graham Moon is professor of Health Services Research at the University of Portsmouth, U.K. He is coauthor of *Health, Disease and Society* (with Kelvyn Jones) and founding editor of the journal *Health and Place*. His current research concerns concepts of place in health policy and comparative health policy.

Blake D. Poland is assistant professor of behavioral science at the University of Toronto and an affiliate scientist at the Addiction Research Foundation of Canada. His teaching and research interests center on qualitative approaches to community health promotion interventions and developing critical social science perspectives on health promotion research.

John Radford is associate professor in geography at York University, Toronto. He has published widely on class and race in nineteenth-century cities, especially Charleston, South Carolina. He has also written on constructs of disability during the asylum era.

Joseph L. Scarpaci is associate professor of urban affairs and planning at Virginia Polytechnic and State University in Blacksburg, Virginia. His research focuses on comparative urban social policy and political economy with special attention to Latin America. He edited *Health Services Privatization in Industrial Societies* (Rutgers University Press) and has recently completed a coauthored book on Havana, Cuba.

Lois M. Takahashi is assistant professor in the Department of Urban and Regional Planning at the University of California-Irvine. Her research interests include attitudes toward homelessness and people with AIDS, community opposition, and the linkages between local mobilization and community health.

Jessica Walsh is a graduate student in the Department of Geography, University of Southern California. Her research focuses on the daily lives of service-dependent families in Los Angeles.

Jennifer R. Wolch is professor of geography at the University of Southern California. She has researched problems of service-dependent people, social policy and human service delivery, and examined the role of the nonprofit sector in the U.S. welfare state. She is coauthor of *Malign Neglect: Homelessness in an American City* with Michael Dear.

Putting Health into Place

1

Introduction

ROBIN A. KEARNS AND WILBERT M. GESLER

Until recently the subdisciplinary label *medical geography* has served to describe those geographers interested in the spatial implications of a range of topics relating to human disease and health and to health care service provision as well. Through the 1980s and into the 1990s, however, medical concerns have become but one necessary, but increasingly insufficient, focus in an emerging geography of health and healing. This book represents a contribution to this expanding of horizons at the intersection of the discipline of geography and the field of health.

The purpose of the book is both intellectual and pedagogic. We have assembled a range of contributions that acknowledge the importance of *theory,* something that most medical geographers have until recently left implicit in their work (Litva and Eyles 1995). Our goal has been to present a range of chapters that self-consciously deal with *health* concerns situated in the context of *place.* In so doing we advance the idea of a reformed medical geography. We use the word *idea* strategically, for this book does not and cannot, outline the definitive shape of a "post-medical geography of health" (Kearns 1993). Rather we provide a resource for those keen themselves to explore, or to teach, beyond the implicit frontiers of medical geography as outlined in earlier texts (e.g., Meade, Florin, and Gesler 1988). We believe that the subdiscipline conventionally known as medical geography is in the transitional phase of a paradigm shift, and this book represents a marker within that change.

The emergent shift in name from "medical geography" to "geography of health" is not a matter of mere semantics. Rather, in the same vein as the seriousness with which places are named, the naming of a field of inquiry is a form of norming (Berg and Kearns 1996). In other words, the name of an endeavor loosely implies the norms of content, epistemology, and research practices. The implications of using our preferred alternative, the "geography of health," are threefold. First, it more faithfully names the focal interests of a community of scholars, a proportion of whom are represented in this volume. This community comprises well-established scholars who have either advocated a reformed medical geography for some time or have more recently taken this new path and several "new voices" among those embarking on their academic careers. Second, the name change places geographers—symbolically as well as practically—closer to the range of social scientists, policy analysts, and planners who evaluate the status of population health and the adequacy of services established to enhance human well-being. Anyone who has read the literature in the social sciences of health and disease over recent years cannot help but be struck by the degree to which mainstream medical geography has lagged behind changes in theoretical perspective. Third, and most fundamentally, the name change legitimates what geographers have for some time been doing: moving beyond the driving metaphors of medicine and disease to embrace issues generated by emerging models of health and disease (in which disease and illness are necessary but not sufficient considerations) (Kearns 1994, 1995). Notwithstanding concern with its more slippery definition (Barrett 1986), health is an attractive rallying point for geographical inquiry, opening research opportunities that move beyond illness and medical interventions to a state of becoming that takes place *in place*.

The "Theoretical Turn" and the Reinvention of Medical Geography

Medical geographers have not been accustomed to thinking in the theory-laden terms of society and space. Rather, the roots of this field are firmly grounded in applied work that focuses on geographic concepts such as central place theory or distance decay and uses such spatial analytic techniques as mapping or location-allocation modeling. Many practitioners retain this orientation. As argued elsewhere, progress in medical geography has tended to be pragmatic rather than theoretical (Kearns 1995). This book represents an expression of the scope of a more progressive medical geography—a medical geography released from the shadow of medicine and reinvented as geographies of health and healing.

Despite the strong influence of social and cultural theory upon other fields of human geography (e.g., Cloke, Philo, and Sadler 1991; Gregory, Martin, and Smith 1994), medical geography has remained relatively immune to this "theoretical turn." The failure to acknowledge and absorb the theoretical influences at large elsewhere in human geography and within the social sciences in general is perplexing, for many of these influences concern the very sites of inquiry for medical geographers—clinics, bodies, landscapes, professions. The dominant tendency has been for people to be viewed as patients, diseases to be disembodied from human subjects, and for geographies of disease and health care to be reduced to dots on maps (Dyck and Kearns 1995).

The apparent aversion of medical geographers to explore the theoretical directions recently imported into geography from elsewhere in the social sciences may well be explained by the subdiscipline's (modernist) concern with explanation and its conflation of explanation with understanding. Overlain on this issue of *epistemology* is the question of *method*. A predominant reliance on quantitative and formal survey-based methods to the neglect of ethnographic and other interpretative methodologies has ensured that, until recently, more nuanced geographies of health and place have been ignored as either invisible or irrelevant.

Although a few geographers have invoked theoretically innovative perspectives such as poststructuralism in their writings about health (e.g., Philo 1986), it is only recently that an engagement with social and cultural theory has been explicitly addressed and an emerging geography of health made more evident (Moon 1995). A recent impetus to putting health into place were papers by Kearns (1993) and Kearns and Joseph (1993) in which they sought explicitly to connect conventional concerns of medical geography with more theoretically reflective views of society and space (Dear and Wolch 1989), and in-place experience (Relph 1976; Eyles 1985). Whereas the latter view emphasized the agency of people in creating their own meanings and experiences, the former perspective (more influenced by political economy) recognized the influential power of institutional and economic structures. Thus, the well-established agency/structure dualism introduced to geography one decade earlier (Thrift 1983) was, at least implicitly, brought to bear on health issues.

These papers were by no means the first attempts to infuse medical geography with broader theoretical concerns. Mayer (1982) explored the links between medical geography's logical positivist heritage with the well-established perspectives of realism (Sayer 1984) and structuration (Giddens 1984). Later, Jones and Moon (1987) employed Marxist explanations of health status inequalities and invoked critical realism (Bhaskar 1975) to reinterpret social epidemiology and to recognize the reflexive relationships between experience, events, and societal structure. In another paper, written in the wake of geography's cultural turn, (Moon 1990) explored the links between community, meaning and structuration. We see the present book as consolidating and extending some of these pioneering syntheses.

The contemporary retheorization of medical geography is most starkly reflected in the debate that followed the publication of Robin Kearns's (1993) advocacy of a reformed medical geography. One pair of commentators dismissed this call for reform on the basis of the perceived adequacy of the disease ecology concept (Mayer and Meade 1994). As applied in practice, however, the disease ecology concept remains largely atheoretical and focused on explanation rather than understanding. Others who responded to Kearns in the *Professional Geographer* agreed with the call for more sensitive readings of place and health and went further in identifying the politicization of the body as one promising direction for a reinvented medical geography (Dorn and Laws 1994). Two observations can be drawn from this invocation of postmodernity and poststructuralism: first, at least implicitly, it drew a closer link between an emerging geography of health and current emphases in the sociology of health and illness (e.g., Nettleton 1995); second, it indicated the distance between medical geography and other currents at large in social and cultural geography. The process of "putting health into place" that concerns this volume, therefore, reconnects the activities of geographers interested in health with not only other colleagues in human geography but also with scholars exploring health elsewhere in the social sciences.

Putting Health into Place

As the first word of our title suggests, we see this as an active volume, one that is part of the process of situating health in the simultaneously tangible, negotiated, and experienced realities of place. Our contributors are among those striving to develop a greater theoretical awareness in their work and, in so doing, to craft the contours of an emergent geography of health. One of the key implications of putting health into place is that a reinvented medical geography must be *social,* given that diseases, service delivery systems, and health polices are socially produced, constructed, and transmitted. As a consequence, we hold that investigations of health and disease should have social relevance. Whereas cultural perspectives on the geography of health have been developed with little comment (Gesler 1991), there have been objections to a self-consciously social medical geography (Mayer and Meade 1994). This book represents a collective commitment to exploring links between social and cultural theory, ideas about place, and discourses on health. Although the chapters represent a diversity of perspectives and themes, within that diversity lies a unity of concern that biomedical concerns issues are a necessary, but not sufficient, component of emergent geographies of health and healing.

Conventionally, there have been two parallel streams of concern in medical geography: disease ecology and health care provision. Until recently, little scholarly interaction between the "two traditions of medical geography" (Mayer 1982) was apparent. With few exceptions (e.g., Pyle and Lauer 1975), there was little interweaving of these streams, which was, perhaps, an echo of the way in which disease research and service planning are largely disconnected concerns for medicine itself. Recently, as the subdiscipline has begun to emerge from within the shadow of medicine, the twin streams of medical geography have changed course and in so doing have mixed with theoretical undercurrents at play within the social sciences (Kearns 1995).

Of central concern in this admixture has been the relationship between *place* and *health.* In their plural form places have long held the fascination of geographers, and the tradition of geographer-as-explorer has bestowed an occupational heritage, endorsing the cataloging of places and their characteristics. The ultimate expression of the geographer's vocation was the reduction of place to a location, a dot on a map. For medical geographers places were where disease agents, vectors, hosts, and culture traits came together or where facilities such as hospitals were located. Whereas places-as-locations (within space conceived as a container) is, therefore, no new concern for geographers, a renewed appreciation of the singularly expressed *place* is.

Beginning in the 1970s, the so-called humanist geographers raised questions concerning the meanings and values that were generated between people and place through the medium of experience. Whereas behavioral geography had effectively made the interactive link between people and place in terms of action and perception, humanists gave currency not only to the full range of senses (e.g., Porteous 1985) but also to dimensions of existence most off-limits to positivist science: emotions, feelings, and spirituality (Buttimer 1974; Relph 1976). For the purpose of making the link between place and health the most useful articulation of place was offered by John Eyles (1985). Sense of place, he proposed, is an interactive relationship between daily experience of a (local) place and perceptions of one's place-in-the-world. This conceptualization sees place as simultaneously center of lived meaning and social position. Place involves an interactive link between social status and material conditions and can be used to interpret a range of situated health effects that imply a link between mind, body, and society.

Within medical geography it has been claimed that existing paradigms satisfactorily accommodate emergent relational views of place (Mayer and Meade 1994). We believe that this is not the case. For the disease ecology tradition it is *disease* that is the fundamental empirical reality and the starting point of inquiry. Although places have been factored into disease-ecologic analyses, place is more than a sum of its parts (Kearns 1994), and it is only the subsumption of medical issues into a broader social perspective that can explain the range of geographical outcomes from inequalities in health (Hayes 1995) to the experience of illness itself (Dyck 1995). For although the biomedical dimensions of such harsh realities as disease, infirmity, and death cannot be denied, there are profoundly *social* ways in which each of these experiences is constructed. The way one sees the world will be largely predicated by the categories that are given preeminence, and we believe that a perspective that uncompromisingly starts with the social and cultural opens horizons to see richer connections between experience, health, and place.

Landscape, Identity, and Well-being

In this section we briefly sketch the theoretical foundations of the three parts of this volume. For each part, we offer basic definitions and discuss the principal underlying perspectives. Thus, our *landscape* focus arises from the concerns of the "new" cultural geography, *identity* relates to certain aspects of postmodernism, and *well-being* is treated in terms of the World Health Organization's well-known definition and critiques of it.

Landscape

The most fundamental concepts are often the most difficult to define, and the word *landscape* is no exception. In everyday speech one talks about enjoying natural landscapes, about landscaping gardens, or about the political landscape. As Gillian Rose (1993) has pointed out, the apparent simplicity of this term—epitomized in seventeenth-century European pastoral scenes—belies origins that are profoundly gendered and classed. For what is seen or depicted in a landscape is very dependent on one's vantage point, and the Dutch painters who pioneered landscape painting carefully selected the objects (e.g., people, houses, and natural features) that were included in any vista. Landscape, however, involves as much what is *ex*cluded as what is *in*cluded in view or perception. This observation is crucially important in developing the connection between landscape and health, for people can believe a place to be healthy when, from their perspective, there is simply an absence of unhealthy elements.

Geographers have used the term *cultural landscape* in three important ways that have a bearing on health. The *first* involves the human transformation of the earth, and this use stems from the Sauerian or Berkeley school of cultural geography. The primary goal of many geographers influenced by this tradition has been to study ways in which societies over time have molded the physical landscape to suit their needs by practicing various forms of agriculture, building cities, or constructing sacred sites. The emphasis is on the material aspects of culture, those objects that are visible in the landscape. From this first perspective a site might be perceived to be healthy if there is a good source of groundwater, and this might be enhanced by the building of a well. The observer, in this case, is objective and an outsider looking in at a scene.

It is this sense of detachment and presumed innocence on the part of the researcher that has recently been questioned by cultural geographers, most prominently Peter Jackson (1993). Indeed, in *Maps of Meaning* (1989) he points to the *second* important aspect of cultural landscape—the recognition that landscape is as much in the head as in the eyes and is ultimately a personal, mental construct. This emphasis on meaning recognizes that one is implicated in a cultural landscape through being an insider, and an active agent in inventing places (Anderson and Gale 1992). Thus, a hospital that may appear to be a neutral element in the urban fabric before an accident may well be reinvented as part of a landscape of fear after a stay that included surgery. To develop this aspect of meaning in their work cultural geographers have sought to obtain insider's perspectives and to uncover the meanings which landscapes have for people, and which symbols are important for them.

A *third* perspective on cultural landscapes is that they are the product of a particular society, the constructions of people living in a particular place and time. Thus, landscape is a social construct that arises from the institutions a society establishes. As these institutions change, so does the landscape and people's perceptions of it. The structuralist or materialist perspective that informs this aspect of the cultural landscape tells one, for instance, that the actual physical content and meaning of precapitalist and capitalist societies are very different (Daniels and Cosgrove 1988). In the example of the location of a hospital this perspective adds political and economic conflicts and negotiations to the traditional medical geographical concerns of, say, distance minimization.

These three perspectives on landscape have given rise to the concept of therapeutic landscape (Gesler 1992; 1993). Therapeutic landscapes are places that have achieved lasting reputations for providing physical, mental, and spiritual healing. The factors that contribute to this reputation vary a great deal over space and time, but some common features appear to persist. These features include such natural characteristics as magnificent scenery, water, and trees; human constructions such as healing temples or spa baths; contributions to sense of place such as feelings of warmth, identity, rootedness, or authenticity; symbolic features such as healing myths; the incorporation of familiar, daily routines into the treatment process; sensitivity to cultural beliefs; and an atmosphere in which social distance and social inequalities are kept to a minimum.

Identity

The identity of geographical work on health has recently undergone change, and part of this change has involved taking greater account of the ways that health status and personal identity are mutually reinforcing characteristics. By *identity* we mean personal and collective self-perceptions that can be summarized as "place-in-the-world." As Eyles (1985) argues, the geographical concept of place can be central to this self-ascription with experienced place both contributing to and being influenced by perceived place-in-the-world.

Further background to our interest in identity is warranted. Unlike the sociology of health (Fox 1993), a self-consciously postmodern geography of health has yet to emerge (Kearns 1995). Postmodern consequences (Dear and Wassmandorf 1993), however, are beginning to be evident in the field. We acknowledge that postmodernism is a highly contested term, but for present purposes we see two important consequences of its influence in the work of geographers interested in health: first, the rejection of "decisive theoretical argument or self-evident truth" (Dear 1994, 2) and, second, the endorsement of difference and the experience of "others." These are related influences. The dominant biomedical model has a tendency to (mis)represent the *persons* who experience illness (or seek health) as *patients.* This distortion not only casts their personhood under what Foucault (1973) calls the professional "gaze" of medicine but also frequently overlooks the issue of *difference* that pervades health experience and that has increasingly prevailed in contemporary social thought (Young 1990).

Increasingly, intellectual space is being made for difference among geographers and the construction of narratives concerned with health as it is experienced in place is one route taken by geographers to develop this space (Kearns 1997). The case studies included in our book contributes to this trend. Although a focus on difference in health outcomes and service opportunities is an established emphasis in medical geography dating from the challenges of political economy (Eyles and Woods 1983; Jones and Moon 1987; Scarpaci 1989), emergent concerns focus on an alternative view of difference: that profound variations in health beliefs, practices and experiences of groups defined by class, "race," ethnicity, sexuality, or gender (or combinations of these identities) must be acknowledged and made visible in research. The feminist challenge represents a key precursor to more recent intellectual endorsement by geographers of identity as shaping health beliefs and practices. Learmonth (1975, 224) commented on the long history of medical geography and the fact that "many of the major contributions have been made by *medical men*" (emphasis added). Invigorated by the legitimation of difference asserted first by feminism, then endorsed by postmodernism, emergent geographies of health are progressing beyond androcentric and "medico-centric" vantage points. We intend the present book to add to this momentum.

Well-being

The optimistic and idealistic World Health Organisation (WHO) definition of health ("a state of complete physical, mental and social well-being, and not merely the absence of disease or infirmity") (WHO 1946) has underlain much work in the health and development field (Phillips and Verhasselt 1994). This is, perhaps, because the links between the physical, mental, and social dimensions of one's humanity and their situatedness within community contexts are thrown into starker clarity in impoverished environments and among peoples less predisposed to the compartmentalized thinking characteristic of Western minds. The holism of the WHO definition of health provides a parallel to the view of place advanced earlier in this chapter. Both concepts are challenging to operationalize but offer a breadth of vision for their engagement with human experience.

One reason that a firmly embodied and placed geography of health has been slow to emerge is that the concepts of health and disease have too easily been located at either end of an imaginary continuum despite the positive health emphasis of the WHO definition ("not merely the absence of disease"). Instead, commentators have pointed out that the WHO definition clearly indicates that "disease and health belong to quite separate universes of discourse" (Kelly, Davies, and Charlton 1993, 163).

Embedded in the WHO definition is a sense of health as *progress,* and this is also implied in two more recent documents: the WHO-sponsored Health for All by the Year 2000' program (WHO 1985) and the Canadian *Achieving Health for All* document (Epp 1986). Whereas progress as an ideology is associated with modernism, the original WHO definition has been interpreted as "unwittingly postmodern" in its depiction of health (Kelly, Davies and Charlton 1993, 163). For although the WHO and agencies and individuals taking up its cause have invariably opted for technical expertise in the quest to address ill health, the positive view of health embedded in the WHO definition begs for an alternative view in which identity, difference, and contingency—hallmarks of postmodernism—surface onto the research agenda. It is noteworthy that holistic indigenous views of health, such as those held by Maori in New Zealand, seem to be "folk-knowledge" precursors to the expert-driven WHO definition.

It must be acknowledged that just as theoretical currents have swept new perspectives and approaches into the social sciences since the mid-1970s, so too medicine itself has changed. Although the biomedical model as an explanatory framework for medicine arguably still holds sway, the social sciences themselves (particularly sociology) have led to a partial reorientation of medicine. The voices of consumer groups (particularly the womens' movement) and the changing profile of morbidity and mortality in Western societies (from predominantly acute and infectious illnesses to more chronic and less life-threatening conditions such as heart disease) have complemented the academic challenges of the social sciences to develop more holistic, humanistic, and socially aware medical practices. Nettleton (1995) identifies a number of transformations observable in health policy and medical practices: from disease to health; from hospital to community; from cure to prevention; and from patient to person, to name a few. We add two transformations that inform this book, both of which arise from and contribute to understanding the shifts Nettleton identifies. These transformations are from space as a container to space as an active agent in the shaping of human (health) experience (Kearns and Joseph 1993) and from place as location to place as simultaneously landscape, center of societal activities and nexus of shared and personal meaning (Relph 1987).

Overview of the Book

The book is divided into three parts that loosely follow our subtitle, "landscape, identity and well-being." Part One, "Therapeutic Landscapes," takes its title from the paper by Wilbert Gesler (1992) in which he sought to infuse medical geography with themes current in the so-called new cultural geography. In this section, places and landscapes that have been imbued with therapeutic qualities are considered, ranging across three national contexts. In chapter 2 Wil Gesler uncovers the development of Bath's reputation as a healing place. He shows how natural beauty, historical events, magnificent architecture, and myths all contributed to Bath's success, but also how the city's reputation for its healing waters, cleanliness, qualified physicians, social leveling, and maintenance of law and order were all contested. Martha Geores shifts our focus to North America in chapter 3, accounting for the development of Hot Springs, South Dakota. She demonstrates the ways in which entrepreneurs, beginning in the late nineteenth century, used a combination of Native American legends, a public relations effort, the newly emerging railroad system, ideas about the healing powers of mineral springs, and the legitimacy bestowed by biomedicine to aggressively sell their healing place. In chapter 4 the locational focus shifts by considerable degrees of latitude with Lessie Jo Frazier and Joseph Scarpaci surveying the connections between state violence, human rights, and mental health as they are embedded within the landscape of contemporary Chile. Although the stark horror of recent political history makes these landscapes less than therapeutic in themselves, the authors point out that symbols of resistance and struggle have been effective in ensuring that history itself has not been buried along with the dead. In other words, mental health is being promoted by both literally and metaphorically exhuming the recent past.

We have titled part 2 "Identity, Difference, and Health" to reflect the ways in which the identities of being ill, "dis-abled," or simply "different"—or perceptions of others as such—can lead to distinctive spatial outcomes in quality of life and the necessity to adjust research relations. In chapter 5 Glenda Laws and John Radford uncover the hidden worlds of developmentally challenged adults in Toronto, revealing ways in which the agency/structure dynamic plays out in the lives of this stigmatized and often misunderstood group. Isabel Dyck follows in chapter 6 with an examination of the implications of feminist geography for the study of embodied subjects, in particular women with multiple sclerosis. Ill-health—whether actual or perceived—carries stigma, and the social distance it creates invariably has spatial correlates. In chapters 7 and 8 two expressions are examined of the "not in my back yard" syndrome in which reaction to difference is etched upon the landscape of urban service provision. In the first Jonggyu Lee, Jennifer Wolch, and Jessica Walsh survey the distribution of shelter and service needs of homeless people in Los Angeles, revealing a distinct link between place and the health chances of the homeless. In chapter 8 Lois Takahashi proposes crucial determinants of "difference" in terms of how outsiders in urban society are defined. She then analyses data from a recent national survey to show how public attitudes to homelessness and AIDS lead to patterns of rejection of the disabled and afflicted. Sheena Asthana completes part 2 with an examination of the relevance of place in AIDS research, focusing on sex workers in Madras. Poverty has predisposed this group toward adopting a deviant identity, and in so doing, hindering efforts to contain the experience of this illness.

Part 3, "Place, Policy, and Well-being," groups together a set of chapters that address the connection between health policy and a range of places (homes, communities, regions). The relationships between housing and health were some of the earliest to be formally addressed in public policy (Smith 1990). In chapter 10 Sophie Hyndman reviews the evidence for links between such housing problems as dampness and ill-health that were first recognized in Victorian England and remain implicit in building codes throughout the Western world. Blake Poland considers the unexpected outcomes of a different set of legal codes in chapter 11—the antismoking legislation that has recently been enacted in Canada. He finds that increasingly smokers are being stigmatized and restricted in their places of social interaction. The next three chapters of this section concern the role of place within recent health reforms in Western countries. In chapter 12 Robin Kearns shifts the focus on identity from the individual to the community and examines implications of New Zealand's national health reforms for a largely Maori community in a remote area. As a result of threats to existing health care services, a protest is mounted, and ultimately these identity politics result in a move toward community provisioning. John Eyles and Andreà Litva examine the relations between place and health care policy more generally in chapter 13, focusing on the conflict between the local and larger scales of service provision and the possibility of citizen participation for in-place decision making. In chapter 14 Graham Moon and Tim Brown complement Eyles's analysis by examining how space and place have been constructed and reconstructed within the language of recent British health policy.

We conclude the book with chapter 15 in which we review key themes traversed in the preceding chapters and consider further directions in which research into place/health relationships might fruitfully proceed.

Part One

Therapeutic Landscapes

2

Bath's Reputation as a Healing Place

WILBERT M. GESLER

Places achieve positive or negative reputations because people perceive that they do or do not fulfill basic human needs such as providing sercurity, a feeling of identity, material wants, or aesthetic pleasure. In particular, humans have a need for physical, mental, and spiritual healing, and they search for that healing within places. Over time, perceptions about fulfilling needs may lead to an "understood truth" that a group of people share about a place. This truth is a cultural construction that arises from experiences, perceptions, ideologies, attitudes, and feelings. Thus, Bath, England, as well as many other spas around the world became famous for healing in different periods of its history.

It must be made clear from the start that the truth of a reputation cannot be tested empirically. Often, in fact, the qualities imputed to a place (e.g., the efficacy of mineral waters to cure gout) may, upon scientific examination, be found to be groundless. Thus, the emphasis on perception in the establishment of a reputation. It is well known that perceptions do not necessarily conform to scientific fact. They may, however, have a strong influence on actual behavior.

Positive reputations result from an accummulation of received ideas that a place satisfies certain needs. Bath achieved its healing reputation through an historical accretion of feelings about the healing powers of its mineral springs. Because reputations come and go, however, it is necessary to examine the social, economic, and political contexts at the times in which Bath's reputation was at its highest levels. Bath's reputation for healing was greatest in the Celtic, Roman, medieval, and Georgian periods.

Reputations are often expressed in symbolic form. That is, they become part of the symbolic cultural landscape. The importance of interpreting symbolic landscapes is well established in the geographic and the social science of medicine literature. This idea is demonstrated by showing how the mineral springs, a healing myth, and Georgian architecture all played symbolic roles in Bath's story.

Reputations are often attacked and subsequently change over time, which indicates at least two of their aspects. One is that they may be false from a scientific perspective. The other is that their very strength may create opposition from those who desire to tear down and control their power for their own ends. Bath's reputation was contested by attacks on its natural setting and on the alleged efficacy of its waters, by an examination of sanitation and hygiene, by questions concerning the qualifications of physicians, and through the two issues of social difference and law and order.

Bath Achieves Its Reputation

Natural Beauty

For many residents and visitors Bath's dramatic natural setting was a key attraction. The city lies in a deep bowl encircled by steep limestone cliffs at the southern end of the Cotswolds in southwestern England. On three sides flows a meander of the rather sluggish Avon (Cunliffe 1969; Gadd 1971; Lees-Milne and Ford 1982). There are magnificent views from numerous vantage points around the town. Perhaps the most essential natural feature for its healing reputation is the hot springs. Bath's thermal waters, which have migrated over thousands of years through permeable rocks from catchment areas in the Mendip and other hills, penetrate fractures and faults in a cover of Mesozoic strata and then gush forth as hot springs. Most of the thermal water emerges at three spots: King's Bath (46 degrees C or 115 degrees F), Hot Bath (49 deg. C or 120 deg. F), and Cross Bath (40 deg. C or 104 deg. F). The combined daily flow at these locations exceeds 250,000 gallons (Cunliffe 1986).

Celtic and Roman Beginnings

It is fairly certain that the Celts were attracted to Bath's waters for religious worship and ritual because the springs were thought to be an entrance to the otherworld and evidence of the beneficence of mother earth (Stewart 1981). For the Romans, who came in A.D. 43 and left in the early fifth century, the mineral springs were the main attraction of the site.

Although Bath was not suitable for military, market, or administrative functions, the Romans found it to be a strategic spot on the periphery of their conquered territory (Stewart 1981). They possessed the engineering and plumbing skills to control the water flow and they practiced Hippocratic medicine, which promulgated the use of water. Building the Sulis Minerva temple complex was part of their strategy to pacify the Celts. The baths became a center for rest and recreation for the Roman army, but it also attracted many middle-class Roman citizens from all over the empire. Tacitus (c. 56–c. 120) claimed that the Romans, led by Agricola (A.D. 78–84) were using the waters to lead a warlike people into idle luxury and vice. "In this way," he said, "people learnt to mistake the path of servitude for the high road of culture" (Wriston 1978, 9).

Medieval Revival

After the departure of the Romans, Bath declined in importance as a healing place. From the eleventh to fifteenth centuries, however, Bath attracted pilgrims to its waters from all over Europe. The Benedictine monks who ran the Norman ecclesiastical complex viewed the springs as a gift from God, which they used to treat charity cases. The *Gesta Stephani*, written in the twelfth century, declared that "sick persons from all over England go there to bathe in the healing waters, as well as the healthy, who go to see the wonderful outpourings of water and bathe in them" (Haddon 1973, 46).

The wool trade that predominated in the fifteenth century introduced a capitalist economy, trade unions, labor disputes, and small-scale mechanization, all before the industrial revolution got fully underway (Haddon 1973). An important change came in the sixteenth century when, after the dissolution of the monastaries by Henry VIII (1535 and after), control of the town lands passed from the bishop and priory to the mayor and city corporation. The new city authorities were entrepreneurs anxious to establish the well-being of Bath and at the same time to line their own pockets. Furthermore, beginning in the sixteenth century, following the continental lead, interest revived in the curative powers of mineral waters. The baths and other amenities fell far short of adequacy, however, at this time. William Turner wrote in 1562 that "there is money enough spent on cockfightings, tennis playing, parties, banquettings, pageants and plays serving for only a short time of pleasure . . . but I have not heard tell that any rich man hath spent upon these noble baths, being so profitable for the whole Commonwealth of England, one groat these twenty-nine years [since the Dissolution]" (Rolls 1978, 47).

Georgian Glory

By the late seventeenth century many English towns were developing as social centers for the local gentry and the middle classes, people who now had enough disposable income to indulge in pleasurable pursuits, often centering around health (either in earnest or as an excuse), but including much else besides (McIntyre 1981). Spa use tended to trickle down from the upper to middle to lower classes with a rough correlation between class and distance traveled (the lower the class the shorter the distance). Springs located near population centers such as London were favored at first, but as they became too accessible to the lower orders the aristocracy and nouveaux riches abandoned them and traveled further afield. Bath, a little more than one hundred miles from London, was ideally situated for the wealthier sort during the eighteenth century, but even it in time became too accessible for the tastes of the wealthy.

In the eighteenth century Jonathan Swift was able to say that "Everyone is going to Bath" (Bezzant 1980, 104). As the century progressed, a small group of architects and entrepreneurs led by John Wood and Ralph Allen began to convince the corporation that they needed to construct buildings worthy of the leading spa (McIntyre 1981; Neale 1973b). Much-improved roads and a canal between Bath and Bristol brought visitors and goods to the city far more easily. To maintain its hold on the idle rich the corporation introduced gambling. At the same time, the corporation saw that something had to be done about law and order if the town were to be made safe for tourists with disposable incomes. Fortunately for them, Richard Nash, itinerant gambler and follower of fashion, appeared on the scene in 1702. Backed by the corporation, "Beau" Nash began to establish both order and a frivolous social life. Bath entered its Georgian Golden Age.

Creating Symbolic Landscapes

Symbols can be used to constrain and control environments (Cosgrove 1987; Rowntree and Conkey 1980), but they can also be employed in positive ways, including healing (Hagey 1984; Kleinman 1973). Two aspects of the symbolic environment of Bath are of special importance: myths surrounding the hot springs and their healing powers and the use of symbols in the built environment, architecture in particular.

The Hot Springs as Symbol and Myth

The springs had strong symbolic power for the Celts (Stewart 1981). Water sources were extremely sacred and the creation of life was believed to have taken place in a boiling cauldron. The Celts also had a firm belief in the other world, which was under the ground and was entered through a cave, cavern, well, mysterious opening, or spring. In Celtic myths there are many stories of journeys to and from the other world, which was a source of both life and death. Celtic deities were closely linked to specific sites. The goddess Sulis, who had curative powers and military prowess, was attached to the Bath waters. In both Welsh and Old Irish *suil* or *sulis* means an orifice, gap, or eye, providing links to the physical attributes of the site and communication with the underworld. The Romans named the site Aquae Sulis (waters of Sulis). Recognizing the similarities between Sulis and their own goddess, Minerva, the Romans made both a symbolic and politically astute move by constructing, in the A.D. 60s, a temple dedicated to Sulis Minerva as the center of their building complex.

Bath waters continued to convey a supernatural aura throughout the Middle Ages, a period when holy wells and springs were used as religious sites, each one dedicated to a saint or used to cure specific ailments (McIntyre 1981; Mitchell 1986). Beginning in the seventeenth century, the waters began to lose their mystical aspect as efforts were made to establish water efficacy on scientific grounds. Nevertheless, a specific myth had grown up concerning the origins of the healing power of Bath's springs. The roots of the myth are pagan, but the story obviously acquired Christian trappings. The first known account was by Geoffrey of Monmouth (d. A.D. 1154) in his *History of Kings;* John Wood, the architect, who was angry with those who scoffed at the legend in his time, brought the tale into his *Essay Toward a Description of Bath* (1765) (Haddon 1973).

The legend is as follows. Bladud, son of a king of the west country, was banished from his father's court because he had contracted leprosy, an often misdiagnosed disease that throughout history has placed a heavy stigma upon its victims. He became a swineherd, and the pigs he tended also became infected with his sores. One day, at a place where the ground never froze, the pigs began to wallow in the mud. Finding that the mineral springs at the future site of Bath had cured his pigs of their affliction, Bladud also immersed himself in the mud, was cured, returned to a warm welcome from his family, eventually became king, and sired King Lear (Winsor 1980; Wriston 1978).

There is, possibly, medical truth in the Bladud legend, but the tale's veracity is not what gives it enduring force. Myths symbolize what a group of people feels to be important in their relationships to their environment, to each other, and to the mysterious powers that created the world (Stewart 1981). Therefore, it is evident that, at least by the time of Geoffrey, the physical, psychological, and social healing functions of Bath and its waters were uppermost in people's minds. Furthermore, the therapeutic function was allied to religious sentiments that included belief in miraculous and supernatural powers. Thus, the Bladud story with its ties to near-supernatural royalty and miraculous cures helped through the years to symbolize Bath's premier position as a healing place.

Although the incidents in the legend were supposed to have occurred in the ninth century B.C., there are clear indications that the earliest tellers of the story were familiar with the New Testament and its tale of the man who was cured when his demons were transferred to a herd of swine and the parable Jesus told about the prodigal son. Thus, the myth might refer to the curing of mental illness, or it could refer to the restoration of broken social relationships. Perhaps, also, the idle rich and middle classes who alternately overindulged themselves at Bath and then sought cures for their gout and other ailments might have found comfort in the prodigal son's forgiveness.

The case has been made that physicians and entrepreneurs in places like Bath used the water as a "commodity fetish" (Rees 1985). That is, the use value of the hot springs was turned into a profit-making venture. To accomplish this the water was given an image of mystery or magic. The waters were promoted as an alternative to establishment medicine while spas gained respectability from their continental origins, recommendations from physicians, and physicians' use of the jargon of the medicine of the day.

Even today, a tinge of the supernatural, the mythical, still hovers about the springs. Dr. George Kersley, a physician to the Hospital for Rheumatic Diseases in Bath for thirty-three years, was determined to free rheumatology from the arcane arts and raise it to a scientific discipline. His efforts gained worldwide recognition, and his hospital became a center of excellence, but he also contributed to the demise of the spa. Now, however, Kersley is one of the most vigorous campaigners for reestablishing Bath as a watering place, saying that he and his colleagues had "knocked the spook out of the waters," meaning, from his perspective, that people had forgotten the placebo effect, the phenomenal effect of mind over matter (Rolls 1988b).

Sacred and Symbolic Architecture

Buildings convey symbolic meaning or help to create symbolic landscapes (Rowntree and Conkey 1980). In addition, studies have shown that housing types and architectural styles may influence personality and social behavior (Bagley 1974; Canter 1986), and may also be important for therapy (Canter and Canter 1979). Celtic dwellings, places of worship, and public works did little to alter the physical landscape permanently around the mineral springs. The Romans, however, harnessed the water and constructed a cluster of monumental buildings centered around the temple of Sulis Minerva. This complex included a sanctuary, the classical tetrastyle or four-columned temple in the Corinthian order, and a large suite of baths. These massive tributes to the engineering and construction skills of the Romans provided the backdrop to the religious, healing, and social functions carried out during four centuries of occupation (Cunliffe 1969).

Georgian Bath, one of a handful of cities that epitomizes a particular age and a prefiguring of the garden city concept, is largely the result of John Wood's dream of a New Rome (Cunliffe 1986). The basic inspiration for the style Wood chose for his masterpieces was Andre Palladio, a late Renaissance Italian architect who simulated ancient Roman buildings (Bezzant 1980). Wood was responsible for bringing an overall cohesion to town planning by using common materials (Bath limestone), a common idiom (Palladian designs), and a common scale, all fitted to the surrounding topography (Haddon 1973). He was a Renaissance man, using in his architecture his self-taught knowledge of astronomy, antiquity, mythology, and finance. His work was innovative and, although he was a provincial architect, his influence on town planning was widespread.

Neale (1973a, 1973b) argues that Wood's creative energy stemmed largely from two pairs of tensions: one between the demands of capitalism and his own creative energy, the other between paganism/antiquity and Christianity. Wood realized that to fulfill his vision of a New Rome he would require a substantial amount of capital, and acquiring it entailed learning how to survive with all the constraints imposed by an agrarian capitalist society: periodic shortages of funds, labor deficiencies, problems with land ownership, and the tastes of a self-indulgent, wealthy, and powerful elite whose members had little knowledge or interest in the finer points of artistic expression. Thus, he became a successful entrepreneur who managed to make a great deal of money from his projects. Yet his artistic side continuously sought expression, and he had a vision of a world that was completely different from the one he lived in. The result was a series of compromises. For example, his son financed the King's Circus, which he designed, with the help of loans from local merchants who were closely connected to the slave and sugar trades in the West Indies.

Wood's interest in the ideas of pagan antiquity was an amazing and fanciful blend of several traditions: pre-Hellenic Jewish and pre-Roman British or Celtic as well as classical Greek and Roman (Neale 1973a, 1973b). In his writings on architecture and ancient mythologies he set forth the idea, wholly unsubstantiated, that Bath was only the core of what was once a city the size of Babylon built by King Bladud (whom Wood claimed was descended from a Trojan prince) around 480 B.C. He wrote of a fantastic landscape that contained Druids, Greeks, and Britons who had built temples, castles, and palaces in the antique style. At odds with his obvious love of antiquity and pagan thought was his deep Christian conviction and attendant fear of paganism. He was troubled by the fact that the work he was able to do was almost entirely secular. The way he resolved this pagan/Christian conflict was to find a divine origin for classical, including Palladian, architecture. He felt that beauty in architecture was the result of God's wishes, which were brought to fruition in buildings such as the Jewish Tabernacle and Greek temples. Thus, he sought to imitate nature and humanity as re-creations of God.

To carry out his task Wood developed a set of symbols that God, the Divine Architect, used to indicate perfect harmony and perfection. The circle, which was often found in both Celtic and Jewish designs, was the preferred symbol; the square was also extensively used. The circle was often composed of three parts, which represented use, strength, and beauty. Humans, made in the image of God, were also composed of three parts, head, trunk, and limbs, and the parts of the body, stretched out, could be encompassed by a square or a circle—thus, the Vitruvian figure of a naked man with limbs extended that Palladio used in abstracted versions in his own religious architecture.

Two of Wood's masterpieces, Queen Square, which he completed in 1734, and the King's Circus, which he started and his son completed in 1758, show how he created his symbolic landscapes. Queen Square has a geometrical design that looks like an abstract Vitruvian figure. The central area is a perfect square and inside this is a perfect circle. The King's Circus was symbolically far more elaborate. It consists of two perfect concentric circles; the outer one's dimensions almost exactly correspond to those of the north-south dimensions of Queen Square and also the chalk wall at Stonehenge, some thirty miles (50 km) to the east southeast. Threefold symbolism is displayed in three ways. There are three sectors of buildings, three street approaches, and three principal Greek orders of columns stacked one above the other. The Doric column on the bottom storey represents Robust Man, the Ionic column above that Grave Matron, and the top Corinthian column Sprightly Young Girl. In these buildings Wood managed to combine mystical feeling with practicality, and the sacred (represented by geometric figures) and the profane (the human figure) (Eliade 1959).

I submit that Wood and other architects were working within the Renaissance view of the world that included a striving for order and harmony represented by the notion of the Great Chain of Being and the metaphor of humanity as a microcosm or model of the cosmos (Bamborough 1980; Mills 1982). According to these concepts, the maintenance of order in human nature was essential to physical and mental health. After the Fall, however, humans were subject to illness and death. Drunkenness, illness, passion, and madness represented disruption of order and harmony. The order and symmetry of the Georgian buildings in Bath can be thought of as attempts to counteract these disruptions. The Vitruvian figure that Wood used in his designs symbolized "two crucial Renaissance commonplaces, one, that the human body is perfect and thus its proportions must be mirrored in all works of art and architecture, and two, that men and women are themselves the image of the cosmos" (Mills 1982, 241). Like the human body, the cosmos goes through the stages of life (recall the figures on the facade of the King's Circus), has physical features such as skin, heart, and stomach, and experiences illness. Thus, one can think of architecture that is based on the human figure as contributing to the health of both the human body and society at large. In addition, I suggest that the circles and squares employed in Wood's designs may represent mandalas, which are composed of concentric forms, link the microcosm and the macrocosm, and have been used in many societies to achieve healing, wholeness, and integration (Arguelles and Arguelles 1972).

Bath's Reputation Contested

It is easy to idealize a city such as Bath, and to focus on its reputed water cures, the wonders of its architecture, and its eighteenth-century social life. A little probing reveals, however, that beneath the facade were conflicts over many issues and ideas. Attempts to control and impose meanings by certain groups were continually contested by others. Reality put Bath's positive reputation as a healing site to the test (and it survived). Illustrations of this theme include the natural setting, water efficacy, sanitation and hygiene, physicians and patients, and civil order versus vice.

Natural Blemishes

The natural setting, as was mentioned above, contributed to the strong sense of place experienced by residents of and visitors to Bath. Obviously, those who profited from visitors seeking healing and pleasure extolled the beauty of the town's physical surroundings. Yet there was disagreement even here. Despite its dramatic natural setting and hot springs, the healthfulness of the physical environment was disputed. John Wood expressed a popular attitude held by eighteenth-century sophisticates when he wrote that Bath was "a place standing in a hole; on a quagmire; impenetrable to the very beams of the sun; and so confined by almost inaccessible hills, that people have scarce room to breathe in the town, or to come at it without danger to their lives" (Neale 1973b, 254). The rugged topography continues to have an unhealthy influence today in the stresses created by having to park on steep hills and some of the worst traffic congestion in England.

Contesting Water Efficacy

Bath had many attractions, but the promise of a cure from the springs remained a dominant motive for visits. The question is, Did the water really cure any ailments? Theories about how or why Bath waters cured altered radically over time (Rolls 1978, 1984, 1988b). Roman physicians used the hot water to adjust the four humors by heating, cooling, moistening, and drying and to ease aches and pains, promote good breathing, relieve fatigue, cure headaches, and soften the body so that it could assimilate the nutrients in food (Jackson 1990). The humoral idea that disease caused by cold and moisture could be cured by applying heat and 'drying' (causing the body to sweat and dry out) continued to dominate medicine up to the eighteenth century.

From Georgian times on the issue of efficacy became the touchstone for a complex web of medical, social, political, and philosophical controversies. Physicians of the seventeenth and eighteenth centuries claimed that Bath waters would cure, among many other things, rheums, palsies, bilious colic, dropsies, skin diseases, green sickness, uterine flours, and forgetfulness (Schnorrenberg 1984; Wroughton 1973). The novelist Henry Fielding declared that the waters were "generally imputed to be almost infallible" (Hill 1989, 17), but Tobias Smollett, a writer and physician (whose medical practice failed in Bath) attacked the baths as unhygienic and the waters as ineffective. In the eighteenth century the notion that water diluted or washed out malicious humors and noxious effluvia came into prominence. Many people thought that certain substances in the water, such as sulfur, bitumen, and nitre, released large amounts of energy into the body and thereby produced curative effects. In addition, it was said that a "volatile creative principle" or an "aerial impregnation" resided in the water, which was lost on cooling. In the 1880s the physiological effects of bathing were deemed most important. In the early twentieth century traces of radioactive radium and radon were hailed as the curative agents, but this discovery was hushed up later in the interest of public relations. A theory that trace elements enhanced the fermentation of the body's digestive juices led to a "zymosthenic index," which was used to rate various mineral waters in the 1920s. A recent idea has been to examine Bath's air for an excess of negative ions. Ironically, the Public Health Department closed the baths in 1978 because a young girl developed fatal meningitis.

From the seventeenth century on the history of the progress of inorganic chemistry can be traced in attempts to analyze mineral spring water (Coley 1982, 1990; Hamlin 1990). In the early days chemistry was simply not technically equipped to make definitive analyses, and, thus, many unsubstantiated claims and counter claims were made by Bath and its rivals. Besides these scientific quarrels, issues of legitimization for spas and spa physicians (Coley 1990; Hamlin 1990; Harley 1990) arose. By the seventeenth century doctors were attempting to replace religious evidence for water efficacy with scientific proofs. Struggles for legitimacy, however, were contested (Coley 1982; Neve 1984; Rolls 1978). At the center of the debate were Bath physicians who strongly asserted that agents such as sulfur were curative versus outsiders who denied efficacy and accused the insiders of fraudulently protecting vested interests.

On another level the debates over efficacy set scientific water analysis against medical evidence of actual cures (Hamlin 1990; Rolls 1978, 1988b). Most chemical analyses showed that there was nothing special about Bath water, yet people and doctors testified to genuine cures. At the same time, from the scientific perspective we know that warm, buoyant water can aid in physiotherapy, and there is evidence that immersion in warm water and drinking water containing certain elements can help to alleviate the effects of lead poisoning. The latter possibility would explain the high success rates at Bath General Hospital for patients suffering from lead palsy in the eighteenth century (Heywood 1990; Mitchell 1986; Rolls 1988a, 1988b).

Questioning Cleanliness

Not much is known about sanitary and hygienic practices until the seventeenth century, although the Romans had a reputation for cleanliness, and we know that the resident Benedictine monks of the Middle Ages were strictly enjoined from bathing. Bath sanitation in the seventeenth century was no worse than in other towns, but it still seems remarkable that a town that staked its reputation on healing could be so negligent about keeping itself clean. Writing toward the end of the sixteenth century, John Harrington (who invented a water closet long before its time and who wondered if he might be rewarded by being named to the Privie Chamber) remarked that "the common sewer which before stood in an ill place stands now in no place, for they have not any at all; which for a town so plentifully served with water, in a country so well provided with stone, in a place resorted to so greatly, methinks an unworthy and dishonourable thing" (Haddon 1973, 74). Bath at this time was a cramped and unhealthy place, and rubbish was left to rot in the streets in the still and humid air. In 1646, when regular street cleaning began, the corporation still felt it incumbent to decree that "no person shall presume to cast or throw any dog, bitch, or other live beast into any of the said Baths, under the penalty of three shillings and fourpence" (Sitwell 1987, 32–33). Fortunately, the city was blessed with an abundant supply of springs that supplied drinking water through underground lead pipes and stone watercourses. Avoiding drinking water drawn from the Avon helped the town largely to escape the plagues that ravaged nearby Bristol at this time.

Hygiene was still a serious problem during the eighteenth century (Lees-Milne and Ford 1982; Rolls 1988b). John Wood complained that the walls of the baths were encrusted with dirt (Rolls 1988b) (some people thought that the filth contained therapeutic sulfur). For many years the mineral water that people drank on their physician's prescription was simply drawn from the water that people bathed in. This danger was finally recognized, and the Pump Room, supplied with an independent water supply, was built next to the King's Bath. It also became the practice to change the waters in the bath once a day to protect against "bath mantle" which was, perhaps, a swimming pool rash. Despite improvements such as these, nineteenth-century Bath had no overall sanitation system although the three city parishes each employed a team of scavengers who swept and collected refuse with horse and cart and took the garbage to the edge of the city to be sold as manure. Most of the sewage left the city through drains that emptied into the Avon. Good water, however, remained a positive public health asset supplied by springs and wells to all except the poor.

Physicians versus Quacks

Bath, particularly in the eighteenth century, provided a lucrative market for physicians of many types (Rolls 1988b; Schnorrenberg 1984). Whereas the ratio of physicians to population in Great Britain in the early part of the eighteenth century was 1:5200, Bath's ratio was around 1:1000. The other two main branches of the established medical profession, surgeons and apothecaries, were also well represented. Many more medical practitioners besides these would have been attracted to the town as well. In fact, there are as many alternative healers in Bath today as those practicing biomedicine. Physicians (distinguished by their university degrees) mixed freely with surgeons, but sometimes were at odds with the apothecaries, who did not confine themselves to selling medicines but diagnosed and prescribed as well. Like London, but unlike most other provincial towns, a relatively large number of Oxford and Cambridge graduates were among Bath physicians. Those with English university degrees, although not considered to be medically superior to other doctors, nevertheless rose higher in their profession and charged higher fees based on their higher social status. Insider physicians with English degrees such as William Oliver also used their academic prestige to substantiate their claims and dismiss outsiders such as Dr. William Baylies (a mere graduate of Aberdeen) and Dr. Charles Lucas (an Irishman) (Neve 1984).

Physicians in eighteenth-century Britain held a far lower status than they do in the Western world today. Nonetheless, they struggled to distance themselves from those they considered to be quacks. Bath naturally attracted those, with or without a medical degree, who prescribed all manner of remedies for disease (Schnorrenberg 1984). Imposters and frauds were known for charging high prices and were often on the move from place to place. Because medical science was so rudimentary and many people felt that doctors were simply out for money and quarreled too often among themselves, physicians were open to a great deal of ridicule. Satirists had a heyday. The essayist Steele (referring to Bath) wrote that "the physicians here are very numerous, but very good natured. To these charitable gentlemen I owe, that I was cured, in a week's time, of more distempers than I ever had in my life" (Schnorrenberg 1984, 195).

Dealing with Social Difference

On the surface and by reputation Bath was the only place where the aristocracy mingled with the bourgeoisie in a relaxed way, so the latter could study and emulate the former (Hill 1989). But this social leveling was rather spurious, causing Smollett to remark that it represented a sort of temporary forgetfulness about social relations, as if the hot springs were the River Lethe (Sitwell 1987). There was, for example, a social distinction based on different prices set for entrance to the various baths that the corporation opened up. King's Bath was relatively expensive and, therefore, exclusive, whereas the others were more accessible and often overcrowded (Mitchell and Penrose 1983). During the Georgian period a new middle class of entrepreneurs, the nouveaux riches, was being created, and this group was in revolt, demanding the freedom to trade, explore, and investigate. Wealth could be gained and lost relatively rapidly in a variety of ventures—building, trade with the colonies, gambling—and so there was a great deal of social flux.

A particular problem faced the corporation: what to do about the poor (Bezzant 1980; Cunliffe 1986; Gadd 1971; Rolls 1988b; Wroughton 1973). In 1572 the Poor Law Act enabled the destitute to come for treatment to two spas, Bath and Buxton. Many were sent by parishes that were only trying to get rid of them. In Bath the poor were cared for at the Leper's Bath, which achieved a popularity that was unwelcome to the wealthy elite. As the town developed a reputation for cures, many of the poor stayed on, making their living by begging. The Beggars of Bath became a recognized social category. In 1601, in an attempt at control, another Poor Law placed the "lazy" in a House of Correction or workhouse. The law also provided for the genuinely needy, however, indicating the dual nature of Bath's attitudes toward the less well-off: a revulsion and rage to control on one hand and guilt and patronizing charity on the other. A poor rate was levied to provide funds for the care of the indigent, and four almshouses were established to take care of the aged and the sick. In 1714 the Elizabethan Poor Law expired; beggars began to proliferate once more, and Bath found it very difficult to distinguish between the truly needy and malingerers. The wealthy became concerned about the loss to agricultural and industrial production of a chronically ill and physically handicapped work force. The solution was to establish a hospital for the poor, which would, at one stroke, salve the consciences of the rich, improve the quality of the labor force, and provide the needed social control (Gadd 1971; Kirby 1925; Rolls 1988a, 1988b).

Bath General Hospital was founded in 1738, and it flourished (Rolls 1988b). Parishes located anywhere in England could send poor patients. They had to come accompanied by a letter of referral setting out their problems, and they also had to pay "caution money" either for their trip back or for funeral expenses. All cases were subject to approval by the resident physicians; those with infectious diseases were sent back home. In the beginning a strong distance decay effect was evident in hospital use, but in later years the friction of distance decreased as reputation came to override concerns for geographic accessibility. In time the hospital became famous worldwide for its treatment and research on rheumatic diseases.

The irony of Bath's eighteenth-century success was that a new political economy had been created that led to its own decline. The newly created middle class found itself in a position of power, and it tried to prevent this power from eroding away. A young, trend-setting, aristocratic, and daring class had given way to a middle-aged, middle-class, timid society with few original ideas (Salter 1972). The aristocrats began to drift away, and seekers of health headed off in new directions. Nineteenth-century Bath was still concerned about the poor and the problems they created, however. In 1805 Lady Isabella King set up a society to, once again, both control the poor and provide charity (Report of the Bath Society 1810).

Two images of Bath remained during the nineteenth century (Wright 1972). One was the pristine spa, the fresh, clean Bath of limestone buildings, Wood's architectural marvels, and a population who lived in good, solid houses and walked along clean and well-ventilated streets. The other image could be seen if one wandered away from the centers of healing and pleasure to the lower and some of the older parts of the city along by the river that Wood and the other builders had ignored. Here the buildings were constructed on alluvial flats, mostly clay, which were subject to flooding and water-borne disease. One medical illustration of the contrast between the poor and the wealthy was the cholera epidemic that reached Bath in the summer of 1832. There were seventy-four cases and forty-nine deaths, not a high toll overall, but 70 percent of the deaths occurred among the poor.

Maintaining Law and Order

At the beginning of the eighteenth century, the streets were dangerous, filled with ruffians, rapacious chairmen who conveyed clients to the baths, and young gallants who settled disputes by the sword; there was also a wide gap between a wealthy clientele and a poverty-stricken underclass. The anonymous author of *A Step to the Bath* described his feelings about the place in 1700: " 'Tis neither Town nor City, yet goes by the Name of both; five Months in the Year 'tis as Populous as *London*, the other seven as desolate as a Wilderness. . . . During the Season it hath as many Families in a House as *Edenborough*. . . . The *Baths* I can compare to nothing but the *Boylers* in *Fleet-lane* or *Old-Bedlam*, for they have a reeking steem all the year. In a word, 'tis a Valley of Pleasure, yet a sink of Iniquity" (Neale 1973a, 39).

In bringing law and order to Bath Beau Nash regulated lodging fees, improved key roads, kept the streets clean, forbade the wearing of swords, stopped street fighting, and brought discipline to the chairmen. He posted a list of rules of behavior in the Pump Room and other public places; the rules were trivial and even comical, but they were obeyed. The rules were not really for the gentlemen and ladies of fashion, who knew them, but for those, aspiring to fashion, who were unaware of such rules. People were told what to wear for every occasion and each day's schedule was set and followed. The effect of all this was to create a society with civilized manners that diffused throughout England.

The Beau may have been unofficially crowned king over his (usually) orderly merrymakers, but he was not unopposed. John Wesley came to preach in the valley of pleasure and sink of iniquity and confronted Nash on a few memorable occasions (Mitchell and Penrose 1983; Sitwell 1987; Wriston 1978). Nash came off rather worse in these quarrels, but he continued to harass Methodist meetings. Still, the Methodists made converts, notably the aristocratic Lady Huntingdon, who opened a chapel and openly proseletyzed, thus putting Nash in an awkward position as enemy of those who would curtail the pleasures of the upper classes.

Assessment of Nash's life and character in many ways reflects the society and place in which he lived (Gadd 1971; *Improved Bath Guide* 1825; Sitwell 1987). He achieved a social status that was far above his humble origins, flashed across the social scene for a brief time, and then died a pauper, spending his later days boring any willing ears he could find in local pubs with his tales of former glory. Chesterfield, commenting on a marble statue of Nash that was placed between busts of Isaac Newton and Alexander Pope in the Pump Room, put Nash and eighteenth-century Bath in their place with this cruel epigram: "The statue plac'd the *busts* between/ Adds to my satire strength:/ *Wisdom* and *Wit* are little seen, /But *Folly* at full length" (Improved Bath Guide 1825, 119).

Summary and Conclusions

It is clear that Bath was perceived to be or understood to be a healing place for more than two thousand years. For many, the natural setting, including rugged topography, spectacular scenes of cliffs and the river Avon, and the unusually voluminous outpourings of the mineral springs, contributed to a feeling of well-being. Bath's growing reputation for healthiness can be traced from Celtic, through Roman, Norman, medieval, and early modern times to the eighteenth century, the Golden Age of the city. Bath gained more and more visitors seeking cures and, by Georgian times, more and more seekers after pleasure. More ample accommodations and splendid architecture also served to attract. Despite a decline in the nineteenth century and devastation in World War II Bath today is enjoying a revival. Its identity as one of a handful of cities that has preserved a substantial amount of its period atmosphere remains very strong. It is one of the most visited spots on the English tourist route. Although it is true that Bath's sense of place rests on more than healing, health was and remains a major factor.

Bath's healing truth was strongly influenced by two sets of symbols: water and architecture. The mineral springs represented powerful otherworldly forces for the Celts; the Romans incorporated the site into their mythology; and the waters maintained a supernatural aura throughout the Middle Ages and even into the twentieth century. Meanwhile, the healing myth of King Bladud, who was cured of leprosy in the springs, grew up in the Middle Ages and was believed by some at least into the eighteenth century. Georgian architecture, stemming largely from the creative energy of John Wood, the self-taught architect, consisted of a series of masterpieces in the Palladian style. Beyond their magnificence, the buildings displayed designs or forms—squares, circles, and the abstract human body in particular—which symbolized order and, interpreted through Renaissance views of the world, health and wholeness.

The strength of Bath's reputation can also be seen through its successful resistance to the attacks made upon it from different quarters. Not everyone agreed that the natural setting was conducive to health; indeed, some found the rugged topography dangerous and the air foul and oppressive. The curative powers of the hot springs became a hotly debated issue from the seventeenth century onward. Chemical science, medical evidence, and the claims of physicians with vested interests were involved in this conflict. The poor state of sanitation throughout much of Bath's history is further evidence that the image of health that Bath's boosters wished to convey was contradicted by actual hygienic conditions. Physicians, who had a relatively low status, struggled to legitimize themselves, marginalize competitors, and raise their status in the eyes of prospective clients. Finally, vice and civil order (both embodied in Beau Nash as gambler and setter of social rules) struggled to gain the upper hand, especially during the Golden Age.

What more general observations can one draw from this case study? Clearly, people perceive that certain places have a healthy environment and that others do not, even though, from a "scientific" point of view (e.g., as measured by how many people with a particular illness were actually cured) this may not be the case. Further, people will travel very long distances to seek out places such as the Mayo Clinic in Rochester, Minnesota, and Lourdes in France (see Gesler 1996a) where the understood truth of healing has taken root.

Health will continue to be a basic human need. Humans striving to meet that need will continue to create understood cultural truths that certain places are healthy.[1] Scientists will attack the validity of healing claims, and rivals will attempt to discredit those claims. Yet, as Bath and hundreds of other healing sites have shown, healing myths survive. They may be suppressed for a time, but they rise again.

1. This idea was suggested by Dr. Stephen Birdsall, Department of Geography, University of North Carolina at Chapel Hill.

3

Surviving on Metaphor

How "Health = Hot Springs" Created and Sustained a Town

MARTHA E. GEORES

The history of Hot Springs, South Dakota, is the history of a town founded by entrepreneurs to sell a commodity called "health." Warm mineral springs were the core of place-making activities, but the founders never limited themselves to the springs. Instead, they adopted a broad perspective from the beginning, steering place-making activities toward the metaphor of "health = Hot Springs." Health is a difficult concept to turn into a commodity because it is so dependent on culture for its meaning. Definitions range from the absence of disease to the presence of a sense of well-being, a subjective and amorphous concept (Kearns 1993). Whether consciously or unconsciously, the founders of Hot Springs left room in the metaphor for it to accommodate changes in both individual and cultural definitions of health which a focus solely on the mineral content of the water as the key to health would not have allowed. Choosing health permitted the process of place making to be ongoing, responsive to changes engendered by medical developments, social class relationships, and changes in transportation.

The founders of Hot Springs were very serious about creating a therapeutic environment (Gesler 1992) by choosing language and exploiting myths (Tuan 1991), and by boldly asserting through ideology and rhetoric that doctors were only a component of health (Gold 1994). The story of Hot Springs is the story of the construction of a place embodying elements of nature, meaning, and social relations in the interest of consumerism (see Sack 1988). Its founders used nature, meaning, and social relations to create the metaphor, "health = Hot Springs." Advertising, the language of commodification, reveals the substantive meaning of the metaphor and chronicles the changes. The majority of the clientele for the spa were not from Hot Springs or even from the surrounding Black Hills region; they were from the Midwest primarily, and considerable advertising was necessary to entice them to Hot Springs. Commodification of the warm mineral springs was, therefore, essential to success of the town. The scenery, climate, and refreshing smell of the town were connected through the mineral springs and provided the context for the new town and the essential metaphor of "health = Hot Springs" beginning in 1881.

Methods and Data

To understand how and why the people of Hot Springs were able to perpetuate the "health = Hot Springs" metaphor it was necessary to learn about the changes in the cultural, political, economic, and historic contexts of the area. Different aspects of meaning contribute to the development and longevity of a metaphor (Kearns 1997). With respect to Hot Springs, some important aspects of the metaphor included the meaning of the place to residents (Relph 1981; Lowenthal 1976), the social meaning evident in the way the landscape was developed (Cosgrove 1984; Ley 1977; Duncan and Duncan 1988), what made the area therapeutic (Gesler 1992), and why health was connected with Hot Springs.

Historical geographer Cole Harris (1978) provides the methodology for this study. He advocates careful and thorough data collection followed by an analysis that tests initial conclusions against a larger and more complete set of information and ideas pertaining to the research question. Because of the variable nature of the data available in historic studies, there really is no standardized way to support conclusions. The researcher must evaluate and interpret the information she has gathered using her own informed judgment. Data sources used in this study included newspapers and magazine articles on Hot Springs, advertising pamphlets produced by railroads, the Hot Springs Chamber of Commerce, and individual spas, local histories, field visits, discussions with a local historian, census data, and economic development plans.

To understand the efficacy of the "health = Hot Springs' metaphor requires a close examination of the qualitative nature of the health concept. Entrepreneurs and advertisers portrayed both health and Hot Springs in a variety of ways, hoping that consumers would be attracted to at least one version and to visit Hot Springs to recover their health, however they defined it.

In this chapter I examine how health was commodified and what the ramifications of commodification were for the commodifiers, the consumers, and the town as a whole. One of the central insights of the study is that the metaphor "health = Hot Springs" always had two meanings. One meaning coincided with whatever health definition was in vogue and would bring health seekers to Hot Springs. The other meaning included all past meanings and was, in a sense, a commodification of the history of health in Hot Springs.

The Beginnings of "Health = Hot Springs"

The Black Hills of South Dakota and Wyoming stand as an oasis of trees in the grassy Great Plains. They contain many resources—gold, timber, and the warm mineral springs, to name a few. "White men," as the Euro-Americans were called in the 1870s, did not "discover" the Black Hills until 1874 when General George Armstrong Custer and his entourage explored them. The Custer Expedition reported a small amount of gold in the streams and exaggerated tales of almost limitless gold reported in the eastern press started a gold rush, even though the Black Hills belonged to the Sioux Indian Nation. In 1876 a true gold rush happened. In 1877, after trying unsuccessfully to purchase the Black Hills, the United States Government appropriated them because there were so many U.S. citizens in the area, even though their presence was illegal (Lazarus 1991). They decided that confiscating the land and placing the Indians on reservations would be the safest course available.

Initially, the entire area of the Black Hills was considered a gold mine by the Euro-Americans. Wherever gold was found there was a boom and bust cycle as miners flocked to veins and rumors of veins and then went on to new finds once the gold was exhausted. Although gold was first discovered near Custer in the southern Black Hills, the largest gold deposits were and still are located in the northern Black Hills, so settlement was concentrated in Deadwood and Lead, which were dominated by the Homestake Mining Company. In the rest of the areas people harvested timber, mined coal, or serviced the needs of the miners. The warm mineral springs in today's Hot

Springs, at the southern end of the Black Hills, were bypassed in the gold rush because they were "off the beaten track" and did not have gold deposits. It was not until 1881 that some enterprising men who already owned a transportation company in the northern Black Hills, went to look at the springs and envisioned a place similar to the European spas of Carlsbad or Baden. These men bought the springs from some "squaw men" who were living near the springs and then obtained enough land from the government to start a town.

The Black Hills were located on the western frontier in the late 1870s and early 1880s, and although there were recreational opportunities, mostly in the form of gambling and drinking, there was a decided lack of interest in the "finer things in life," including a health spa. The people who became "the locals" were not the target group for the spa at Hot Springs. Instead, recruiting was concentrated in the Midwest and East from the beginning.

A Ready-made Reputation

Before the warm mineral springs were commodified as part of the "health = Hot Springs" metaphor, they were a sacred healing place to several Indian Nations. The earliest, and probably most central part of the "health = Hot Springs" metaphor was the Indian lore surrounding the healing use of the warm mineral springs. Indians from many tribes and nations made treks and pilgrimages to the warm mineral springs known in the Lakota language as Minnekahta which translates simply as warm springs (Clark 1927). Use of Indian lore in building the metaphor was problematic for the entrepreneurs. On the one hand, the Indian use "proved the healing powers of the springs," but, on the other hand, no white man at that time wanted to base a business venture on what could be Indian superstition.

There are several versions of the Indian legends about the healing springs, each of which serves a certain purpose in its retelling in later promotional literature. Badger Clark's (1927) version contains some very important elements for the establishment of the "health = Hot Springs" metaphor. His account describes pre-Columbian Indians finding a canyon with red walls and rim rocks of a peculiar conglomerate and a warm, clear mountain stream. An old squaw who had leg pains immersed herself, and pain was relieved. She refused to come out and then realized that the pain was really gone. "Verily," intoned the medicine man, "verily, a mighty god dwells in the water of the spring, and he has driven the evil spirits out of her legs. Behold what it is to have a wise medicine man who can lead you to the very abode of the gods" (Clark 1927, 2).

Plains tribes from the Missouri River, 250 miles east of the Black Hills, had used the springs for centuries before Columbus. Clark considers that "their regard for the strange warm waters had a superstitious element in it, so 'the canyon walled in with big rocks made out of little rocks' became a religious shrine as much as a watering place." (Clark 1927, 3) This part of the legend establishes the healing quality of the waters, the Indian belief that the springs were a sacred place, that the whites considered the Indian beliefs about the waters superstitious, and that no particular Indian nation "owned" the springs. It is noteworthy that no tribal or national identity is given to the squaw who was healed by the warm springs. As with most places sacred to Indians, they did not reside at them but only visited for specific purposes.

A second part of the Indian lore involves contested claims to the springs between the Sioux Nation and the Cheyenne Nation. When the Sioux migrated west, they used the springs and named them Minnekahta (Clark 1927). The Cheyenne, who had been using the springs regularly were surprised to find the Sioux claiming them because they felt they had a prior claim based on inheritance and immemorial usage. The Sioux asserted ownership based on a superior culture, invoked their gods, and claimed manifest destiny. A battle ensued, which the Sioux won, but Clark reports that after the battle a peace conference was held and both nations signed a declaration that the springs would be under a perpetual flag of truce with a neutral radius where no man should unsheathe a knife or pull an arrow from the quiver, and red willow bark was smoked to seal the deal. The Sioux controlled the surrounding area, but once in the sacred zone, no fighting or personal grudges were allowed. "The canyon became forever a place of peace and sparkling rapids of warm creek and have never been reddened with human blood since that distant day" (Clark 1927, 5).

Leffingwell's (1894) version of the Indian lore varied considerably from Clark's. His version was contained in a publicity booklet published by the *Hot Springs Herald,* and in it he described medicine men taking water from the springs to sick people in animal skins. Only in extreme cases were the patients led by a circuitous route to the springs to keep the location secret. Later, the people figured out that the water, not the medicine man, furnished the cure, so they went on their own. Leffingwell claimed that the Cheyenne had lived near the springs for generations and called the area the Happy Hunting Grounds. "Then the Sioux found out about the springs and the buffalo, so they donned their war bonnets and sallied to the Black Hills to exterminate the Cheyennes, and obtain ownership of the hills" (Leffingwell 1894, 5). The Sioux won and kept the Black Hills until they were ceded to the United States in 1876.

Leffingwell's version is important in its historic context. Ownership of the Black Hills (including the springs) was very much contested, and in his version he discredits the Sioux claim. The sacred nature of the waters is questioned, and he reports Cheyenne living near the springs. Leffingwell's emphasis on the aggression of the Sioux people speaks to the tension of the time. It was written only four years after the 1890 Wounded Knee massacre at a time when it seemed very important for whites to establish control over the entire Black Hills.

Rezatto (1989) reports a legend that the waters of Minnekahta healed all of the tribes of North America afflicted with a terrible epidemic. The Great Spirit had blessed the waters and led the tribes to them. Some tribes stayed in the area, and some went home after being healed. Again, one of the themes seems to be that the sacred waters of Minnekahta belonged to all of the Indians of North America, discounting the claim of the Sioux. This same legend was reported in more detail in an advertising booklet that began by saying that superstitions about the springs had magnified their healing properties into miraculous manifestations of the Great Spirit (Cook 1888). According to the legend, 257 years earlier a virulent epidemic had attacked all of the Indians of North America, and they were in danger of being wiped out. The Indians already knew about healing waters, and they had tried the waters in the east and the south without success. When they had given up hope, a messenger arrived from the "Great West" with news of a wonderful water, which he said had been touched by the finger of the Great Spirit and would cure all manner of diseases. Indians went in droves to the healing waters at Dakota Hot Springs from that time until 1888. Cook also reports that it is well known that the Indians believe that the Black Hills are the abode of the Great Spirit. Cook's version of the legend included the observation that a bathtub in the shape of a moccasin had been carved for bathing. Cook's booklet was republished in its entirety in the 4 April 1946 edition of the *Hot*

Springs Star. Others considered the rock bathtub a natural formation carved only by the action of the elements.

The Sioux legend, as compiled by the workers of the South Dakota Writer's Project in 1941, mentions the springs as follows:

> *Paha Sapa,* or the Black Hills, have long been regarded by the Sioux as their holy land. Each year tribes came from great distances to cure illnesses in the warm springs, and to hunt wild animals. A legend of the Sioux, still firmly believed, is that the dark of night turns the rocks into spirits that sing strange songs, awakening the echoes. From holes in rock walls healing waters flow and the people fill their buffalo-horn cups with the clear water and drink it to become pure." (Workers of South Dakota, 1941, 109)

It was very important to include Indian classification of the springs as a sacred healing place because it was the foundation for the commodification process that led to the metaphor of "health = Hot Springs." Indians held a certain fascination for whites, particularly among the upper social classes. To Euro-Americans it was exotic that the mineral springs resort had so recently been sacred healing springs for the Sioux, and the founders of the resort used that fact in crafting the metaphor of "health = Hot Springs." There were disadvantages in trying to commodify the concept of health based on the Sioux beliefs in sacred mineral waters because Indian-white relations were still tense when the springs were purchased and the land was surveyed and marked off into plots for the establishment of a town. Therefore, the founders thought that it might be better to downplay the currency of the Indian use of the springs and to couch the legends as if they had happened a very long time ago instead of in the present.

Establishing the Metaphor

In the process of place making a considerable amount of work was needed to dissociate Hot Springs from some of the negative stereotypes held about the Great Plains and the frontier. The stereotype concerning the climate gave the developers the most cause for concern. A health resort would have limited appeal if it were perceived to be buried under three feet of snow in the winter or roasting in summer temperatures over 100 degrees Fahrenheit. In fact, Hot Springs did have a very peculiar climate compared to the rest of the Great Plains. It did not have the continental climate of extremely cold winters and oppressively hot summers that one would expect and find elsewhere in South Dakota and Wyoming. The average annual temperature was about 60°F, mediated by the altitude of the area (3,500') and the wind pattern set up by the Black Hills (Bureau of Publicity 1895; Passenger Department, Chicago and Northwestern Railway 1916). The promoters of Hot Springs dealt with the climate issue by publishing the temperatures, rainfall, snowfall, and number of cloudy days in detail in the publicity pamphlets (Bureau of Publicity 1895), comparing the climate with other areas of the Midwest (Publicity Committee 1924). Even in the summer months, evenings were cool. The mineral springs and the peaceful atmosphere in the canyons and hills exuded health and inner peace, according to all the pamphlets and advertisements (e.g., Cook 1888; Hot Springs Commercial Club 1928; Mueller and Petty 1983).

After purchasing the springs and demarcating a town, the entrepreneurs still had many obstacles to overcome in creating a health resort. The "aboriginal resort qualities of Minnekahta" were an interesting part of history and could be incorporated into the sense of place they were trying to create, but they were not enough to bring people. One problem was that the few white people who populated the Black Hills in the 1880s were mostly miners and speculators who did not come from cultures that appreciated fine health resorts. The entrepreneurs needed to create an image of Hot Springs as health that included more than testimonials from Indians.

Changing the town's name from Minnekahta to Hot Springs in 1883 was one of the first pragmatic decisions (Mueller and Petty 1983). This was a marketing decision in at least two ways: it distanced the resort from its Indian predecessors in title, and it took advantage of the reputations of Hot Springs, Arkansas, and Hot Sulphur Springs, Virginia. In this way naming was a form of norming (Berg and Kearns 1996) and the entrepreneurs could reap benefits by association with established resorts. They targeted their market for a healing place as the Midwest or the eastern United States where people would be familiar with the benefits of the other hot springs. They also distinguished the Dakota Hot Springs from the Arkansas ones; in Arkansas doctors were necessary for a cure, but in the Dakotas the water alone was sufficient. The springs that were the best temperature in Arkansas were open to the public and, therefore, were not sanitary, whereas the Dakota Hot Springs were the perfect temperature for bathing. Dakota Hot Springs catered to an exclusive clientele instead of the general public because of the sparse local population and the expense connected with traveling a long distance for a stay of at least several weeks at elegant hotels (Dakota Hot Springs Company 1888). These types of disassociations were necessary for the creation of the image of an upper-class resort, an important consideration because health resorts at the time catered to the upper classes.

When the founders of Hot Springs laid out the lots of the town, they actually planned for an upper and lower town. Health resorts, hotels, and springs were in the upper town, and the residences of the local folk and necessary businesses were in the lower town. This design fitted the natural landscape because Hot Springs is in a canyon with the Fall River flowing through it, which narrows significantly near the middle of the town. Clark (1927) reported that Hot Springs set a high moral tone for the resort by prohibiting gambling and banishing its practitioners and other disreputable people. This tone is in marked contrast to the development of the northern Black Hills, particularly Deadwood (Parker 1966). This social stratification was an attempt to develop the resort in the European style. Fred Evans, the primary developer, had traveled widely and was familiar with European resorts such as Carlsbad in the Czech Republic and Baden in Germany, and he did his best to emulate them. The trappings of gentility were advertised as proof of operation in the civilized European model. The hotels were described as gracious and palatial with baths constructed in the finest continental tradition, "accommodations befitting people of culture and refinement" (Leffingwell 1894, 16).

The Publicity Bureau's Work

The Hot Springs Publicity Bureau and the railroad companies were the most active forces in establishing the "health = Hot Springs" metaphor. They supplied newspapers with information for a constant barrage of articles that referred to Hot Springs as the Carlsbad of America in the early years of the resort. Part of the commodification of the "health = Hot Springs" metaphor was, therefore, conscious association of Hot Springs with Carlsbad. Curiously, Carlsbad was never described in the promotional literature or even referred to as the world's leading health resort. Only on occasion was it mentioned that Carlsbad was in Europe. It was a code word: if you knew what it meant, promoters wanted you at Hot Springs; if you did not know, it appears that you were not part of the target population.

One of the themes that the Publicity Bureau chose early was the establishment of a direct link between Nature and Health. Using this theme required considerable work to dispel popular beliefs about nature in Hot Springs, South Dakota. The climate was one point of great emphasis discussed above. Slogans such as "The Carlsbad of America, Hot Springs, South Dakota, in the Famous Black Hills, Climate and Waters Combine to Heal the Sick, Health for the Invalid, For the Tourist Pleasure" all appeared on the cover of one pamphlet of the Publicity Bureau in 1895. On the cover of a 1924 pamphlet was, "Fascinating Climate All Year Round" followed inside the pamphlet by a description of the crisp mountain air filled with the smell of birch and pine, cool summers, mild winters and dryness of the air, "truly an ideal climate for one of delicate constitution" (Publicity Committee 1924, 7).

Railroad companies published glowing accounts of how beautiful Hot Springs was in their effort to paint a positive picture and to encourage people to come to the area. They pulled out all the stops, praising the natural wonders of Hot Springs. The Burlington Route railroad brochure described Hot Springs as the place where civilization had just commenced, so nature was relatively undisturbed. The physical beauty contained in the smells and sights around Hot Springs created a "paradise for the health seeker." The air was clean and free from malaria.

The NorthWestern Line's (1910, 2) pamphlet quotes a "well-known medical expert of Chicago" as saying:

> There is no other place in the United States which combines the *three great essentials* of comfort and health in so perfect a manner as they are combined at Hot Springs and in the Black Hills:
>
> 1st. A reasonably increased altitude above sea level.
>
> 2d. Waters tempered to man's normal heat, charged with Nature's best remedies and given out in great purity and abundance.
>
> 3d. A pure atmosphere, a clear sky and sun-purified conditions.

Railroads had an obvious stake in promoting Hot Springs as they tried to build up passenger service between midwestern cities and the Black Hills. If vacationers were going to be attracted in the late 1890s and early 1900s, Hot Springs was one of the drawing cards.

They were trying to sell a commodity and the most attractive one was health.

Nature, health, and Hot Springs were further linked by the use of local building materials, which blended the town into its natural surroundings. The founders had not only planned for the stratified town but also for the hotels and bathhouses to be built of natural sandstone. The pink hue of the sandstone added to the beauty of the resort area but also contributed to the emphasis on naturalness, which, in turn, contributed to the "health = Hot Springs" metaphor.

The Waters Themselves

The founders and maintainers of Hot Springs took a multifaceted approach to the mineral springs. Initially, as discussed above, belief in the healing power of the springs attested to by the Indians was accepted by the Euro-Americans. The Sioux reportedly were mildly amused that they could be healed in an hour, but white people had to soak in the springs a week. It was said with pride in the early days of the resort, that doctors were not needed. This made Hot Springs, South Dakota, superior to Hot Springs, Arkansas. At the same time that these claims were being made, however, chemists were carefully measuring the mineral content of each spring, and the results were reported in most brochures about the resort. Each spring had a slightly different chemical composition, but the waters could cure a broad spectrum of illnesses. An 1888 booklet listed the following diseases that could be cured:

> Rheumatism, acute inflammatory and sciatic; syphilis in all its stages; diseases from use of mercury; neuralgia of the head, face, stomach or limbs; catarrh; ascites, or dropsy; hemorrhoids, or piles, dyspepsia, or chronic indigestion; constipation; nephritis and other diseases of the kidneys, urinary difficulties; eczema, psoriasis, and all other diseases of the skin. . . . In addition to the above, it is known that the following diseases have been very much relieved, and in some cases cured, viz.: Female complaints of various characters, diseases of the stomach and alimentary canal, liver complaint, and Bright's disease of the kidneys" (Cook 1888, 16).

Despite that listing the emphasis of the booklet was by no means on disease. Rather it was on the luxury of the town, the services offered, and health and happiness attributable merely to being in the beautiful Black Hills. The idea that medicinal waters were useful was not by any means an artifact of the late 1880s. In 1946 the State Geological Survey prepared a report entitled "Medicinal Waters of South Dakota" for the Natural Resources Commission as part of a state development plan. The report showed the presence of medicinal salts in several of the springs in Hot Springs.

There was competition among the springs as to which one had the best water and which one had the best bathhouse. The rivalry was not related to medicinal qualities of the water as much as luxurious, yet sanitary, recreational qualities. Mammoth Spring claimed to be the most sanitary plunge because it had constructed a swimming pool with a smooth, hard bottom that could be "frequently and completely cleansed." In one of the Mammoth Springs pamphlets was the explanation that bathing gives off refuse particles which "sink to the bottom and mingle with the water, giving off offensive odor. . . . And if water so polluted gets into the eyes or mouth, the condition is intolerable and most unsanitary" (Mammoth Spring 1909, 3). The smooth bottom eliminated accumulations, and the water could be shut off occasionally and the entire basin cleaned. The promoters of Mammoth Plunge claimed that the U.S. Department of Agriculture had approved the cement floor. This floor is only important in contrast to the natural pebble floor of Evans Plunge, which was also claimed to be the cleanest bathhouse because of the swift spring flow that completely replaced the water in the pool eight times each day. In Evans Plunge the spring water bubbled up around the pebbles, which was considered an added attraction. Although the springs competed with each other for guests, the competition was subdued. Owners of all the springs recognized that they were all dependent on all of Hot Springs to attract visitors.

Disease, Doctors, and Hospitals

Curing disease was a part of the "health = Hot Springs" metaphor. Certain constraints, however, were placed on the diseases that were welcome at Hot Springs. Excluded from the long list of diseases the waters could cure, cited above, were all contagious diseases. For example, an annual report for Our Lady of Lourdes Hospital boasted of all the people who had been cured but stated unequivocally that "patients with contagious diseases were not admitted" (1910–11, 9).

In the early days of the resort there were boasts, such as those cited earlier, that the waters alone could cure, but even if the founders of the resort believed these assertions, they hedged their bets by encouraging doctors to establish clinics in Hot Springs. This openness to different methods for obtaining health was actually a very shrewd marketing strategy for the metaphor because it extended the potential market to include people who wanted to be healed just by water and people who felt the need for a doctor's care. Advertising pamphlets from the Publicity Bureau and the railroads contained advertisements for several types of healing modalities (see Hot Springs Commercial Club c. 1909; Bureau of Publicity 1895; Cook 1888). At Evans Plunge and Sanitarium one could have a "Russian bath, Turkish bath, fomentation, vapor, needle baths, plain mineral baths, mud baths, in fact every bath which is conducive to health" in addition to Swedish movement massage (Bureau of Publicity 1895). None of these treatments required a doctor, although doctors did have offices at the Evans.

In an astute move to guarantee the success of the "health = Hot Springs" metaphor, the railroads sponsored medical conventions for their doctors at Hot Springs, and the doctors in turn passed resolutions praising Hot Springs as a place for a cure (Hot Springs Chamber of Commerce c. 1893) and later as a place for rehabilitation recommended by physicians from the Mayo Clinic (Hot Springs Commercial Club 1924, 6). By 1924 the Commercial Club was saying that "the development of a medical community [in Hot Springs] is seen as science becoming Nature's ally" (1924, 5). In this way doctors, clinics, and hospitals were explicitly embraced within the metaphor.

Hospitals became very important in Hot Springs and in some ways probably ensured the survival of the town. Hot Springs has more than its share of hospitals if one calculates by permanent population. Most of the population of South Dakota lives east of the Missouri River, and the extreme western part of the state, including Hot Springs and the rest of the Black Hills, has always had a much smaller population. By playing on the metaphor Hot Springs was able to obtain the territorial soldier's home for veterans of the Grand Army of the Republic in 1888 and a national hospital for veterans in 1902 known as Battle Mountain Sanitarium (Julin 1982). The waters of Hot Springs and the natural environment were instrumental in the federal government's decision to locate the veteran's facility in Hot Springs.

In 1893 a "test" was conducted by the government to see if Hot Springs was really a place that restored health. Thirty veterans with chronic diseases being treated at Fort Leavenworth were sent to the State Soldiers Home in Hot Springs for sixty days to see if their conditions would improve. It was reported that "8 rheumatic cases were practically cured, and all the other patients except one were improved" (Battle Mountain Sanitarium 1909). People in Hot Springs were sure that if the veterans had stayed six months instead of two, the cure rate would have been higher.

"Endorsements"

One of the marketing ploys used by the Hot Springs Commercial Club was to claim endorsement by anyone who praised the town and springs (e.g., individuals writing letters of thanks for a wonderful stay) or who located a facility there (e.g., the state and federal government). The Battle Mountain Sanitarium created such an endorsement by the federal government. A NorthWestern Line railroad pamphlet from 1910 read, "South Dakota Hot Springs Endorsed by the U.S. Government Through the Construction of the Battle Mountain Sanitarium." A 1928 publicity pamphlet (Hot Springs Commercial Club 1928) said, "National Health Resort, Hot Springs South Dakota in the Black Hills." The basis for entitlement to use the National Health Resort title, in addition to the Veterans Administration (VA) Hospital, was set forth in a 1924 pamphlet entitled "Black Hills Health Resort Hot Springs, South Dakota, . . . Endorsed by the United States Government as a National Health Resort":

> No city in the world is more worthy of the title for here are combined every weapon, both natural and artificial, to attack the strongholds of disease; an all-wise Providence has provided a panacea for every ill to which the human race is subject. Medicinal herbs and plants, healing waters, radio-active minerals, together with the variations in altitude and climate, are Nature's restoratives, which have only to be wisely administered to become effective. Thus Nature provides and Science applies the remedies that eliminate disease and restore our well-being. (Hot Springs Commecial Club 1924, 8)

Chicago and NorthWestern Railway's cover of their advertisement in 1916 contained a picture of Battle Mountain Sanitarium and the words "The So. Dakota Hot Springs Endorsed by the U.S.

Government as a National Sanitarium" (Chicago and NorthWestern Railway 1916).

The real heyday of the resorts was before World War I, but Hot Springs never died. Despite national economic trends related to the effects of World War I the Publicity Bureau still kept the metaphor of "health = Hot Springs" alive. The railroads were replaced by cars, and the target market was no longer exclusively the upper class. Hot Springs was now within the reach of anyone with a car.

In 1932 the Publicity Committee was still using the National Health Resort title, but an endorsement from the American Automobile Association (AAA) had been added (Hot Springs Chamber of Commerce 1932). The 1932 pamphlet was a recreational advertisement aimed at tourists, not people seeking cures, but the recreation was couched in terms of health. The VA Hospital and the chemical composition of the springs were mentioned, but no cures were promised from the waters. Hiking along Fall River was as important as drinking from it or playing golf. Evans Plunge was seen to be a major recreational asset. People in the town never gave up on the idea that the hot springs could be their ticket to redevelopment. The 1946 report from the South Dakota Department of Natural Resources counted the warm springs as potential economic (re)development sites. Automobiles, however, made other hot springs as accessible as the South Dakota springs.

Is the Metaphor Still Alive?

The "health = Hot Springs" metaphor is not entirely gone, but it no longer defines the town. Hot Springs is long past its heyday, but it still has mineral springs and more hospitals than one would expect in a town of its size. The widespread acceptance of modern medical techniques hurt belief in the healing powers of the waters, and certainly the polio epidemic in the 1950s discouraged many people from going to the spas. But Evans Plunge continues to operate and still has a natural pebble bottom to the pool and slides and ropes much as it did in the late 1900s. It is endorsed by AAA and its brochure says, "The Water's Fine. Evan's Plunge Hot Springs, South Dakota, The City of Healing Waters." In 1961 it was serving between one thousand and fifteen hundred visitors per day (Hot Springs Chamber of Commerce 1961). The 1992 brochure is very much like the 1961 pamphlet.

In June 1974 Hot Springs was designated a Historic District by the National Register (Aberdeen, South Dakota, *American News,* 7 May 1975). The story reporting this designation blamed the decline of Hot Springs on World War I and the lure of more famous resorts, but it reported cause for optimism in the booming business of Evans Plunge. Today Evans Plunge is a health club in addition to being a major tourist attraction in the summer.

In a pamphlet designed to attract new industry the emphasis was "our history can be your future" (Hot Springs Chamber of Commerce 1986). It highlighted the Richardsonian Romanesque style of architecture and suggested that the opportunities that the Dakota Hot Springs Company (*sic*) discovered still existed, but it did not mention health. Instead, the pamphlet mentioned the low wage rate, the right to work laws, and the large percentage of women in the labor force. Clearly, the health metaphor no longer defines the town. From 1977 to 1980 Hot Springs participated in the Main Street Pilot Program through the National Trust for Historic Preservation to see if economic development could be fostered (Skelcher 1992). The emphasis was on the Lakota sandstone buildings built in the Richardsonian Romanesque style. Architecture, not health would define the town according to the planners. The project was not successful. Skelcher blamed the failure on the need for long-term monitors to encourage preservation of the built environment (1992). More likely the project was unsuccessful because the history of Hot Springs is not in sandstone buildings alone but in a metaphor of "health = Hot Springs." Without the metaphor the buildings lose their context.

Conclusion

For much of its history Hot Springs has embodied the metaphor "health = Hot Springs." Health was commodified through the appropriation of mineral springs, red canyons, fresh air, and all of nature. From the beginning there was room for different definitions of health and different means of obtaining health at Hot Springs. The common goal, however, was to promote health. The Indian legends were part of the history and the meaning of health in Hot Springs, but they were not part of the commodity. Most likely their absence from active participation in the commodification process reflected the political situation surrounding the appropriation of the Black Hills. The founders of Hot Springs used the European resorts of Carlsbad and

Baden as their models during the heyday. The several changes of ownership during its early years suggest that the resort was more socially than economically successful.

The inclusiveness of the definition of health was extremely important and was a wise move from a development standpoint. Most articles about Hot Springs concentrate on the heyday that essentially ended in 1919. The metaphor lived on for many years past that date, however, Evans Plunge, the sole surviving commercial spring, still uses healing waters in its advertising materials. South Dakota tour books include the history of Hot Springs and recommend a visit to Evans Plunge. In light of this history, it is somewhat puzzling that "alternative" medical practitioners have not used the springs. It may be that the population of Western South Dakota is just too small to support that type of health practice.

Hot Springs is a place constructed through the commodification of health. Since the 1960s it has lost its vigor, and the package of attractions no longer finds a market among health "consumers." Rather, Hot Springs is known for its historical associations and recreational potential.

4

Landscapes of State Violence and the Struggle to Reclaim Community

Mental Health and Human Rights in Iquique, Chile

LESSIE JO FRAZIER AND JOSEPH L. SCARPACI

Mulchén, no hubo guerra
¡¡Fue matanza, todos fueron asesinados!!
Lonquén, no hubo guerra
¡¡Fue matanza, todos fueron asesinados!!
Laja, no hubo guerra
¡¡Fue matanza, todos fueron asesinados!!
Pisagua, no hubo guerra
¡¡Fue matanza, todos fueron asesinados!!
Colina, no hubo guerra
¡¡Fue matanza, todos fueron asesinados!!
Derramaron la sangre
¡¡Ahora, quieren borrar su culpa!!
No habrá perdón ni olvido en la tierra!!
Pinochet es culpable. Juicio y castigo a todos los culpables!!

—Sebastian Acevedo Movement Against Torture

Lessie Frazier received research support for this chapter for field work conducted in Chile (1990, 1991, 1992–94) from the National Science Foundation, Fulbright, Wenner-Gren Foundation for Anthropological Research, and Rackham Graduate School, History and Anthropology Program and Latin American and Caribbean Studies Program fellowships at the University of Michigan. She thanks Mine Ener and Julie Hastings for their comments and suggestions. Joseph L. Scarpaci acknowledges support from the Summer Social Sciences Program in Chile sponsored by Virginia Tech.

The above passage highlights a litany of places in Chile where the remains of the victims of the Pinochet dictatorship have been recovered: Mulchén, Lonquén, La Laja, Pisagua, Colina. The litany insists that "it wasn't a war, it was a massacre, all were assassinated" and, finally, "They spilled the blood—now they want to erase their guilt. There will be neither pardon nor forgetting in the earth—Pinochet is guilty. Justice and punishment for all of the guilty." This litany is also an example of the struggle over whose history of the dictatorship would achieve credibility and which regimes would be considered legitimate. We refer to the military dictatorship of General Agusto Pinochet Ugarte who, as a member of a junta, started a coup d'état against the government of President Salvador Allende Gossens on 11 September 1973. After a plebiscite and election, a coalition of Center-Left parties assumed governmental power in 1990.

During its 1973–90 rule the Chilean military claimed to have won a civil war fought against the forces of global communism, whereas the human rights movement referred to a long history of repression of the Chilean people. The exhumed bodies became artifacts of this struggle over history as forensic scientists traced the stories of torture and execution encoded on the corpses (fig. 4.1). Each additional mass grave site mapped out a topography of state terror (Miranda 1989).

In a 1990 protest in downtown Santiago members of Sebastian Acevedo lay silently on the ground in the main pedestrian thoroughfare, holding signs for each of the grave sites throughout the country. The silent presence of the protesters, representing the wordless testimony of the bodies in the graves, provided an arena for people to speak of their history. A woman cried out over the bodies and signs, "Pinochet murdered my nephew, there is no pardon on this earth!" Other bystanders called back across the way, "Calm yourself, here is the truth." Through the geography of urban protest, the demonstrators and the crowd reshaped public discourses of national history—a history grounded and evidenced in an archaeology of state terror.

Corroboration for these and other civil protests over human rights abuses stems from the discovery of clandestine graves. During seventeen years of military rule (1973–90) the Pinochet regime was anxious to purge the country of "enemies of the state." Under the guise of being at war civil liberties were ignored and military rule superseded civilian processes of law and order (Scarpaci 1991). Death from torture or assassination led the armed services to dispose of forensic

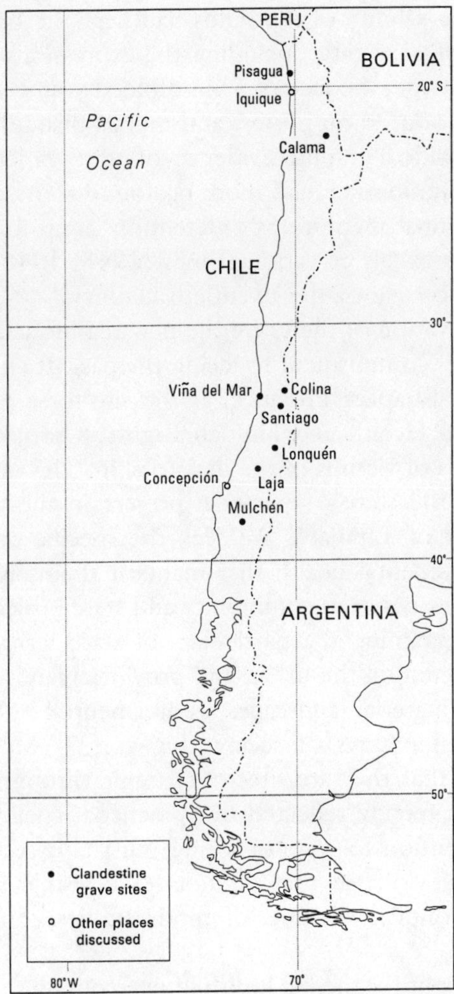

Figure 4.1. Clandestine grave sites in Chile created during Pinochet regime, 1973–1990.

evidence quickly, and clandestine grave sites served that purpose. The first grave excavated in the time of regime transition was in June 1990 in the northern desert province of Tarapacá. The grave found in a cemetery in the nearly abandoned nitrate port of Pisagua riveted the nation's attention for two reasons. First, not only was it the first mass grave to be excavated but the abundant video and photographic documentation of the site made its impact unavoidable. The lack of moisture and the salinity of the sands had kept the bodies in a state of near-perfect preservation, including the expressions on their faces. One particular image, the face of a blindfolded young man grimacing in pain, was reproduced on posters and murals throughout the country. Pisagua provided graphic evidence of state violence heretofore denied. But its significance had more profound roots. Pisagua is also infamous in national memory as a detention camp for political prisoners and homosexuals at various times (1943, 1948, 1956, 1973, 1984) over the course of the twentieth century.

With the excavation of the grave the new regime seized the opportunity to show its commitment to facing the past. It chose the nearby city of Iquique, Tarapacá Province, as the site for a pilot reparation program, Mental Health and Human Rights, a project intended to address the needs of victims of the dictatorship. This chapter presents a case study of the state's reparation project in the context of the social geography of Tarapacá. We seek the specific connections between place and mental health that manifest themselves in conflicts and contradictions between community and state projects. To address these issues we examine the particulars of state terror and popular resistance as enacted on the urban and provincial landscapes of Chile. We affirm that "material landscapes are not neutral but reflect power relations and single ways of seeing the world" (McDowell 1994, 161). We assert that they are sites of struggle through which power relations are not merely reflected but practiced, challenged, and reconstituted. Attention to ways of seeing must also account for technologies of state violence that do not leave visible scars, but also render internal connective tissues of minds, bodies, communities, and places.

The Chilean fight for mental health in overcoming repression forms part of a mental health and human rights movement spanning the Americas. Iquique provides a case study of the processes by which a military regime reshapes urban landscapes and community, and, subsequently, how a community struggles to reclaim its spaces and well-being through protest, testimony, and the search for mental health and integrity. Hence, we outline the features of local historical geography in the pursuit of antiessentialist depictions of place and locality recognizing no authentic places, but nexuses of social relations grounded in struggles (Massey 1994). Whereas medical geographers contend that the politics of state health policies operate on specific local terrain (McLafferty 1989; Mohan 1989), we seek to explain the struggles for mental health and the contradictions of regime transition and neoliberal insertion within a global system.

The Archaeology of Landscapes of State Violence

In the first few months after the transition to formal democracy (March 1990) the human rights movement focused attention on the discovery of mass graves holding the remains of disappeared (Gómez 1990; Verdugo 1990) or executed people.[1] Information on possible grave sites had been collected over the years by the Catholic Church's Vicary of Solidarity. Given the more favorable political conditions of regime transition, the vicary began to uncover the sites. A representative along with a sympathetic judge—with shovel and video camera—investigated each alleged site. As soon as a grave was uncovered, the team called in the press immediately so that publicity would inhibit any military attempt to close off the site (as had occurred during dictatorship). As the forensic anthropologists identified the bodies, whole communities gathered to hold funerals that served as occasions for collective mourning and for political demonstrations. The ultimate symbolism of these funerals was the reburial of President Allende's remains in the National Cemetery in 1990. Although his family was allowed to bury the body in a small cemetery in Viña del Mar on the Pacific coast, the nation was not given an opportunity to bury and mourn properly. Holding the second burial service in the nation's capital and in the main public cemetery underscored the role of prominent public places in healing Chile's "landscapes of terror." Mourners throughout Chile, demanding "Truth and Justice," called upon the government to confront the past and to attempt a degree of moral resolution. In this way the human rights movement began to map out the history of state terror across the country.

Human rights groups insisted that Chileans acknowledge the grave sites—covering the entire country and dating from various points during the dictatorship—as evidence of the systematic and institutionalized

1. The movement adopted the name of Sebastian Acevedo, a father whose sons disappeared. To draw attention to their plight this father immolated himself in Concepción, Chile. His sons were eventually released. In late 1990 the group split into two over the issue of the degree to which the democratically elected government of Patricio Aylwin should be pushed on human rights issues. By 1992 it had ceased to exist, not from a lack of issues (i.e., the continuing human rights abuses) but from the stress of an ambiguous political arena.

nature of human rights abuses under the Pinochet regime. Through protests on the streets human rights groups challenged not only the legitimacy of the military's rule but also the authority of recently inaugurated President Aylwin's administration to control violence and to assert command over the history of that violence. In addition, the human rights movement attempted to make this history available to the Chilean people through media, posters and murals, public demonstrations, cultural events, and vigils.

In light of the persistent demands by the Chilean and international human rights movement President Aylwin named a commission to collect evidence of human rights abuses and to publish an official report much like the *Nunca más* (Never again) reports issued in Brazil, Argentina, and Uruguay (Argentine National Commission 1986; Dassin 1986; Weschler 1990). Although known as the Rettig Commission, Aylwin also dubbed it the Commission of Truth and Reconciliation. The commission, as representative of the ruling coalition of political parties, deliberately chose not to call itself the Commission of Truth and Justice. This choice was indicative of the precarious negotiation of regime transition in Chile (Valenzuela and Valenzuela 1986; Drake and Jaksić 1991), that is, strong popular and international support for a democratic government in the face of an aggressive—and nervous—military.

Throughout the process of regime transition sectors of the human rights movement called for (1) the recognition that torture was systematic and institutionalized (versus the excesses of a few officers); (2) the understanding that torture left lasting physical and psychological scars on the Chilean people (thus, survivors of torture and indirect victims should be recognized); and (3) the government's recognition of international conventions against torture.[2] These resolutions arose largely in response to the Rettig Commission's limited scope of inquiry. It gathered documentation for the cases of victims who died and ignored survivors of torture. It then presented those findings to the government. Pursuit of individual cases was beyond

2. The groundwork for this analysis and for projects on mental health and human rights was provided by the work of several human rights associations. *Persona estado poder: Estudios sobre salud mental Chile: 1971–1989* (Santiago, 1989) published by the organization Comité de los Derechos del Pueblo (CODEPU) elaborates a political project for the recuperation of individual and collective mental health. Of particular scholarly interest is the work of the Instituto Latinoamericano de Salud-Mental y Derechos Humanos (ILAS) (Becker and Lira 1989; Lira and Castillo 1991).

the charge of the commission; family members of the missing or deceased had to file court cases and seek judicial review of those cases if they so desired. Activists recognized that over the decades of the dictatorship power had become institutionalized in the government and police in ways that were left intact under the transition to formal democracy. The archaeology of state violence in the excavations of the mass graves to a certain extent had displaced the need for an archaeology of violence as manifested in living bodies. Torture as an ongoing process in the minds and bodies of survivors, not to mention cases of brutality since transition, became the hidden text of a "truth" defined by the politically possible.

Thus, the concerns voiced by the human rights community could not outweigh the enormous pressures on the new government to limit the range of questions asked by the Rettig Commission. These pressures were revealed in the responses to the Rettig Report that were approved by the military before being made public. Officials of the Unión Democratica Independiente Party (UDI), the extreme right-wing party of the *pinochista* ideologues, gave their stamp of approval. Party president, Julio Dittborn, pronounced, "It is fair to recognize that the study was made with prudence, and our fears that the information would reach public opinion distorted did not come true" (CHIP News 1991). Dittborn said that the actions the commission studied were products of the Unidad Popular (Allende) government. He added that the report "will not be new, because everyone knows that there were war councils—which are established by legislation—executions, and human rights violations" (CHIP News 1991). Concern over international accords involved an appreciation for a set of universal standards of human rights. In the context of ferocious nationalism the National Security Doctrine served as a powerful ideological tool and a justification for human rights violations. In other words, national security concerns, it was argued, superseded any international accord to which Chile might be a signatory nation. Recognition of international versus national doctrine, moreover, made it look like Chile was giving preference to foreign versus national (right-wing, anticommunist) concerns. In Chile, human rights groups successfully used the international arena and created local forums to challenge the legitimacy of the authoritarian state. Thus, a Chilean government human rights discourse that emphasized national reconciliation above universal moral standards of justice seemingly negated many of the gains brought by international alliances and universalistic moral stands.

The political party leaders of the new government—in an attempt to mediate between the military state and Chilean society—believed that the survival of political democracy in Chile depended on a project of national reconciliation. This ability to "turn the page" of history—as the government wished—was based on attaining a consciousness and then transcendence of national history. Thus, they advocated truth and reconciliation. This call for reconciliation as healing unwittingly reinforced the military's metaphor of opposition groups as Chile's "cancer" that had to be surgically removed. Medical metaphors for political processes in Chile were mobilized for violence, the Chilean military's organic and geopolitical notion of the state (Lebensraum), and liberatory projects (Scarpaci and Frazier 1993). The government saw "justice" as tantamount to another coup and felt it had no choice but to hope for the intrinsically liberatory function of history. Human rights activists charged that it was the government that pursued a politics of forgetting. The human rights movement made demands that the government felt it simply could not meet.

Thus, the human rights movement took a politically daring stand when it reinscribed public spaces with memories of concrete human beings. Activists insisted that the dead not only deserved a place in the present but also a revindication of their identities as Chilean citizens; doing so would restore their honor. They argued that truth and reconciliation are ephemeral, rhetorical concepts unless they are linked on the ground with a project of justice and social democracy. In spite of the disappointment wrought by the Rettig Report human rights groups continued to insist on a more complete truth and on the continuous remembrance of the past—a sort of justice through the refusal to allow the guilty to forget. Chilean forensic anthropologists continued the painstaking labor of excavation and identification of the remains of the victims of the dictatorship: "It's one thing to identify the murderers and another to bring them to justice," one Grupo de Antropología Forense (GAF) anthropologist said. "But if only for the sake of history, we are obliged to continue" (Browne 1992).

The Historical Landscapes of Iquique and Tarapacá

Iquique was Pinochet's "pet" city, a place whose development via a free trade zone was to become the international paradigm of the benevolence of military rule and neoliberal economics. Paved, watered, urbanized, and blessed with a bounty of imported consumer goods, the city was a cornerstone in Chile's model to ward off deindustrialization in the 1970s and 1980s (Scarpaci 1990). This desert port remains Pinochet's retreat when assailed by the demands of democratic transition. Yet Iquique's streets and neighborhoods bear the scars of the dictator's attentions. Since the coup d état of 1973, the military population of Iquique has been housed in residential compounds strategically built around and within neighborhoods once famed as "the cradle of the Chilean Left." Streets and neighborhoods were renamed in an effort to erase the progressive legacy of this mining boom town (although changes in toponyms happened throughout Chile during military rule). In 1973 dissidents were concentrated in the nearby, isolated port of Pisagua in a prison camp of a consciously fascist design.

Pisagua was used as a detention camp at various times during the twentieth century. With the collapse of the nitrate industry in the 1930s development schemes to save Pisagua from depopulation called for the construction of a penal fishing colony. Pisagua was lauded as a "natural prison" because of the attributes of its absolute location—a small beach surrounded by an almost vertical rise of a coastal mountain chain. The lack of land meant construcing a few buildings such as the municipal theater over the water. As a result, prisoners did not necessarily have to be locked up. Its relative location also enhanced Pisagua's role as a military prison: if a detained person could escape by sea or overcome the immediate precipice, a waterless desert would almost certainly deter their flight.

With the discovery of a mass grave in 1990 Pisagua once again became a key national symbol of the search for truth and justice. The associations of former political prisoners and families of the disappeared and executed demanded reparation, including health care for the victims of state terror. Iquique became the site of the United States Agency for International Development (AID) funded pilot health program for victims of the dictatorship. The success of this program inspired its adoption by the Ministry of Health and implementation throughout the country. The incorporation of issues of human rights and health into a state project represents an enormous achievement for those who—during decades of repression and with marginal resources—worked steadily to confront the legacies of state terror.

National political and economic conflicts have been inscribed on and through territory. The northernmost frontier province of Tarapacá has played a particular role in Chilean state formation. The late nineteenth and early twentieth century struggle over nitrate wealth in the desert and the control of nitrate workers shaped the social geography of Tarapacá and its place in the nation. Battle sites of the War of the Pacific (1879) in which Chile conquered the nitrate rich north from Peru and Bolivia and of the civil war when Iquique became the stronghold for British-backed antigovernment forces make Tarapacá a key site in Chilean military history. Yet community and place in Tarapacá also represent the connection between people's lives and their ways of making a living in this inhospitable land. It is known as the birthplace of the Chilean labor movement and of most of the contemporary political parties (de Shazo 1983; Loveman 1988). State terror worked in this place by strategically using its contradictory histories and reinscribing it as "Chilean." Here guardians and benefactors were the military, and there were attempts to erase other legacies of popular struggle.

Tarapacá is a case study of landscapes of terror both in direct state repression and an oppressive interaction of the community with its economic environment. In the late nineteenth century nitrate-processing stations (*oficinas*) sprang up throughout the Atacama Desert, which runs through the heart of Tarapacá. High evapo-transpiration rates gave the desert floor rich layers of chemicals that could be easily mined by scraping the surface. Although the oficinas served a key role in the world fertilizer and munitions industries one hundred years ago, today these ghost towns litter the landscape rendered useless by the synthetic processing of nitrogen from the atmosphere. The northern mining towns were the sites of bitter and violent labor-management confrontations, giving rise to the first medical programs for workers in key industries that provided the nation with significant hard currency (Scarpaci 1988). Nonetheless, the nitrate industry powered Chile to unprecedented levels of wealth during its heyday.

In the 1980s the region rose again to national prominence. Regional economic policies of the dictatorship involved an "opening" up to the world via a free trade zone, the fencing off of the coastline for the private benefit of the fish meal industry, the continued dismantling and selling off for scrap of the old nitrate communities, and a collusion with weapons-dealer Cardoen that resulted (1984) in a weapons factory explosion just above the city whose victims remain to this day uncounted and uncountable. In the spirit of fiscal accountability and cost-recovery that characterized the Pinochet regime, authorities in Tarapacá set out to dismantle old oficinas and to sell the scrap metal from roofs, homes, stores, and industrial complexes. Almost all of the oficinas were ghost towns except for a few die hard inhabitants. The dismantling of the oficinas also deprived former residents and friends of periodic visits to these frontier mining outposts. Perhaps the most celebrated organized group to visit these places was the Hijos de Salitre (Sons and Daughters of Nitrate) who would make annual pilgrimages to certain old mining towns as a tribute to a bygone era and their loved ones who had toiled in the mines.

Given the legacies of the economic and political history in Tarapacá, the geography of popular protest became critical in resistance to this "landscape of terror" (Scarpaci and Frazier 1993). Iquique's urban geography differed from that of other Latin American cities (Griffin and Ford 1980) and from the capital city of Santiago (Scarpaci, Gaete, and Infante 1988; Scarpaci 1994). The cathedral is not located in the main plaza or any plaza at all for that matter. Instead, it sits off to the side of a minor town square, Plaza Condell, which is named for a hero of an important naval battle held off the coast of Iquique during the War of the Pacific. Because of its historic significance, Plaza Condell has been a site for political meetings and rallies of local and national import. Iquique's city hall is also located on this secondary plaza, yet another atypical feature of Iquique's built environment. The main town square is Plaza Prat, named for a national hero who was the martyr of the battle of Iquique. Plaza Prat is the site of a well-known military procession each Sunday. It is framed by an ornate neoclassical theater built of Oregon pine (with sculptures of the four seasons that, ironically, only exist as artistic symbolism in this tropical climate). English nitrate barons built the landmark theater, but it was restored by Pinochet's appointed city mayor. Other buildings on this main town square include an elegant hotel, banks, and private clubs founded by the foreign capitalists of the nitrate boom years (1890–1930) such as the Spanish Club (an ornate Moorish style building with elaborate interior murals of scenes from Don Quixote) and the Yugoslavian Club. Thus, the urban geography of Iquique has more to do with British-led investment than with Spanish colonial iconography.

Protests usually began at Iquique's Cathedral and ended at a local school in the center of the city that was the site of a massacre of nitrate workers in 1907. In 1957 a small monument was inaugurated by the unions and provided an anchor for subsequent urban protests. The anniversary of the massacre, 21 December, became a day of protest during the dictatorship, linking generations of suffering and struggle. Demonstrators frequently incorporated songs from a cantata about this massacre composed by a local son during the Allende years. In spite of the logistical difficulties of travel in this militarily occupied region protesters began to make annual pilgrimages to Pisagua as early as 1983 to commemorate the experiences of the former political prisoners and to search for the graves of the executed and disappeared. The human rights movement in Tarapacá drew together its local histories of struggle to challenge powerfully the legitimacy of the military.

The local human rights movement creatively connected issues of mental health, community, and place in the kinds of demands it made during regime transition. The democratic regime's ambiguous response to these demands marks an inability or unwillingness to attend to the peculiarly local connections between place and mental health. Community in Tarapacá has been difficult to reclaim because of contradictory and complex relations of community and nation, yet this history is precisely the rich material from which the components of collective, resisting identities are drawn.

Modernity and Mental Health

National attention turned north in June 1990 when the mass grave containing executed and disappeared persons from 1973 was excavated by local human rights activists. The site was at the edge of an old cemetery in the nearly abandoned nitrate port of Pisagua. As discussed previously, the mass grave at Pisagua was the first of a series of graves to be excavated throughout the country in 1990. These graves mapped in a very concrete way the extent of state terror in Chile. The visual documentation of the open graves, which appeared in posters, magazines, murals and documentaries, and forensic anthropologists' "readings" of the histories of torture and execution inscribed on the bodies provided tangible artifacts of the history of state terror as an institutionalized system at a crucial moment in the earliest stages of regime transition.

The grave both revindicated the anti-Pinochet movement and challenged and pushed the Aylwin administration when it might have moved more cautiously toward formulating its own relation to Chile's political past. Members of mental health organizations in Santiago and the newly inaugurated Aylwin presidency had been considering a reparation program for victims of the dictatorship. The events at Pisagua riveted national attention at a crucial moment in the transition. More importantly, local human rights activists, former political prisoners and their families, and committed medical personnel began to pressure the government for just such a program. The Rettig Commission provided a template for government action when it recommended that the state "provide to families of the victims the legal advice and necessary social assistance whenever necessary" (*Comisión Nacional de Verdad y Reconciliación*, 1991, 2:873, our translation). The government seized the political moment and decided to start a pilot project immediately in Iquique, the primary port city of the province. Gradually, the program expanded to cover other cities and regions. The project became known as Programa de Reparación y Atención Integral de Salud y Derechos Humanos (Human Rights and Integrated Health Service Reparation Program [PRAIS]), and funding for the first three years of the project came from AID. Mental health as development complemented the new government's project of "cultural modernization" designed to mold Chile into the form of Western liberal democracy in a neoliberal economy.

The PRAIS program services family of executed and disappeared *retornados* (returned exiles) and former political prisoners (many of whom are also retornados and *relegados*, people exiled internally) and their immediate families. It provides basic primary care and access to specialists as well. The resources are limited; patients must go to great lengths to obtain appointments; and referrals to higher levels of care are complicated. In Iquique, between September 1990 and December 1993, the project attended 798 patients. About 77 of these were members of thirty-six families affected by situations of execution or disappearance. On a national scale, PRAIS estimates that it has reached 37.8 percent of potential patients from such families (Domínguez 1994), suggesting that PRAIS operates with an ideal model of both the patients and the process of recovery. The program, as with other policies of reparation, privileges family members of a deceased individual (executed or disappeared). The ideal process of recovery then is that of mourning in which the family (as the foundational unit of civil society) will come to terms with its loss and then move on. As with the Rettig report, this ideal model both fails to account for surviving individuals who were detained, tortured and exiled and to account for the direct participation and repression of family members in resisting the dictatorship.

This discomfort in tracing the history of repression as inscribed on the living (a counterpart to the forensic analysis of those found in the grave) shows itself in the disagreements between staff and patients about the connection between current complaints of a generally aging population and the physical and psychological traumas experienced over the preceding twenty years. The former political prisoners attribute diabetes, stress-related disorders, cancer, alcoholism, and other common illnesses to physical abuse and torture in the prison camp and detention centers.

On a national level, PRAIS estimates a 28.4 percent relation between diagnosis and the repressive situation under which patients lived. When considering mental illness apart from other complaints, however, PRAIS found a 48 percent connection between mental illness and individual history of repression with only 12.8 percent relation for physical problems. Overall, 47.5 percent of diagnoses were for mental disorders. Physical problems tended toward the osteomuscular system and connective tissue (6.8 percent) and the circulatory system (5.2 percent). The predominance of mental as opposed to physical diagnoses was particularly notable among women (Domínguez 1994). The PRAIS staff in Iquique are reluctant to draw those conclusions, and their general skepticism frustrates the former political prisoners to the point where they refuse to discuss past traumas and even current symptoms with the staff. The following account illustrates this gap in the mental health care delivery system between the staff and the former political prisoners.

In an interview with the general physician of PRAIS in Iquique, one of us asked about the medical basis for the former political prisoners' insistence that their current physical and mental problems stemmed from torture at Pisagua. The doctor replied that torture was not really an issue in Pisagua because the camp operated early in the dictatorship before methods of torture were perfected, and most of the guards were mere conscripts not trained to torture. In a session with a committee of the former political prisoners who were interested in putting together their own book on Pisagua, one of them insisted that an entire chapter should be devoted to their torture experiences because torture was central to the fundamental purpose of the camp, that is, to force prisoners to betray/renounce their political loyalties. The fact that people had not told the military what they wanted to hear represented a victory for the survivors. The others emphatically agreed, and for the first time recounted in detail their experiences to us.

How do we understand the physician's denial of torture? Our answer must of necessity be partial and tentative. This doctor (who lost many friends to repression) comes from a family long devoted to Allende and progressive politics. Working with intense dedication in the PRAIS program was a way to fulfill a personal sense of obligation and responsibility. Perhaps the inability to listen reflects the difficulty of representing the same state—albeit a new regime—that perpetrated the violence. In demanding that the state via the PRAIS staff acknowledge the specificity of violence in Tarapacá the former political prisoners reconstruct themselves as historical agents and reclaim their community, not in opposition to, but with a particular relation to the state and national history.

During regime transition the PRAIS program represented the only direct link of this community to the state, and it was a tenuous connection at best. After a cautious trial period, in 1994, the program was formally and permanently incorporated into the Ministry of Health as the program on Mental Health and Violence that addressed issues of domestic violence, rape, child abuse and molestation in addition to its former role in treating victims of political violence. The program staff in Iquique, however, resolutely refused to expand their mandate beyond the realm of strictly political violence. In response to this stand the state has allowed them to continue working solely with victims of "political" violence. That the program is carried out in sparsely settled northern Chile is significant because Tarapacá, like the southern Mapuche territory, was one of the most repressed areas of Chile during the dictatorship. The national security interests of these remote corners of the country—perceived to be dangerously vulnerable to foreign aggressors—had become central to the military's notion of itself as the guarantor of civilization and the integrity of the Chilean nation-state.

In some ways Iquique was an unlikely place for the pilot program. Most nongovernmental organizations working in mental health and human rights operated primarily in the capital, Santiago. In a country spanning three thousand kilometers the logistics of governmental and nongovernmental programs are no small matter. With almost one-quarter of the population concentrated in the central, metropolitan region most programs have few ambitions beyond the capital. Yet in a country historically centralized in economic and political power and administrative bureaucracy frontiers have played a central role in state formation. The political process of regime transition, or democratization, has not proved exceptional in this area. The timetables for transition factored in a period of national healing that culminated in reconciliation. Iquique's resistance to the easy incorporation of the PRAIS program into the bureaucracy of the Ministry of Health highlights the contradictions inherent in this model of regime transition as healing.

The local PRAIS health care professionals protested that they could barely meet the needs of current patients let alone take on whole new categories of potential clients. The Ministry of Health agreed that Iquique, unlike other sites in the country, was not experiencing a decrease in patient visits and, thus, still had much work to do with recuperating of victims of the dictatorship. People in Iquique view the program as a concession that they won through great struggle and make specific demands of the democratic regime largely through this program because it is one of the few direct links they have to the state. They are proud that their struggle has served as a mental healthcare delivery model for the rest of the country. They see the continued demand for the program as a positive sign of the strength of their community forged in struggle. The state sees it as a sign that these people are still sick, trapped in the past, and have yet to meet the goals of reintegration. Broadening the scope of the program was a way of signaling that Chile had put its history behind itself, that reconciliation was complete, and that government concern could move on to nonpolitical social problems in a project of cultural modernization (Brunner, Barríos, and Catalan 1989). Through mental health treatment this community of outcasts had the possibility of participating fully in the national project of modernity. The existence of an alternative notion of community and its relation to the past and to the state is a source of conflict for the new regime.

The human rights community in Iquique is rife with bitter divisions. Factions surfaced among the founders of the association of families of disappeared and executed and widows (some of whom remarried to military officers) who took over the group when reparation became available. Almost all agree, however, on the importance of the PRAIS program in their daily lives and claim it as the fruit of their own struggles as a community rather than as the result of the benevolence of the state. They make constant demands of the program and challenge that it has an excessively top-down, paternalistic model of health care. They also use the program selectively in terms of which health services they use, how much they reveal to the staff, and which members of their families participate.

In addition, the local staff of the program also emphasizes the distinctiveness of Iquique both as a place and as a therapeutic program in Chile. The community has suffered from the stigma derived from uncovering the graves. Moreover, the absolute location will never go away and stands in mute testimony to the crimes of the past. Iquique health-care professionals feel that everything they know they have learned on their own with little support from the administrative offices in the capital who see them as a source of data. They talk of their sense of isolation and harassment by other medical staff in the hospital (for being "reds") in the first years of the program. The staff has been intransigent in their refusal to take on the broadened mandate of institutionalization and the Mental Health and Violence Program. They plead lack of resources and the fact that the needs of their "political" patients have not diminished. The reparation program had been constructed as a temporary measure until the victims of political repression "recover" and are "reintegrated" into Chilean society. In spite of the conflicts between patients and providers they maintain a united front toward the state and its claims of proprietorship. They have demanded and been conceded the uniqueness of their community and its mental health needs.

Mental Health and the Human Rights Movement

The Mental Health and Human Rights movement spanning the Americas holds exciting possibilities for transnational struggles for justice. The movement expands medical anthropology and medical geography's concern with the individual and practice in the "clinic" to seeing individuals' health as inseparable from collective health and politics. Those concerns, moreover, are grounded in clearly defined places whose historical geography brings a great deal to bear on the conceptualization of illness, treatment, and well-being. Mental health has been reformulated beyond pathology to include positive processes of growth and well-being. For the most part, mental health and human-rights activists have operated on the margins or in direct opposition to the states in the region. The conflicts and challenges when their insights are taken up in state projects have been the subject of this chapter.

It is significant that the Chilean government of transition began to fulfill its commitment to reparation first and foremost through a health program. Although many families of the executed and disappeared have received one-time cash compensation and some educational grants, the PRAIS program remains the most far-reaching initiative in offering services to the survivors of repression as broadly defined.[3] As pointed out previously, health as a metaphor for politics and, in this case, the safest means of enacting a politics of reparation, has certain troubling implications. Political repression as pathology and reparation as therapy do not necessarily confront the configurations of power that made a long-lived and, to a certain extent, quite popular dictatorship take hold and endure.

A psychologist from a prominent U.S. treatment center for the victims of torture visited Iquique in hopes of including it in an overview of mental health and human rights in Latin America. He had heard of Iquique's fame as a focus of particularly terrible repression. In a meeting with the Association of Former Political Prisoners he suggested that international assistance to their group could be mobilized best with a complete account of the challenges they have faced in organizing. They began with tales of the "shameless" who siphoned off international solidarity funds during the dictatorship. In addition, they told of the take-over of the Association of Family Members by pro-military widows only interested in the rewards brought by transition (the reparation money). The psychologist explained to the former political prisoners that one insight of political psychology has been to assert that *they* are not the mentally ill, rather they are people responding in a normal way to extremely adverse circumstances and it is society that is demented. He suggested that these widows suffer from an overidentification with their oppressors and that through therapy they would come to see the error of their ways.

After the meeting, one woman—who is internationally recognized as a founder of the human rights movement in Iquique, who had lost her son to torture and a firing squad, had seen years of organizing swept aside by the usurpers, and had been forced to abandon the organization of family members altogether—turned aside and said

3. In 1993, Iquique also became the pilot for a government small business loan project for former political prisoners, as Iquique has one of the strongest organizations in the country. This project has heavily negotiated between the association of former political prisoners of Pisagua and state officials in Santiago and their local representatives.

"that idea is crazy." She rejected the psychologist's dismissal of moral culpability as pathology. For if politics is pathology, then there are *only* victims—the politically subversive and those whose paranoia required their destruction.[4] Yet imagine the possibilities if the PRAIS program had begun under the supposition that it was the military and its many supporters who required psychological first aid before they could be reincorporated into moral, civil society? This approach would have entailed a profound dismantling of structures of repression, a task made impossible in the regime transition as imagined and managed by Chilean political and economic elites and the military.

Healing the Wounds in Landscapes of Fear

Clinical psychologists working in Argentina and Chile have found that ill-health and place are inextricably bound in Chile's human rights calamity. Victims, their loved ones, and the torturers and soldiers can benefit from reconciling (ill)health and place. Victims who survived often return to places of detention. The opportunity to see the place of detention is an important part of their postdetention therapy. It can heighten details and clarify events that, although mostly negative, may allow them to gain a sense of empowerment over place, a key therapeutic step in overcoming trauma.

Place has served as both a sense of affirmation and rejection in Pisagua. On the one hand, many make an annual pilgrimage to Pisagua in October. They hold a ceremony at the mass grave site. A cultural act is held in the former theater of the prison camp, the same camp where the prisoners were forced to perform for the officers and soldiers of Pisagua. Picnics are held during these pilgrimages, and acts and offerings are made before a statue of the local Virgin who is highly venerated in the region. Such activities reaffirm the heinous crimes that took place at Pisagua and help the process of bereavement. On the other hand, land uses have changed. The camp no longer functions, and the main building in the camp has been turned into a hotel, complete with the original graffiti on the walls as it was carved by the prisoners. The new private management of the hotel

4. This notion of political instability as an unfortunate pathology has been reinforced by journalistic and scholarly analyses of *fear* in Chile, which argue that all sectors of Chilean society have been gripped for two decades by mutual fear and misunderstanding. Repression and resistance, thus, can be seen as a collective overreaction of a nation unacquainted with itself.

makes no attempt to hide the building's history and uses the graffiti as a marketing ploy in the hotel's interior design. Adding insult to injury, the new private management will not allow former prisoners to enter the premises, and will certainly not permit any group ceremony to be held in the hotel.

Loved ones of these human rights victims benefit by knowing where the victims were kept and how they may have spent their final days or hours. Since the return of democratic rule in Chile, however, no full forensic reports have been released to the families of the detained and disappeared; military rule seems to be immune from any civil effort that tries to put these documents into the hands of civilians. In the Pisagua saga, for instance, some former detainees who survived their internment returned. This strengthened the victims' cases against military personnel who participated in human rights violations. One accused intelligence agent was Osvaldo Pincetti, a secret police hypnotist, who, although he did not work at Pisagua, would hypnotize prisoners so that they would write self-incriminating statements. Revealing this to victims' loved ones is helpful because although they had assumed that confessions were extracted by coercive means, knowing whether the coercive means was by torture, hypnosis, or some other force plays a key part in "filling in the pieces" in this heinous puzzle of detention. Other examples include the case of a solider, Miguel Nash Saez, who was executed shortly after the 11 September 1973 coup d'état in Pisagua. The mother of the soldier, Ana Saez, wrote to President Arturo Frei stating: "The Army told me that my son was dead, and that they had buried him in the old Pisagua cemetery. I just want his remains to be transferred, to give him a decent burial. . . . I'm not even asking for justice. I don't know what that is" (CHIP News 1994). As Ana Saez pieced together the account surrounding her son's death, she found that he and a socialist leader were forced to run toward a hill and were told that the first one to reach it would be saved. As they started running, however, they were shot from behind by antiaircraft weapons. Details such as these—however horrible—help bring closure to the process of grieving as does the ceremony of a proper burial.

Even the torturers and military officers and soldiers who indirectly helped the junta carry out their mission of terror profit—psychologically and monetarily—from joining place and health. Military officers often used place to justify their positions. One such group is the

National Association of Soldiers of Silence. Members of this group are former security agents who feel betrayed by their military leaders and countries. Although clandestine, the association sends menacing messages and even death threats to human-rights lawyers and activists who continue to press for justice in the courts. Intelligence sources under the democratic government of President Patricio Aylwin reported that the association met in Iquique in mid-November 1992 to organize a right-wing terrorist group (CHIP News, 1 Jan. 1993). Other torturers and military officers seek pecuniary rewards for disclosing the sites of clandestine grave sites. Unscrupulous persons will contact the family members of the detained and disappeared and offer to tell them whether their loved ones are buried, but only for a price.

Conclusions

Through the particular shape that reparation has taken in the Chilean transition from dictatorship to formal democracy in the context of deepening neo-liberal economic transformations, health and place have become central in the constitution of community. In Tarapacá Province in northern Chile, the human rights community insists on the historic specificity of its needs and relation to the state. Activists see this history as inscribed in the scars that the dictatorship left on their bodies, minds, and landscapes. They allege the ongoing connections between those scars and the contemporary political order. In so doing, they demand that the public health system facilitate their efforts *not* to recover and/or get over from the past and be reincorporated into a seamless national narrative but to recuperate the voice and integrity of their community.

The process of creating landscapes of state violence is complex. In this chapter we go beyond the current norm in medical geography by showing how the "interconnection between global forces and local particularity" alter the relationships between identity, meaning, and place (McDowell 1994, 166) to see how local struggles impinge upon state projects. In the case of Iquique—a frontier community of internal strife—the demands made on the Chilean state during regime transition have resisted a centralization of suffering and have challenged the very foundational models of reparation and healing. For the survivors of Chile's human rights travesty and their families and loved ones, however, the process of healing the wounds has only just begun. A first step in that healing process is grounding illicit events in specific places and then making the connection between place and health.

Part Two

Identity, Difference, and Health

5

Place, Identity, and Disability

Narratives of Intellectually Disabled People in Toronto

GLENDA LAWS AND JOHN RADFORD

In this chapter we respond to Kearns's (1993) recent call for a realignment of the focus of medical geography and also acknowledge one of the most important lessons of recent feminist and postcolonial contributions to social theory, namely, the need to listen to the voices of the Other (Bhaba 1990). We feel that this is a necessary step if Kearns's search for a renewed understanding of the role of place in human well-being is to be achieved.

Human geography has largely abandoned its former one-dimensional view of society and has come to recognize the importance of such factors as class, "race," ethnicity, and gender in influencing the environmental and spatial aspects of human behavior. Further, an increasing number of studies have emphasized the role of small group and individual attributes in shaping urban life (Eyles and Smith 1988). "The practice of everyday life" (de Certeau 1984; Smith 1993) and the everyday routines in peoples' lives—their action spaces, their perceptions of neighborhood and community—are regarded as significant components of social geography (Buttimer 1976; Ley 1977; Entrikin 1991). Feminists have recently joined humanists in calling for sensitivity to the routine and domestic aspects of everyday life

This project was one of the last that Glenda Laws worked on before her tragic and untimely death in June 1996. Glenda played a key role in the humanizing of medical geography, and the sense of loss we continue to experience is both personal and professional.

(McDowell 1992). Places, including homes, neighborhoods and cities, are therefore analyzed, on the one hand, not as a set of supposedly objectively defined statistical areas but as congregations of the individual life-worlds of their inhabitants; on the other hand, places are conceptualized as the product of a layering of collective political struggles over the practices of everyday life (see Johnston 1991).

Those who have adopted the lessons of social theory have continued to ignore people who are labeled "mentally handicapped." Even Golledge (1993), a major contributor to disability studies in geography, has yet to do full justice in his research to the richness of people's experiences. In this essay we focus on the ways in which places are constructed by and for people with "mental handicaps." Such people have been largely overlooked in comparison, for example, with those labeled "mentally ill." Historically, they were "put away," falling victim to modernity's emphasis on the ordered society and to the Enlightenment's worship of truth, beauty, and intellect, both of which emphasized "abnormality" and indicated the necessity for segregation (Radford 1994). Since the early 1980s people with developmental disabilities have come to have a visible presence in neighborhoods within most major North American cities. During the 1970s and 1980s the concept of "normalization," which eroded the dogma of enforced segregation (and often involuntary sterilization) was implemented in varying degrees within jurisdictions throughout Western Europe and North America. First articulated in North America between 1969 and 1972, normalization advocated the provision of as normal an environment as possible (Wolfensberger 1972). Normal daily, weekly, and annual rhythms, normal social contacts, and the expectation of a normal life cycle would, it was argued, provide an environment within which individuals could develop their fullest potential. By the 1980s normalization and community integration had become the bywords of mental handicap policy. Out of this development have grown more recent initiatives, including a human rights approach and self advocacy (Bleasdale 1994; Rioux 1994). One manifestation of this change has been a deinstitutionalization movement comparable with that in the mental illness sector (Simmons 1982; Bruininks et al. 1981). Another has been a reduction in the incidence of intellectually disabled dependents remaining in the parental home into adulthood. In place of such arrangements a variety of residential alternatives have been established, including group homes, cooperatives, and other types of ordinary housing (Ontario Ministry of Community and Social Services 1987; Willer and Intagliata 1984). A new presence has also evolved selectively in public settings such as schools and workplaces. It is clear that in some jurisdictions these trends have been cost-driven. Lack of adequate funding provision for "community care" has prompted criticisms of the scale and rapidity of deinstitutionalization and has contributed to increases in the homeless population.

Described in its early stages as "a vast experiment" (Landesman-Dwyer, Stein, and Sackett et al. 1978), deinstitutionalization of people with an intellectual disability began, and to some extent is still being conducted, in something of a research vacuum. Until recent years medical information on intellectual disability was based overwhelmingly on research conducted on institutionalized populations. Anthropological and sociological work has expanded knowledge along three main lines. First, numerous studies of the effectiveness of community residential alternatives appeared during the 1980s. These are usually based on survey data, sometimes including questionnaire surveys completed by, or on behalf of, residents. In most cases the researchers strive for methodological rigor in sampling procedures and experimental design (Heal and Fujiura 1984). Many of these survey-based studies also incorporate what may be identified as a second type of approach—so-called ecological studies that focus on interrelationships between disability groups and the surrounding community (Richardson 1981; Gollay et al. 1978; Sinson and Stainton 1990). Contrasting with these is a third set of ethnographic studies by anthropologists who compile detailed life histories through prolonged and intensive contact with small groups and individuals (Langness and Levine 1986; Dudley 1983). This approach is designed to counteract the problem of the "disappearing individual" in survey research by providing an "inner view" of the experiential basis of disability. Informed by many of the same ideals as those expressed by geographers such as Buttimer (1976) and Ley (1977), the focus of this work is heavily biographical and intensely personal, with a special emphasis on early socialization experiences (for a particularly dramatic example of this type of biographical study see Smith 1995). Cross-disciplinary research has examined the situations of people with disabilities within the broader social matrix (Castellani 1987). Rioux and Crawford (1990), for example, have examined the relationships between disability and poverty. In a similar vein Torjman (1988) and Salisbury, Dickey, and Crawford (1987) have studied the problems of income insecurity and service brokerage.

Despite this recent literature the issues surrounding the integration of intellectually disabled people into the community remain neglected by geographers, especially in comparison to studies of other marginalized groups such as the mentally ill (Dear and Taylor 1982; Dear and Wolch 1987; Smith and Giggs 1988). Too little is still known of any distinctive ways in which intellectually disabled people perceive their environments and to what extent these perceptions are colored by individual life chances and experiences. As a result only a slender body of knowledge has existed on which to base the implementation of community-based policies. That so many individual projects achieved a measure of success is a tribute to the intuition and involvement of care workers and those in the voluntary sector.

However, a literature has begun to emerge that attempts to gain a fuller insight by providing an opportunity for people with an intellectual disability to express their views on their lives in institutional settings and on their experiences with community living (Schwier 1990; Whittacker, Gardner, and Kershaw 1991; Collins 1992; Jones 1992; Ballard 1993). In this chapter we build on these studies to illustrate some of the ways in which place affects the life experiences and well-being of our subjects. We take a broad view of well-being that includes satisfaction with daily life circumstances: with housing, employment opportunities and experiences, social networks and social attitudes. We report on a study in which we ask intellectually disabled people questions about the nature of their lives in the community. The aim is to formulate generalizations about their experiences within supposedly integrated settings in a major urban area, the greater Toronto region of southern Ontario. We focus on the question of whether disabled individuals do participate and whether *they regard themselves as participants* in the life of the wider community. We begin by briefly outlining our perspective on the relationships between well-being and place. We then comment on some of the methodological considerations of the study before discussing our findings by presenting aggregated results. Results are followed by some in-depth profiles of our respondents. In the concluding section we address the question of how well disabled people are integrated in the community and outline some of the directions our future research will take.

Well-being and Place: Some Methodological Issues

As Kearns (1993) has noted, the links between health and place have long been recognized though not always centralized in studies which might broadly be referred to as medical geography. Our focus is upon individual well-being. We believe this bodily centered focus is important because it is the individual who must experience the negative consequences of stigmatizing social practices and attitudes (Edgerton and Bercovici 1976; Gale, Ng, and Rosenblood 1988; Scheper-Hughes and Lock 1987; Odette 1994).

Places are important in the creation of individual identities. It is in particular places that individuals interact with and react to other people who may or may not label them in one way or another. We draw from both humanistic and structuralist traditions when we conceptualize places as the loci of social relations and practices. These relations operate between people with different degrees of power (e.g., employer and employee, male and female, parent and child) and between peers (colleagues, friends, family members). Each of these two broadly defined sets of relations are both embodied and emplaced to shape simultaneously an individual's identity and experience of place. The embodiment of identity is important when we consider well-being (Dorn and Laws 1994). The bodily appearance of old age (Laws 1994b, 1995), disability (Dorn 1993), homelessness, femininity, or race can make a very real difference to the ways in which an individual is perceived and to the ways in which other people react. Kristeva (1982) describes the ways in which people create some bodies as abject and repulsive, whereas Proctor's (1988) analysis of racial hygiene in Nazi Germany shows the deadly consequences of such constructions. Less extreme, but still the basis for discriminatory behavior and attitudes, are the ways in which the population at large stigmatizes the bodies of the disabled and older people.

The stigmatizing and "abjectioning" potential of the larger population has been recognized for some time now, and great efforts have been made by professionals to reverse older oppressive policies through mainstreaming. Normalization theory and, more recently, the insistence on human rights have been translated into social practices that "integrate" the people back into the community with the purported goals of two-way education. If places are, as we have argued, concentrations of social relations and social practices, then an investigation of these relations and practices should provide some insights into the links between place and well-being. We have found this a particularly useful window through which to view the position of our study group, a nonrandom sample of developmentally disabled adults in Toronto. We use the word *window* deliberately; as social scientists, we are, in fact, voyeurs, gazing into a world of which we are not entirely a part but a world that we nonetheless help to construct. Choosing to bundle together a group of people as the "researched" immediately establishes us as the party responsible for the construction of the object, for the construction and imposition of a certain identity. But we remedy some of the faults of traditional academic voyeurism by hearing and listening to the voices of our respondents rather than by statistically analyzing their life experiences.

Studies of the experiences of individuals can provide the basis for a useful guide to future planning. We are not, however, advocating a focus on the individual at the expense of the environment; rather we want to consider the environment as viewed through the individual. Moreover, the only true judge of successful adjustment to environmental factors, of the significance of life experiences, of the quality of life is the individual person with a developmental disability. The opinions of professionals, caregivers, and even immediate family may provide useful complementary material, but they are no substitutes for allowing people with disabilities to speak for themselves. We are not naïve enough to believe that this chapter truly represents the voices of the Other. In the process of interviewing and writing we have obviously been selective in what we report, an issue with which we have grappled but one that is not uncommon to research that relies heavily on qualitative approaches (Burawoy, Burton, and Ferguson 1991).

Interviewing people with developmental disabilities poses special problems (both practical and ethical) that have prompted a small but provocative literature (Birenbaum and Re 1979; Sigelman et al. 1980, Singelman et al. 1982; Flynn 1986). Particular attention has been paid to high levels of acquiescence that have been noted in the survey research and that may be explained by fear of the consequences of complaints or by a desire to cooperate with the interviewer. In particular, a yes/no format may produce higher response rates than open-ended questions, but it has been found to yield responses that are more at variance with information provided by caregivers. Sigelman et al. (1982) have suggested that a multiple choice format is the most useful compromise, but they admit that their studies reveal more about how *not* to interview mentally handicapped people than about proven techniques.

Our own research was based on a structured interview schedule, the design of which closely followed that used by Dear et al. (1980) in their study of mentally ill people. Questions were asked about the respondent's living situation, employment, recreational activities, and income because each of these factors is obviously an important component of anyone's (disabled or otherwise) experience of place. Yes/no, multiple choice and open-ended formats were all used in an attempt to elicit responses as detailed as possible on the daily activities of the respondents and their degree of involvement in their communities. No attempt was made to identify a random or representative sample. It is doubtful whether such a concept is even plausible, given the definitional problems that plague the study of mental disability. Rather than risk allowing the project to become stuck in the labeling quagmire, we simply selected respondents from among those that society had clearly stigmatized as "handicapped." The procedure used was a snowball design, the interviewers building on contacts from one respondent to another.

Three interviewers were hired, each having wide experience in interacting with people with a developmental disability and more than willing to listen to stories if necessary rather than expecting exact, precise, or succinct answers to questions. Although we provided them with a structured questionnaire, the interviewers were encouraged to use it as a guide rather than a prescription and, particularly, to allow open-ended discussion that would yield narrative information. As might be expected, the interviewers' notes, scrawled on the margins of the schedule, were often as revealing as the answers that they recorded to the prearranged questions. These notes usually reported comments made by the respondent rather than interviewer observations. Space was provided at the end of the survey schedule for the interviewers to record any comments that they felt were relevant. Such information included whether another person was present at the interview, particular problems encountered in the interview, and any observations made as a result of the interviewers' training (all had experience in working with people with developmental disabilities). The interview sessions averaged more than two hours. Fifty-seven interviews were completed, the majority of these taking place in the respondent's homes. No refusals were encountered, mainly because the possibility of becoming a respondent was allowed to evolve gradually. Ethical guidelines on research involving human subjects were closely adhered to, and individual questions were sometimes set aside when reluctance to answer was evident.

Basic demographic information about our group is shown in table 5.1. It is made up of adults only, slightly more women than men.

Table 5.1

Intellectually Disabled Sample Characteristics

	N	%
Age distribution		
18–30	21	37
31–45	23	40
46–60	11	19
> 60	2	4
TOTAL	57	100
Marital status		
Single	48	84
Married	4	7
Separated/divorced	3	5
Missing	2	4
TOTAL	57	100
Level of education		
Did not complete grade school	6	10
Completed grade school	5	20
Completed junior high school	8	14
Completed high school	7	12
Humber College CICE[a] program	7	12
Missing	24	42
TOTAL	57	100
Sex		
Male	25	43
Female	30	53
Missing	2	4
TOTAL	57	100

[a]Humber College offers a diploma program, Community Integration through Cooperative Education.

Because of the age profile of the group, we have a significant number of people who have spent some time in an institution and have experienced firsthand the process of deinstitutionalization. The questions we asked, however, focused on their community experiences, so we make no attempt to comment on the institutional experiences of these people, except where they volunteered information. Only two members of our sample were more than sixty. It is possible that people in this older age group have had very different life experiences than the younger respondents have had. Only four of our respondents were currently married (they constituted two couples) although another three had been married at some time. The information on education levels suffers from an extremely high number of missing observations (42 percent), many of these reflecting a lack of formal school education that until recent years was replaced by "training." However, Of the thirty-three individuals for whom grade level education information is meaningful, one-fifth had completed high school and another one-fifth had gone on to complete a special program at a local community college. Almost 60 percent, however, had an education of junior high school or less.

With respect to the residential experiences of our respondents, 60 percent lived in the municipality of Metropolitan Toronto, the remainder living in newer suburban subdivisions in the Greater Toronto Area. Almost 80 percent lived in either a house or an apartment. Thirty-seven percent of the respondents lived with one or both parents; another 26 percent lived in group homes and 23 percent in independent apartments. In most cases these apartments were located in complexes developed for senior citizens, even though only two of our respondents were over the age of sixty. This result is a function of provincial housing policy which allows handicapped people to live in publicly funded senior citizens' housing. Of the thirteen individuals who lived in independent apartments, four were living with their respective spouses (i.e., the two couples in our sample) while others lived by themselves. Six respondents had been placed in a supported independent living program designed to allow as much freedom as possible, but with supervisory backup when necessary. Finally, one respondent was currently in an institution and one was living in a boarding house. We realize that these figures in no way represent the extent of institutional experiences or boarding house situations in which developmentally disabled people find themselves, but within the constraints of this phase of the project we were unable to extend our search.

Perhaps the most important question we asked was, "Do you feel comfortable in your neighborhood?" The response was overwhelmingly positive. It was also remarkably consistent throughout the Greater Toronto Area. A little more than one-quarter of our respondents suggested that they had some reservations about their neighborhoods. Some were concerned with traffic and noise, and others were aware of neighbors who labeled them. It is also interesting to note that a little more than half the respondents who answered the question said that they would consider moving. Those who said they would move were largely interested in upgrading their accommodations: more space, the desire for privacy, and the wish to own a home were some of the reasons cited for the wish to move.

The answers about employment revealed that almost two-thirds of the respondents worked outside the home in paid employment. It should also be noted that 49 percent of our sample (or 80 percent of those who worked) were employed full time. Of these, most worked in manufacturing jobs in sheltered workshops that pay less than market wages. Other jobs included work in cafeterias, ushers at cinemas, and shop assistants. One of our female respondents managed a small shop and jewelry manufacturing operation owned by her mother. Half of those who were employed traveled to work by regular public transport and another 28 percent by special buses provided by Metro Toronto or private agencies to ferry handicapped (both physically and mentally) individuals to and from work and services that they require. Forty-one percent of those who were working had been employed for less than two years, suggesting that for the other 60 percent, at least, employment was a relatively stable feature of their daily routines. We should note, however, that 35 percent of the total sample was not working. One-quarter of the total sample (or 36 percent of those who were working and who responded to our question) reported difficulty in finding a job. Seventy percent of those who were working reported that they had had some assistance in finding employment. Such assistance came from a variety of sources including counsellors and social workers. Eighty-six percent of the working sample said that they "fitted in" at work, suggesting very positive perceptions of their environments.

Despite this relatively high level of comfort with their work environments, less than 30 percent of respondents said they socialized with their workmates. This might well be a reflection of the fact that 28 percent of our sample use special bus services to get to and from work and this might limit some of their opportunities for after-work activities. It quite probably also reflects the stigma experienced by developmentally handicapped people. In response to questions about free-time activities 56 percent said that they felt they had enough to do in their free time, whereas 35 percent answered no to this question. Fifty-seven percent reported that they regularly did things with their friends (although not their workmates), and 79 percent had regular contact with their families. Various activities were mentioned, but watching television was by far the most common.

Even though a high proportion of our sample did work for wages, it should be noted that only 14 percent told us that wages were their major source of income. Fifty-six percent said that the majority of their money came from income-maintenance programs such as the provincial Family Benefits Allowance (FBA) or pensions of one sort or another. For 24 percent of the respondents a combination of wages and these income-maintenance payments provided their financial resources. It is difficult to draw conclusions about the respondents' levels of satisfaction with the amount of money available to them. The group is almost equally divided between those who feel they have enough and those who do not. A clear majority (65 percent) of the sample look after their own money. This result may be a function of the biases created by our sampling method. By contacting people known by those who had already answered the survey we found that, in general, we were interviewing a relatively independent group. Had we found more individuals in more structured residential settings, we might have found a lower proportion who responded positively to questions regarding financial independence.

Profiling the Respondents

Rowe and Wolch's (1990) paper on the lives of homeless women in Los Angeles is an excellent example of how geographers can use peoples' stories of their day-to-day lives to shed some light on the urban experience of groups who have been neglected in the literature. Rollinson's (1990) work on the elderly who live in single room occupancy hotels also points to the value of ethnographic research in geography. We are concerned, however, that attention focused on a visibly marginalized population such as homeless people, a group whose plight has been publicized by the media, might detract attention from less-visible groups who are hidden from view within the complex structure of cities. People with "mental handicaps" seem particularly vulnerable to becoming invisible. In part, this is a function of the fact that they are more likely to receive the sympathies of the public and their families and are, therefore, likely to receive support that prevents them from becoming a visible part of the street population. The stories we offer below shed light on the lives of our respondents, the "voices from the shadows" who recounted their experiences for us. The names have been changed in all cases, but these are individual stories, not composites. They were chosen as fairly representative of the profiles that emerged.

Sarah is forty-one years old and lives alone in an apartment in the northern suburbs of Toronto. As a child she simultaneously contracted tonsillitis and measles, and complications arose that left her with some brain damage. She was then labeled as a slow learner and was placed into an "opportunity class" designed to meet her special needs. Before moving into her current home, a bachelor apartment in a seniors' building, eight years ago, Sarah had been living in a group home in suburban Toronto. She heard of the opening through REENA, a nonprofit service agency that assists handicapped persons living in the community.[1] Even though the move was coordinated by this organization, Sarah found certain hostilities toward her when she moved. The seniors living in the complex did not want "young people" (Sarah's words) living in the apartments. REENA helped challenge this attitude, and an agreement has been reached that the people placed by REENA in the building will be working or looking for work. In Sarah's words, "We can't just stay around here all day." When she was asked about the neighborhood, the only complaint was that "sometimes the seniors label us, but we can't do much about it."

When asked if she was thinking of moving Sarah answered, "No." She said, however, that she only said "no" because she cannot afford to move. "If I had the money I would buy a condo downtown. I would like to have a dog, but no pets are allowed in this building." Even with these desires Sarah finds independent living in the apartment very attractive because she has a place of her own, doesn't have to share, can cook and buy the food of her choice, and can have guests whenever she wants.

1. REENA is an agency founded by members of the Toronto Jewish community who took the organization's name from a Hebrew word meaning joy. This name symbolizes the joy of people coming out into wider society as full participants.

Sarah works from 10:30 A.M. to 4:30 P.M. each day in a restaurant at a large education center in northern Toronto. She has been there for twelve months and previously worked in a cafeteria at one of the city's universities but was laid off during the summer. She likes the people she works with but does not socialize with them. When she does go out, Sarah's activities are relatively limited. Once each month she attends meetings of People First (an international self-advocacy organization of people with an intellectual disability) at a community center within walking distance of her home. As a member of the executive committee of this group, she also meets with other executive members monthly at their homes. Twice each week she plays bingo with friends or with the seniors in her apartment building. She always stays in the northern suburbs of Toronto and either walks or uses public transit to get to these places. During the interview she told us that she goes home after work, indicating little if any variation in this routine. She told the interviewer that she was not bored but would like to do more things although she did not know what other things she would like to do.

Sarah has no contact with her family, so relies on her friends and organized support groups for social activities. She does, however, lead an independent life managing her limited income herself. She receives a wage supplement from the government but still remains in the very low category of income levels. When asked about her "typical" day, her responses indicated that it revolves around a routine of work, bingo and television.

Jonathon is a forty-six-year old single man who was born with cerebral palsy, which left him with poor vision and impaired hearing. Consequently, he was labeled as a slow learner. He finished grade 6 at a "regular school" and then completed grades 7 and 8 at a vocational school. For the past four years he has lived independently in an apartment designed for seniors, single parents, and handicapped people in Etobicoke on the western edge of Metropolitan Toronto. A social worker helped him find the apartment, and Jonathon has no complaints about his apartment or the neighborhood. He finds that the area offers him all the amenities he needs: shops, banks, dry cleaners, shoe repairers, and other services. At the time of the interview, he was between jobs and hoped he could find a job as a bookkeeper or as a photographer. He realizes that he has several problems in finding employment: his age, his hearing and visual impairments, his inability to drive a car, and his slow learning. Yet he was being assisted by several agencies in his search for work.

Like Sarah, Jonathon is an active member of People First and attends monthly meetings and a weekly Friday dance. His activities with People First means that he commutes into the City by the Metropolitan Toronto public transit service (TTC) quite frequently. Jonathon perceives himself as having no friends and would like to be able to go to a movie or sit and talk with a friend. He says, "Sometimes I have time on my hands." At Christmas and over the summer he is able to travel out of the province to visit relatives. But his day-to-day life is characterized by watching television, reading the newspaper, relaxing, sleeping, the occasional sporting event, and "doing my own personal bookkeeping" once a week. While he is unemployed, Jonathon must survive on Family Benefits Allowance, so is financially restricted, but he feels he has enough money.

Michael is a twenty-six-year-old resident of a boarding home for people with psychiatric histories. He was born with cerebral palsy and lived in many different foster homes until he was eleven. He was on his way to an institution when he was adopted by a family. His adopted mother successfully struggled to have the label "developmentally disabled" removed and cerebral palsy is now his only diagnosis. For the last ten months he has lived in a boarding home where he shares a room with one other man and the house with twelve others. His mother has tried to have him moved, but he wants to stay despite several serious problems with his living situation. Michael's reply to the question of what he dislikes about the house is a telling one: "I want to have my TV in my bedroom but they won't let me. They want us to take the pictures down from our walls. I want to have a key to the house." He likes the neighborhood and cites the presence of doughnut stores and a soup kitchen as making it attractive. He also wants to remain close to the library.

Michael is keen to draw and expressed disappointment that he could not attend art classes locally because the classes scheduled at the community center were canceled. He formerly worked at McDonald's but now attends a community college. He receives welfare payments, but his landlady and social worker manage his money, most of which goes to pay rent. The shortage of money is problematic for Michael. He is disappointed that he cannot afford to buy art supplies, and he would like to "go out to the Art Gallery, Museum, and movies." Even though Michael is attending a community college, he reveals a limited group of friends. He reported that "my friends are the people in my support circle." He is only too aware of his "segregated" status. He walks to the local soup kitchen for meals and fellowship with "other poor people in Parkdale" or to the local doughnut store for coffee with members of his support circle.

Jane is a married woman in her late thirties. She and her husband, Rod, are among the few people in our sample who have spent a considerable time in a large institution. Both are labeled as slow learners. Married for ten years, Jane rents a one-bedroom apartment with Rod in a seniors' building, again in northern Toronto. She has been living here for two years and moved from her last home because she "was too ashamed to take people in." As with many of the other accounts we heard, Jane reported two major problems in finding an apartment. First, the costs of renting an apartment in Toronto are extraordinarily high. Second, she "didn't know where or how to look for a place." Her husband, Rod, also answered our survey, and he gave us more details of the problems they encountered:

> I had applied to Ontario Housing years ago and received a letter saying that subsidized apartments were for seniors only but I should get a medical form from my doctor stating that I am handicapped. I did this, but something happened to our file and no one ever helped us. Finally, our social worker got our file opened, and we were given three choices as to where to live. We would have preferred a townhouse but were told because we have no children we could not get a townhouse.

The hassle of moving means Jane is happy to stay in the apartment she is currently in, even though she has several complaints: "The space is too small for us. It is cockroach infested, and even though they give us cockroach houses, they don't work. I want a second bathroom." Rod, however, said that he wanted to move: "If we could get a townhouse, a second bedroom, and more space, I would move. It would have to be rent-geared-to-income. I want to have a garden and be able to control the cockroaches." He described the windows of their current apartment as not well insulated; the apartment, therefore, gets cold at times. He did not feel safe crossing at the nearby lights; there have been a number of accidents because people go through red lights. He also wished that the sidewalks were salted in the winter.

Jane would like a secretarial job that involves collating or photocopying. But she has encountered problems in finding a job, saying "I am a slow learner, and for me learning the job takes some time.

I am shy, and I don't know enough people to help me. I don't know where to look for a job." When asked how long she had been unemployed, she told the interviewer: "It feels like years and years. I feel like I have never had a job. When I was at [ ] School I had a job placement at a Kresge store, but the woman complained that I smelled bad, and I was so hurt that I never went back. It involved lifting heavy boxes, which was too much for me." Unlike some of our other respondents, Jane is not active in any social groups. This means that her day is largely "empty." When she was asked if she had enough to do in her free time, Jane said, "I am not sure what free time is because I am always home and just do everything there; it is all just what I do at home." At home she paints ceramic figurines, cleans the house, knits, and watches television. She would like to paint more figurines, go shopping more often, and garden. Jane relies on her family for support and visits her mother in Northern Ontario. According to Jane, she has "almost no friends," so her social network is restricted.

Her husband, however, does work and is far more active, even though he too is labeled a slow learner. He works part time as an usher at one of Toronto's largest downtown entertainment centers. Rod describes his hours of work as "steady," and he travels by public transport to work, but if he is returning late in the evening, he takes a taxi. He had only been working at this job for two months when we spoke to him, but before that he had been working as a security guard, a job he gave up because he did not like it. Before that job, he had been employed in sheltered workshops. Like others in our sample, Rod reported that he had trouble finding a job because he "did not know the right people to help him." He went to Project Work, a program that develops job-searching skills, which "taught [him] how to find a job and what tools to use, like a résumé and references." Rod likes the people he works with and reports that he is "treated just like everyone else." But he does not socialize with any of his work colleagues because "they haven't asked me." In spite of this lack of response he has a positive view of his interactions with people: "I like working with the public. I like seeing all the shows for free. People do not label or belittle me. I like working with university students. I like educating people about People First. I like knowing that people will help me if problems arise."

Rod's social life is also more active than his wife's. He is a member of People First and a board member of the Ontario Association for

Community Living and a committee member of the Canadian Association for Community Living. In these capacities he has traveled across Canada speaking about the group's work. During his free time Rod watches television and shops with his wife. He said he does not have enough to do with his free time, "There aren't enough requests coming in for me to do speaking engagements."

Rod was one of the more articulate of our respondents, but he speaks for many others when he says: "I want to get off Family Benefits Allowance. I want to restore my dignity. I don't want to live with my hand out asking for money. Because of how the system is, I am stuck in the middle between FBA and real wages to live on, and I hate it."

The preceding profiles are indicative of people who have greater degrees of independence than some members of our sample. Because of the snowball design we used, we do not yet have stories from mentally disabled people who live in the full range of possible housing situations in Toronto. We do, however, have a few cases of people who are more-or-less institutionalized and some cases of young people who continue to live with their parents. It is to these examples that we now turn.

Janine is the only one of our respondents who reported an episode of homelessness. She is a thirty-eight-year old woman who has suffered from cerebral palsy since birth and has lived in a nursing home, a group home, and a woman's shelter before moving into her current room four years before we interviewed her. The facility she now lives in is a group home for persons with cerebral palsy. She described the problems she had in finding this room in a downtown boarding house with eleven other intellectually disabled people: "I was really out on the street, and it is hard to find a place when you are in that situation. I had tried to get into [her current home] another time, but because I had a nervous breakdown, they wouldn't take me. I didn't know any places where I could live. A social worker helped me." She is not happy with her living arrangement:

> [This] is not a good place to be. I want more privacy. I feel trapped at [this house]. The rules are awful. This place is not accessible enough for me. I know I would go outside more if I lived somewhere else—I feel trapped here. . . . It is good to have a roof over my head after the hostel experience. Other than that I don't like anything about my home.

Her complaints are at least in part about the lack of wheelchair accessibility. The local bank, for instance, is not accessible to her. Janine does not work but she goes to an adult-upgrading school three days a week. She has been unemployed since 1980 when she previously worked for the March of Dimes charity. She is now dependent upon Family Benefits for her income, which she manages with some assistance from her boyfriend. Her social life is very restricted. She visits the hospital regularly for physiotherapy, has a volunteer tutor visit once each week for two hours, and once each month or more attends meetings of a support circle at a support person's home. Janine feels she does not have enough to do in her free time because she "didn't know any other things to do." She said she would like to go out with her boyfriend more often and do some volunteer work.

We had only one other respondent who was currently institutionalized, living in a downtown chronic-care hospital. Fifty-two year old Lynda suffers from cerebral palsy and because of psychiatric problems was, at the time of our interview, in a locked ward of the hospital (where she had been for two years) with three other people, but she told the interviewer: "I am on a list to move to ward 4, which is not a locked ward. After that I want to move out, but there are no places that are affordable now."

The trail of events that led to her presence in a locked ward are interesting and reveal something of the lack of control that people labeled as handicapped have over their life experiences. Lynda previously lived in a group home in downtown Toronto with eleven other people. One of the questions on our survey schedule was not quite appropriate to Lynda's case, but her response was interesting. When asked if she had any problems finding a place to live, she replied, "No, because I didn't know I was coming here" and continued "I went to the hospital from my group home for a medical reason, and when I was able to leave the hospital, I was brought to this chronic care hospital—it was quite a surprise to me."

Despite being in a locked ward Lynda continues to work, from 9:00 A.M. to 3:00 P.M., at a sheltered workshop where she assembles mufflers. She has held this job "on and off" for five years. Lynda is connected with friends and families and socializes with them. Unlike some of our respondents, her social contacts included people outside her support network. Her major source of income is a "government check," which is managed by the hospital. From this check she is given $1.00 per day to buy a drink at the workshop. Interestingly,

Lynda lives in the most structured of environments, yet she is one of the few people that one interviewer felt compelled to describe as "quite capable and self-directed" and wondered why such a woman would find herself in this institutionalized setting.

Graham is one of our respondents who has first-hand experience at the "deinstitutionalization process." At age nine and a student in grade four, Graham was placed in an institution for the mentally retarded in Orillia, north of Toronto. His mother had contracted multiple sclerosis and could no longer look after him at home, and his father placed him in the institution after his school principal described him as "learning disabled" because he would "repeat words a lot." Graham grew up in the institution, and his education never continued beyond the grade four level he had reached before being admitted. He told us that the staff "called you retarded." "If you said you weren't, they would laugh at you." He used to do a lot of jigsaw puzzles at the institution, and these would be framed and hung on the walls. Graham says that when the staff saw that he could do the puzzles, they decided he wasn't retarded and sent him to a group home in Toronto. With the assistance of the Metropolitan Toronto Association for Community Living (fomerly the Association for the Mentally Retarded), he has worked through various degrees of independent living to the point that, for the last year and one-half, he has lived alone in a bachelor apartment.

He wants to move to a one-bedroom apartment in a cooperative building he knows of in downtown Toronto. The building he is in, says Graham, is not in good condition, needs painting and repairs to the ceiling, and is dark. But, as we heard often, he likes it because "it's mine." Graham has worked full time for three months with a company that prints crests on T-shirts. Staff at Project Work helped him find the job, which he likes even though "sometimes people pick on me and poke me in the ribs when I am trying to relax. I think it is just to get my attention, but I get nervous when they do that. It is mostly one person." The staff at Project Work continue to support him, for example, by giving him a wake-up call each morning. Besides this job, Graham does other part-time work. He helps an old friend of his mother's by cleaning the floors and doing her shopping. He also works around his mother's house on alternate Saturdays.

We have many more stories from our interviews. With few exceptions they point to the same general conclusions: people in Toronto who are labeled as developmentally handicapped have a very restricted social network. Their major contacts are family, social service workers, and workmates. Very few report strong networks of friends. This translates into a rather routine use of the city's resources. There is a sense of frustration with how little there is to do with free time.

Recall that a large proportion of our respondents lived with one or both of their parents. In some cases these were the younger respondents although in several instances individuals were of an age when it might have been expected that they would have moved into independent living arrangements. Almost without exception these respondents expressed a high degree of satisfaction with their living arrangements. In several cases, however, one or other of the parents was present at the interview, so the question of acquiescence must be kept in mind when considering the responses. We found, also, that in almost every case where the respondent was earning money, the parent(s) would take responsibility for its management. Several of the people who lived with their parents and worked had daily routines similar to some of the more "independent" individuals we profiled above. They spent the better part of their day working and would return home for an evening that was dominated by television. Their daily schedules, however, differed in small ways. For example, they were not responsible for the preparation of meals or laundry.

Craig, for example, is a twenty-eight year-old man living in Rexdale with his mother and father. He takes a bus to work daily at a nearby shopping mall where he is responsible for various janitorial duties such as grass cutting, trash collection, sweeping the floors, and decorating stores. He likes his job a lot because he gets to know all the people running the stores in the mall and because he earns some money. His work week contrasts with his weekends, which he describes as "dull" because he "needs more people." Craig also gets a small grant from FBA, and his mother manages his money for him. Like several of our other respondents he described his evening as "watching TV" after supper.

Twenty-one-year-old Lori also lives with her family, and her routine is much the same as Craig's. At the time of the interview Lori had been working for six months at a workshop after having been at home for eighteen months. Unlike other respondents who were willing to volunteer some positive information about their jobs, Lori's response to our question about what she liked in her job was "its better than being in my room." She wants to do more things socially although she attends organized trips to the movies and bowling. Her major source of income is FBA payments, which are managed by her parents.

(Well)-being in Toronto

Before hastily concluding that intellectually disabled people lead lives with which none of us are familiar, we draw attention to the fact that the temporal dimension of their daily life-paths is not unlike that of most people, at least in the case of those who are working. We began the task of constructing time-space prisms for individual respondents and found common daily paths for those who worked, those who attended some form of school, and, to some extent, for those who were unemployed. Employed handicapped people get up in the morning, go to work, and come home in the evening, a pattern familiar to most workers. Social events are restricted to occasional evenings and the weekends. The opportunities for work and socializing, however, seem to distinguish our sample from the general population and from other "special-needs" populations. Most social activities were those that were organized by the support groups who serve people with disabilities in Toronto. In this way they differ from the social activities of the "normal" population, but they also differ from, say, the homeless, who have a less-formal support structure to offer recreational activities. Similarly, the daily routines of the respondents who attended school were similar to those of other students. School would occupy the day from about nine until three in the afternoon when the respondent would return home. The most conspicuous difference was the fact that our respondents were dependent upon special buses to get them to and from school. In addition, several of our respondents who were attending school were beyond the regular school age. Although some attended "regular" schools (where they were sometimes taught in segregated classes), several of our student respondents attended programs designed specifically for disabled people. Such programs are not available in all parts of the city, as is also the case with sheltered workshops that offer employment. The opportunities for work and education, although limited, combine with a supportive transport service geared toward their needs to produce time-space networks that spread over a larger area than those found for other special-needs groups such as the homeless

(Rowe and Wolch 1990). This is because many of the disabled people whom we interviewed must travel relatively long distances to reach their jobs and schools.

Being employed makes a real difference to the urban experience of people with disabilities. When we examined the time-space profile for the married couple, Rod and Jane, the relative isolation of Jane, who remains housebound, was clear. Again, however, we raise the point that such a pattern is probably mirrored in any number of typical households where for various reasons a woman remains at home. Unemployed men and women in our sample have similar daily routines. It is dominated by visits to case workers, therapists, hospitals and drop-in centers, and watching television when at home. To visit the professionals with whom the developmentally disabled interact and the drop-in centers geared to their needs often means several trips by public transit around the city. The limited mobility of some wheelchair-confined respondents means dependence upon special bus services, the priority of which is to get people to and from work and school. The very limited spatial ranges of some of our respondents was striking.

The difference between the nondisabled population and our sample appears to be in the degree of choice or control they have over their lives. We found repeatedly that social events for the respondents are often dominated by other disabled individuals. It seems that of all the labels they wear (wife, lover, workmate, woman, middle-aged, sports fan, etc.), it is the handicapped or disabled label that most clearly defines the social network in which the members of our sample move. In contrast, members of the nondisabled population might be involved in any number of social networks (e.g., as a professional, as an athlete, as an aunt, as a movie buff, etc.). Of course, these networks overlap but disabled people seem not to have as many overlapping choices.

The intellectually disabled population in Metropolitan Toronto (and other cities) is relatively small, and it is not a highly politically organized population. Public policy concerns with the efficiency of service delivery (a response to a more political general population) mean that the points of service delivery for this population will be relatively few. The Metropolitan Toronto public transit service is not accessible to people who are severely physically disabled and in lieu it operates a special bus service, known as WHEELTRANS. This is a positive service because it allows people to go to work and to attend adult upgrading schools that would otherwise be inaccessible. Such a 'special service' however, hides the disabled from the public view and further segregates them.

Our interviews showed us that people involved in support groups had a more active social life than those who were not. The monthly or weekly activities of groups like People First ensured members the opportunity to meet with others and to attend social functions that were not reported by nonmembers. These groups also offered chances for members of the disabled community to hold offices (e.g., board membership) that are important to any individual's self-confidence. There was a clear difference between the longer-term life-paths of the two different groups. The monotony of the daily schedule of home-work-home (dominated by television) was broken up by a monthly, or in some cases, weekly outing for members of such groups.

Our surveys confirmed what several other studies have found. The needs and desires of so-called special-needs groups are not so different from the so-called normal population. For example, with respect to housing, we heard requests for privacy in a home that is not infested by cockroaches and that is affordable. The often-heard comments regarding the wish to do more things in free time or the desire to have more friends reflects the needs that everyone has for companionship. And, in more than a few instances, we were told that knowledge of *how* to find jobs was needed, again something that most people take for granted but is, after all, an acquired skill.

Conclusions

Responses to our questions can be read at several different levels. Superficially, they show a high degree of satisfaction at work and in the community. The fine print reveals a much more complex situation. Part of this discrepancy can presumably be attributed to the high degree of acquiescence noted in similar contexts by other researchers. Because, however, our interviewers were sufficiently experienced to be able to minimize the sense of threat and to detect the effects of a desire to please, undetected acquiescence stemming from these motives is likely to have been small. The expressions of satisfaction may simply reflect low levels of expectation—of resignation to the inevitable. For if there is one thing that stands out from the profiles illustrated here, it is the long-term *marginalization* of the respondents. Low levels of interaction with the so-called normal world, small action spaces, attenuated life worlds, and precarious finances all point to a life on the outer fringes of the daily round of a major metropolitan center.

For us, this project has reinforced the need to conceptualize places as bundles of social relations and practices. It is these relations, attitudes, and behaviors that shape an individual's experience of place, and without a doubt this is central to well-being. It is important to individuals' satisfaction with their lives, and thus to their well-being, to feel part of a community, part of a caring social network. Places are the point at which those communities and networks come together. When choices are available, people often choose to develop their identities in accordance with particular places: the downtown-living yuppie, the suburban family, the seashore retiree. These identities are also imposed by social relations and practices over which individuals have little control. Our interviews suggested that people labeled as disabled rarely have choices available to them. Several respondents expressed the desire to live elsewhere, to have a different home, to live in a different part of town. But the identity that has been thrust upon them restricts the places where they can live. We do not imply a grand conspiracy here. The social workers and professionals who place developmentally disabled people in group homes act in good faith. But the consequences of such actions may be devastating, reproducing images of the disabled as dependent and incompetent. The dissatisfaction about living arrangements expressed to us by many of our respondents (despite more positive answers to the structured questions) suggest that individual well-being is not being maximized in certain places. The social relations at work in the sheltered workshop, the group home, or the boarding house are not ones that promote autonomy and self-esteem.

Our most useful information was gleaned from the qualitative data obtained during the discussions between the interviewers and the respondents. We believe that the feelings expressed in these conversations are more useful than the compilation of descriptive statistics. This result suggests the utility and, indeed, the necessity of an ethnographic approach to understand the experiences of people with disabilities. We propose to continue our research in an ethnographic vein, collecting and collating personal stories. This exercise will serve two purposes. First, it will fill a gap in the social geographic literature by including perspectives of people with disabilities in studies of sense of place. To ensure a comprehensive study, we intend to extend the study to include small urban centers and rural communities and some institutional settings in order to contrast the community experience, a larger number of older people, and school-aged children. Second, by giving disabled people an opportunity to express their opinions, we hope to contribute constructively to ongoing policy discussions around community integration.

In studying the routines of Torontonians labeled "mentally handicapped" we are confronted to a large extent with a picture of the everyday life of people who are at the margins of society not only in terms of their assumed or "measured" intellectual ability (the basis for their selection as respondents in the first place) but also socially and economically. This conclusion is not unprecedented. Indeed, associations such as these have frequently been used to construct highly deterministic rationales for the inevitability of poverty and environmental deprivation. A national survey in 1986 found that almost two-thirds of persons with disabilities had annual incomes under $10,000 (Canada, Secretary of State 1986). Yet it is discouraging that in a province that prides itself in the comprehensiveness of its medical and social services the interrelationship between disability and poverty is so apparent (Rioux and Crawford 1990). As our study proceeds and the representativeness of our sample broadens, our challenge will be to identify some paths toward more equitable residential provision, community services, and employment opportunities consistent with the original ideals of normalization and the renewed insistence on human rights. Studies that listen to the voices of those who are the object of policy decisions, promise to allow policymakers, practitioners, and others to gain a deeper appreciation of individual needs and desires. They demonstrate the difficulties disabled people have in "making it" under certain conditions and, thus, may be able to assist those with power in making places that are more accommodating to the needs of all residents. Finally, a study such as this exemplifies the complex interrelationships between health and place, between social well-being and the absence of stigma that inspired Kearns's call that we "bring the work of the geographer of health into close association with the broader fields of social and cultural geography" (Kearns 1993, 145).

6

Women with Disabilities and Everyday Geographies

Home Space and the Contested Body

ISABEL DYCK

The insistence that space is socially constructed, dialectic, and of unstable meaning has brought new interests and methodologies to medical geography research agendas, and a reflective moment to the subdiscipline. Questions formulated within the dominant categories and methodologies of disease ecology and health service traditions of research have been joined by approaches informed by social theory that decenter geometric space and confront an unproblematic use of biomedically driven categories and concerns (Eyles 1993a; Gesler 1992; Jones and Moon 1993; Kearns 1993; Kearns and Joseph 1993; Scarpaci 1993). As with geography's other subdisciplinary fields, the influences of feminist and poststructuralist thought have introduced a concern with diversity and difference as the exclusions of modernist intellectual thought are identified and the certainties of "objective" knowledge are questioned (Kearns 1995). With these shifts in enquiry the experiences and views of health care consumers have attracted interest, so previously hidden and alternative geographies of health and health care are being uncovered (Dyck 1995; Gesler 1993; Kearns 1995; Lewis and Kieffer 1994). Among these geographies are those of women.

Opening up space for women on the medical geographical agenda requires engagement with feminist theory, including attention to the embodied subject and local knowledges. An emerging agenda identifies the socially constructed body as central to the investigation of geographies of health and health care; geographies of the "deviant" body, alternative health movements, and the complex links between space, power relations, the body, and the constitution of identities replace biomedically driven concerns (Dorn and Laws 1994; Moss and Dyck 1996). In this chapter I discuss a study concerned with women's experiences of living with multiple sclerosis (MS) with a specific focus on their home space. I aim to show how the women's responses to both the diagnosis of MS and its physical manifestations are linked to a complex interplay of space, struggles around identity, and relations of power that describe and define normative expectations of the gendered body. The reconstitution of home space is shown to be closely interwoven with the women's renegotiation of their bodies and of their identities after diagnosis with MS.

In the chapter I begin by tracing the implications of feminist geography for the study of the "diseased body" in a postmedical geography; in particular I discuss the notion of the embodied subject and its close alliance to the "reading" of space. I go on to discuss the reconstitution of the home as a material space and one imbued with social meanings as the women's experience of a physically changing body intertwines with the "marking" of their bodies through biomedical representation. In the final section I explore the implications of the analysis of the everyday spaces in which illness is experienced for ways of thinking about health care in the context of a postmedical geography of health and health care.

The Embodied Subject and Hidden (Medical) Geographies

The Geography of Health and Health Care and the Inclusion of Diversity

In his invitation to medical geographers to reform their subdiscipline Kearns (1993, 145) suggests that it "remains an unnecessarily placeless endeavor and that a re-placed geography of health will be more easily gendered and inclusive of all maps of meaning." This latter notion implies an oppositional stance to the dominant biomedical map of meaning with its disease-focused categories, so directing a shift of investigation to the lived geographies of those experiencing ill health and alternative views of health and illness.[1] Further explication of a medical geography inclusive of diversity has followed this initial questioning of how place and space can be inserted in understanding health and health care issues.

The introduction of a relational view of space, with recognition of its social construction and complex interaction with social relations, has opened up different angles from which to view health and illness, adding to the more traditional concerns predicated on geometric space and questions of location (Kearns and Joseph 1993). Centering place in enquiry and working with a more nuanced and theoretically driven understanding of space also introduces greater reliance on nontraditional methodologies, such as a variety of qualitative methods, as a way of addressing new concerns, including the situated experiences of health and illness. Models of health using ethnographic approaches and in-depth interviews are provided in earlier works that reveal the close association between place and lay perceptions (Cornwell 1984; Donovan 1986; Eyles and Donovan 1986).

Using interpretive approaches in exploring the consumer's point of view requires engagement with epistemological issues concerning the production of knowledge about and representations of health and disease. Discussion of the admissability of the "subjective" as evidence in explanation in medical geography (Poland 1992) has been followed by further critique, influenced by postmodernism and feminist theory. This critique attempts to destabilize the taken-for-granted certainty of biomedical knowledge and its categories and questions the notion of "objectivity" that has been the cornerstone of an approach centered on the medical model (Dorn and Laws 1994; Kearns 1995; Moss and Dyck 1996). To include diversity, then, is not just a matter of adding other voices on, such as those of women, but one of questioning usual ways of constructing knowledge, and rethinking what might constitute the objects and subjects of enquiry.

The decentering of the medical model in research also requires attention to the social categories brought to analysis. Antiessentialist theories emphasize the social construction and instability of categories of, for example, gender and "race" and direct attention to how

1. The insertion of theorized place and space into medical geography has not gone uncontested, as evidenced by the debate in the *Professional Geographer* of 1993 and 1994 in response to Kearns's invitation to reform medical geography through a centering of the concept of place.

diversity or social differentiation becomes interpreted as "difference." Entangled with this concern is the question of how identities are constituted, acted upon, and become "fixed" or maintained. Feminist geographers are particularly interested in how space and place enters into how one understands the diversity of experiences within the category "woman" as their positioning within different relations of power shape experience. In this chapter my focus is on the category of "disabled woman." I find poststructuralist feminist work on the body and feminist geography's careful consideration of space provide useful ways of looking at the "disabled body" outside the narrow confines of a purely biomedical interpretation.[2]

The "Disabled Body" and Feminist Geography

In biomedicine the concern with causal explanation, diagnosis, and treatment of dysfunctions of the physical body, and a reliance on positivist science approaches preclude serious engagement with social context and subjectivity. Yet as a dominant discourse about the body, its knowledge may have profound implications for people's access to opportunities and movement in space. Foucault's analysis of the exercise of power through discursive and material practices, for example, has been important in understanding how scientific ideas about the body have been used to control bodies in space (Foucault 1973, 1978). Feminists influenced by Foucault's ideas have also been interested in the subtle and complex interplays of power in the constitution of embodied, gendered subjectivities. The body in such readings is understood to be a site of disciplinary power with interpretations of its corporeality subject to historically and culturally specific criteria and constructions. Culturally contingent meanings of the gendered body, for example, varying over time and across space, will shape expectations of what particular bodies can or should do.

A poststructuralist perspective also suggests that the body is usefully understood as a surface of inscription "marked" by discourses that mediate our experiences of the body (Butler 1990; Grosz 1994). The body may be inscribed in different ways, affording a multiplicity of "scripts" to draw on in interaction; as Bordo comments (1992, 167), "We thus have no 'direct,' innocent, or unconstructed knowledge of

2. Discussion of poststructuralism within feminist geography can be found in Bondi 1990, 1993; Bondi and Domosh 1992; McDowell 1991, 1993b; Pratt 1993.

our bodies; rather we are always 'reading' our bodies through various interpretive schemes." Women's identities are not unitary, but multidimensional and constructed within the historically specificity of relations of power and in relation to particular places (de Lauretis 1990; Ferguson 1993; Gatens 1992; Haraway 1990). There is, therefore, no universal "woman," but various possible enactments of "womanhood" with certain strands of identity having greater salience according to specific contexts.

That space has much to do with women's multiple positioning and the ways in which their subjectivity is constituted is demonstrated by feminist geographers working in various ways with ideas from time-geography, humanistic geography, cultural geography, Marxist geography, and postmodernism (Rose 1993). A feminist critique also suggests that places and spaces are not universally knowable and are gendered in their representations and in how they are experienced as well. Work concerned with the everyday geographies of women, for example, has revealed spaces and ways of interpreting these that have not appeared in dominant representations of space and place. Furthermore, a focus on the "ordinary" shows complex interdependencies between home, community, and workplace that cut across dichotomous representations of urban space as productive or reproductive or as public or private (Dyck 1989; Hanson and Pratt 1988; Mackenzie 1989; McDowell 1993a; Pratt and Hanson 1991). Women's experiences of these spaces also vary according to their different positioning within sets of social relations, in addition to gender, such as the social relations of "race" (Collins 1990; hooks 1991). Everyday spaces of the home, streets, neighborhood and workplace, however, are not merely "experienced." Such spaces and women's identities may be integrally involved in the constitution of each other while the practical and ideological aspects of being a woman in a particular place are negotiated in the course of carrying out everyday responsibilities and demands. Women, for example, remake and bring specific meanings to home and neighborhood spaces as they use them in changing ways (Dyck 1990; Mackenzie 1989).

Women's embodiment has implicitly run through analyses of women's experience and restructuring of space by virtue of a focus on mobility and the day-to-day life activities of women. But it is a taken-for-granted body, most notably "marked" by its gender than by other forms of inscription. Variations in corporeality, however, are also shown to be significant to women's experience of the environment, such as in the cases of pregnant women and women with disabilities (Longhurst 1994; Dyck 1995). Actual bodily changes are also inscribed in relation to ideological notions of the gendered and able-bodied "norm" so that although barriers to spatial mobility for the physically changed body at first sight may appear as "neutral" physical limitations, they are rather embedded in a complexity of physical, social, and cultural understandings of the body and its positioning in different spaces. For instance, the appearance of the "deviant" body is accepted as natural in a hospital or clinic but may be responded to quite differently in the "public" spaces of the workplace or community.

Attention to the embodied subject is a useful way of reconceptualising illness behavior as "situated" experiences in particular places that are not completely knowable "objects" but exist for people in the context of their own spatial and social positioning. In the rest of the chapter I discuss examples from my research to explore how women manage and reread their home space in light of changes to the corporeality of the body and its representations. It is here in the home that we can begin to see the complex intertwining of cultural constructions of the body, physical symptoms of disease, and women's negotiation of their identities.

Uncertain Bodies, Uncertain Spaces

Reinterpreting the Body

The taken-for-grantedness of the body comes under threat from the time of a woman's diagnosis with MS or its precursor of a period of transient and variable symptoms. MS is a chronic neurological disease that strikes about 130 of 100,000 people in Canada with women about twice as prone to the disease as are men (Poser et al. 1984; Wakesman, Reingold, and Reynolds 1987). Symptoms vary, but most commonly include profound fatigue, motor and sensory impairments, and visual disturbances. The course of the disease is unpredictable and may be characterized by remissions and relapses or by progression. Resultant disabilities range from minimal impairment of activity to severe mobility difficulties and functional problems. Its typical onset is in young and middle adulthood, commonly affecting a person actively engaged in wage and/or domestic labor and childrearing.

There is no known cure for MS and little authorized guidance on managing the psychosocial dimensions of living with the disease on a daily basis. It is a disease, however, that attracts intense medical interest and research about its definitive diagnosis, cause, course, and possible treatment.[3] This body of knowledge, including the elaboration of the physical consequences and typical progression of the disease, is usually made available in some form to those diagnosed. This description and definition of the disease acts as a further "script" that is added to existing ones that may be drawn on by the individual. Embedded in this script is the realization that the body may fail, sometimes unpredictably, in carrying out usual household, community, or paid work activity. The uncertainty of the body is a central concern for many of the women who participated in the research.

The analysis is based on the accounts of fifty-four women recruited to the study through a branch of the Multiple Sclerosis Society and a hospital clinic specializing in the diagnosis and treatment of MS. All participated in in-depth interviews about their experiences since being diagnosed, including changes in the workplace, community, and home.[4] The women had various degrees of disability. Some women had "hidden" disabilities, whereas others had considerable mobility restrictions and other functional problems, requiring use of mobility aids such as a cane, wheelchair, or motorized scooter. Although those with visible disabilities were less likely to be working than those without, this was not always the case. At the time of the study nineteen women were in full-time employment and twelve in part-time employment. The women varied in age, but most were in their thirties and forties. They also varied in educational level, marital status, and ages of children. Consistent with the incidence of MS, all the women participating in the study were white.

Many of the women found some relief in receiving a diagnosis, particularly as most had endured a period of symptoms that were transitory, variable, and had defied naming in previous medical visits. At the same time, however, the lack of a known cure and the

3. Blackford's (1993) analysis of newsletters of the Multiple Sclerosis Society of Canada shows the power of physicians to shape research directions and the underrepresentation of women's concerns, especially as mothers.

4. In the study I conducted with Lyn Jongbloed, we explored women's workplace experiences in some depth and included a quantitative component, using a mail survey to identify specific features in the workplace that affected women's ability to work. The findings of these other aspects of the study are beyond the scope of this chapter.

unpredictability of the course of the disease or its likely severity also brought considerable uncertainty to the women's lives. One woman said, "As soon as they tell you you've got something like that, it's like the whole world changes; the sky looks different." Whether the women were experiencing relatively minor symptoms or more severe disabilities at the time of the study, previously taken-for-granted spaces presented uncertainties for the women as they navigated a differently experienced body through the course of a day. Physical negotiation was one dimension of traversing particular spaces, but this was complicated by a changing experience of social relations of power predicated on a differently "scripted" body. Spaces come to be known in different ways. As shown in the rest of the chapter, the home and its reconstitution was important to how disability was experienced and responded to and was a central site in the renegotiation of a woman's identity.

The Fractured Meaning of Home

The construction of the home as private, feminine, and domestic has been the ideological core of an analytic dichotomy in geography of space as public or private. Yet empirical work showing the fluidity of the boundaries between home and work and the different meanings the home may have for different women questions a universal understanding of home space (see Rose 1993). For the women of the study the experience of the home changed although this varied in quality and extent according to the severity of their illness and disability, household composition, and how they associated the home with their identities. A single career woman, living alone, for example, might be more concerned with independence, security, and her home as a retreat from the public management of her symptoms than would a married woman in a two-parent family with children, whose concerns about the performance of her identity as mother and wife and in many cases as worker as well are central.

Although identities are multifaceted, the ways in which the women talked about their disabilities or transient symptoms of illness showed variation in the prominence accorded to the "disabled" dimension of their identities. Although the severity of disability was of central importance to what a woman was able or not able to do, time since diagnosis and particular experiences of remissions, exacerbations, or rapidity of physical deterioration also were a part of how women responded to changes to the material body. For all, however, their self and social positioning as women at a particular juncture of the life course mediated how such functional limitations were negotiated. In focusing on the social dimensions of the women's lives I do not intend to diminish the centrality of women's experiences of illness, pain, and physical limitations in their lives, which Morris (1992) states tend to be denied in approaches that challenge the medical. Rather my aim is to show the inseparability of the personal experience of disability from the social and the spatial. In the following examples I aim to show how the home is reconstructed as women attempt to accommodate their changing physical abilities and struggle to maintain valued strands of their identities.

The Home as a Site of Struggle

For most of the women the home presented physical barriers to their ability to carry out household chores and sometimes childrearing and self-care. Refiguring home space was one strategy in accommodating declining abilities. This was particularly the case for women with more severe disabilities, although not exclusively so. Commonly used strategies were a move to a single level home, the installation of entrance ramps, and modifications of bathroom and kitchen. With such housing adaptations entry into the home and movement within it was made easier so that women could continue to carry out some if not all household tasks. Other nonstructural alterations, such as a rearrangement of furniture, the use of a microwave, or purpose-made gadgets also facilitated usual activities. Some of the women who had severe disabilities could do very little in the home and relied on other household members or homemakers to carry out domestic labor.[5] A few lived in wheelchair accessible apartments or in suites designed specifically for people with disabilities in subsidized coop housing. Coop housing was particularly attractive to nonhome-owning single women because subsidized rents and security of tenure provided stability for unemployed women or those uncertain of the length of

5. More detailed description of the range of strategies used in restructuring of the home and delegating household tasks is contained in an account focused on women who had left the paid work force (Dyck 1995). A small minority of women depended on others for most of their needs and either were hospitalized or had daily, extensive home support.

their employability. Long waiting lists, however, precluded this as an immediate or universal option.

The importance of restructured home space was expressed in different ways by the women according to their specific situations but varied most according to household composition and marital status. In common, however, as women expressed their responses to reduced accessibility and mobility, these notions were linked to their attempts to maintain continuities in value-laden activities. For married women, being able to carry out household tasks and to participate actively in children's activities were important considerations. It was distressing, for example, for one woman who was not able to change her baby's diapers for a time. Women with school-aged children were concerned when their illness made it difficult for them to continue mothering and other activities in a way they saw as important to maintaining their part in family life. One woman who had been unable to climb the stairs of her home commented, "You cannot look after two teenage children from your bedroom upstairs." A further concern for women was letting go of their "ownership" of familiar household work. A change in the division of domestic labor was common in nuclear family households when a woman's symptoms prevented her from carrying out heavier tasks, such as laundry and vacuuming, or when stairs acted as a barrier to particular work areas in the house. Marilyn's words were typical of women experiencing shifts in domestic work:[6] "Right now I can still make the stairs, but a one-level house—that's what we want because I think it would be better for me, and a smaller piece of property, less gardens and that, so we can equalize the work a little more. Right now it all falls on my husband's shoulders." The two-story suburban house, inscribed in the landscape as a mirror of tenacious cultural constructions of the nuclear family, no longer necessarily supported the task of managing the home, work that was already complicated for women who were also in paid employment. Residential moves and restructurings of the internal space of the home and its immediate surroundings were common ways of attempting to match declining physical ability with a home space that could support activities closely allied to their valued identities as wives and mothers.

6. The names used are pseudonyms. Because of limitations of space, the quotations used were chosen as typical of women's accounts and are intended to illustrate particular points rather than to exhaust all views.

Single women, either never married or divorced or separated lived in a variety of household arrangements and types of housing stock, including single-family dwellings, condominiums, and apartments. Most lived on their own or with their children, but a few lived with partners, parents, or friends. For women on their own, addressing accessibility issues had some similarities in purpose to those of married women's, but there were also different dimensions of meaning. These women talked of housing in a variety of ways, including expressed concerns with financial stability, independence in self-care, and personal security. One woman managed all these concerns by moving into subsidized, cooperative housing after a period of living in a group home that she had found a depressing experience: "I've moved into a—this is a handicapped suite . . . so that if I have a relapse, which I did three years ago . . . I can get around in a wheelchair, so that's important. That's security. . . . So this has been good. I'm independent. I can look out for myself. [There are] people around." It was among this group of women, who were living on their own, that the potential for further progressive or exacerbating symptoms was most commonly voiced as a concern. Some, for example, were not currently experiencing significant problems but saw a change in housing as a strategy for guarding against a future when their physical status might deteriorate. Elaine, a thirty-two-year-old single woman said: "Actually I moved in here . . . thinking in the back of my mind, geez, if anything ever did happen, maybe I'd be able to get into a subsidized unit if worse came to the worst. And that's one reason for coming into a coop." Other women living alone were also thinking ahead of possible moves because of reduced income through unemployment or a need to be close to social support in case of increasing physical vulnerability. Two younger, single women in their twenties read their relationship to home space differently again. One planned to move out of her parents' home in order to share an apartment with a friend. She considered this accommodation more accessible for her in that it was in a less-hilly area and closer to stores, a community center, and a bus route with buses accessible for wheelchairs. She and the other young woman were keen to establish their independence away from their parents and to pursue a lifestyle that approximated those of their age peers, which took them into a grey area of trading off security and daily support for independence.

As women talked about the accommodations they made in relation to the home as a social and material space, their expectations of what it is to be a woman at a particular point in a normalized, "average" life course were juxtaposed with their performative abilities as these were experienced and defined through a material body.[7] Remaining a competent being involved not just physical performance but also a sense of who one was socially as defined by a woman's particular situation.[8] One woman with invisible symptoms, for instance, described her anxiety about disclosing her illness in the following way: "I think it's my able body, my attachment to being strong, tough. I mean most of my life I was the one who had a lot of energy. . . . I just don't want to identify with the disabled."

In general, women were unwilling to give up the nondisabled strands of their identities without a struggle of which an attempted physical matching of body and environment was a part. Housing was an area over which most felt they could exert control as they managed their illness. Restructuring of space, however, was not confined to a simple equation between physical experience and environment. It was also a reconstitution of the home according to a woman's reading of her new self as couched in the language of biomedical knowledge describing the disease process. This reading included mapping future possibilities as well as current experiences in material space. The women's experiences of their bodies, however, and their expectations of change according to its biomedical representation was not just an individual matter as they negotiated their self-identities. Identities were also imposed by others, who also read the women through new scripts.

Women stressed continuities in their identities as they struggled with changing bodily experiences in the home, but these were not always accepted in the context of heterosexual relationships because cultural expectations attached to gendered identities were destabilized. The study's main concern was not with the intimate relationships of the

7. These different aspects of the self are exemplified in McCuaig and Frank's (1990) detailed ethnographic study of a woman with severe speech and mobility difficulties who was living independently in the community. For her the "able self" consisted of being considered "mentally able, physically capable, and socially competent" (229).

8. Twenty-three of the women were married, fifteen single, and sixteen separated or divorced. Of the latter not all the women attributed their separation or divorce to their illness, and it is not within the scope of this analysis to draw definitive conclusions about any one relationship. A few had married or started new relationships after diagnosis and disease symptoms.

women, but their stories of struggling to remain "competent women" showed that disability added stress to relationships in different ways. Although some marriages and relationships foundered, others remained intact. There were as many examples of supportive husbands, partners, and boyfriends as stories of men who had left relationships. Statements of husbands who "couldn't handle it," who were resentful of things a woman could no longer do, or menfriends who left after a woman disclosed her diagnosis were countered by other women's accounts of caring and encouraging husbands and partners.

How the stress of diagnosis of multiple sclerosis and its manifestations were handled in a relationship clearly differed, but those women who did separate or divorce often experienced considerable shifts in how they could live with their disabilities. Some moved out of the family home, one woman then living apart from her children, and several experienced a decline in income and financial security as they moved outside the umbrella of the "family wage." These dislocations in social relationships and living circumstances were reminders of discontinuities of identity as subjectively lived and defined by others.

The Public Body in "Private" Space: Ambiguities of Bodily Inscription

The biomedical representation of the body is drawn upon by the women as they chart their home lives in new ways, but accommodations of home space have further implications for women as workers in the paid labor force. Shifts in the meaning and experience of the home occur with women's changing experiences of work. It is beyond the scope of this chapter to explore the nuances of women's changing relationships to the workplace, and I retain a focus on the home in looking now at how the definition of the body, as mediated by scientific discourse about the disease, further complicates the interdependencies of public and private space that feminist geographers have rehearsed. There are contradictions for the women because the legitimization of their functional limitations through biomedical authority may both enable opportunities and pose difficulties for a woman with an identity in flux.

The entry of the public into the most private domain of a woman's living space occurs in various ways as women find they can no longer perform routine household tasks despite physical restructuring of the home. Although other family members may take these over for a time, some part of domestic labor was in many instances delegated to private cleaners or publicly subsidized homemakers. The severity of a woman's disability and the length of time she had been unable to continue with certain tasks shaped her response to the entry of figures from the public sphere into her day-to-day activities. Some women with little by way of occupation welcomed the sociability that such workers might bring although others resisted losing their independence and control of home space. One of the main advantages mentioned was the freeing up of time and energy for women to pursue other activities with their husbands and friends. Delegating household work also enabled some women to continue with their paid employment or to participate in volunteer or advocacy work. This was particularly important for women dependent on their personal incomes to maintain themselves and whose work was central to how they saw themselves. Deirdre, for example, whose adapted housing and homemaker services facilitated her return to work after a period of unemployment said, "I didn't feel myself, you know; I wasn't the old working [me] that I'd been before."

Gaining access to homemaker services, adapted housing, and grants to make structural alterations to existing accommodation could, thus, be closely related to a woman's continued participation in the workplace as well as activity in the domestic sphere. Further access to services, such as subsidized mobility aids and parking placards reserving handicapped parking spots, may also enhance a woman's ability to get to and work within her place of employment. In all these cases, access to resources was mediated by a gatekeeping process informed by representation of the body as "deviant" in terms of the norm of the able-bodied. The external verification of a diseased body through biomedicine and being labeled as disabled resulted in the provision of some benefits to women, even as they actively countered the disabled strand of their identities in other situations.

The representation of disability as an individual medical problem is, however, not a benevolent or even "neutral" representation, for it is an important dimension of the power relation of "expert" knowledge that may override women's own subjective experiences. As critics of the medical model of disability claim, the translation of this model into social policies also directs policy solutions away from the social processes underlying the cultural construction of disability (Bickenbach 1993; Oliver 1990). Similarly, the creation of the category of disabled takes on an essentialist hue as particular representations of the body are used in differentiating among people in relation to eligibility for resources provided within the welfare state (Laws 1994a). The power of external representations of the women's bodies was, therefore, potentially far-reaching. For women in the study access to disability benefits was commonly through government pensions or insurance schemes through their places of employment. Because this type of income is based on eligibility rather than need, the area of disability benefits caused anxiety for some women who were concerned about their future financial security. Dealing with this issue was another route by which public representations of the body entered the women's use and experience of their homes.

Although the notion of the home as haven or refuge has been critiqued in feminist scholarship as other ways in which women experience home have been uncovered, this dimension of the home was important to some women in the study. It was a place of recuperation and rest for women meeting the demands of paid work. For women with invisible symptoms who had not disclosed their illness at work, it might also have the additional meaning of a place of concealment. Two examples illustrate how the power relations of the workplace and a biomedical scripting of the body combine in shaping the meaning of the home in this way.

One woman who worked in a private company found her job more stressful and demanding after her workload increased as a result of personnel changes. Although she did not experience symptoms at work, by the end of the day she was usually very fatigued, had difficulty climbing stairs, and sometimes experienced slurred speech. She had to curtail her social activities during the week, but no one in the workplace was aware of her symptoms or diagnosis. The home was important for her as a space hidden from public view. Disclosure was an issue for the woman because she feared she might lose her job and might be denied work elsewhere if she disclosed her illness in interviews. She talked of her worry about her future as a single woman, now in her early thirties, with the prospect of many years of supporting herself. A second woman, Maria, also was worried about disclosure. In her fifties, her symptoms were becoming more pronounced, and she was prepared to quit work. She was concerned, however, about the reduction of her income this would entail. Her place of employment was introducing a disability insurance scheme, but this was not yet in operation. If Maria disclosed in the meantime, she believed she would not be eligible for disability benefits and so devised various ways of concealing her symptoms. Part of her job routinely involved handwriting notes that her secretary then typed up. But because of her increasingly shaky handwriting, she transcribed the notes herself on her home computer.

For both these women the home was a place that enabled them to conceal symptoms that they understood would jeopardize their access to income because of eligibility rules. The authorized representation of their own experience intervened in their lives in a way difficult for them to control. The home was a site in the process of the women's resistance against the official designation of "disabled," which mattered to them at this particular time in the specific conditions of their workplaces. In Maria's case it also became a direct extension of her workplace because she used it for completing work tasks. Although the home as workplace has been discussed in accounts of different forms of home working (Ahrentzen 1992; Mackenzie 1989; Oberhauser 1995), this had not been a significant option for the women of the study. One had worked at home, linked to the office by computer, for a short period before quitting work altogether, something she said was possible because of her track record at the place of employment and a positive relationship with her employer. It was, however, a more significant base for volunteer work, an area unregulated by authorized representations of the body. For these women, the use of home space for clerical and other sedentary work supporting community organizations could signal a view of themselves as contributing members of society. The subjective experiences of the body could be worked around in a secure and controlled space.

Conclusion

Changing perspectives in medical geography include the decentering of the medical model in exploring the complex relations between health and place. In this analysis of women's changing experiences as they live with disability, the medical model still appears but has been shifted to the same plane as, rather than separate from, other discourses that can be employed in untangling the multidimensional experience of disability. The study was informed by feminist theory and methods intended to reveal the "consumer's" views of their health experience. This approach opened a window through which to explore the close alliance of the spaces of women's day-to-day lives with how they managed destabilized identities. Interviews with the women suggested that although the physical experience of multiple sclerosis was of central importance to how they were able to carry out their day-to-day activities, it was not readily separated from the discursive dimensions of the women's experiences. Bodily changes were also experienced in light of their construction as "deviant" through biomedical discourse and dominant cultural understandings of gendered activity.

The relationship between the women's illness, space, and their identities is complex and difficult to disentangle, but this study suggests that the home is a site and part of a process in which the threat of disability to the valued strands of a woman's identity is contested and negotiated. Its part in this contestation varied, however, according to the women's different situations. Furthermore, the biomedical script, although carried by the women, will have more or less salience in the various contexts of day-to-day interaction. When boundaries between disability and able-bodiedness are at stake, for example, in the allocation of services and benefits, the "marking" of the body as diseased may hold ambiguity for the women. Living with a body that is represented as deviant and changing physically as well involves experiencing power relations in a changed way. Increased vulnerability may be experienced in sites where social practices are informed by dominant cultural constructions around gender and notions of the able body, for example, as women experience unsettled heterosexual relationships, unpredictable responses in the workplace, and increased involvement with the state. Power relations, however, are not unidirectional, and the interviews showed women actively engaged in social practices through which power was negotiated. The everyday space of the home is not static in this process but is intimately involved with the experience of disability as it is reconstituted in a web of changing meanings and social relationships. The home, rather than being merely a container of women's attempts to manage disability, is, thus, integral to the complex processes through which space, identity, and material practices are remade.

Although this close focus on the home may seem distant to health-care planning, it does emphasize the central importance of everyday spaces and nonmedical sites to how disability is experienced and interpreted. It also suggests that one cannot understand spatial mobility and the associated access to opportunities without attention to the body's representation as this is interpreted both by those suffering illness and those mediating access to resources. In biomedical discourse the body's ability to function is set against a concept of the "normal" universal body moving in universal space. But the close relation between embodied subjectivities and the "reading" and experiencing of space suggests that the use of the decontextualized body without a subject in medical approaches will provide a limited perspective on how disability is lived. The psychosocial issues that people with severe illness face, as one instance, are not separate from the interweaving of the discursive and material body. It is important that the problems of those with disabilities are not universalized and stripped of the underlying power relations that construct them, through their bodies, as "deviant", by containment within a discourse of physical mobility and impairment. Approaches that can reveal the embodied local geographies of people suffering from illness help one understand the complex webs of meaning about people-place relationships that are an integral, if unrecognized, part of living with ill health.

7

Homeless Health and Service Needs

An Urban Political Economy of Service Distribution

JONGGYU LEE, JENNIFER R. WOLCH, AND JESSICA WALSH

Homelessness emerged during the 1980s as one of the most critical problems facing the United States. Contemporary homelessness results from a combination of socioeconomic changes, government policies, housing market dynamics and individual vulnerabilities (Wolch, Dear, and Akita 1988; Shinn 1992; Hertzberg 1992; Wright 1989; Hoch and Slayton 1989). Because people can become homeless for a number of different reasons, a range of services is needed to reintegrate homeless people into mainstream society. In addition to shelter services, counseling and empowerment services, employment and income programs, food and nutrition, and a range of substance abuse, outreach, rehabilitation, case management, and transport services are often needed.

Effective health care is critical for homeless people because they are often more susceptible to illness than is the general public. Health problems such as chemical dependence and mental disabilities may precede and contribute to homelessness, but more often than not, homelessness itself increases the risk of ill health (Institute of Medicine 1988; Dear and Takahashi 1992). Because the health of homeless people is so integrally tied to their diverse service needs, the provision of health care alone is not enough to improve general health. Health care must be part of an integrated shelter and service system designed to provide longer-term opportunities.

The development of an appropriate system of service resources geared to the specific needs of the homeless population requires a complete identification of homeless service needs and existing service types. Yet if services are to be used, they must be geographically accessible. Hence, an effective shelter/service delivery system must address two distinctive dimensions: *functional* and *geographical.* Our purpose in this chapter is to evaluate the extent to which shelter and service provision meets the health and human services needs of homeless people and to consider how this distribution might be improved. We focus on the functional and geographic distribution of shelters and services in one major metropolitan area—Los Angeles.

We begin by tracing the evolution of homeless service needs, focusing in particular on the functional links between health services and broader service needs. In part 2, we evaluate the current geographic accessibility of these services in Los Angeles County, using traditional functional/spatial approaches in medical geography (following, e.g., Shannon and Dever 1974). Finally, in part 3, we examine the prospects for improving service delivery to homeless people, given the obstacles posed by the political economy of homeless shelter and service siting. Here, we look to the "new" geographies of health to consider the impact of ongoing redevelopment of Skid Row areas, community opposition to the siting of controversial facilities, and continuing privatization of services on prospects for a more equitable planning and delivery of homeless services.

Shelter and Service Needs of the Homeless

The growth of homelessness in America has been explained by such structural factors as deinstitutionalization, welfare state restructuring and the concomitant privatization of social services, a loss of low-income housing, and poverty caused by economic restructuring. In this context personal crises also contribute to homelessness. Eviction, domestic violence, divorce, job loss, discharge from an institution, and loss of welfare benefits have all been shown to contribute to episodes of homelessness (Hoch and Slayton 1989; Rossi 1989; Wright 1989; Wolch, Dear, and Akita 1988).

Because of these different paths into homelessness, a variety of services is needed. These include subsistence-level social services, such as shelter, food and health care, and government cash income benefits, such as General Assistance (GA),[1] Temporary Assistance to Needy

1. This program is known as General Relief (GR) in California; it will be referred to as such in the empirical portion of our analysis, which focuses on Los Angeles.

Families (TANF), and Supplemental Security Income (SSI). Other services essential for survival in everyday life and for reentry into mainstream society include employment services, advocacy, empowerment services, and other generic community facilities. A substantial literature now details these services (Dear and Takahashi 1992; Institute of Medicine 1988; Mowbray et al. 1992; Wright 1989). Here we specifically address the health care needs of the homeless.

Health Care Needs of the Homeless

Rates of mental disability are high among homeless people. The homeless possess many of the characteristics known to increase the risk of mental disability, such as poverty, membership of minority ethnic groups, minimal social support, and general disenfranchisement. Mentally disabled homeless people need more than just shelter, food, and basic necessities. Psychiatric services are usually needed to treat disabilities ranging from severe personality disorders to schizophrenia (Mowbray et al. 1992). These homeless people are often in danger because of the severity of their mental disabilities and inability to live independently, but generally they respond positively to treatment. Still, appropriate psychiatric care is typically not available at shelters. For the chronically mentally disabled homeless, housing is particularly necessary because a lack of appropriate accommodation has been shown to result in high relapse rates (Drake, McHugo, and Noordsy 1993; Rosenfield 1991).

In addition to the prevalence of mental illness homeless people suffer greatly from the most common illnesses, such as hypertension, other arteriosclerotic cardiovascular illnesses, and major infections. Homeless people are also disproportionately affected by those common health problems that have serious consequences when untreated. These include infestations such as scabies and lice, problems such as hypothermia arising from exposure, nutritional and vitamin deficiencies, and peripheral vascular diseases such as cellulitis and leg ulcers (Weinreb and Bassuk 1990; Institute of Medicine 1988; Surber et al. 1988). Moreover, homeless individuals are more likely to suffer multiple diagnoses, that is, a complex web of illnesses such as mental disorders, alcohol abuse, illicit drug abuse, and other chronic or acute physical illnesses (Brooner et al. 1993; Empfield, Cournos, and McKinnon 1993; Drake, McHugo, and Noordsy 1993).

The high incidence of acute and chronic diseases amongst the homeless population makes comprehensive health care imperative (Mowbray et al. 1992; Institute of Medicine 1988). Improved community-based treatment and outreach programs to the places where homeless people congregate are essential (Empfield, Cournos, and McKinnon 1993). Such health care should include primary health services (such as pediatric, prenatal, dental, podiatric, and dermatological care), treatment of venereal diseases, hypothermia and hyperthermia, and the mental health services that are more frequently needed by the homeless population. Shelter-based clinics and mobile medical teams can provide the most accessible health care for homeless populations, and integrating substance abuse treatment into mental health programs may also be effective because of the high comorbidity of mentally disabled patients (Drake, McHugo, and Noordsy 1993, 328; Brooner et al. 1993).

Of course, health needs vary with the specific characteristics of homeless people. Homeless mothers, for example, often need periodic gynecological examinations, screening for major infections and venereal diseases, and contraception and counseling and education programs concerning nutrition, substance abuse and AIDS as well. Homeless children need adequate nutrition, immunization, and sometimes acute physical treatment, and the elderly need geriatric care (Weinreb and Bassuk 1990; Dear and Takahashi 1992; Institute of Medicine 1988). Enhancement of national programs such as the Veterans Administration's Domiciliary Care for Homeless Veterans (DCHV) and Homeless Chronically Mentally Ill (HCMI) can provide better treatment for homeless veterans (Rosenheck and Leda 1991).

Yet homeless people often fail to obtain health care because of inadequate income, social alienation and fear, and limited public health care opportunities. Mental health policies such as deinstitutionalization and restrictive hospital and clinic admission policies further contribute to severe underutilization of services by many vulnerable people (Institute of Medicine 1988).

A Functional Typology of Homeless Services

To provide appropriate health and social services to homeless people it is necessary to understand how service needs change at different stages of homelessness. Generally, extremely poor people who become homeless experience several distinctive stages in the path into and (ideally) out of homelessness: entry into homeless status; survival; stabilization; and, finally, reentry to the homed community. To evaluate the shelter/service resources needed to sustain and assist the homeless, we identified three levels of service categories: *gatekeeper*, *coping*, and *other human services* (fig. 7.1). Gatekeeper services are targeted to the extremely poor who are on the brink of homelessness or the newly homeless. Gatekeeper services typically comprise emergency services geared to meet the immediate support needs of such people. Emergency shelters, emergency meals, and the Food Stamp program, disaster services (to assist people dislocated by natural disaster), transient services, emergency housing assistance, and government cash assistance programs (TANF, GA, SSI) fall into this category.

Coping services help homeless people survive on a regular day-to-day basis and typically include various homeless sustenance and transitional services, such as temporary housing, counseling services, health/mental health services, crisis intervention services, vocational rehabilitation services, employment-related services, and other generic community facilities. Some of these services may assist the homed as well as the homeless population.

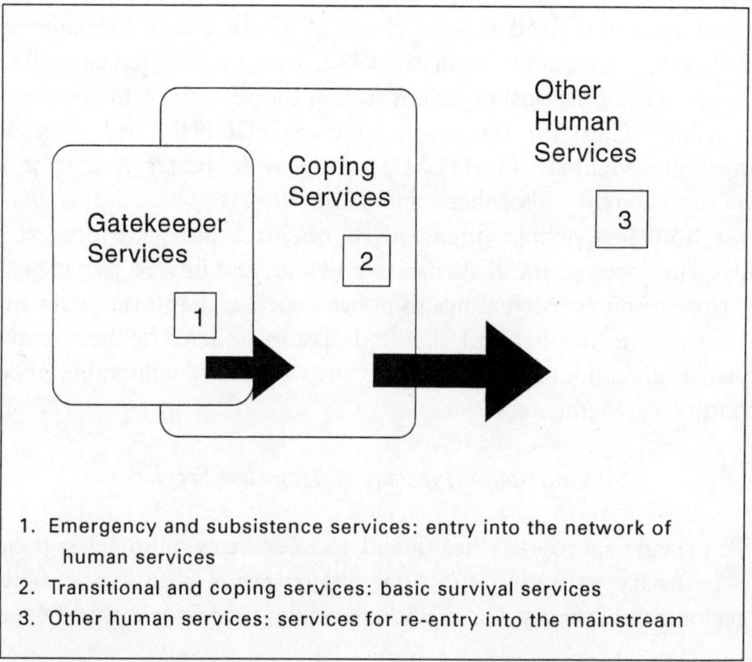

Figure 7.1. Hierarchy of homeless shelter/services.

Other human services comprise a broader range of more generic community services in the human service environment that are not included in the gatekeeper and coping service sectors and that are not explicitly targeted to the homeless but are universally available to the general population. Services in this sector are usually transitional or permanent social services such as long-term affordable housing, education, job training and counseling, and political advocacy activities.

The Geography of Homelessness and Shelter/Service Resources in Los Angeles County

A spatial analysis of service providers and clients can reveal the extent of mismatch between the location of resources and those most in need of services. Although accessibility of services does not ensure that they will be used, studies revealing the limited extent of homeless mobility suggest that a lack of local availability in most cases constitutes a powerful barrier to utilization (Wolch, Rahimian, and Kroegal 1993). Thus, understanding the geography of social service resources is a critical starting point for any assessment of the adequacy of homeless services provision. In this section we use our three-tiered categorization of service resources to identify the extent of equity in shelter and service provision within Los Angeles County.

Data Resources and Methods of Analysis

The data are divided into *service needs* and *shelter/service provision* data. Because it is notoriously difficult to determine the actual numbers of homeless people and their location (Appelbaum 1990; Kondratas 1991; James 1991) and because people on the verge of homelessness often need services also, we use a proxy to represent service need. People living below 75 percent of the poverty line are identified as extremely poor, using the U.S. *Census of Population and Housing* (Summary Tapes Files 1a, 3a) and in this analysis represent the level of homeless service need.

Shelter/service provision data are mainly drawn from the Info-line database supplemented by other major human services directories for Los Angeles County. Info-line is a nonprofit organization (funded by the Los Angeles County Department of Public Social Services and the United Way) that provides twenty-four-hour telephone information and referrals to callers seeking human services. The Info-line database provides a variety of information about individual service programs, including a brief description of functional characteristics and street addresses. It should be noted that service data refer to programs rather than facilities; more than one program may be resident in a single physical facility. One weakness of the Info-line database, however, is that it does not indicate program size and, hence, the volume of clients potentially served.

A total of 23,044 programs were identified in the database (table 7.1) as part of the shelter/services system for the homeless and other

Table 7.1

Homeless Service Programs, Los Angeles County, 1992

Category	*Program Category*	*Number of Programs*	*Percentage*
Gatekeeper	Domestic violence shelter	25	6
	Transient services	13	11
	Disaster services	28	0
	Emergency food	154	13
	Emergency shelter	263	2
	AFDC[a]	26	100
	Food stamp application	23	100
	General relief	14	100
	Emergency housing assistance	3	33
	Refugee cash assistance	1	100
	Social security offices	47	97
	Homeless target group	29	6
	TOTAL	626	27
Coping services	Basic components	467	33
	Crisis intervention	222	21
	Advocacy	252	38
	Health services	835	21
	Vocational rehabilitation	223	65
	Generic community facilities	607	82
	Mental health services	1,085	21
	TOTAL	3,691	36
Other human		18,727	43
	GRAND TOTAL	23,044	42

[a]Aid to Families with Dependent Children.

populations in Los Angeles County. In the shelter/service hierarchy, other human services provide 81 percent of the total programs, whereas gatekeeper and coping services provide 3 and 16 percent respectively. This distribution is not surprising, given the broad range of services included in the Info-line database, most of which are targeted to the general (nonpoor) population.

Any spatial analysis of these homeless shelter/ services and homeless proxy population distributions requires a set of geographical divisions of the study area. Our study area, Los Angeles County, is large, heterogeneous, and displays an enormous need for social services. By the early 1980s it had become known as the "homeless capital" of the United States; more recent estimates suggest that only New York City may surpass it in extent of homelessness (Wolch and Dear 1993). Los Angeles is also the largest county in the United States with a 1990 population approaching nine million (U.S. Bureau of the Census 1990).

We divide the study area in the first stage of our analysis into six subregions and 128 cities and communities to demonstrate the spatial distribution of shelter/services across the county. The six subregions of the county (Central, Westside, San Gabriel Valley, San Fernando Valley, South Bay, North County) are derived from the major statistical areas delineated by the Los Angeles County Department of Regional Planning. The community-level divisions are based upon three local administrative classifications in the county: the 83 incorporated cities; the 35 community-plan areas designated by the Los Angeles City Department of City Planning, and the 10 remaining unincorporated clusters.

The broad geographies of homeless shelter/services that emerge at these subregional and community scales of analysis are useful for policy discussions about the equity of service provision. To explain adequately the distribution of shelter/services across the county, however, a more fine-grained, neighborhood-level analysis is required. Thus, in the second stage of our study, we use census tract level data to identify the socioeconomic, demographic, and land-use correlates of shelter/service locations to grasp better the determinants of service distribution and access within the county's subregions and communities.

Lastly, we explore the question of service availability versus levels of service need. To characterize the basic patterns of geographic mismatch between services and needs we return to the broad subregional and community levels. This approach reveals that deep disparities in service needs across the county combine with an uneven development of service resources to create a distinctive landscape of service-rich and service-poor communities and associated dilemmas of sociospatial justice.

The Spatial Distribution of Homeless Shelter/Services in Los Angeles County

There are significant differences in the overall demographic and socioeconomic makeup of the county's six subregions. According to the 1990 census, the Central subregion contains some of the poorest communities in the county. Two-thirds of the subregion's residents are nonwhite, almost one-quarter of the population lives in poverty, and two-thirds are renters. At the opposite extreme, the Westside subregion contains the county's most affluent communities with only 8 percent living below the poverty line and a predominantly white population. The San Fernando and San Gabriel Valley areas and the South Bay region are more alike in demographic and socioeconomic characteristics. In these subregions white population ranges from 61 percent to 71 percent, and only about 11 percent of the populations of all three subregions live below the poverty line. In both the South Bay and San Fernando Valley subregions almost one-half of the households are renters, whereas the San Gabriel Valley comprises mostly homeowners. Both the San Fernando Valley and South Bay subregions are more heterogeneous than the San Gabriel Valley with pockets of intense poverty and segregated minority areas. Finally, the North County area contains newer suburban fringe communities and is predominantly populated by white homeowners; few of North County's population live below the poverty line.

With respect to shelter/service resources, the Central subregion of the county has the highest concentration of all types of services, providing 45 percent of gatekeeper services, 36 percent of coping services, and 37 percent of other human service programs (table 7.2). Conversely, the newly developed North County and the affluent Westside have the lowest proportions of all categories of homeless shelter/service programs. Significant proportions of coping services are found outside of the Central subregion in the San Gabriel Valley area, and a large number of other human services locate in the San Fernando subregion.

Gatekeeper services provide the point of entry into the broader human services system and are, therefore, a necessary starting point

Table 7.2

Subregional Distribution of Homeless Shelter/Services, Los Angeles County

Subregion	*Gatekeeper Services (%)*		*Coping Services (%)*		*Other Human Services (%)*	
Central	285	(45)	1,316	(36)	6,863	(37)
North County	32	(5)	124	(3)	558	(3)
San Fernando	75	(12)	575	(16)	3,118	(17)
San Gabriel	103	(16)	755	(20)	3,784	(20)
South Bay	99	(16)	600	(16)	2,810	(15)
Westside	32	(5)	321	(9)	1,594	(8)
TOTAL	626	(100)[a]	3,691	(100)	18,727	(100)

[a]Percentage sum may not be 100 because of rounding.

for newly homeless people in need of assistance. Figure 7.2 represents the spatial distribution of these services across the subregions and communities of Los Angeles County. Within the poor Central subregion several communities have particularly high concentrations of gatekeeper services. Most notably, two central communities, Southeast Los Angeles and Central Los Angeles, have more than forty gatekeeper service programs each and are surrounded by smaller concentrations of gatekeeper services. Long Beach in the South Bay subregion also has a significant number of gatekeeper services. Other relatively high concentrations of gatekeeper services are scattered throughout the county in communities such as Santa Monica, Pasadena, and Lancaster. Many of the more affluent fringe suburban communities, such as Palos Verdes Estates and Agoura Hills have no gatekeeper services.

Clearly, a "zone of dependence" exists in the Central subregion of the county where all services, but particularly gatekeeper services, are numerous. This finding seems consistent with evidence of human service ghettoization in central cities across the United States. In the decaying inner districts of most large cities skid row areas have developed as crucial coping zones for poor and marginalized groups, and many human service agencies, missions, shelters and other support facilities concentrate here (Dear and Wolch 1987).

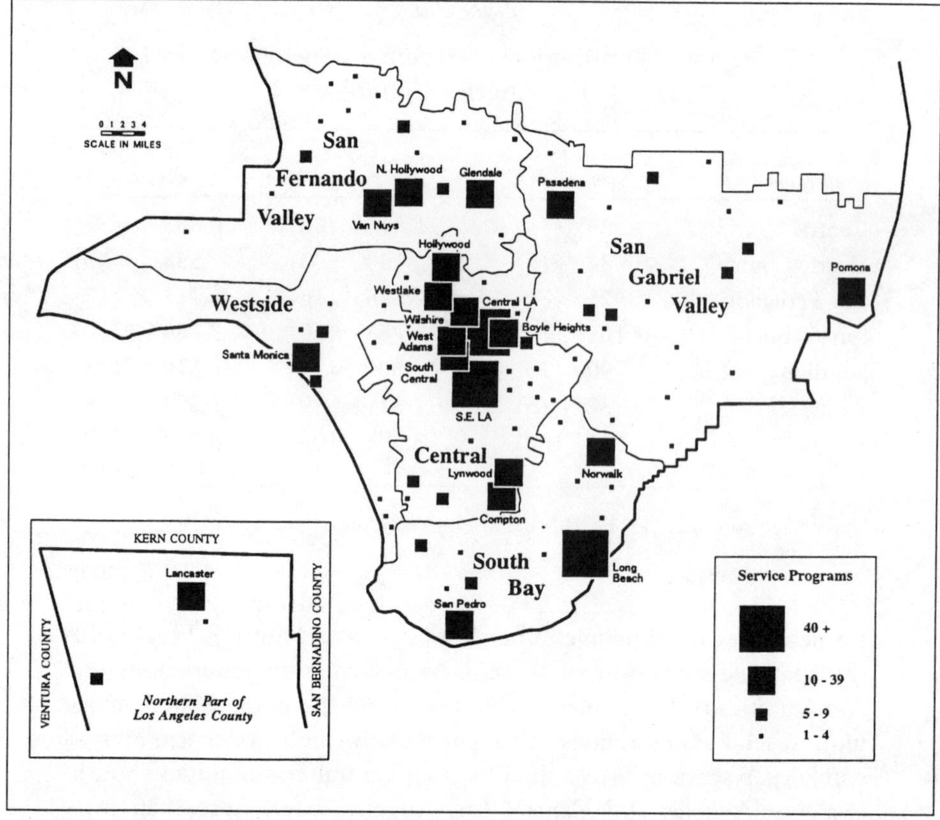

Figure 7.2. Distribution of gatekeeper service programs by subregion and community, Los Angeles County.

At one level such a concentration of human services can benefit clients because services located in close proximity to one another provide valuable and accessible resources for people in need of assistance. The relative dearth of social services in other densely populated parts of cities, however, generates an inevitable drift of service-dependent populations to the inner city. A self-reinforcing cycle of co-location of service-dependent populations and human services can result, perpetuating the spatial confinement and marginalization of service-dependent people in zones of dependence.

At the same time more-affluent communities are relieved of their responsibility to provide those social services that may be perceived to have negative spillover effects, such as the presence of 'undesirable' people. Poor communities are, thus, left to shoulder the burden of providing human services rejected by other communities. To explain this distribution we turn in the following section to a closer examination of the local characteristics associated with different levels of shelter/service provision across the county.

Determinants of Shelter/Service Location

To identify clearly the determinants of shelter/service locations we used the Info-line database and 1990 census variables to construct multivariate regression models relating service distributions with socioeconomic, demographic, neighborhood, and housing characteristics. For this analysis the county's 1,652 census tracts provide a more useful geographical subdivision because they afford insight into the locally conditioned determinants of service location.

Our multiple regression analysis (table 7.3) suggests that, as we might expect, gatekeeper services are positively associated with many poverty indicators such as low-income, high black unemployment, low educational attainment, high rent-to-income ratios, and poor housing quality. Many of the housing units in these areas lack complete kitchen facilities, suggesting that single room occupancy hotels (SRO) may be a common housing type. Short journey-to-work travel times are also a significant characteristic of gatekeeper service locations, suggesting areas of mixed land-use patterns or low-income inner city areas in which workers reside close to employment opportunities (or both).

Coping service programs similarly tend to locate in areas close to employment centers and are characterized by the presence of low-income minorities, rental units, large family sizes, and public school attendance. In these areas residents tend to be employed in relatively low-wage professional or related services. Other human service programs are more likely to locate near residential areas dominated by finance, insurance, and real estate industry workers. They are negatively associated with white homeowner households and private school attendance, tending to be found in minority areas where nonfamily households are plentiful and jobs are close by.

All programs in the three-tiered shelter/service hierarchy are, therefore, likely to cluster in relatively low-income minority areas. In these low income areas, residences and workplaces are relatively proximate; hence, travel time is short. Given that low-wage workplaces are mostly

Table 7.3

Regression Analysis of Shelter/Service Distribution, Los Angeles County

Independent Variables	*Dependent Variables*		
1990 Census Regressors	*Gatekeeper Service Programs (N)*	*Coping Service Programs (N)*	*Other Human Service Programs (N)*
White occupied housing units with no vehicles		0.17	0.0043
Housing units lacking complete kitchen	0.29 (2.82)[a]	0.05	0.05
Separated, widowed, and divorced persons		0.25 (2.24)[a]	1.00
Persons enrolled in private school	−0.14	−0.09	
Journey-to-work less than 10 minutes	0.26	0.09	0.24
White owner occupied housing units			−0.16
Hispanic renter occupied housing units			0.66
Finance, insurance, and real estate employees			0.33
Persons in college dormitories	−0.03	0.05	0.19
Female-headed families with related children		0.07	0.08
Black renter householders, $750 or more rent			0.11
Persons in nursing homes		0.18	
Persons residing in the same house in 1985		−0.51	
S-night homeless population		0.02	0.06
Professional or related services employees		0.41 (5.19)[a]	
Hispanic persons, income above poverty level		0.24	−0.05
Persons 18 years+ with 12th grade education	0.15 (2.22)[a]		
Black unemployed persons 16 years and over	0.10 (2.40)[a]		
Rental units with gross rent less than $300	0.49 (2.96)[a]		
Workers 16 years+ who walk to work		0.14	
Persons per family		0.48 (5.69)[a]	
R	88.88%	76.71%	78.97%
F value	131.88	97.50	186.09

Notes: Second stage, best linear unbiased estimates provided. The reported results are derived from a two-stage best linear squares model used to eliminate heteroscedasticity. All coefficients are standardized. T-statistics are in parentheses.

[a]Parameter estimates are significant at $p = 0.05$.

concentrated in or around the Central business districts (CBDs) of cities and communities, or in downtown Los Angeles, shelter/service proximity to employment centers suggests concentration in, or adjacent to, inner-city zones of dependence or zones of transition.

The identification of socioeconomic, demographic, and neighborhood characteristics associated with the distribution of shelter/service resources is an important step in understanding the equity of service distributions. The analysis thus far suggests that the low-income inner-city communities that are most in need of services are, in fact, well endowed with a range of emergency and transitional services. In particular, low-income inner-city communities seem to be well served by gatekeeper shelter/services.

Abundance of service resources in a locale does not guarantee access to services, however. Access is a function not only of the number of programs available in a given locale but also of the volume of clients attempting to negotiate services there (Pinch 1979; Powell 1992). In short, congestion can act as an effective rationing device, blocking service utilization; in the case of those on the brink of homelessness, congestion of critical gatekeeper and coping services can push people onto the streets.

Accessibility of Service Resources

To examine more closely levels of client access to services across the county we use the notion of "service-rich" versus "service-poor" environments. Service-richness describes the degree of service availability adjusted by the amount of service need in a given locale. This concept reflects the reality that an area may be characterized by a concentration of services, but it may not be service-rich if it is also an area of high need. In our analysis service-richness is measured by calculating the ratio of service programs per ten thousand extremely poor people (those living below 75 percent of the federal poverty line). This measure should not be construed as an absolute standard for adequate levels of service provision in relation to need; specification of such an absolute standard is not possible, given variations in program size and individual human service requirements. The analysis, however, can identify those areas where human service levels are likely to be inadequate, given differing levels of poverty and deprivation across the county.

This analysis demonstrates that the poverty-stricken Central subregion, despite having a large number of service programs, has the lowest numbers of shelter/services in relation to extremely poor populations as compared to all other subregions (table 7.4). Only the San Fernando Valley area shares similar levels of gatekeeper services (approximately six gatekeeper programs per ten thousand extremely poor residents); however, the Central subregion has about one-half the adjusted coping and other human services of the San Fernando subregion.

The Central subregion does not approach any other subregion in proportions of coping and other human services adjusted for extremely poor population. Most notably, the Westside subregion has almost three times the other human services, and more than three times the coping services per ten thousand extremely poor residents as does the Central subregion.

Because gatekeeper services are the crucial point of entry into transitional and long-term services, it is important that very poor and homeless people have access to areas which are gatekeeper service-rich. Figure 7.3 shows the distribution of gatekeeper shelter/service programs per one thousand extremely poor residents of the communities of Los Angeles County. The figure also indicates that the Central subregion is not as well served as it appears in the simple frequency distribution of service programs highlighted in figure 7.2. The service

Table 7.4

Service-Rich and Service-Poor Subregions, Los Angeles County (Programs per 10,000 Extremely Poor Residents)

Subregion	*Gatekeeper Services*	*Coping Services*	*Other Human Services*
Central	6.0	27.6	144.0
North County	18.0	69.7	313.7
San Fernando	6.4	49.4	267.7
San Gabriel	7.2	53.1	265.9
South Bay	9.8	59.3	277.9
Westside	9.9	99.3	492.9
TOTAL	7.1	41.6	211.1

Note: Extremely poor = below 75 percent of federal poverty line.

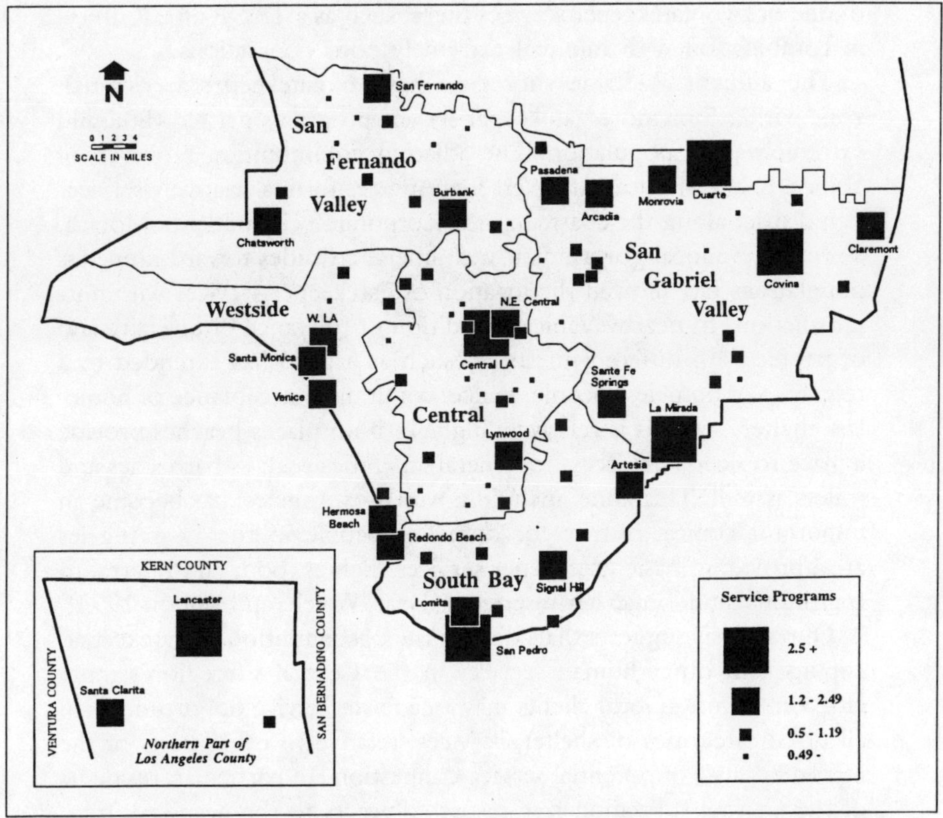

Figure 7.3. Adjusted distribution of gatekeeper service programs by subregion and community, Los Angeles County.

concentration apparent in the Central subregion in figure 7.2 has contracted, and only the communities of central and northeast central Los Angeles remain rich in gatekeeper programs in relation to extremely poor population. Communities that appear to be well endowed with gatekeeper services, such as southeast Los Angeles and Long Beach in the South Bay subregion, are revealed to be service-poor communities relative to the potential need for such services there.

Some areas with few gatekeeper services have high proportions of such services per one thousand extremely poor residents. In the San Gabriel subregion, Covina, Duarte, and La Mirada are service-rich, as is Lancaster in the North County. The service-rich nature of these new suburban fringe communities may be explained by the location of one or two gatekeeper services there, such as a TANF or GR office, in combination with minimal extremely poor populations.

The affluent Westside subregion has no gatekeeper service-rich zone with 2.5 or more gatekeeper service programs per ten thousand extremely poor population. The adjacent communities, however, of Venice, Santa Monica, and West Los Angeles form a relatively service-rich district along the coast. In the incorporated city of Santa Monica, a progressive local government with liberal attitudes toward homeless populations has allowed the location of gatekeeper services within its jurisdiction. In nearby Venice a tradition of tolerance of diversity and of people with different lifestyles (such as artists) has extended to a tolerance of homeless people; hence, community acceptance of homeless shelter/services is relatively high. In both places beaches provide a place to sleep and access to general amenities such as barbecues and toilets as well. This zone, including west Los Angeles, has become an important coping district for homeless people in the Los Angeles area, providing basic gatekeeper services such as food, and referral to transitional and longer-term services (Dear, Wolch, and Wilton 1994).

Our analysis suggests that, despite the concentration of gatekeeper, coping, and other human services in the Central subregion's inner city communities, local clients may face fewer service opportunities in all three categories of shelter/services, relative to other parts of the region because of potential service congestion. In particular, residents of the Central subregion face restricted access to the necessary transitional and longer-term services. Homeless people in this subregion thus lack the continuum of care necessary to facilitate reintegration into the homed community. These homeless people in need of coping and other human services are likely to be either dislocated from their Central area communities in a search for appropriate services, forced to make burdensome trips to service-rich areas, or simply denied access to necessary services.

A basic service-richness measure sharply reveals the distributional inequity of service program location across the county. Thus far, our analysis suggests that low-income communities tend to attract a range of services, particularly gatekeeper services, but that service levels may be overwhelmed by levels of need in these communities. Meanwhile, in the more-affluent communities availability of emergency services is limited, whereas access to coping and other human services is relatively high.

The Political Economy of Shelter/Service Siting

Our analysis suggests the existence of a spatial mismatch between those at risk of homelessness and the full continuum of necessary support services. The study, thus, reinforces findings from other research that points to the ghettoization of services for the homeless and other dependent populations in many cities and communities, a pattern that strongly influences the everyday lives and life chances of inner-city residents and service clients. Increasingly, too, the homelessness crisis has spread to the suburbs, where those at risk have difficulty finding immediate assistance and face the difficult choice of trying to survive on the streets without benefit of services or moving into an unfamiliar and often threatening inner-city skid row zone.

A "fair-share" approach to human services provision has been proposed by Dear and Wolch (1987) as a way to remedy the problems posed by ghettoization of human services. This approach requires that society as a whole take responsibility for service-dependent populations. Every region and community, in this view, should participate in the provision of appropriate services. The best way to achieve such sociospatial justice is through the careful design of *service hubs* (Dear, Wolch, and Wilton 1994) located throughout a metropolitan region. Service hubs comprise groups of small-scale community-based facilities that can share the benefits of proximity and provide integrated services for clients. Because service hubs are to be distributed along "fair-share" principles, inner-city ghettoization of services is avoided.

A fair-share approach to the homeless shelter/service distribution we have described for Los Angeles would require the selective addition of coping and other human services to those gatekeeper facilities already concentrated in the inner city. In this way, existing emergency services would be supplemented by the artful addition of transitional and longer-term facilities to ensure the continuum of care necessary for the reintegration of homeless people into mainstream society. At the same time gatekeeper facilities would be added to coping and other human services concentrations in more-affluent areas to ensure that all communities assume responsibility for, and offer some capacity for, the support of homeless people. The creation of integrated service hubs in this way should also prevent the displacement to skid row districts of those on the verge of homelessness in more-affluent communities.

Fair-share service-hub planning, however, is obstructed in Los Angeles, as elsewhere, by three dynamics common to the political economy of contemporary cities. First, many cities are experiencing threats to those existing service concentrations, particularly skid row areas, which could function as effective service hubs if a broader range of programs were integrated with existing facilities. Second, the increasing success of oppositional tactics employed by communities seeking to prevent the siting of particular facilities considered to be dangerous or undesirable (such as homeless shelters and group homes for the mentally disabled) is part of the dynamic underlying the present service distribution, simultaneously posing a significant barrier to the realization of fair-share planning goals. Finally, the proliferation of nonprofit services that exhibit different locational patterns from public programs can frustrate efforts to achieve fair-share distributions of human services across cities. Each of these dynamics is considered in turn.

Destruction of Skid Rows

Skid row areas have traditionally provided resources needed by homeless people to cope with life on the streets. These resources include social services but also the social networks that homeless people forge (Rowe and Wolch 1990) and a variety of commercial and retail services geared to the very low-income population (Hoch and Slayton 1989). In the post–World War II period, however, demolition of skid rows has been promoted by urban politicians seeking to "clean up" the inner city and to remove the threats posed by its social "disorganization" (Groth 1994). For the homeless, however, redevelopment of skid row districts implies the loss of vital services and affordable accommodation to upscale land uses with few alternatives provided.

In Los Angeles this trend has taken the form of a policy of "containment" of skid row land uses and populations rather than wholesale destruction. Although this policy has protected (and in some cases improved) some share of remaining low-cost accommodation for the homeless such as SROs, it has also had the adverse effect of isolating and confining the homeless within a high-density zone of intense suffering and poverty. Simultaneously, more-affluent areas of the city have been relieved of responsibility to provide services for the homeless (Wolch 1992).

A fair-share approach to service siting for the homeless would protect skid rows as valuable coping zones. But such districts would become only one of many dispersed service hubs rather than isolated service ghettos. According to our research, most service agencies are still located in inner-city communities; if our data had reflected service *capacity* (e.g., number of beds), the skid row of Los Angeles would be even more striking as a primary locus of homeless services in the region. However crucial such high-density service zones may be as a coping mechanism for people in need of help, particularly as a site of emergency and crisis assistance, their lack of full-continuum care means that homeless people are routinely "churned" from one gatekeeping agency to another, in an ongoing cycle that involves repeated "failure" on the part of homeless people to reenter the mainstream and greatly prolongs homeless episodes. Clearly, for skid rows to function as part of a system of dispersed service hubs, longer-term and transitional services must be added to existing configurations and the worst aspects of most skid row neighborhoods—such as dilapidated buildings, lack of green open space and other amenities and conveniences taken for granted elsewhere in the city—must be remedied.

Community Opposition to Controversial Service Siting

The second obstacle to a "fair-share" distribution of homeless shelter/services is the prevalence of "not in my backyard" (NIMBY) sentiments. Shelter/services for the homeless tend to confront severe community opposition (Takahashi 1992). As we have seen in Los Angeles, homeless service distribution patterns are directed to low-income minority neighborhoods and to the central part of the county. These general patterns appear to stand in contrast to the long-standing "underclass hypothesis," which suggests that public facilities and/or service distributions discriminate against minorities or the poor (Lineberry 1977).

Our findings are, however, consistent with those of Segal and Aviram (1978) and Dear and Taylor (1982) who found that NIMBY sentiments are strongest in homogenous suburbs that tend to reject difference, whereas in the diverse inner city further addition of facilities is likely to go unnoticed or, at least, unopposed. Similarly, a national survey revealed that the profile of a person typically exhibiting NIMBY sentiments is of a high-income, married, male home-owner, who is well educated and has a professional position and lives in a large city or its suburbs (Daniel Yankelovich Group 1990). This profile clearly relates to the distribution of socioeconomic and political power across cities. Power relations are reflected through the degrees of resistance to siting facilities for controversial or noxious human service facilities.

Against this general political-economic backdrop, however, the importance of service characteristics and, in particular, the perceived extent of negative externalities must not be overlooked. Specifically, gatekeeper service programs are more likely to locate in socioeconomically marginalized minority communities than coping and other human services, indicating that the nature of the service type is a critical factor in determining differing locational outcomes. Conversely, we found that areas rich in coping and other human services are positively associated with higher income and suburban white homeownership areas.

From a NIMBY perspective this is not surprising because regressive siting of *noxious* facilities is a long-standing pattern (Wolpert 1976). Gatekeeper programs are targeted to those in most desperate (and often most visible) need of basic survival services, who may be stigmatized by a variety of personal characteristics (e.g., mental disability) and who are typically (and inaccurately) perceived by community residents as "outsiders" rather than neighbors. They are, thus, seen as burdensome and threatening to the health and well-being of the community. Coping and especially other human services, in contrast, cater to a much broader range of clients; in the case of other human services only a portion of the clientele may be poor. In addition, the physical facilities themselves are apt to differ across the service typology with more gatekeeper services involving a residential shelter component that is often the most problematic from the standpoint of generating community opposition.

The Threat of Privatization

Finally, a fair-share distribution of homeless shelter/services may be compromised by ongoing privatization of social and health services. In response to changing global economic conditions and declining rates of domestic welfare spending, U.S. states and localities and the federal government as well are accelerating the privatization of services to the for-profit and, especially, the voluntary sector (Wolch 1990). In Los Angeles, as elsewhere, this restructuring of the welfare state into a "shadow state" apparatus through contracting out, program reductions, and facility closures has led to a crisis in health and social service provision. Reduction in cash welfare provision itself contributes to homelessness (Wolch and Dear 1993), but changes in the organization of service delivery also limit the types and locations of services available to people on the brink of homelessness.

Research on the differential siting patterns of public versus nonprofit services indicates that services provided under these two auspices exhibit different locational and functional characteristics (Lee 1993). Many gatekeeper programs are publicly provided (e.g., TANF, GR), and these services are typically concentrated in areas of high need. The more-generic coping services and other human services, however, are more likely to be provided by the voluntary sector (typically with state funding). Such services are often directed toward more-affluent populations, suggesting that the distribution of the voluntary sector service system is more likely to reflect factors aside from the distribution of potential clients. Voluntary organizations are often concentrated in middle-income communities affluent enough to supply donations and volunteers, but not so wealthy as to be able to fill service needs strictly through market provision, for example, by attending private psychiatrists (Wolch and Geiger 1983). Poorer districts, in contrast, often have low levels of donative resources and, thus, little in the way of voluntary sector infrastructure upon which to build additional government-supported service capacity.

Thus, privatization and shadow state development can reinforce existing inequitable patterns of service provision. Because voluntary organizations are often stand-alone facilities (rather than networks) and face no locational constraints related to coverage or minimum travel distance for clients (as do many public facilities), implementing a fair-share siting pattern for shelter/service resources may face even greater obstacles under policies promoting privatization.

Conclusions

We began this chapter by showing that the health of homeless people is integrally tied to their diverse service needs. Increasingly, geographical research demonstrates that the provision of health care alone does not guarantee health (Hayes 1994). This is particularly true of homeless people, for whom access to a broad range of services, such as adequate housing and employment opportunities, is imperative to their attainment of adequate health status and to their reintegration into mainstream society.

It is clear from our analysis, however, that those most in need of such services are often geographically barred from receiving them or face the possibility of congestion in overburdened facilities. Moreover, the concentration of shelter/services and the clients who rely upon them for survival further burdens those communities in which they are clustered. In the Los Angeles context these are places whose residents are already facing challenges to health and safety as a result of poverty, overcrowding, environmental hazards, and the depredations of gangs and drugs. And, although the inner-city poor have access to emergency facilities, transitional and longer-term services are often concentrated in more-affluent and less-accessible neighborhoods. We have suggested that this spatial mismatch is deeply rooted in the social and economic foundations of society.

Spatial patterns of homeless shelter/services, then, are not autonomous from socioeconomic and political spheres of everyday life (Horvath 1992; Dear and Wolch 1989). Political economic conditions in part determine the geography of homeless shelter/service resources. In particular, threats to inner-city zones of dependence, the ability of affluent communities to resist the location of unwanted facilities, and ongoing privatization of human services delivery confront attempts to institute fair-share planning of homeless services.

The homelessness crisis will not be solved in the near future because of the deep-seated structural forces that underlie the severe marginalization of society's most vulnerable people. Service provision policy for the homeless population must, therefore, be diversified and comprehensive. The provision of health and mental health care for homeless people must be accomplished simultaneously with and geographically proximate to the provision of housing, employment, and other support facilities and services. To reach these goals shelter/service distributions must be reformulated to ensure that support burdens are shared fairly and that homeless people and those most at risk of homelessness can enjoy easy access to the full continuum of shelter/service resources.

8

Concepts of Difference in Community Health

LOIS M. TAKAHASHI

In traditional models of health care delivery the degree of access of poorer populations to service facilities such as hospitals and clinics has often been regarded as an important determinant of population health. This type of assumption has increasingly been called into question (e.g., Evans, Barer, and Marmor 1994). Explanations of inequalities in health that directly link health status and service facilities have typically neglected the role of place as it affects client well-being. With respect to health care the notion of place includes local historical elements (such as the neighborhood's experience with deinstitutionalization and other social policies), the local political and institutional setting (such as the relationship between service providers and residents), and the existing physical structure (such as existing and proposed land uses) (e.g., Dear and Taylor 1982; Seley 1983). Place has always played an important role in clients' ability to obtain services and to cope with everyday existence. This role has become much more important in the wake of increasing local opposition to human service facility siting.

Local opposition, especially toward controversial human services such as homeless shelters and facilities for persons with AIDS, has been on the rise since the late 1980s. This increase can be traced to wider social trends, most especially, an increasing population who need health care services and rising grass-roots and other local activism. Such trends suggest that local opposition toward health care facilities shows no signs of decreasing. Given this growing hostile environment for health care facilities and their clients, the importance of place has grown significantly. In essence, the connection between place and client well-being appears to have become a vital element for effective health care provision.

In this chapter I argue that to understand population health the dialectic between place and client well-being must be fully incorporated into theory and practice. For example, effective provision of health care services, especially for those groups having few economic and other tangible resources, requires an understanding of the local community context, especially residents' responses to varying clients and facilities. The argument is that understanding this place-client dialectic may, in the short term, facilitate the siting process for health care services and, in the long term, encourage health promotion for both communities and clients.

To explore this perspective, I present a formulation of the dialectic between place and client well-being, using the notion of *difference* drawn from postmodern debates in social theory. This section is less concerned with abstract theorizing and more concerned with one vital component of place—community response to clients and facilities. I then use a framework to analyze this dialectic, using three methods: hierarchies of acceptance, socioeconomic and spatial variations in attitudes, and regional variations in attitudes and behavior. I analyze a recent national survey in the United States to show how public attitudes toward homelessness and AIDS play a significant role in community rejection of the disabled and afflicted. Finally, I speculate about how understanding this dialectic might lead to more effective and appropriate solutions for health-care planning.

The Dialectic of Place and Client Well-being

Social theory debates concerning the merits and dangers of postmodernism have often focused on the definition and use of *difference.* Difference in these debates has encompassed multiple issues (including identity, subjectivity, citizenship, and justice) and has suggested both emancipatory and reactionary possibilities (e.g., Cloke, Philo, and Sadler 1991; Flax 1993). An increasingly popular notion for scholars, the discussion of difference has become a "boom industry" for various academic disciplines (Giroux 1993, 66).

The preoccupation with difference has tended to be more reactionary in the wider public. Since the late 1980s, for example, society has witnessed a growing rejection of difference. Such rejection has been manifested explicitly in ongoing public policy debates at differing geographic scales across the United States. At the federal level there are efforts to intensify welfare state restructuring, emphasizing the reduction and denial of benefits to individuals who do not comply with increasingly restrictive eligibility requirements. At both the federal and state levels there are calls for the reappraisal of the need for and equity of affirmative action policies that aim to provide employment and education opportunities for women and underrepresented minority groups. And, in the state of California, an initiative was recently passed (Proposition 187), that would deny public services, including health care and education, to undocumented immigrants.

At the scale of the community, the family, and the individual, difference is used daily to define outsiders. The definition and perpetuation of individuals as outsiders depend upon the interactions between large-scale systems, such as identity, politics, and economy, and microlevel institutions, such as the neighborhood and the family. Three particular issues, central to the concept of difference, provide a basis for a formulation of the dialectic of place and client well-being: representation, power relations, and marginalization.

Representation of individuals becomes very important when selected individuals become outsiders in specific places. For human service clients, in particular, the definition of specific individuals as outsiders often stems from equating them with disability or illness (Katz 1981; Kleck 1969). Following this categorization, disability or illness becomes the primary point of self-characterization for both clients and wider society (Gibbons 1986; Jones et al. 1984). This characterization of self means that the person with an illness becomes an extension of the illness itself with the ill person embodying the representation of disease (Fine and Asch 1988; Gilman 1988). Everyday examples are common: "the mentally disabled," "the homeless," "AIDS patients." For such clients their representation as the embodiment of disease often results in stigmatization and exclusion by neighborhood residents. Such stigma, in turn, tends to perpetuate biased representations, or stereotypes, of individuals. The popular understanding of such stereotyped individuals is that they behave and appear inherently different from the general population. For clients such difference is then equated with unpredictability and dangerousness in the minds of community residents, resulting in their being perceived as a threat to the community (Berdiansky and Parker 1977; Coates 1981; Fischer 1988). The stereotype thus acts as a social code, indicating to the community that clients are to be avoided and, moreover, that they should be excluded from the neighborhood.

Relations of power are very important in constructing and reinforcing such stigmatizing definitions of difference. Political influence, monetary and informational resources, and informal uses of power are very significant in defining and controlling difference in society. Communities having access to political influence and other resources, for example, are often extremely successful at keeping difference at bay. Those having access to political and monetary resources often do not need to resort to overt public demonstrations of rejection to prevent unwanted human services and clients in a community. Instead, they may use existing channels of political influence to block facility siting (Graham and Logan 1990). Informal and everyday uses of power are also used by communities to "discipline" difference by delineating acceptable behavior and appearance and, more broadly, by maintaining specific relationships of control and domination. These small uses of power normalize behavior for all members of the community (Foucault 1977; Fox 1993). Thus, because of these norms, which serve as social codes of acceptance, and the ongoing exclusion of unwanted facilities and clients, difference becomes easy to identify and very visible.

Marginalization of specific groups is made possible through this identification and visibility of difference. As a contextual process, marginalization is highly dependent on the current and place-specific definition of normality. Those who do not meet the standards of acceptable physical traits, personal autonomy, or sexual orientation are assumed to be inferior. The definition of these groups as inherently inferior leads to a dehumanizing by the community (Goffman 1963b). Members of such identified groups lose their individual identities, becoming instead, symbols of disease and deviance. Specific groups and individuals have been subject to more frequent marginalization because of characteristics that readily identify them as different. Four broad categories, for example, which are often used in marginalizing homeless individuals and persons with AIDS are race/ethnicity, gender, sexual orientation, and illness/disability (see, e.g., Bean et al. 1989; Dear and Gleeson 1991; Herek and Glunt 1988).

A Framework for Analyzing the Place-Client Dialectic

Although this theorization of the place-client dialectic is necessary for understanding contemporary sources of rejection, the level of abstraction inherent in its formulation does not translate easily into quantitative analysis. This difficulty creates a need for developing a middle-level framework to bridge the gap between abstract theorization and the analytical techniques available for exploring numerical data. Providing a portrait of the place-client dialectic through such an analysis accomplishes two objectives: first, a quantitative presentation of the constitution of the dialectic provides a different illustration to the theoretical formulation; and, second, a quantitative analysis may indicate where the current theoretical formulation should be adapted. Place is operationalized in this chapter as the community context, specifically the responses of residents in particular places to human services and their clients. This section presents an analytical framework for illustrating the place-client dialectic through three related methods: hierarchies of acceptance, sociodemographic and spatial variation in attitudes, and regional variations in attitudes and behavior. These three methods highlight various portraits of attitudes and behavior and suggest how perceptions of difference have affected community response. They, consequently, provide a partial, but important, insight into the interactions of place and client well-being.

Variations in acceptance toward different client groups and facilities have often been represented through *hierarchies of acceptance* (Blissland and Manger 1983). Hierarchies of acceptance are rankings of facility types or client groups according to their relative acceptability in the neighborhood. They are not monolithic, but change over time and space, and vary by facility type or client group. Such change can be divided into two components: volatility (the inclusion of new client groups and facilities) and synergy (the relational shifts in acceptance). The volatility of change is readily illustrated by the rapidity with which new client groups and facility types are included in hierarchies of acceptance.

In a 1970 study, for example, the least acceptable group was composed of alcoholics, former convicts, and mentally disabled individuals (table 8.1, Tringo 1970). People having common physical ailments and disabilities (such as ulcers and asthma) were the most acceptable. A survey conducted in 1980 in Ohio, however, indicated that the elderly and the physically disabled engendered the least opposition,

Table 8.1

Hierarchy of Acceptance, 1970

Ranking	*Type of Condition*
1	Ulcer
2	Arthritis
3	Asthma
4	Diabetes
5	Heart disease
6	Amputee
7	Blindness
8	Deafness
9	Stroke
10	Cancer
11	Old age
12	Paraplegic
13	Epilepsy
14	Dwarf
15	Cerebral palsy
16	Hunchback
17	Tuberculosis
18	Former convict
19	Mental retardation
20	Alcoholism
21	Mental illness

Source: Tringo 1970.

followed by terminally ill and mentally retarded persons (table 8.2, Solomon 1983). The least-acceptable group in 1980 was composed of mentally ill persons, alcoholics, and drug addicts.

Although these two hierarchies cannot be compared in detail because of the variation in sample and survey methods, several general characteristics about changing acceptance of difference can be noted. For example, hierarchies of acceptance tend to remain defined over time by the degree of difference from socially established norms. Those persons considered to be the most different are consistently

Table 8.2

Hierarchy of Acceptance, 1980

Ranking	*Type of Client*	*Percentage of Respondents Opposing the Facility*
1	Elderly	4
2	Physically handicapped	6
3	Terminally ill	12
4	Mentally retarded	21
5	Mentally ill	39
6	Parolees	48
7	Troubled adolescents	51
8	Alcoholics	55
9	Drug addicts	78

Source: Solomon 1983.

located at the bottom of the hierarchy. Although there is some stability in response over time, hierarchies also show volatility as evidenced by the distinct hierarchies in 1970 and 1980 with the introduction of new client groups and with shifts in perception about existing client groups.

These two hierarchies also illustrate the synergy in changing acceptance for clients and facilities. New client groups that are introduced into the hierarchy can alter the relative acceptance of other groups by creating a new datum or benchmark for evaluation. In essence, the synergy of new client groups with other more established groups can serve to change visibly the character of such hierarchies. The introduction of drug addicts in 1980, for example, established a new benchmark by which the rest of the client groups could be evaluated. In addition, the relative position of other groups shifted. Notably, whereas alcoholics remained near the bottom of the hierarchy in both surveys, the position of mentally disabled persons shifted substantially.

A second method used to explore variations in attitudes toward difference has been to focus on the *sociodemographic and spatial variations in resident perceptions.* Sociodemographic and spatial characteristics have often been used to analyze the connections between neighborhood type and resident attitudes toward human service facilities (Green, McCormick, and Walkey 1987; Segal, Baumohl, and

Moyles 1980). With respect to mental disability, accepting neighborhoods have been characterized by large proportions of unmarried, younger, and renting individuals (suggesting a more transient population), whereas rejecting communities have been more homogeneous in race, income, and education (Trute and Segal 1976). In addition, studies have indicated that suburban communities have largely rejected human service facilities (Taylor, Dear, and Hall 1979).

Suburban communities, having greater resources and opportunities, have been better equipped to reject facilities for marginalized groups. The overall result of such effective neighborhood rejection has been that facilities serving less-stigmatized groups have been commonly sited in middle-income suburban areas (Sundeen and Fiske 1982). Conversely, more controversial human service facilities have tended to be concentrated in transient and minority neighborhoods, such as inner-city communities and skid rows (Dear and Wolch 1987). Although these sociodemographic and spatial variables help to characterize the uneven provision of human service facilities, such characteristics alone cannot predict whether a neighborhood will reject or accept a facility. In combination with the study of attitudes and other contextual factors, however, the use of such characteristics becomes a powerful tool for understanding the potentials for behavior.

Regional variations in attitudes and behavior constitute the final method of the analytical framework used in this chapter to explore the place-client dialectic. The characterization of resident behavior is important in understanding community response because although attitudes appear to influence resident behavior strongly, they do not appear to determine them. The linkage between attitudes and behavior thus constitutes an existing problematic. One way to explore the problematic of the attitude-behavior link is to define more clearly the connection between regional variations in attitudes and behavior. This regional linkage in attitudes and behavior has not been previously investigated largely because of the limitations of case study data, which have constituted the primary source of information about resident attitudes and behavior.

Hierarchies of acceptance, sociodemographic and spatial variations in attitudes, and regional variations in attitudes and behavior have all been used to develop typologies of accepting and rejecting neighborhood residents. In such studies, however, sociodemographic and spatial characteristics have been seen as primary determinants of acceptance and rejection (e.g., Dear and Taylor 1982). Thus, suburban homeowners tend to be seen as *essentially rejecting*, whereas renters in inner-city neighborhoods have been characterized as accepting. Such characterizations of residents based upon their sociodemographic and spatial characteristics, however, minimize the dynamic relationship inherent in the place-client dialectic. For example, suburban homeowners may be rejecting of specific client groups defined as being different, but such rejection may depend in large part on how difference is currently defined by those residents. Thus, although it may be true that suburban residents are highly rejecting of difference in general, it may also be true that the definition of difference is highly variable, leading to the notion that not all clients will be equally rejected by all suburban communities. These three methods can inform the place-client dialectic by rethinking how results from such methods should be interpreted. Hierarchies of acceptance, sociodemographic and spatial variations in attitudes, and regional variations in attitudes and behavior point to rejection among residents but, in addition, also indicate how residents define difference. Thus, these methods can be used to formulate current conceptualizations of difference among varying types of neighborhoods across the United States to understand better how place matters in community response to controversial human services.

Understanding Community Response: Results from a National Survey in the United States

To investigate the contemporary hierarchy of acceptance, the sociodemographic and spatial variations in attitudes, and the regional character of attitudes and behavior I analyze the first national survey of attitudes conducted in the United States. This survey was conducted by the Daniel Yankelovich Group (DYG) on behalf of the Robert Wood Johnson Foundation. These data were recently released for scholarly inquiry (Daniel Yankelovich Group 1990).

DYG used a random probability sampling technique to obtain a stratified sample of all adults more than twenty-one years of age in the continental United States (N = 1326). A sample of operating telephone exchanges in the United States was prestratified according to the following criteria (presented in the order of stratification): the nine divisions defined by the United States Bureau of the Census, states within these divisions, metropolitan statistical areas (MSAs) versus nonmetropolitan county areas, and the division of places into cities, towns, and rural areas. A random digit selection process was used to include both listed and unlisted telephone numbers. Approximately 3,016 persons were contacted to achieve the goal of 1,326 interviews (a 44 percent response rate) between 1 and 11 December 1989.

The population surveyed by DYG consisted of a relatively homogeneous cross-section of the nation. The surveyed population appeared in general to be less ethnically mixed, older, and having larger numbers of homeowners than the nation as a whole (table 8.3).

The *hierarchy of acceptance* for this national sample has been constructed using the median and mean acceptability scores of individual respondents. The acceptability scores are the responses given on the Likert scale to questions concerning the acceptability of fourteen human service facility types. Values on this scale range from one to six, with "one" meaning "absolutely would not welcome" a facility in the neighborhood, and "six" meaning "absolutely would welcome" a facility. Definitions of values between these two extremes were left to the respondent.

Median scores of acceptability are used to define large tiers in the hierarchy, whereas mean scores are used to rank facilities within these tiers (table 8.4). The most acceptable facilities in the national survey have the highest median and mean scores and consist of the following

Table 8.3

Demographic Characteristics of National Sample Comparison with U.S. Census

	Daniel Yankelovich Group (1990)	*United States (1990 Census of Population)*
Gender	50% male	49% male
Race/ethnicity	86% white	80% white
Median age	40 years	33 years
Income	58% at least $30,000	43% at least $35,000
Marital status	63% married	55% married
Education	20% bachelor's degree or higher	20% bachelor's degree or higher
Housing tenure	70% own homes	64% own homes

Source: U.S. Bureau of the Census. 1990. Statistical Abstract of the United States. Washington, D.C.

Table 8.4

National Hierarchy of Acceptance

Facility Type	*N*	*Median Score*	*Mean Score*
School	1,316	6	4.75
Day care center	1,319	5	4.69
Nursing home for elderly persons	1,318	5	4.65
Medical clinic (eyes/allergies)	1,319	5	4.40
Hospital	1,317	5	4.32
Group home/mentally retarded persons	1,315	4	3.98
Alcohol rehabilitation facility	1,318	4	3.80
Homeless shelter	1,316	4	3.73
Drug treatment center	1,320	4	3.61
Group home/mentally disabled persons	1,312	3	3.51
Group home/people with depression	1,315	3	3.47
Mental health outpatient facility	1,313	3	3.45
Independent apartment/people with mental disabilities	1,319	3	3.30
Group home/people with AIDS	1,317	3	3.20

facility types: schools, day-care centers, nursing homes for elderly persons, medical clinics treating eyes or allergies, and hospitals. Respondents are less accepting of facilities in the middle tier of the hierarchy, consisting of group homes for mentally retarded individuals, alcohol rehabilitation facilities, homeless shelters, and drug treatment centers. These middle-tier facilities represent either more-ambivalent or more-polarized attitudes toward human services than in the top tier of acceptance. The facilities in the bottom tier are least accepted by the national sample. These least acceptable facilities have the lowest median and mean acceptability scores and consist of group homes for mentally disabled persons, group homes for persons with depression, mental health outpatient facilities, independent apartments for mentally disabled persons, and group homes for persons with AIDS.

Homeless shelters and group homes for persons with AIDS provide clear examples of the volatility and synergistic characteristics of resident attitudes. For example, both facility types are new additions to the hierarchy when compared to the 1970 and 1980 hierarchies discussed earlier. The inclusion of these new facility types illustrates the volatility in attitudes toward difference that become important in any given place and time. At the time of the survey both homelessness and AIDS had reached crisis proportions in the public consciousness. The two facility types are perceived differently, however, in terms of acceptability. Homeless shelters are located in the middle tier of acceptance and are very similar in acceptance to drug treatment centers and alcohol rehabilitation facilities. This proximity in acceptance among homeless shelters, drug treatment centers, and alcohol rehabilitation facilities should not be surprising given the amount of publicity given in the popular media to the association between homelessness and substance abuse. This hierarchy of acceptance indicates that homeless shelters represent a middle ground in terms of acceptance and rejection of facilities; that is, respondents tend to accept homeless shelters less than facilities such as schools and day-care centers and tend to accept them more than mental health care facilities and group homes for persons with AIDS. Indeed, group homes for persons with AIDS are less accepted than are all other human service facilities, suggesting the threat and danger associated with this group of clients.

These two facility types also exhibit the synergy in attitudes that exists among various facility types in the hierarchy. This synergy is best illustrated using group homes for persons with AIDS. As a new facility that represents the least acceptance in comparison to all other facility types, this facility establishes a new benchmark by which the acceptance of all other facilities is evaluated. When compared to the 1970 and 1980 hierarchies, for example, other client groups tended to be perceived as being the least acceptable (mentally ill persons in 1970 and drug addicts in 1980). Thus, these least-acceptable groups defined difference in its extreme. The nature of difference, however, appears to have shifted in the 1990s with the introduction of persons with AIDS as a widely visible client group. This hierarchy of acceptability implies that, currently, facilities for persons with AIDS define difference in its extreme, leading perhaps to a more-accepting view of mentally disabled persons and substance abusers. Thus, substance abusers and mentally disabled persons have become less different to respondents in part because of the introduction of persons with AIDS.

The acceptabilities of homeless shelters and group homes for persons with AIDS are used to explore the contribution of *sociodemographic and spatial variation* to attitudes (table 8.5). There are

Table 8.5

Acceptance for Homeless Shelters
by Sociodemographic and Spatial Characteristics

Variable	*Coefficient Estimate*	*Standard Error*	*Standard Estimate*	*Probability* $>|z|$
Demographic				
Age[b]	0.0179	0.0060	–2.992	0.003
Education level	–0.0552	0.0402	–1.373	0.170
Gender[b]	0.3563	0.1181	3.016	0.003
Grandchildren	–0.3345	0.1736	–1.927	0.054
Race	0.1340	0.0845	1.586	0.113
Housing/household				
Household income	–0.2207	0.1466	–1.505	0.132
Household income comparison[a]	0.1646	0.0717	2.295	0.022
Own/rent residence[b]	0.3665	0.1412	2.596	0.009
Employment				
Employment status	–0.0792	0.0508	–1.559	0.119
Location				
City size[a]	0.2236	0.0898	2.490	0.013
Metropolitan or not	0.2193	0.1489	1.472	0.141
Suburban neighborhood or not	0.0015	0.1262	0.012	0.991
Measure of model quality				
Log likelihood = –1618.5	Chi-squared = 88.4 with 12 df (p = 0.0001)			

Notes: Dependent Variable: Acceptability for Homeless Shelters (6-point Likert scale).
[a]$p < 0.05$
[b]$p < 0.01$.

two reasons to focus on these two facility types. First, they represent relatively new additions to the hierarchy of acceptance when compared with prior studies. And second, homelessness and AIDS have become widely understood as social crises during the 1990s in the United States.

To analyze the contribution of various sociodemographic and spatial variables to attitudes toward homeless shelters and group homes for persons with AIDS the multivariate statistical method of ordered logit is used. This method is used to account for the ordinal nature of the dependent variable (the acceptability based on the six-point Likert scale for homeless shelters and group homes for persons with AIDS).[1] The independent variables (the sociodemographic and spatial characteristics) were checked for correlation, using Pearson correlation coefficients, to minimize the chance of multicollinearity; none of the variables was highly correlated.

Each of the statistically significant characteristics indicates a particular relationship with facility acceptance while controlling for the other variables. Several characteristics appear to be very important in explaining the variation in attitudes toward homeless shelters: age, gender, respondents' perceptions of their household incomes as compared to the incomes of the rest of the nation,[2] homeownership, and the size of the city where the respondent lives. Older respondents tend to be more rejecting of homeless shelters; men tend to be more rejecting than women; respondents who believe that their household incomes are higher than those of most other residents are more rejecting; homeowners tend to be more rejecting of homeless shelters than are renters; and respondents living in larger cities are more rejecting. Thus, for older respondents, men, respondents believing they have higher incomes, homeowners, and those living in larger cities, homeless shelters may represent difference to a significant degree. In other words, their degree of rejection indicates that homeless shelters appear to be more threatening to them than they are to other groups. This perception of threat might be traced to the vulnerability that such respondents might feel in terms of property (for homeowners and for respondents believing that they have higher incomes property issues may be very important) and personal safety (for older respon-

1. The ordered logit procedure estimates an underlying score as a linear function of the independent variables (the selected sociodemographic and spatial characteristics) and a set of cut points based on the categories of the dependent variable (the six-point Likert scale used to measure attitudes toward the facility types). This procedure is a generalized version of a more standard two-outcome logit model. The Log Likelihood statistic indicates whether the model is statistically sound or not.

2. Household income did not significantly explain the variation in attitudes toward homeless shelters, and there was no significant correlation between respondents' perception of household income and their actual household incomes. This result suggests that self-perception about socioeconomic status may be as, or even more, important than actual socioeconomic status.

dents and for those respondents living in larger cities greater concerns for personal safety might lead to fear concerning homeless shelters).

Fewer sociodemographic and spatial characteristics prove useful in explaining the variation in attitudes toward group homes for persons with AIDS. Only gender and homeownership are statistically significant in explaining acceptance toward these facilities with women and renters tending to be more accepting than men and homeowners. These results support other studies that suggest that women and more transient residents tend to be more accepting of human services such as mental health care facilities (Smith and Hanham 1981). The lack of explanatory power of the sociodemographic and spatial characteristics included in the survey could be the result of the widespread rejection shown toward this facility type. That is, because most people tend to reject group homes for persons with AIDS, there is little variation in attitudes to explain. Consequently, group homes for persons with AIDS appear to constitute a strong definition of difference for most respondents in the national sample. Such widespread rejection may be traced to the association of persons having AIDS with homosexuality, promiscuity, and substance abuse (Blendon and Donelan 1989; St. Lawrence et al. 1990). Contributing to the intense fear and stigma of persons who have AIDS have been the widespread belief that AIDS can be contracted through casual social contact and the rising incidence of AIDS in the United States, particularly among minorities, heterosexuals, and persons believing they are at low risk (Selik et al. 1989).

Regional variations in attitudes toward the fourteen human service facility types indicate how place contributes to perceptions of difference. The four United States census regions (Northeast, North Central, South, and West) are used to compare regional differences in attitudes across the nation. The aggregations are made so that small samples in several states will not bias the overall results.

Regional patterns of acceptance emerge when the mean acceptability scores are compared across the four census regions (table 8.6). On the one hand, region appears to have very little association with attitudes toward highly acceptable facilities (such as schools, day-care centers, nursing homes, medical clinics, and hospitals). These facilities appear to be accepted in similar ways across the United States. On the other hand, for facilities that are less acceptable by the national sample, there is much more differentiation among regions. The Northeast, for example, is much more accepting of group homes for

Table 8.6

Regional Ranking by Facility Type
(Rank and Mean Acceptability Score)

	Region			
Facility	*Northeast*	*North Central*	*South*	*West*
Alcohol rehabilitation facility1 (3.97)	4 (3.73)	3 (3.75)	2 (3.79)	
Day care center	1 (4.85)	4 (4.56)	3 (4.66)	2 (4.71)
Drug treatment facility	1 (3.75)	4 (3.53)	2 (3.61)	3 (3.56)
Homeless shelter	1 (3.90)	2 (3.79)	3 (3.64)	4 (3.61)
Group home/mentally disabled	1 (3.75)	4 (3.36)	3 (3.44)	2 (3.53)
Group home/mentally retarded	1 (4.25)	4 (3.84)	3 (3.91)	2 (3.98)
Group home/people with AIDS	1 (3.79)	4 (3.72)	3 (3.75)	2 (3.79)
Group home/people with depression	1 (3.58)	2 (3.48)	4 (3.39)	3 (3.48)
Hospital	1 (4.48)	3 (4.27)	2 (4.31)	4 (4.23)
Independent apartment/ people with mental disabilities	1 (3.46)	2 (3.28)	4 (3.22)	3 (3.26)
Medical clinic/eyes or allergies	1 (4.58)	3 (4.31)	2 (4.43)	4 (4.29)
Mental health out-patient facility	1 (3.70)	2 (3.43)	3 (3.39)	4 (3.29)
Nursing home for elderly persons	1 (4.76)	4 (4.54)	3 (4.63)	2 (4.67)
School	2 (4.81)	4 (4.62)	3 (4.73)	1 (4.85)

Note: Statistically significant differences among regions at $p < 0.05$.

mentally disabled persons, group homes for mentally retarded individuals, and group homes for persons with AIDS than are the North Central and the South. This result suggests that difference, as defined by mental disability, mental retardation, and AIDS, may be perceived as being less threatening and dangerous by respondents in the Northeast region than by those in other regions across the country.

This national survey suggests that few respondents have actually been involved in local action surrounding a facility siting controversy (table 8.7). Only 6 percent of the surveyed population report that they were involved in opposition against a facility in the neighborhood. The absence of individual involvement is also reflected in the small proportion of respondents (about 8 percent) supporting a facility. The proportion of respondents directly acting to support a facility is about the same as the proportion acting to oppose one, indicating that supportive actions may be as widespread as the more highly publicized not in my back yard (NIMBY) activities.

An analysis of the ***regional variations in behavior*** indicates that both oppositional and supportive behavior are rare across all regions in the nation (table 8.7). Those respondents living in the West and Northeast regions have been slightly more supportive in their activities than have respondents living in the North Central and Southern regions; however, these variations are not statistically significant. There is less variation among regions in individual opposition toward facilities. When comparing supportive to oppositional behavior within

Table 8.7

National Dimensions of Behavior Toward Facilities

Survey Question	*N*	*Percentage "Yes"*
Have you, yourself, ever taken any action to support the placing of a facility in your neighborhood?	1,315	8
Have you, yourself, ever taken any action to oppose the placing of a facility in your neighborhood?	1,320	6

	Supporting the Placing of a Facility in the Neighborhood		*Opposing the Placing of a Facility in the Neighborhood*	
Region	*(%)*	*(N)*	*(%)*	*(N)*
Northeast	9.0	(290)	6.9	(292)
North Central	8.1	(335)	5.9	(337)
South	7.2	(431)	7.2	(432)
West	10.0	(259)	5.4	(259)

regions, the results indicate that respondents in the South and North Central regions appear to be less supportive than in other regions and, in the South, appear to be more oppositional. Respondents in the Northeast, however, appear to be involved in both supportive and oppositional activities with 9.0 percent supporting a facility in the neighborhood and 6.9 percent opposing a facility. The Northeast, therefore, suggests a relatively active group, both supportive and oppositional, when compared to other regions.

Health Care and the Place-Client Dialectic: The Changing Institutional and Structural Context

These analytical results suggest that the place-client dialectic is strongly related to location and to facility type. Representation, for example, appears to vary for homeless shelters and for group homes for persons with AIDS. The hierarchy of acceptance implies that homeless shelters are much more acceptable than are group homes for persons with AIDS, indicating that facilities associated with AIDS and persons having AIDS are seen as being more threatening than are facilities for homeless individuals. The degree of acceptance is not monolithic across residents, however. Older respondents, males, people believing that they have more income than most Americans, homeowners, and respondents living in larger cities tend to be more rejecting of homeless shelters than are younger respondents, females, people believing that they have less income, renters, and respondents living in smaller cities and towns. Location also appears to play an important role in the marginalization of difference. The national data indicate, for example, that the northeastern region of the United States appears to be the most active in terms of individual respondents both supporting and opposing facilities in their neighborhoods.

Such variations in the perception of difference cannot, however, be divorced from the wider context of institutional and structural change, which has, since the 1960s, framed society's views concerning difference, acceptance, and health care delivery. Two aspects of institutional and structural change have particularly impacted resident attitudes and responses toward human service facilities in particular places. The first concerns the dramatic increase, over the 1990s in particular, in the numbers of people needing health care and other human services. This growing population has begun to encroach upon communities that have never before encountered them. The second aspect of change affecting community response has been the increase in local activism across the country. This development has meant that neighborhoods and local jurisdictions are taking a more active role in health care delivery, particularly in preventing new facilities from being sited and in closing facilities that exist.

The *rapidly increasing numbers of persons needing health care* and other human services stem from multiple sources. Five developments have, since the 1960s, significantly increased the vulnerability of individuals and families to health crises, thus adding to the growing numbers needing health care services: deinstitutionalization of the mental health care system, welfare state restructuring, economic restructuring, homelessness, and AIDS.

Deinstitutionalization, the movement initiated during the 1950s and 1960s to move mentally disabled individuals out of large-scale institutionalized care to community-based care, has long been criticized as not fulfilling its mission (Bassuk and Gerson 1978). Problems in implementing deinstitutionalization policies, such as the lack of funding for community-based facilities and the absence of coordination between services, have meant that an organized, long-term community-based health care system never fully materialized. The lack of services has, in turn, been implicated in the significant growth in the number of mentally disabled persons who have become homeless.[3] Reinstitutionalization of mentally disabled persons through an expansion of state hospitals has increasingly been touted as a viable solution to this issue (Plotnick 1986). In practice, however, reinstitutionalization has more often resulted in placing homeless mentally disabled persons in already overcrowded prison systems than in providing appropriate and adequate care (Abrahamson 1991).

The lack of preventative and other human services can also be traced in part to the ongoing restructuring of the nation's welfare state. Restructuring of the welfare state has been realized through national strategies of privatization, cutbacks in programs and funding, and changes in eligibility requirements for receiving benefits. The overall result of these various strategies has been a transfer of program and funding responsibilities to the state and local levels. Such transfers of responsibility to lower tiers of government and efforts at privatization have meant that, increasingly, local health care is being provided through an often chaotic system of private, nonprofit, and

3. This argument, however, has been disputed by Blau (1992).

informal sector sources. The state of California, for example, by the early 1980s reorganized its Medi-Cal benefits system, resulting in a privatized system of hospital contracts for services and a shift in responsibility to the county level for medical care for indigent clients (Wolch and Dear 1993).

Cutbacks in funding and programming for health care by various levels of government have made the outcomes of economic restructuring critical for many client groups. Economic restructuring, in general, is reflected in the growing dependence of private firms on "flexible" work organizations. Such built-in flexibility and adaptability has resulted in increasing part-time and contractual employment at the expense of full-time permanent positions, a lessening of the influence by labor unions, diminishing real wages, and the shrinking or eliminating of benefits such as health insurance (Harrison and Bluestone 1988). In addition, corporate strategies to boost profitability, made more difficult by globalized competition, have resulted in a massive growth in the number of service sector jobs, many at low wages. Service sector employment along with strategies for improving corporate flexibility have contributed to an increasingly bimodal distribution of income, instability in employment opportunities, and fewer resources emanating from the private sector.

One result of economic and welfare state restructuring and the deinstitutionalization movement has been a visible and drastic increase in the incidence of homelessness. The failures of deinstitutionalization have led to a rising number of mentally disabled persons who have become homeless. In addition, economic restructuring has created a growing population at risk of becoming homeless through illness, eviction, job loss, divorce, or other personal crises (Wolch and Dear 1993). Growing numbers of individuals and families have already become homeless, drastically increasing the need for affordable housing and social services.

During the 1990s, AIDS has also reached crisis proportions in the minds of the public. Emphasis on AIDS education and awareness strategies by the public sector, disclosure of HIV infection by athletes and other highly visible individuals, continuing media coverage of the HIV-positive status of persons other than homosexuals and intravenous drug users, and ongoing controversy concerning the distributions of condoms in public schools have kept the issue of AIDS in the forefront of public consciousness. At the federal level the devastation of the condition has elicited strong policy responses in prevention and treatment. At the local level, however, although communities have often responded with sympathy, they have also often rejected persons who have AIDS and opposed the potential siting of facilities associated with AIDS.

The second aspect of change that has significantly influenced community response to health care facilities has been the overall *rise in local activism* over the 1990s both by neighborhoods and by municipalities. Increasing local activism can be traced in part to the disillusionment that residents and localities have felt concerning the bureaucracies of the state and federal political systems. Disillusionment has been spurred by recurring scandals concerning politicians, the inability of legislatures to balance budgets and to pay their bills, and, most recently, the lack of fiscal responsibility associated with municipal bankruptcy. Politicians and political institutions are often regarded as corrupt, ineffective, or irrelevant. One consequence of such disillusionment has been the circumventing of formal political apparatuses. In California, for example, ballot initiatives are being increasingly used as a means to bypass the legislative process. More generally, at all levels of government, term limits have become a popular means of reestablishing citizen control over a seemingly huge and unresponsive state.

Growing neighborhood activism has also resulted in a concomitant growth in locational conflict. Such locational conflict has occurred along horizontal and vertical dimensions. Along the horizontal dimension, adjacent jurisdictions, municipalities, and communities have increasingly competed over the siting and distribution of health care and other facilities. Debates concerning the "fair-share" allocation of facilities across municipalities have resulted in conflict among local municipalities and regional political institutions, often around the issue of facility saturation. Residents in many communities believe that their vicinities are already saturated with health care and other human service facilities, especially in relation to other neighborhoods. These neighborhoods have often been targeted for multiple facilities because of their greater acceptance or because the community was unable or unwilling to protest the siting. Saturated areas have typically been composed of racial/ethnic minorities or populations having low incomes. Neighborhoods hosting multiple facilities become, at worst, service "ghettos," concentrating facilities and clients in transient and dilapidated areas such as skid rows (Dear and Wolch 1987).

To prevent facility siting and to garner greater control over other land-use issues some communities have physically and legislatively delineated themselves from larger political jurisdictions. For example, many local governments have enacted protectionist legislation such as growth control initiatives and incorporation measures. These strategies have allowed local municipalities to disengage themselves from the issues and problems of larger jurisdictions by defining themselves as separate political and economic entities. Other communities have resorted to "gateing" (erecting iron fences and gates around their neighborhoods) in an effort to keep outsiders from entering their neighborhoods and to define and control the behavior of insiders.

Vertical conflict has occurred among the various tiers of the government hierarchy. Intergovernmental conflict has increased as the responsibility for programs and funding has shifted from the federal level to the state and local levels. Welfare state restructuring is one example of a more general trend to shift responsibility to state and local tiers of government through "new federalism" policies enacted during the 1980s. These policies were often accompanied by a reduction in programs, cutbacks in funding, and tightened eligibility requirements for federally funded welfare programs. The developing fiscal crises at various tiers of government have further fueled intergovernmental conflict. While federal and state governments have shifted their emphases toward policies of privatization and local response, local governments have been reluctant or fiscally unable to provide full funding to implement programs.

The Future of Health Care Planning

In this chapter I have explored the dialectic between place and client well-being to explain the current hostile environment for siting health care facilities. The institutional and structural shifts discussed in the previous section imply that health care planning in the United States will continue to be difficult. In addition, other changes in the institutional and structural context suggest that the upsurge in the numbers of persons needing health care and human services will not diminish, especially given current state and federal initiatives that would deny health care and other services to specific groups, such as undocumented immigrants and families currently receiving welfare benefits. Given this hostile climate, health care planning will continue to be a difficult task in terms of available program funds and political will. This analysis, however, has illustrated the important role that place can play in health care planning. In particular, a varied landscape of acceptance and rejection currently surrounds health care facilities and clients. This variation in response to difference implies that there are opportunities for gaining acceptance that need to be brought more sharply into focus.

Two concepts would contribute to improved understanding of the place-client dialectic building on the analysis presented here. The first seeks an expansion of the place-client dialectic to include "race" and culture, and the second involves an incorporation of client self-characterization and definition of health promotion. First, there is a great need to investigate residents' definition of difference further, especially given the growing diversity in "race" and ethnicity currently being experienced in the United States. For example, homelessness and AIDS and other issues critical to contemporary population health must be viewed in a context of changing cultural norms. Cultural understanding is vital, especially given the rate at which minority racialized and ethnic groups are growing across the nation, particularly in states such as Florida, New York, and along the Pacific Rim (Bureau of the Census 1990). Beyond the moral imperatives brought forward by an increasingly diverse society, such rapid growth in minority populations across the United States dictates that health care planners incorporate the needs and attitudes of minority populations in order to produce effective programs.

Further exploration of difference may help health care planners to design and implement health care services for a changing population. This examination is becoming ever more important in a context where many different groups are becoming clients of health care and human services. HIV infection, for example, has become the leading cause of death for young adults (between the ages of twenty-five and forty-four years) in many cities across the United States (Selik, Chu, and Buehler 1993), indicating the importance of providing appropriate preventative and other health care services. Services that incorporate specific ethnic and cultural norms may be increasingly necessary, especially given the trend that minority populations, African-American and Hispanic in particular, have disproportionately high rates of contracting HIV and AIDS (Selik, Castro, and Pappaioanou 1988).

These trends suggest important issues for health care planning specifically around the issues of HIV and AIDS. For instance, the disproportionate numbers of minorities acquiring HIV may imply minority residents may be unaware or unsure of the characteristics associated with HIV and AIDS. Thus, there may be a need to develop many different types of programs to address the varied needs of these groups. In addition, the disproportionate number of minorities having HIV and AIDS indicates that minority residents have a greater exposure to persons having AIDS than do other groups. Often, however, exposure and knowledge may not translate into greater acceptance. Because of prevailing social norms concerning homosexuality, and the strong association that many communities still hold between homosexuality and AIDS, a family member having HIV/AIDS and even dying of AIDS may not influence household attitudes toward AIDS. Anecdotal evidence suggests, for example, that family members may attribute the death of a family member from AIDS to a more "acceptable" source, such as pneumonia or cancer, primarily because of the deeply embedded cultural stigma against homosexuality (Takahashi 1994).

A second concept which would help elaborate the place-client dialectic concerns the emphasis on clients' views of their self-characterization, overall health promotion, and their definition of difference. Although in an increasing number of studies the needs of various client groups have been outlined, many from the clients' point of view (e.g., Dyck 1992), a more comprehensive conceptualization of the place-client dialectic needs to focus more on the facets of health and health promotion expressed by the clients themselves. Health care plans will not match client need without such an emphasis on client perceptions. Such mismatches between policies and client need often occur. For example, homeless individuals placed in permanent housing may often give up this resource because such housing tends to separate them from their familiar and supportive social networks. Although the shelter component of homelessness has been addressed by the solution of providing permanent housing, the social support needed by many homeless people to cope with everyday life often becomes dislocated. Thus, the homeless person must choose between a permanent housing option and social support from a peer group (Rowe and Wolch 1990). An understanding of homeless persons' definitions of the constitution of health promotion might help to resolve these mismatches between service provision and visible need.

The development of effective and appropriate health care services is especially important given the current hostile political climate concerning health care services, particularly for those having few economic resources. Mismatches such as the one just described could be used as evidence to support stereotypical images of client groups and, consequently, be used to argue that housing and health care services for homeless individuals or persons having AIDS are unnecessary or unwanted by the clients themselves. One pessimistic scenario might be that such representations of client groups might be used to relegate individuals permanently to an underclass of outsiders. A better understanding of the place-client dialectic might help realign such views of difference.

9

The Relevance of Place in HIV Transmission and Prevention

The Commercial Sex Industry in Madras

SHEENA ASTHANA

Despite recent interest in the role of social theory in medical geography (Gesler 1992; Kearns and Joseph 1993; Jones and Moon 1993), the field continues to be strongly influenced by a positivist philosophy (Litva and Eyles 1995). Nowhere is the spatial tradition more in evidence than in geographical studies of HIV and AIDS. Since 1988, when one of the first geographical works on the AIDS epidemic was published (Wood 1988), medical geographers have focused almost exclusively on the spatial distribution and diffusion of HIV and AIDS (Kearns 1996). By contrast, relatively little attention has been paid to sociocultural, economic, and political dimensions of the disease nor to the ways in which individual risk behaviors are related to nonspatial processes in particular geographical settings (for a notable exception see Brown 1995). As health policymakers are increasingly recognizing the need for locally specific HIV interventions, geographers could more usefully contribute to HIV/AIDS research by adopting a place-sensitive perspective. In this chapter I do just this. After a theoretical critique of spatial approaches to HIV and AIDS, I use the example of the commercial sex industry in Madras to illustrate how factors operating at the national scale work together with local conditions to make HIV transmission a very local and place-specific phenomenon.

The Place of Geography in HIV/AIDS Research

Since the first clinical descriptions of acquired immune deficiency syndrome (AIDS) in 1981, there has been an explosion of scientific and popular literature on its origins, spread, disease process, control measures, and future impact. By 1991 nearly forty thousand papers on HIV and AIDS had been indexed by Medline and an estimated $5.4 billion had been allocated by governments of the ten major industrialized countries for HIV/AIDS research (Mann, Tarantola, and Netter 1992). A vast proportion of this investment has funded biomedical and clinical research into the virology, immunology, pathology, and pharmacology of the disease. Although considerable advances have been made in identifying the HIV virus, analyzing its genetic structure and variability, devising diagnostic tests, and developing drugs to prevent and treat certain opportunistic infections, the search for a vaccine or cure for AIDS has been unsuccessful.

In the absence of vaccines and treatments the only way to combat AIDS is to prevent exposure to and transmission of HIV infection. Methods of prevention have been identified, including the screening of blood products, the control of sexually transmitted diseases, the use of sterile equipment by health workers and injecting drug users, and the use of condoms during penetrative sex. In spite of the availability of effective prevention technologies, however, rates of HIV infection are continuing to rise rapidly, particularly in parts of the developing world. Thus, in contrast to industrialized countries such as Australia and the United Kingdom, where cases of HIV infection and AIDS have not reached the high levels predicted in the mid-1980s, earlier projections of HIV infection in Asia have proved highly conservative.

The fact that AIDS researchers and policymakers have been limited in their ability to predict accurately the course of the HIV epidemic and to mount effective strategies to prevent the spread of the virus has fueled criticism of the medically sophisticated but behaviorally naïve paradigm that has shaped the AIDS agenda (Ankrah 1989; Packard and Epstein 1991; Seidel 1993). Sexuality and sexual behavior, for example, are extremely complex and must be placed in their social, historical, economic, and cultural context (Standing 1992). In practice, however, little attention has been paid to the ways in which sexual behavior varies across space and time. Focusing predominantly on HIV transmission at the individual level, epidemiological research has reduced sexuality to a question of coital frequency and positions (Schoef 1991). Questions are not asked about the situations that lead to multiple partners or unsafe sex nor about whether individuals have the power to resist unwanted sexual activity or to modify their sexual practices. Drug injectors are similarly treated in a social vacuum. As a result, very little is known about the social construction of injecting drug use.

The failure to identify the wider determinants of risk behaviors has had a number of unfortunate consequences. First, it reinforces the impression that HIV spreads simply as a result of individual behavior. This places responsibility for the disease on its victims and results in the further marginalization and stigmatization of vulnerable individuals. Second, it impedes the design and implementation of effective HIV interventions (Zwi 1993). Prevention efforts have focused primarily on changing individual behavior through information campaigns. The dissemination of information about risk practices, however, is not in itself sufficient to change risk behavior, especially when targeted groups feel that they have little control over their lives. Information needs to be transmitted in a way that is culturally sensitive and appropriate to the target audience and efforts made to ensure that individuals have not only the knowledge and means but also the motivation and power to implement and sustain behavioral change. Research and intervention strategies should, therefore, focus upon the social, cultural, and economic factors that give rise to risk behaviors and that constrain less-risky activity.

To this end Zwi and Cabral (1991) propose replacing the current emphasis on high-risk behaviors with a concern with *high-risk situations.* Because this change involves an appreciation of the ways in which structural determinants of risk interact with local conditions in specific geographical settings, geographers are well placed to embark upon such research. With notable exceptions (e.g., Ford and Koetsawang 1991; Wallace 1990), however, medical geographers have been less interested in the connections between HIV and specific places than in spatial aspects of the disease, most particularly diffusion. Proposing that levels of social interaction (including contact leading to HIV transmission) conform to gravity model and friction of distance principles, several studies have applied diffusion theory to describe and analyze the origins and spread of HIV and to predict its future distribution (Wood 1988; Gardner et al. 1989; Shannon and Pyle 1989; Loytonen 1991, 1994; Smallman-Raynor, Cliff, and Haggett 1992; Gould 1993).

There are theoretical, practical, and ethical drawbacks to this perspective. With insufficient information about the rates and distribution of specific risk factors HIV transmission is depicted as a function of population distribution, occurring where population clusters in large cities and spreading through population movement between places in the urban hierarchy and between centers and their surrounding hinterlands. Empiricist observations of hierarchical and expansion diffusion have fueled suggestions that there is a "spatial logic" to HIV and AIDS (Gould 1993, 70). Few would dispute that, once the HIV virus has been introduced to a population, spatial interaction has a bearing on the pattern and pace of its spread. The primacy accorded to geometric space is very problematic, however. First, it suggests that the spatial distribution of risk factors is a function of the spatial distribution of the general population. Second, it obscures the role of nonspatial processes and locality effects that, given the social construction of sexual and drug-injecting behaviors, are more relevant to risk than mere proximity.

At a practical level, spatial approaches to HIV/AIDS suffer from problems of data scale and reliability. Spatial representations of disease distribution are only as good as the data sets on which they are based. Yet seroprevalence data are usually aggregated to such a crude geographical scale that maps of HIV distribution cannot portray geographical variations at anything but the most generalized level. Data on HIV cases are also known to be both incomplete and unrepresentative. In many developing countries, for example, surveillance systems have been characterized by the lack of a systematic sampling strategy, wide regional variations in numbers and proportions of different categories screened, and inconsistencies in the reporting and processing of information. Subject to biases in both sample selection and sample size, such data cannot be used to make precise estimates about seroprevalence levels in specific groups or regions.

If many maps of the HIV epidemic tell more about surveillance than the true distribution of the disease, questions must be raised about the value of this approach. This is important because of the ethical implications of AIDS-related research. Surveillance data may be useful for epidemiological and spatial studies. However, their production is highly controversial. In many countries so-called high-risk groups continue to be singled out for testing, a process that contributes to their stigmatization. It is doubtful whether the consent of screened individuals is always obtained and whether they have the knowledge and freedom to refuse testing. Pre- and post-test counseling is often inadequate and, because of insufficient resources, little is available in the way of social, psychological, and medical support. Finally, the collection of seroprevalence data raises problems of confidentiality. In India, for example, information about people's HIV status is frequently leaked to the press, which has not only named HIV-positive individuals but printed their photographs.

Spatial analyses also lead no further in understanding the underlying social causes of HIV transmission. Like epidemiology, this approach decontextualizes individual behavior. It, therefore, fails to challenge the dominant behavioral model that has shaped the research and policy agenda. As outlined above, the tendency to view AIDS as a behavioral problem and the subsequent neglect of the sociocultural and economic context of HIV transmission has left planners poorly equipped to design and to implement HIV prevention strategies. Geographers can and should contribute to HIV/AIDS research to further the identification of more appropriate forms of health promotion. There is a strong case for arguing that this would be better achieved by drawing upon particular geographical understanding of *place*.

In this chapter I adopt such an approach in assessing the potential of HIV-prevention strategies among commercial sex workers in Madras. In view of the need for HIV interventions that are place-specific the local circuits of commercial sex in the city are examined in some detail. The situation in Madras, however, cannot be divorced from its broader context and, thus, the national pattern of HIV in India and the cultural, economic, and political factors underlying the epidemic are first explored. This case study, I argue, does not merely illustrate how Madras constitutes a particular locale within which these broader factors are played out but demonstrates how the place itself must be seen as a "process" (Thrift 1983; Pred 1984) in which individual practices together with institutional and structural forces actively shape the nature of the local commercial sex industry and patterns of HIV transmission in the city.

HIV Transmission in India: National and Regional Trends

Although the numbers of recorded cases of HIV and AIDS in India are still relatively low, the rapid increase in seropositivity rates among low-risk populations suggests that the scale and pace of HIV transmission in the country is already significant. By June 1994, 2,096,053 people in India had been screened for HIV infection, and 15,399 were found to be seropositive using the Western Blot method (NACO 1994). Twenty-four of the states or union territories in the country, however, have already reported HIV infection, and, extrapolating data on HIV prevalence rates in pregnant women and blood donors, the government of India and WHO suggest that by the end of 1992 more than one million people in the country were infected with the virus. This figure was expected to double or even triple by 1996 (NACO 1993).

Analysis of the spatial distribution of HIV in India is subject to problems of data reliability. A national program of serological surveillance was established in 1986. Sentinel studies were not attempted until 1990, however, and these were biased toward urban areas and toward people seeking health care. The vast proportion of surveillance data has, thus, been collected unsystematically from "captive" populations (e.g., sexually transmitted disease [STD] patients, prisoners, and women detained under the prostitution laws, blood donors, and hospital patients). Because access to the latter depends upon the extent to which individual surveillance centers can liaise with hospitals and social welfare or police departments in their states, screening efficiency and intensity vary widely. In Delhi, for example, the percentage of positive samples collected by eight centers that had screened more than 10,000 individuals by June 1994 ranged from 0.0003 to 0.05. The pattern of surveillance is also highly uneven at the regional level, rates of screening ranging from 5,157 per 100,000 population in Pondicherry to 10 per 100,000 in Bihar.

Bearing these reservations in mind, clear regional trends in HIV infection can be discerned (fig. 9.1). The highest rates of HIV have been recorded in the northeastern state of Manipur where cheap, good quality, and easily available heroin is fueling an HIV epidemic among injecting drug users (Naik et al. 1991). By June 1994, 120 per 1,000 people screened in the state were found to be HIV positive, yielding a rate of 1,160 positive tests per million population (NACO 1994). The neighboring states of Mizoram and Nagaland are also recording steady increases in HIV. High rates of injecting drug use in this region have been associated with its proximity to the "Golden Triangle" of Burma, Laos, and Thailand where 20 percent of the world's heroin is estimated to be grown and processed.

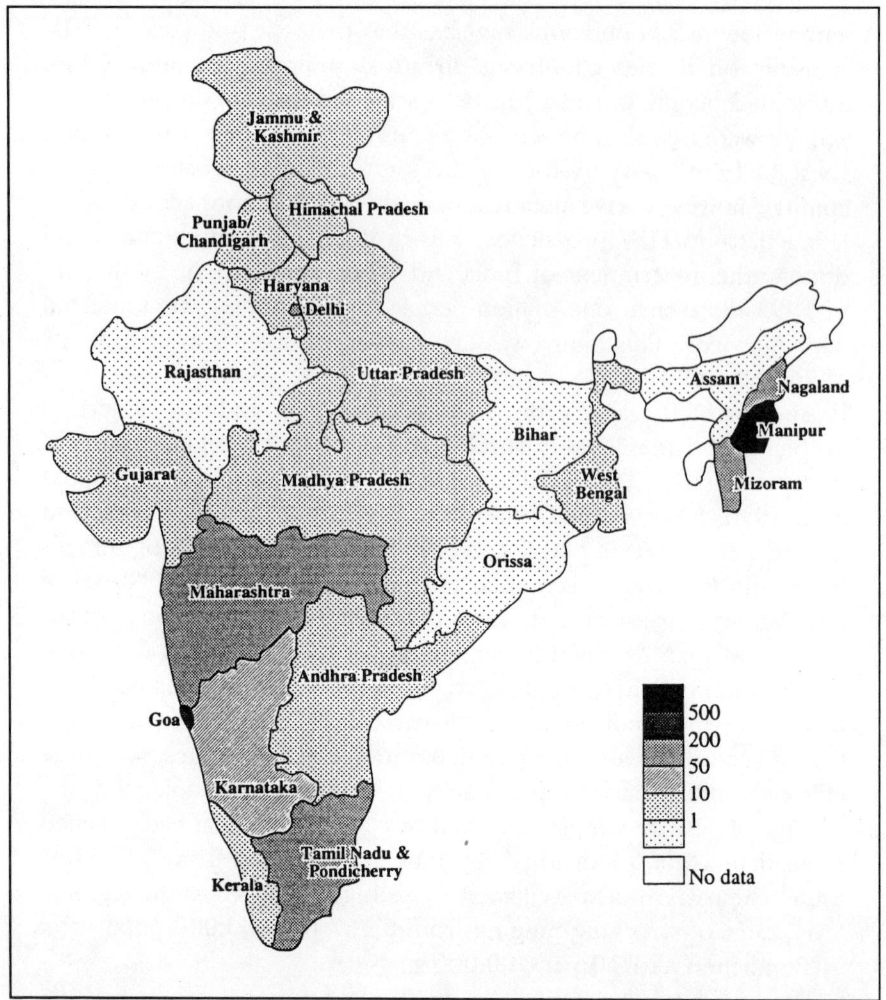

Figure 9.1. Recorded HIV positive cases per million population, India, June 1994.

Intravenous drug use is not confined to the northeast, however. Of the estimated 2 million drug users in India, 50,000 are believed to inject drugs (Jayaraman 1992), and in Delhi the recorded seropositivity rate among injectors rose from 43.5 per 1,000 in 1993 to 333.3 in the first six months of 1994 (Pioneer 1994).

The northeastern states of India (which comprise 0.44 percent of the total population) account for 15 percent of recorded cases of HIV. A further 65 percent are located in the southern and central states of Tamil Nadu (including Pondicherry), Karnataka, and Maharasthra, which comprise 21 percent of the population. This pattern confirms earlier reports about the key role played in the Indian HIV epidemic by the commercial sex industries of Madras and Bombay. Nevertheless, care must be taken in interpreting the figures. The three states also account for 49 percent of people screened under the surveillance program. Thus, if the data are adjusted to take account of numbers screened, high prevalence rates are also found in the neighboring states and territories of Goa, Kerala, and Andhra Pradesh together with Uttar Pradesh, Punjab/Chandigarh, and Delhi in the north (fig. 9.2).

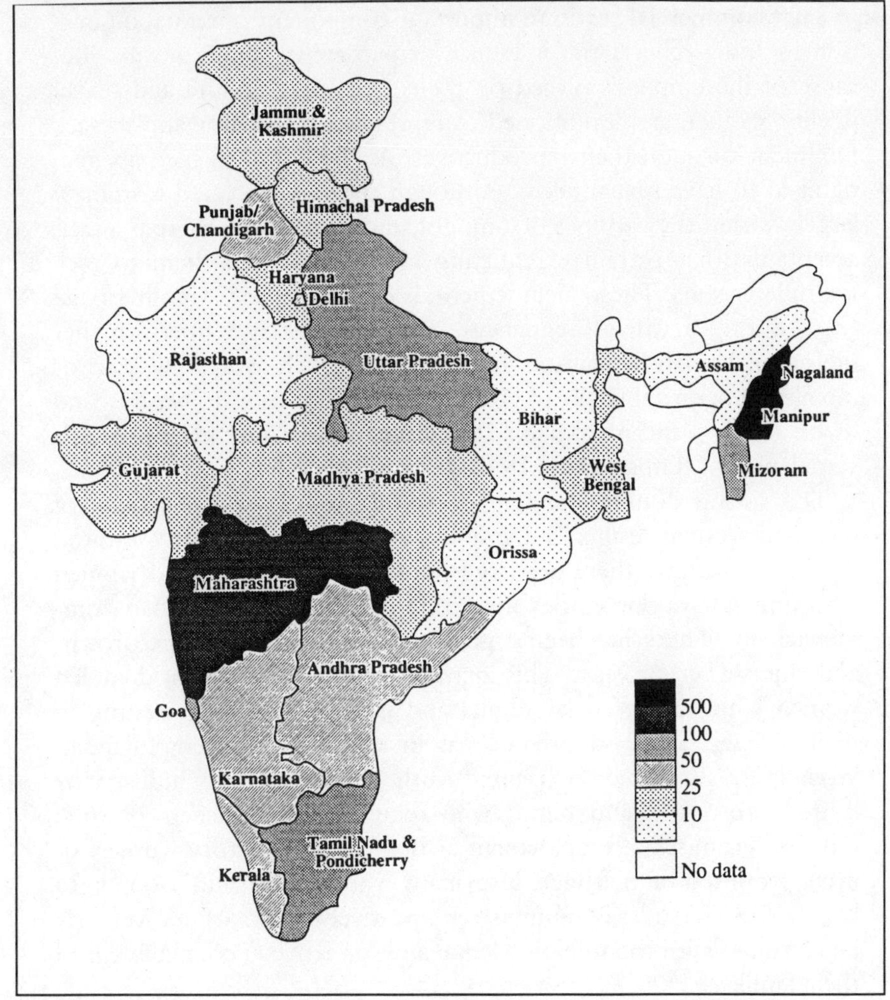

Figure 9.2. HIV positive cases per 10,000 cases screened for HIV infection, India, June 1994.

Although trends in HIV prevalence among injecting drug users (IDUs) and commercial sex workers (CSWs) have commanded the most attention from both the Indian media and government officials, evidence suggests that HIV is firmly entrenched in the general population. The number of people infected by blood and blood products is unknown although this factor probably accounts for more HIV infection than intravenous drug use. The dominant mode of HIV transmission, however, is heterosexual intercourse, CSWs and their clients providing points of contact between large numbers of otherwise disconnected people.

That commercial sex is an important component of sexual interaction in India reflects the influence of patriarchal family norms. Because of the emphasis placed on their premarital chastity and sexual fidelity, women are conditioned to repress their sexuality and to seek fulfilment through their reproductive role. By contrast, men are recognized to have sexual needs. Although they are expected to remain largely within the confines of a monogamous marriage, there is a tacit acceptance that certain extenuating factors may lead them to seek multiple liaisons. These include periods of abstinence within marriage (e.g., during a wife's pregnancy), a wife's inability to perform her biological, social, or status-enhancing roles (such as bearing sons or mobilizing her natal family to give high value "presents" to her husband or his family), and a woman's inability to satisfy fully her husband's sexual needs (Ramasubban 1990).

The strong double standard pertaining to the sexual activity of men and women results in a sizable demand for female prostitution. At the same time, there are large numbers of impoverished women who find few opportunities for economic survival other than commercial sex. There has been a growth in female migration to towns and cities in recent years. This increase includes deserted or divorced women who, facing social stigma and lacking economic security in their villages, arrive in urban areas in search of new employment. Women are also directly recruited to the commercial sex industry by retired prostitutes and pimps who regularly tour pockets of rural poverty. Promises of employment as domestics or factory workers or even promises of marriage lure many young girls and women to brothels. Some are as young as ten and twelve years of age yet may be recruited with the full knowledge and/or active encouragement of their families.

The Indian Council of Medical Research (ICMR) estimates that up to one million women are working in the commercial sex industry throughout the country (ICMR 1992). Approximately one hundred thousand female prostitutes work in Bombay alone. Trafficking in women and children takes place over very long distances (Rozario 1988). In Bombay, for example, a substantial proportion of CSWs hail from Nepal. Patterns of migration, however, are highly complex. Brothel-based women are moved not only between individual establishments but between cities and states. Male migration is also an important component of the complex flow of commercial sex. From college students seeking premarital sexual experience to businessmen on short city trips, truck drivers on interstate highways, and migrant laborers from poor rural areas, the client population is large, diverse, and very dispersed.

Low levels of condom use have facilitated the rapid transmission of HIV among CSWs and their clients. By 1991 approximately 30 percent of prostitutes in Bombay were believed to be HIV positive (ICMR 1991) and in Madras, where the first case of HIV infection in the country was detected, seroprevalence levels among CSWs had reached 10 percent by August 1992 (Pers. comm. Dr. S. Solomon). Because condoms are associated with contraception rather than with disease prevention and are presumed to affect sexual pleasure negatively, they are rarely used in encounters between CSWs and their clients. Indeed, sex workers may be abused for insisting upon their use. The negative image that clients hold about condoms partly reflects the poor quality of condoms that have dominated the Indian market. Medical attitudes and practices regarding family planning, however, have also played a role. Sterilization and intrauterine devices (IUDS) are the most popular forms of contraception advocated by family-planning agencies, who assume that barrier methods are too unreliable to be widely promoted among low-income and illiterate groups. Given that IUDs are contraindicated for women who are at risk of contracting HIV, the active promotion of this form of contraception is unfortunate.

Several other factors relating to the health system in India have also been implicated in the HIV epidemic. These factors include the inadequate provision of STD services and the poor regulation of blood and blood products. Because genital ulcer diseases such as chancroid, genital herpes, and syphilis facilitate both the acquisition and transmission of the HIV virus, the prevention and control of sexually transmitted diseases (STDs) is essential for HIV prevention. Available surveys indicate, however, that STDs are a major health problem in India. A study commissioned by the National AIDS Control Organization found 10 percent of antenatal clinic attenders in Madras were suffering from a sexually transmitted disease and 2 percent from syphilis. Six percent and 4 percent of rural men and women tested in Tamil Nadu state were also affected (NACO 1993). At present, clinical services for the diagnosis and treatment of STDs are provided in specialist urban- and district-level clinics. Only a very small percentage of patients attend these public facilities, the majority seeking clinical care from private doctors, going directly to drug sellers (where both diagnosis and case management tend to be inadequate), or resorting to self-medication. Women are particularly likely to go without treatment, first because they are more likely to overlook symptoms and second because of the fear and stigma attached to seeking care for an STD. Those in rural areas are further disadvantaged as a result of the lack of female doctors and problems of physical access to health facilities.

Infected blood and blood products probably constitute the second largest risk factor in India, preceded only by multiple-partner sex. HIV was first detected in a professional blood donor in 1987, and in 1989 the screening of all donated blood and blood products became mandatory. Three years later, however, an estimated 85 percent of the nation's blood supply was not being screened for HIV (Baweja and Katijar 1992). Blood banks in smaller towns and cities lacked access to screening centers, and few had the skills or equipment to undertake testing themselves. Although linkages had been established between blood testing centers and government blood banks in metropolitan cities and large urban centers, many private blood banks were not sending their samples to be screened. The private sector includes commercial blood banks, which in 1989 supplied 24 percent of the nation's blood supply and which are estimated to rely on professional blood donors for 94 percent of blood collected (NACO 1993). Seropositivity rates among this sector have risen very steeply, perhaps because professional donors have been exposed to the HIV virus during the process of plasmaphersis (Girimaji 1992). It is, therefore, likely that a significant proportion of infected blood has been missed by the screening program. There is also evidence to suggest that professional blood donors responded to the tightening up of screening procedures in metropolitan areas by migrating to smaller towns and cities.

Although efforts to improve blood safety have been stepped up since 1992, obstacles are formidable to ensuring that all donated blood is screened. Delays have occurred in the implementation of the Blood Safety Programme at the state level because of the failure of state Finance Departments to release centrally allocated funds and, as acute shortages remain in the nation's blood supply, unregistered blood banks continue to operate. Nevertheless, improved surveillance of donated blood has already had an impact on HIV transmission through blood transfusions, at least in the metropolitan areas. According to the head of the Delhi AIDS cell, the rate of infection in blood recipients had fallen from 20 per 1,000 in 1993 to 10.5 per 1,000 in 1994 (Pioneer 1994).

That the Blood Safety Programme is one of the more successful components of the National AIDS Control Programme (NACP) testifies to the inadequate response mounted by the government to the growing challenge of AIDS in India. Although the program, launched in 1987, was responsible for health education and care and screening and surveillance as well, more emphasis was placed in its early years on surveying so-called high-risk groups for HIV antibodies than on developing strategies to prevent the continued spread of the disease. Cultural taboos about openly discussing sex fostered a reluctance to initiate AIDS awareness campaigns. Official apathy and indifference were also linked to the belief that AIDS would be confined to highly marginalized groups. Selective surveillance reinforced this impression and strengthened calls for discriminatory legislation. Although most attempts to pass HIV/AIDS related laws have been rejected on the basis of human rights, this has not prevented the application of highly discriminatory measures in practice. A number of Indian states have illegally detained HIV and AIDS sufferers and people suspected to be at high risk of infection as well. In 1988, for example, HIV-positive sex workers arrested under the Immoral Traffic Prevention Act in Madras were kept under detention even after serving their official sentences. The case provoked a strong response from local activists, and in 1990 the Madras High Court ordered the release of five prostitutes who had been detained at the government vigilance home (Nataraj 1990).

In the face of both international and national pressure the government of India has revised its AIDS policies. In 1992 the National

AIDS Control Organization (NACO) was established and the more comprehensive National AIDS Prevention and Control Programme (NAPCP) launched. This represented a turning point in Indian AIDS policy. Although some emphasis is still placed on targeted surveillance, NAPCP now acknowledges the need to promote greater awareness among the public as a whole to ensure a policy of nondiscrimination toward individuals with HIV or AIDS and to focus more resources upon HIV-prevention activities. Considerable progress has been made in establishing the structure and mechanisms of a coherent national AIDS prevention and control program, which now comprises STD control, condom promotion, and information, education and communication (IEC) activities in addition to the existing surveillance and blood safety programs. NACO officials have, thus, confronted highly sensitive issues and have demonstrated a willingness to challenge cultural taboos surrounding sexual behavior in India.

The progressive approach of national-level policymakers has been countered, however, by conservative forces at the state and local levels. With important exceptions state governments have shown a reluctance to launch health education campaigns that talk openly about sex and condom use. Bottlenecks have occurred in the distribution of funds for AIDS projects and in the recruitment of personnel. Because of the stigma attached to working with high-risk groups, especially in the context of AIDS, many government officials are happy to pass the responsibility for HIV-prevention activities to the nongovernmental sector. Although this move has paved the way for more innovative and challenging projects, it has permitted the growth of nongovernmental organizations (NGOs) that seek little more than funds and prestige. Problems of implementation have also stemmed from conflicts of interest between different state sectors. On the one hand, health departments are expected to take an inclusionary approach to groups such as CSWs and IDUs. On the other, state bodies in charge of public order and law enforcement are expected to arrest them.

The tensions that exist between central and state governments, different ministries, and departments and between governmental and nongovernmental organizations are unfortunate. Although the wider economic, cultural and political context of the HIV epidemic suggests the need for a political commitment to fundamental social change, regionally specific factors also play a significant role in HIV transmission. Prevention activities, therefore, need to be decentralized so that appropriate action can be taken by state and district authorities and by local NGOs. The development of effective, context-specific interventions also requires a thorough understanding of how such national and regional political tensions, economic conditions, and cultural contexts are actually expressed in particular locales and of how these locales acquire their own dynamic. It is, thus, to the local scale, the setting within which structure/agency interactions are situated, that the discussion now turns.

The Commercial Sex Industry in Madras

In 1986 a commercial sex worker in Madras became the first Indian national to be diagnosed as HIV positive. The case provoked a media outcry, led to the vilification of women engaged in prostitution for "importing" the disease by having sex with foreigners, and resulted in the massive expansion of surveillance efforts in the state of Tamil Nadu (which accounted for 43 percent of all people screened in India by October 1989). Finding relatively high rates of HIV, the CSWs of Madras were identified as an important "reservoir of infection." Until 1993, however, no HIV-prevention activities were targeted at this sector. The few programs that were initiated by NGOs in the city focused either on raising awareness among the general population or among potential clients of sex workers.

That CSWs have been overlooked in prevention efforts stems partly from a lack of relevant information. Until recently, little was known about the commercial sex industry in Madras. To a perhaps unusual extent research efforts have been hindered by problems of identifying, gaining access to, and eliciting cooperation from sex workers and their affiliates. A local research team established in September 1992 under the Tamil Nadu State Government AIDS Cell and WHO thus became the first to illuminate patterns of prostitution in the city (Oostvogels 1992). Using ethnographic research, the team gradually gained detailed knowledge about this hitherto unresearched area. A detailed map was produced of pick-up points, cruising areas, brothels, lodges, and other locations where commercial sex takes place. An inventory of numbers of female sex workers, customers, and affiliated target groups of brokers, pimps, brothel keepers, and police in the city was also compiled.

The team found that the nature and organization of commercial sex in Madras differed from those in other metropolitan cities in a number of respects. Because of the relatively conservative nature of

Tamil culture, which condemns the display or discussion of sexual matters in public, the institutional response to commercial sex in the city is extremely repressive. Sixty percent of arrests under the Immoral Traffic Prevention Act (SITA/ITPPA) are made in Tamil Nadu State alone. At the city level Madras ranks second in the country in arrests, preceded only by Bombay, which has a much higher concentration of sex workers. Thus, whereas only three thousand women are estimated to work in the city on a regular basis, fifteen hundred cases are registered annually under SITA/ITPPA. This figure does not include the many women who are caught while soliciting or during police raids on brothels but who pay off police officers in cash or kind.

Local actors in the commercial sex industry have been highly creative in their response to repression, taboo, and social stigma. Prostitution is dispersed throughout the city, which, unlike Delhi, Calcutta, and Bombay, lacks a geographically discrete red light area (fig. 9.3). Much of the sex trade takes place in an underground circuit, access to which is controlled by various forms of "middlemen." Thus, although street prostitutes can be approached directly, they account for less than one-quarter of the CSW population. The vast majority of sex workers are engaged in disguised prostitution. Referred to as "family girls," these women continue to live within regular households and often sell sex without the knowledge of their families or neighbors. Gaining access to clients through female brokers or "aunties," many family girls do not consider themselves "prostitutes," but decent women making some extra money for their households. They, therefore, distance themselves from street workers and brothel-based women who are open about their profession and who service larger numbers of clients.

Brothel-based prostitution is also largely hidden. The few brothels that are "declared" in the sense of being known and tolerated by the authorities enjoy political patronage. Other establishments regularly shift their premises in response to police raids or complaints from neighbors. As a result, brothels are smaller than those commonly found in Indian cities, most establishments housing no more than three to four women at any one time. Many pose as ordinary family homes comprising a "couple" and their "daughters." Because of the secretive, shifting nature of brothel prostitution, clients are normally procured through brokers.

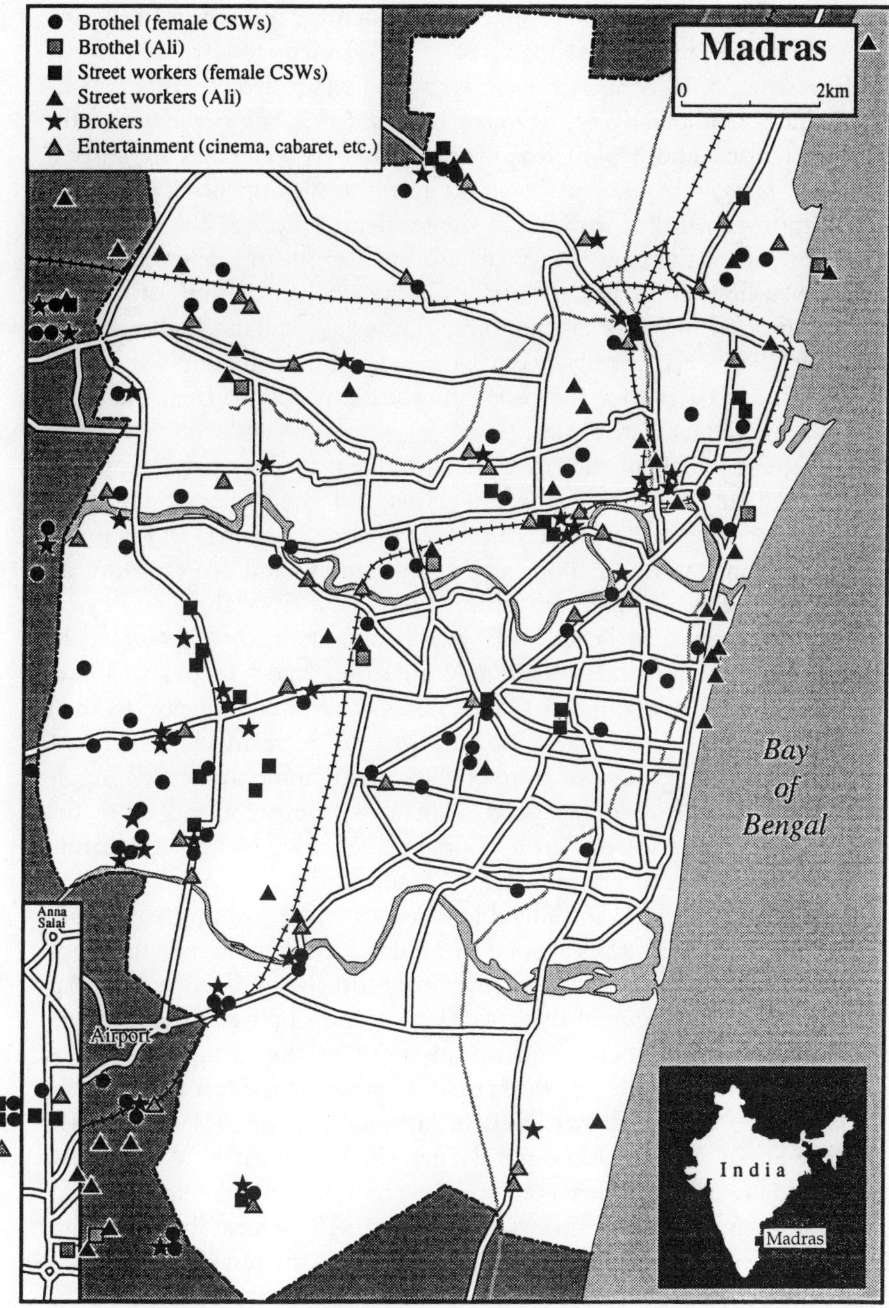

Figure 9.3. Distribution of commercial sex outlets in Madras.

Although street workers are easier to identify, this sector of the sex worker population is also scattered as the women seek to avoid arrest. Nevertheless, local areas can be identified where street workers concentrate. Comparatively cheap sex is provided in the beach area, railway stations, and Mount Road (on which several cinemas are based). Here, sex often takes place at or near the pick-up point itself. By contrast, prostitutes working in the residential areas to the south and southwest of the central city (where bus depots are commonly used for pick-up points) and at Parry's Corner, the central hub of the old city, are of a higher socioeconomic status and demand higher prices. Their clients are usually taken to a lodge or small hotel where, in addition to paying for the room, they are expected to treat the prostitute to dinner and drinks.

Because much of the sex trade is hidden, brokers play a key role in mediating contacts between CSWs and their clients. Full-time brokers "hang out" in front of cabaret theatres, cinemas, and massage parlors, and at bus depots and train stations and try to cultivate regular clients. A significant proportion of the city's auto- and cycle-rickshaw drivers, however, work in this capacity, taking passengers to brothels, street workers, or family girls they know in the area. Because both clients and sex workers usually pay a commission to their intermediaries, commercial sex in Madras is relatively expensive. Consequently, groups of four or five men commonly book a single street worker or brothel-based woman for the night and share the costs. This practice of "group bookings" is another unusual feature of the commercial sex industry in Madras.

Although there is considerable diversity in the working conditions of different types of sex worker in Madras, and although factors such as the high turnover of clients among brothel-based prostitutes may lead to varied potential risks of HIV infection between the different categories, a number of factors place all of the groups at risk. A survey of fifty female sex workers undertaken by the research team in January 1993 found that levels of knowledge about HIV and AIDS were abysmally low. Although 81 percent knew that HIV was transmitted by sexual contact and 62 percent by contaminated blood, misconceptions were also very common: 43 percent believed that AIDS could be transmitted by mosquito bites (the rest did not know); 29 percent by infected food or water or by sharing toilets; and 52 percent that AIDs could be spread by kissing. Only 52 percent agreed that an infected needle could transmit the disease. A survey of eighty clients found similar gaps in knowledge. Although 97 percent had heard about AIDS, and 79 percent knew that it could be sexually transmitted, 54 percent identified kissing as a cause of transmission, and only 31 percent believed that anal sex was riskier than vaginal intercourse.

Low levels of knowledge about AIDS are compounded by even lower rates of condom usage. Eighty-seven percent of the sex workers surveyed claimed to have used condoms in the past. Only 4 percent, however, did so in every client encounter. The fact that 73 percent relied on their clients to bring condoms confirmed qualitative reports that the choice of whether to have protected sex or not lies overwhelmingly with the customer. Unfortunately, the client survey revealed little enthusiasm for safe sex, only 9 percent of respondents claiming to use condoms in every encounter with sex workers and 20 percent occasionally. The vast majority of nonusers (40 percent) claimed that condoms affected their enjoyment of sex; a further 37 percent rationalized their behavior by claiming to only visit girls who looked healthy. For many clients, particularly those who hire the services of a prostitute in a group, it is simply not macho to use a condom. Neither clients nor sex workers associate condoms with protection against STDs or AIDS, instead relying on a mixture of folk remedies and antibiotics to control sexually transmitted disease. Many brothel owners, for example, arrange for their girls to have weekly injections from private doctors. Other women and clients rely on less-scientific solutions such as washing one's genitals after intercourse in urine, soda water, or lime juice.

Prospects for HIV Prevention in Madras: The Need for Locally Specific Interventions and Structural Change

Given the high turnover of clients and the low levels of condom use that characterize the commercial sex industry in Madras, there is a pressing need for interventions designed to prevent the transmission of HIV among sex workers and their clients. This may, however, prove problematic, for although there is a growing consensus that community-based strategies involving peer educators and support groups provide the best means of gaining access to, communicating with, and empowering marginalized groups, the evidence presented in this chapter suggests that the specific nature of the commercial sex trade in Madras may not be conducive to such an approach.

Community-based intervention strategies rest on the principles of changing peer norms and strengthening community action to attract local participation in prevention and care activities. Thus, an important goal of grounding HIV prevention efforts in community networks is to make risk reduction an expected and accepted norm. One problem that arises in Madras is that CSWs lack the autonomy to exercise control over their sexual encounters. The choice of whether to have protected sex or not lies overwhelmingly with sex workers' clients. The latter, however, do not constitute a readily identifiable "community" for outreach efforts.

Apparently, there is little scope for community participation amongst sex workers themselves. Because family girls obtain their clients through small circles of contacts, they have limited contact with other CSWs. Brothel-based women are also highly isolated because of the small size of brothels in Madras, the fact that women are moved regularly between different establishments, and the numbers of young migrants represented in this sector who, unable to speak or understand Tamil, are highly dependent upon their brothel-keepers. Finally, although the greater experience and occupational autonomy of streetworkers offers more opportunities for the development of informal support structures, they are too dispersed and mobile to establish many ties. Moreover, informal gathering is risky because of fear of arrest.

The unusual organization of the commercial sex industry in Madras reflects the local juxtaposition of relatively harsh policing policies, a strong cultural antipathy toward the discussion of sex, HIV, and AIDS, and a well-developed tradition of small-scale and dispersed prostitution supported by brokers, procurers, kingpins, and political patronage. It is, in other words, impossible either to understand the nature of the sex industry or to address the problem of HIV transmission without careful regard to place—the setting within which actions are situated and social processes emerge. Equally, solutions must be sought which address the peculiarities of particular places. Thus, given the potential obstacles to recruiting effective peers from CSWs themselves, health promotion strategies may have to begin by using aunties, brothel keepers, and brokers as outreach workers. Although this would entail using the very people who exploit sex workers, it may be unrealistic to ignore such players because of the key role they play in defining the sexual practices of CSWs in Madras. HIV prevention in the city, however, cannot be achieved by individual- and community-level efforts alone. Cultural taboos must be overcome and publicity campaigns mounted to raise public awareness about HIV and AIDS. Institutional changes will also be necessary to challenge the very policies that drive prostitution underground, lock sex workers into unequal power relations, and undermine the potential of community-based strategies of education and empowerment.

At a more fundamental level the vulnerability of CSWs in Madras cannot be separated from broader gender and development issues. In the Indian context this means confronting double standards that result in the strict control of women's sexuality, sexual freedom for men, and commercial sex for large numbers of impoverished women; challenging political attitudes that have resulted in the discrimination against people who are vulnerable to HIV; and addressing the economic inequalities that deprive large numbers of people of access to adequate health and education facilities and that result in the entry of impoverished men and women into the commercial blood and sex industries.

Part Three

Place, Policy, and Well-being

10

Making Connections Between Housing and Health

SOPHIE HYNDMAN

There used to be a piece of graffiti in the East End of London that read, "Think twice, most doctors don't live on the Isle of Dogs." The Isle of Dogs is situated in Tower Hamlets, one of the more deprived areas of London. The graffiti illustrated the somewhat cynical, but common-sense connection that the "artist" had made between living in a poor housing environment and health. When considering health, housing as a "place" has an important role to play. People spend a large proportion of their lives inside their homes; indeed, elderly, unemployed, and ill people may pass most of their time at home.

Housing and health can be connected in a number of ways. Most commonly, people think of ways in which poor housing may affect people's health. Since the 1980s, there has been a renewed interest in this area. Evidence of such interest includes: a series of articles in the mainstream *British Medical Journal* (see Lowry 1991); professionals expressing a continued concern about inequalities in health; and a recognition by some that housing has a central role to play in the "new public health." More broadly, it is important to remember the role of housing status and the way it can affect access to health care and that health status can affect housing opportunities (Smith, Knill-Jones, and McGuckin 1991).

The very existence of a poor housing environment should be sufficient reason for it to be improved; no one can really believe that a damp, moldy home is pleasant to inhabit. Although no one should ignore the importance of how a person subjectively responds to poor housing conditions, this is, regrettably, not always enough to achieve change. Those responsible for housing will be more inclined to improve poor conditions if they have objective "proof" that an environment is detrimental to a person's physical or mental health. Similarly, those responsible for health may be more likely to succeed in rehousing a person on medical grounds if specific housing factors are known to affect health adversely. An examination of the literature, in particular, the work linking dampness in the home to health, reveals that the more specific the definition of *poor housing* used, the clearer the connections with ill health become.

Definitions: Housing and Health

The potential links between housing and health are evident when one looks at the WHO concept of health, "A state of complete physical, mental and social well-being and not merely the absence of disease and infirmity" (quoted in WHO 1961, 6), alongside the WHO definition of *residential environment,* "The physical structure that man [*sic*] uses for shelter and the environs of that structure including all necessary services, facilities, equipment and devices needed or desired for the physical and mental health and social well-being of the family and individual" (1961, 7). Along the same lines, Britten (1942, 193), who examined tuberculosis, wrote, "If under a definition of housing we choose to include crowding, proper sanitation, playground space, and home environment in general, and if at the same time we choose to include under health the maintenance of a state of physical, mental and social efficiency, the causative relation becomes quite obvious."

There are no difficulties in seeing common-sense connections between housing and health, therefore, when the definitions of housing and health are all-embracing, but there always seems to be an element of doubt about whether the connection can be shown scientifically. For example, Heginbotham wrote that "it seems axiomatic that poor housing should lead to poor health, yet there is little hard data on the links between housing per se and physical and mental illness" (1985, 218).

This hesitancy has been generated quite reasonably by an academic debate that recognizes the problems of disentangling the effect of one factor, namely, poor housing, among many in what Stein (1952) termed the *social complex.* Engels observed in *The Condition of the Working*

Class in England in 1844 that "there is ample proof that the dwellings of workers who live in the slums, *combined with other adverse factors*, give rise to many illnesses" (cited in Jacobs and Stevenson 1981, emphasis added). Researchers examining housing and health have also highlighted the problem: "Health is not an easy area in which to disentangle cause and effect, since an individual is affected by many different factors, such as genetic predisposition, age, sex, smoking and drinking habits and employment history. Some of these are also likely to be linked to housing conditions. People who live in the poorest houses also tend to take up the least healthy employment, live in the worst environments and consume the poorest diets" (Keithley et al. 1984b, 8). Britten went so far as to say that "the interrelation of socioeconomic facts with housing, on the one hand, and with health, on the other, would make impossible any clear-cut determination of the effects of housing per se on health" (1942, 193).

This debate is understandable but limiting. First, it assumes that poor housing conditions are always associated inextricably with other features of "multiple deprivation," which is not necessarily true. Not all aspects of poor housing need relate to multiple deprivation at all, for example, the possible problems of radon or electromagnetic radiation in the home (Lowry 1991). Second, not everyone is multiply deprived. People do not universally experience *every* aspect of poor housing *and* undertake all health damaging behaviors *and* work in poor environments *and* suffer from a lack of nutrition. It is this variability that enables a certain amount of unraveling to take place. In some housing and health research, therefore, the inability to link housing and health scientifically arises through a lack of a clear definition for housing. *Poor housing* is often referred to when, in fact, it means *multiple deprivation*. This chapter is concerned with some aspects of housing that are traditionally related to deprivation, and discusses how the various housing factors contributing to ill health—in particular, housing dampness—can be, at least in part, distinguished.

Deciphering the Social Context

From Broad to Specific Definitions of Housing

The broader the definition of housing under investigation, the more open any relationship to health is to confounding variables. To examine specific relationships between housing and health, therefore, a first consideration is to state clearly what is meant by *housing* at any one time. Until such identification, the exposure suspected of causing ill-health is not clear and it is not really possible to construct studies to look scientifically at specific aspects of housing and health. Until this is done, one cannot determine the type of association (e.g., whether it is causal).

In the following section some of the literature that has sought to investigate relationships between housing and health is classified by the definition of housing used (see fig. 10.1). More specific definitions enable study design (e.g., natural experiments and carefully selected populations and multivariate statistical analyses) to elucidate housing and health relationships.

Housing Deprivation and Health

The associations between lower social class and ill health are well established (Townsend and Davidson 1982; Whitehead 1987). A broad definition of housing approximate to *social class*. Studies of housing tenure and health, for example, show strong associations: "For respiratory diseases, circulatory diseases and malignant neoplasms, people in owner-occupied accommodation had the lowest and local authority tenants the highest SMRs (standardized mortality ratios), irrespective of age or sex." (Fox and Goldblatt 1982, 66).

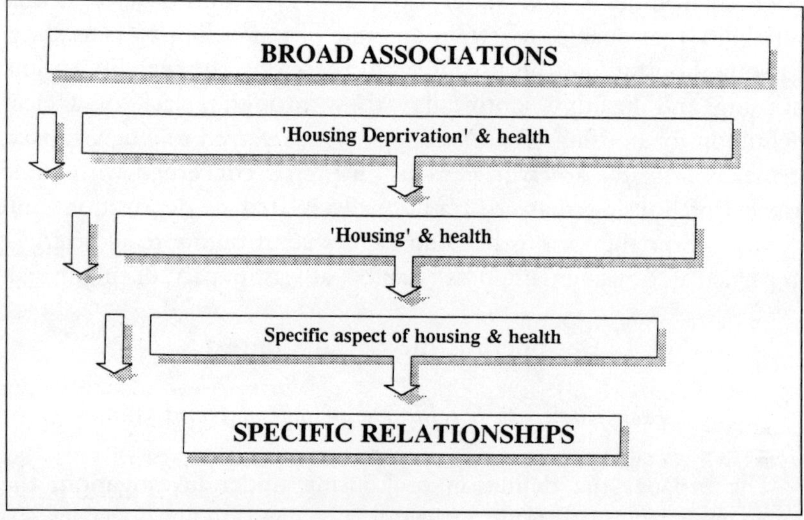

Figure 10.1. Definitions of housing.

Along the same lines, Spivey and Radford (1979) found higher rates of illness in inner-city black children in public compared to private housing. McGregor (1963) observed that in London and southeast England, the infant mortality rate was 18 per 1,000 live births where there was also the lowest percentage of slum property. Northwest England, by contrast, had an infant mortality rate of 26 per 1,000 live births and the highest percentage of slum property. Similarly, Burt (1945) reported that the infant mortality rate was two times as high, infectious diseases were three times as high, and infantile paralysis was four times as high in an inner suburb with "lower housing standards" in Melbourne compared to an outer suburb with "higher housing standards." These relationships are interesting, but the definition of housing is too broad and cannot be divorced from other social factors that could also be influencing the aspect of health in question.

Housing and Health

Changing the housing environment as a whole while "putting on hold" other social factors is one approach that removes this group of variables that may relate to deprivation out of the analysis. Robinson (1955), for example, showed how a group rehoused from a slum area in Newark, New Jersey, showed a decreased incidence of tuberculosis and childhood diseases. Wilner et al. (1962) reported that after three years a group of rehoused individuals showed improved health with fewer infectious and parasitic diseases, digestive disorders, and accidents. To consider other factors in such studies, one could argue that a change in housing environment may lead to changing social circumstances. For example, there may be a positive change in aspirations, which, in turn, may change other aspects of the social environment. The initiating factor in producing this chain of change, however, could be attributed to the improved housing.

Other studies, although still using a fairly broad definition of poor housing, have tried to disentangle it from other socioeconomic factors. For example, Keithley et al. (1984a, 1984b) found consistent differences in self-reported morbidity between individuals from "good" and "bad" housing areas. Using multivariate statistics, they showed that when controlling for age and sex, for all age groups up to sixty-five years, those living in "bad" housing areas reported poorer general health, more long-standing illness, and more respiratory disease and depression than those living in "good" housing areas. Taking into account age, smoking, income, type of housing (e.g., flats compared to houses) and occupational experience, people living in "bad" housing areas still suffered more respiratory conditions than those in "good" areas.

Brennan and Lancashire (1978) also conducted an analysis of different socioeconomic factors, this time in relation to mortality in 0–4 and 5–14-year-olds in the county boroughs of England and Wales in 1971. Using Kendall's partial correlation technique, keeping the effects of social class and unemployment constant, they found that at ages 0–4, a significant and positive relationship remained between mortality and high-density housing and inadequate housing facilities. These approaches allow a distinction to be made between physical housing as a whole and other factors contributing to multiple deprivation. They do not, however, allow an examination of specific aspects of housing that may contribute substantially to ill health in their own right.

Specific Aspects of Housing and Health

By being still more specific in the definition of housing it is possible to look in more detail at relationships between aspects of housing and aspects of health. In this section housing dampness is used as an example of a more specific housing factor that has been successfully looked at in relation to health.

Table 10.1 summarizes a number of studies that have undertaken an examination of the relationship between damp housing and ill health. Two approaches have been adopted. Some studies have tried to eliminate by design at least some confounding variables (e.g., by examining a population restricted in some way). This is most commonly done by selecting a population of a more limited social class variability. For example, Melia et al. (1982a, 1982b), Strachan and Elton (1986), Martin, Platt, and Hunt (1987) and Platt et al. (1989) concentrated their work in local authority housing or deprived areas. In this way the health of occupants of damp and nondamp homes can be compared while controlling at least some social confounding variables. Hyndman (1990a, 1990b) studied an even more limited population of British Bengali council tenants in East London. The members of this group were in similar social and economic positions and had a limited age range and distinctive cultural similarities (e.g., limited

Table 10.1

Studies of Housing Dampness and Health

Study	Population	Type of Measurements for Dampness and Health	Potential Confounding Variables Discussed	Significant Associations with Damp/Mold
Burr, St. Leger, and Yarnell 1981	Males and females, aged 20-44, with and without history of respiratory symptoms, in a South Wales town	Reported history of respiratory symptoms and reported dampness	Sex, smoking, presence of coal fire, social class	Yes: reported dampness/reported respiratory symptoms
Melia et al. 1982a, 1982b	5- to 6-year-old children, local authority housing in urban area, N. England	Objectively measured relative humidity; reported respiratory symptoms	Age, sex, social class, smoking, nitrogen dioxide levels	Yes: objectively measured dampness/reported respiratory symptoms
Strachan and Elton 1986	7- to 8-year-old children, deprived area of Edinburgh	Reported respiratory symptoms, GP consultations for respiratory ill health; reported damp and mold	Sex, family history of wheeze, family size, other children, crowding, heating, night-time window opening in bedroom, gas and coal applicances, parental smoking	Yes: reported mold/reported respiratory symptoms But: no significant association between reported damp/mold and GP consultations for wheeze
Martin, Platt, and Hunt 1987; Hunt, Martin, and Platt 1986	Adults and children in a deprived area of Edinburgh	Independent assessment of dampness (observation and measurement); reported health	Overcrowding, age of tenants, number of children, previous poor housing, duration of tenancy, move to present home because of health, household income, use of Calor gas, smoking	Yes: assessed dampness/reported respiratory and other health symptoms mainly in children
Strachan 1988; Strachan and Sanders 1989	6 and 7 year olds, Edinburgh	Reported damp and mold, objectively measured damp and objectively measured lung function	Smoking, housing tenure, number of people/room, gas cooking, heating type	Yes: reported damp and mold/reported respiratory health But: no association between objectively measured respiratory function/reported or objectively measured dampness

continued on next page

Table 10.1 (continued)

Study	*Population*	*Type of Measurements for Dampness and Health*	*Potential Confounding Variables Discussed*	*Significant Associations with Damp/Mold*
Wagemaekers et al. 1989	Adults and children from Katwijk, The Netherlands	Reported dampness; fungal spore count in subsample of 36 homes; reported health	Sex, age, smoking, heating system, closed/open kitchen, pets and carpeting in living room and bedroom	Yes: adults and children—reported dampness/reported respiratory symptoms; for children—reported dampness/other reported health symptoms and fungal spore count/reported respiratory symptoms
Platt et al. 1989	Adults and children in local authority housing in Edinburgh, Glasgow, and London	Independent assessment of dampness, spore counts; reported health	Gender and marital status of respondent, smoking, household income, over-crowding, employment, number of children, house-hold size, pets, previous ten-ancy characteristics, use of Calor gas, time at current ad-dress, other housing problems	Yes: adults and children—assessed dampness and fungal spore counts/reported respiratory and other health symptoms
Hyndman 1990 a, b	British Bengali adults and children, tenants of local authority housing in East London	Objectively measured and reported respiratory health/other reported health symptoms/objectively measured and reported dampness, cold, mold	Age, sex, smoking, social class, occupational exposure to dust, overcrowding, gas cooking cold	Yes: reported and objectively measured dampness, mold and cold/reported health symptoms But: no association between objectively measured housing conditions/objectively measured respiratory health
Dijkstra et al. 1990	Children, S.E. Netherlands, aged 6–12	Reported dampness, ob-jectively measured pulmonary function over more than two years/reported respiratory symptoms	Parental education, parental respiratory symptoms, ex-posure to tobacco smoke, nitrogen dioxide levels	Yes: reported damp with mold/reported respiratory symptoms But: no clear association between lung function or lung function growth and reported dampness
Dales, Burnett, and Zwanenbug 1991	Adults throughout Canada	Reported dampness/reported health	Three groups of potential confounders relating to (1) Sociodemographic variables; (2) Important ex-posure variables; (3) Possibly important exposure variables	Yes: reported dampness/mold and range of reported health symptoms
Spengler et al. 1994	Children throughout North America, aged 9–11	Reported respiratory symptoms/reported moisture	City, sex, parental education, asthma, chronic obstructive pulmonary disease; other housing variables also examined	Yes: reported dampness/mold and reported respiratory symptoms

smoking, large family sizes), which meant a range of confounders could be controlled between people in damp and nondamp homes.

A second approach, often used with the first, is to distinguish relationships by means of multivariate analysis. Partially confounded variables associated with housing characteristics or with specific health symptoms can be examined using logistical and multiple regression techniques. An example of this approach is Dales, Burnett, and Zwanenbug (1991) who selected thirty communities throughout Canada in a study that involved 14,799 adults aged at least twenty-one years. Independent variables were divided into three subgroups: socioeconomic variables (age, gender, ethnic group, maximum parental education, crowding, region, and occupation), "exposure variables of importance" (e.g., several factors relating to cigarette smoking, use of wood stoves and gas ovens) and "exposure variables of possible importance" (e.g., hobbies, pets, use of portable gas/kerosene heaters, use of fireplace or gas stoves to heat and forced air heating). Each group was entered into a multivariate logit model with dampness/mold as an independent variable and the symptom/disorder as the dependent variable. Once each group was examined separately, the subgroups of significant variables ($p<0.01$) were combined into one model. Significant associations were still found between a whole range of respiratory and other symptoms and the presence of damp/mold.

Establishing Causality in Housing Dampness and Health

Having refined down a "housing" exposure suspected of causing ill health to dampness and having reviewed a number of studies constructed to examine it, can one say that housing dampness *causes* ill-health? What is meant by *causal* in this context? For medicine and public health Lilienfeld and Lilienfeld (1980, 295) suggest what they term a *pragmatic concept of causality* that seems appropriate to apply to housing and health: "A causal relationship would be recognized to exist whenever evidence indicates that the factors form part of the complex of circumstances that increases the probability of the occurrence of disease and that a diminution of one or more of these factors decreases the frequency of that disease." Epidemiological research methods can be used to examine the effect of factors on health, and a number of criteria can be applied to help establish whether an observed association between an exposure and a health outcome is causal. Experimental techniques such as the randomized controlled trial, go a long way to demonstrate causal associations, but these methods are almost certainly unethical and impractical in the study of housing and health. The best that can be achieved in practice, therefore, is the observational studies described in table 10.1. These studies offer a convincing *association* between exposure to damp housing and ill health. To help indicate whether this association is causal, the following epidemiological criteria can be used: biological plausibility, consistency of association, strength of association, specificity of association, and dose-response. There are various pros and cons to using these criteria (Lilienfeld and Lilienfeld 1980), and although finding evidence of them will *help* establish causality, they are not necessarily conclusive or essential (Jones and Moon 1987).

Biological Plausibility

The evidence that damp (high relative humidity) per se has a direct negative effect on health is not easy to find, but damp *housing* is not the same as dampness alone. A home combined with damp can give rise to potentially harmful agents that would not arise with dampness in isolation. If a causal chain is constructed, dampness must be viewed in the context of housing, and in that context it leads to the propagation of house dust mites and fungal spores and possibly has an effect on respiratory microorganisms and the off-gassing of chemicals from housing interiors.

Respiratory Problems

Perhaps the most plausible and well-established links between damp housing and respiratory health relate to the indirect effect of higher humidities on house dust mite populations and molds. There are very well-established clinical associations between house dust mites and molds with a variety of allergic diseases. For mites these include rhinitis, asthma, and dermatitis (e.g. Platts-Mills and Chapman 1987; Sporik et al. 1990; Lau et al. 1989; Fain, Guerin, and Hart 1990; Korsgaard 1983). A variety of molds have also been associated clinically with respiratory ill health, including asthma, rhinitis, and (largely in occupational environments) hypersensitivity pneumonitis (e.g., Salvaggio and Aukrust 1981; Gravesen 1979; IEHO 1985). These clinical associations would help explain the common association of dampness with wheezing, asthma, and rhinitis.

From a number of studies, however, damp housing seems to be associated with respiratory symptoms in apparently nonatopic populations (e.g., Burr, St. Leger, and Yarnell 1981; Dales, Burnett, and Zwanenbug 1991; Spengler et al. 1994). The reason for this fact is less clear. In the literature in which the role of humidity on the viability of respiratory microorganisms is examined it appears that both low (below 40 percent) and high (more than 70 percent) relative humidity may increase the viability of infective microorganisms (Arundel et al. 1986). Most of the epidemiological studies in this area appear to have been concentrated on the potential ill effects of low rather than high humidities. Higher levels of humidity may increase the mucous flow and hence help expel respiratory organisms from the respiratory tract (Green 1979) and reduce the infectivity of microorganisms by causing them to clump together (Green 1975). High humidities, however, may also increase the chance of droplet infection (WHO 1987). Ross, Collins, and Sanders (1990) could not find a relationship between upper respiratory tract infections and domestic temperature or humidity. The levels of humidity in the study homes, however, were not excessive. More research to examine the effects of humidity on the viability and infectivity of respiratory microorganisms clearly is required. Higher humidities may also have a role to play in the off-gassing of, for example, formaldehyde, which can be found in indoor building materials and has been associated with adverse health effects, including respiratory disorders (NAS 1981, quoted by Arundel et al. 1986).

Other Health Effects

A number of studies describe associations between nonrespiratory symptoms and dampness/mold (Martin, Platt and Hunt 1987; Platt et al. 1989; Waegemaekers et al. 1989; Hyndman 1990; Dales et al. 1991). Common observations that require more research are the relationships between damp/mold and diarrhea and vomiting and aches and pains. It has been postulated that mycotoxins may play a part in these problems (Martin, Platt, and Hunt 1987). Platt et al. (1989) report a study by May et al. (1986) in which symptoms of fever, muscular pain, chest tightness, cough, and headache were found to be caused by organic toxic dust. It was suggested that this pulmonary mycotoxicosis could represent a systemic reaction to inhaled fungal toxins. Although this was an acute reaction observed after massive doses of organic dust, Platt et al. suggest that possibly similar, although less severe, symptoms might occur as a chronic response to prolonged exposure to lower concentrations of such material. Although damp housing is popularly supposed to predispose occupants to rheumatism, Lawrence (1977) asserts that there is a paucity of objective data on this link.

Consistency of Association

Jones and Moon suggest that "if the same results are found in laboratory beagles, vegetarian Trappist monks, cannibals, and Welsh males, you know you are on to something" (1987, 133). The association between dampness and ill health has been noted in a wide range of populations, if not quite as wide a range as Jones and Moon identify. In the studies shown in table 10.1, the populations include Welsh adults, children in the North of England and Edinburgh, adults and children in the Netherlands, British Bengalis in East London, and two large populations in Canada and the United States (in both apparently atopic and nonatopic groups). In all these studies associations have been consistently found between respiratory and other aspects of general ill health and damp or moldy housing conditions or both.

Strength of Association

Strachan (1988) has reported that "the prevalence ratio for wheeze in the past year when homes with and without mould were compared is remarkable in view of the lack of correlation of most social or environmental variables with childhood asthma" (1988, 1,225). Strachan found a highly significant association between reported mold in the home and wheeze, with an odds ratio, adjusted for a number of confounders, of 3.00 (1.72, 5.25). In an earlier study Strachan and Elton (1986) also found a highly significant association between reported mold and reported wheeze ($p<0.01$). Waegemaekers et al. (1989) found the majority of respiratory symptoms for adults and children and a number of other symptoms for children were more prevalent in homes reported to be damp. For example, in adults damp homes were strongly associated with wheeze ($p<0.01$); in children, with morning cough, runny nose, bronchitis, pneumonia, allergy, tiredness, and nausea/vomiting ($p<0.01$). Dales, Burnett, and Zwanenbug (1991) reported an odds ratio (adjusted for a range of confounders) for adults for upper respiratory symptoms of 1.50 (1.39, 1.61), for lower respiratory symptoms, 1.62 (1.48, 1.78); for chronic respiratory disease, 1.45 (1.29, 1.64), and for asthma, 1.56 (1.25, 1.95). Spengler et al. (1994) found reported mold to be associated significantly with, for example, bronchitic symptoms (odds ratio 1.74; 1.54, 1.97) adjusted, once again, for a number of confounding variables.

One reservation about these studies is the possibility of respondent bias in reporting housing conditions or health. Although no study has shown a significant association between "objectively" measured health and "objectively" measured dampness, studies have shown significant associations between objectively measured dampness and reported health and objectively measured health and reported dampness, adjusting for a range of confounding variables. For example, Melia et al. (1982b) found a significant association between measured relative humidity (75 percent and above) and respiratory illness ($p<0.05$); Platt et al. (1989), using a surveyor's report of dampness, showed a number of significant associations between dampness and reported health (e.g., in adults significant associations between housing dampness group and "bad nerves," aching joints, nausea and vomiting, backache, blocked nose, fainting spells, constipation, and breathlessness; $p<0.05$). Hyndman (1990a, 1990b), using thermo-hygrographs to measure humidity in respondents' homes found a strong relationship between reported chest health and degree of humidity (relative risk of 3.86; 2.35, 6.34, for an average weekly humidity 65 percent or more compared to an average weekly humidity of less than 50 percent). Significant results were also found with objectively measured humidity and other reported symptoms and objectively measured and reported cold and reported and observed (percentage mold cover in worst room) mold in the home and reported health. Hyndman (1990b) reports an earlier survey (not shown in table 10.1) of tenants in more than two hundred local authority homes where reported dampness was found to be associated with a small but significant reduction in peak flow among British Bengali participants ($n = 84$; $p = 0.018$).

Most studies in which objective measurements of housing and health are used do so to help validate and, therefore, add weight to reported measures; they do not question their importance. If people feel unwell, it will be this, after all, that determines whether they consult their doctors. The fact that fairly strong associations have been found between damp housing and aspects of health by using a mixture of measurements and that reported and objectively measured variables have been found to be related significantly (e.g. Hyndman 1990a, 1990b), strengthens those studies that rely on self-report and strengthens the argument that damp housing is deleterious to human health.

Specificity of Association

Epidemiologists argue that there would be an increased likelihood of a causal association if, for example, housing dampness were only related to one disease or to one disease more strongly than to others. Housing dampness is, in fact, associated with a range of health problems—respiratory problems (in individuals with and without reported atopy), aches and pains, diarrhea and vomiting, "nerves," depression, and headaches to name a few. Because of this fact, it might appear that housing dampness does not necessarily fit this criterion. Jones and Moon (1987), however, regard specificity as a poor criterion on which to judge relationships because diseases can be caused by more than one agent. Respiratory illness is obviously caused by many factors, and housing dampness itself may have more than one effect (see section on biological plausibility), each of which may cause different diseases.

Dose-Response

The results in a number of studies in table 10.1 do demonstrate an apparent dose-response relationship. For example, Platt et al. (1989) showed a significant tendency for increasing severity of dampness to be associated with a greater prevalence of a range of symptoms for both adults and children. Hyndman (1990a, 1990b) found that respondents in homes with an average weekly relative humidity of 50–64.9 percent were 2.94 (1.81, 4.77) times more likely to report poor chest health; those in homes with an average relative humidity of 65 percent and above were 3.86 (2.35, 6.34) times more likely to report poor chest health than were respondents with average humidities of less than 50 percent ($p<0.0001$). Dales, Burnett, and Zwanenbug (1991) found that a range of symptom prevalences increased with increased numbers of reported mold sites, and Spengler et al. (1994) showed that odds ratios for respiratory problems were higher when two or more rooms were affected with mold as compared with one affected room.

Using Lilienfeld and Lilienfeld's (1980) "pragmatic concept of causality" and these epidemiological criteria, therefore, damp housing does appear to be associated causally with ill health. The effects seem to be indirect rather than direct but still clearly form part of a causal chain leading to ill health (see fig. 10.2). It is fair to say that no one study has addressed all possible confounding variables, but without randomizing people into damp and nondamp conditions this task is almost impossible. Undoubtedly, work remains to explain certain associations more clearly.

Cold and Damp

Using epidemiological techniques to distinguish dampness from other social and environmental factors in the social complex is possible because these other factors are not *always* associated with dampness (i.e.,

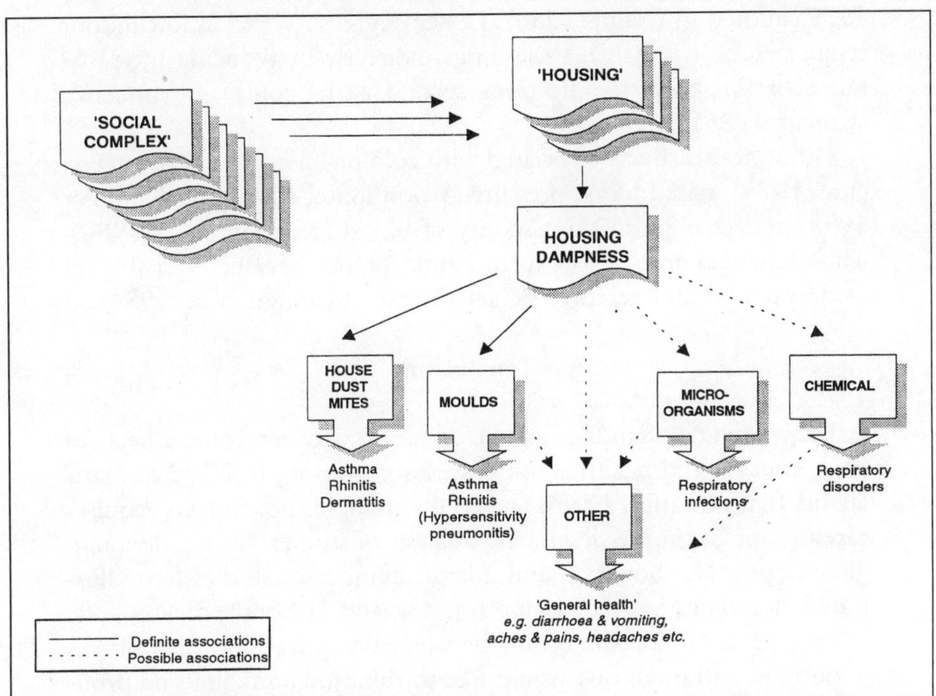

Figure 10.2. Associations between housing and health.

they are partially rather than completely confounded). Damp housing, however, is very frequently associated with cold housing (especially condensation dampness), and the effects of these two factors are not always separated in studies. It is potentially possible to have a damp, warm home, so theoretically a distinction could be made, but of the studies in table 10.1 only Platt et al. (1989) appear to have examined cold in combination with dampness; Hyndman (1990a, 1990b) considered the effects of dampness and cold separately. Problems associated with colder temperatures may be exacerbated by, for example, damp clothing. A layer of cold, wet air requires more energy to warm than a layer of dry air. It is worth briefly considering, therefore, the ways in which cold, and cold and damp housing may produce ill health.

Some evidence exists that very cold outdoor air and cold misty air may have an effect on respiratory health (Collins 1986). Cooling of the nasopharynx in cold weather may be a contributory factor in winter epidemics of cold and influenza (Collins 1987). Cold air is also considered important in exercise-induced asthma (Deal et al. 1979, quoted in Collins 1986). Lesser degrees of cold in low indoor temperatures may damage the lungs indirectly by reducing the resistance of the body to infections secondary to colds and influenza (Collins 1986).

Other health affects associated with cold include hypothermia (Fox et al. 1973), raised blood pressure (Woodhouse, Khaw, and Plummer 1993) and changes in the viscosity of blood (Keatinge et al. 1984). These changes may help explain some of the seasonal variation in cardiovascular and cerebrovascular disease (Keatinge et al. 1984).

Conclusions

Establishing a scientific causal association between some aspects of poor housing and health is not easy. Poor housing is linked to many factors that can affect health and to disentangle these effects requires careful thought in the design and analysis of studies. Such a disentangling is possible, however, and a large number of studies have illustrated clear links between damp housing and ill health, for example.

Proving a causal connection between dampness and ill health is important. Although one would like to think that any housing problem as unpleasant as dampness would be dealt with, regardless of whether it affects health, this is not necessarily the case. At a time when resources are difficult to come by, short cuts will be taken where possible. At the individual level, according to United Kingdom law, at least, obtaining improvements to homes with condensation dampness can be difficult for tenants where specific disrepair may be difficult to show unless a link with health can be proved (Luba 1986). More generally, if firmly grounded building and environmental standards are to be recognized and enforced, then the need for them will have to be proved. If there are no standards, then a supply of sufficiently dry and warm homes will not be forthcoming.

The benefits to health that would result from improving housing could be enormous. Although the prospect of undertaking this task may appear financially daunting, it would almost certainly be cost effective both in savings to health services and improvements to individual quality of life. A lack of proof in this area can be viewed as an excuse for inaction. Making clear connections between poor housing and ill health is, therefore, an important step toward better housing and better health for all.

11

Smoking, Stigma, and the Purification of Public Space

BLAKE D. POLAND

Increasingly, governments in Canada (as elsewhere in the Western world) are turning to public policy legislation to assist in the reduction of cigarette smoking. In addition to the taxation of tobacco products, controls on tobacco advertising, and raising the legal age at which cigarettes can be purchased, governments at all levels (federal, provincial, municipal) are enacting more restrictive legislation regarding where smoking can occur in indoor environments outside the home. These areas I loosely refer to as *public space*. They are often publicly used but privately owned as in restaurants, shopping malls, and the workplace. My intention is not to describe the evolution of these policies nor to account for them with reference, for example, to the emerging interest in "healthy public policy" within health promotion, which has been well described by others (see, e.g., Leichter 1991; Goodin 1989).

Rather, this chapter represents an analysis of the mechanisms by which institutional initiatives (specifically, tobacco policy interventions to restrict smoking in public places) attempt to produce social change. The arena of tobacco control is a particularly interesting one in which to examine these issues because smoking has become a politically charged issue that involves considerable financial and other vested interests on both sides of the debate and because the political correctness of the tobacco control agenda in Canada may obscure the essentially socially constructed and political nature of the "problem" and its "solutions" (Eakin et al. 1994). In this examination of the social geography of tobacco control my interest, in particular, is on the ways in which the social construction of smoking as a moral social problem is partly predicated on (although also facilitative of) the legal control of space. This control involves the exercise of power, which is directed at the manipulation of individual behavior through the selective criminalization of smoking on a territorial basis and which is experienced interpersonally as the stigmatization of smoking behavior.

In this chapter I account for some of the complexities and contradictions arising from my interviews with smokers, tobacco control advocates, and others, which formed part of a qualitative evaluation of a large community-based smoking cessation intervention in Brantford: the community intervention trial for smoking cessation (COMMIT).[1] Although I draw on the testimony of those interviewed, my hypotheses extend well beyond the data and are only loosely grounded in it because (1) many of the ideas for this chapter developed after the interviews and focus groups were complete and (2) the regulation of public and private space was only one of many topics explored in the interviews (whose focus was primarily on the nature of the assistance the Brantford COMMIT intervention provided to smokers interested in quitting). The ideas in this chapter are, therefore, presented as a set of propositions in need of further investigation and are intended to stimulate debate about the spatial dynamics of tobacco control in North America.

The remainder of this chapter comprises two principal sections. In the first I address the lived experience of tobacco control at the interpersonal level, drawing on symbolic interactionist perspectives, particularly Goffman's work on stigma. In the second section more formal (legislative) restrictions on where people can smoke are explored as an illustration of class-based conflicts over the purification of public space.

1. The Community Intervention Trial (COMMIT) for smoking cessation, sponsored by the U.S. National Cancer Institute, concluded four years of intervention in the fall of 1993 and was the largest randomized control trial of a community-based approach to smoking cessation ever mounted. In Brantford, the extensive standardized (and largely quantitative) evaluation protocol was supplemented by an ancillary qualitative evaluation study to attempt to understand better the impacts of the trial locally as part of the author's doctoral research. A range of qualitative methods was used, which included individual depth interviews and focus groups with intervention staff, project volunteers, and other key informants and with a cross section of members of a smokers' network established by COMMIT for smokers interested in quitting, the analysis of program documentation, and direct observation. For a fuller description see Poland 1993a and Poland et al. 1995.

Smoking as Stigma: Social Norms and Behavior in Public Places

Federal, provincial, and municipal legislation in Canada has made a growing number of public shopping malls, restaurants, aircraft, buses, trains, and other public environments smoke-free or has limited smoking to designated areas. In the absence of formal enforcement, sanctions are maintained primarily through interpersonal social relations and social norms. Indeed, one focus of intervention has been the use of social marketing and community mobilization strategies to attempt to engineer changes in community social norms (e.g., the aforementioned COMMIT trial). Survey research now indicates that a majority of smokers are supportive of restrictions on smoking in public, viewing it as a reasonable courtesy to nonsmokers (e.g., Pederson et al. 1989; Ashley, Bull, and Pederson 1994). In addition to the collective social recognition of the right of nonsmokers to smoke-free air the tendencies in Canadian culture toward politeness, to do what is expected, and to obey the law, would appear to contribute to the success of antismoking regulations. These observations are consistent with Foucault's claim that many so-called advanced societies are characterized by social control based on self-censorship (internalization of the panoptic gaze) rather than by displays of brute force (Foucault 1980). It is, therefore, possible that many of the legislative reforms such as restrictions on smoking in public succeed in the main because of this tendency toward self-censorship coupled with subtle cues from nonsmokers signaling inappropriate behavior.

Erving Goffman (1959, 1963a, 1963b, 1971) has written extensively on the nature and social regulation of behavior in public places. Goffman turned his attention not to the perpetrators of inappropriate behavior, but to the rules and social circles that are offended by such transgressions. As his contemporary Howard Becker wrote in the seminal book *Outsiders: Studies in the Sociology of Deviance,* "Social groups create deviance by making the rules whose infraction constitutes deviance, and by applying those rules to particular people and labeling them as outsiders" (1963, 8). Goffman explicated a complex and implicit social order of moral norms regulating human behavior of which public order was a subset concerned with conduct in public. The public realm can be defined as "those nonprivate sectors or areas of urban settlements in which individuals in copresence tend to be personally unknown or only categorically known to one another" (Lofland 1989, 453). One class of interactional principles governing public behavior pertains to the social etiquette of movement, such as how to negotiate crowded streets or to find a seat on a bus, relating to physical contact and personal space between strangers. Another class of unwritten rules of social conduct more directly concerns interpersonal exchange, three of which Lofland (1989) identifies as predominant. The first interaction rule is civil inattention: that is, acknowledging the presence of others but not routinely engaging them in conversation (neither staring at nor completely ignoring others). Second, people function as audiences for each other and for activities that surround them in public settings. The third interactional principle identified by Lofland is being civil toward what one would usually find offensive by not drawing undue attention to it or approaching the person directly.

These so-called rules are more than mere conventions in that social competence is demonstrated by abiding by them; they are fundamental to social and cultural identity. Because the meaning of acts varies according to the context in which they occur, the apparent "freedom of choice" within a class of possible accepted behavior obscures from view the constraints regarding the nature of the choice set in the first place (Goffman 1963a). In terms of smoking it is crucial to understand that these three interactional principles create a situation in which people are generally reluctant to "make a scene" or to draw attention to themselves by raising objections to someone else's inappropriate smoking.

Generally speaking, in Canada it is not usual to approach strangers about their behavior; in fact, one has to "get up the courage" to do so. Instead, often somewhat subtler means are used to the same effect. Goffman (1963a, 1963b) has outlined a number of (primarily nonverbal) ways in which people act to enforce social behavioral codes that operate precisely *because* of the principle of civil inattention. For example, staring is impolite and causes discomfort to the recipient. It is, therefore, often an effective tool to bring others "into line" by indicating that their behavior is the object of unusual attention. Likewise, sideways glances, body language, throat clearing, moving away, and other actions can be cues that someone's smoking is not appreciated. These are not direct verbal communications, however, and the targets of such disapproval can, in pretending not to notice these cues, succeed in getting the offended parties to desist because they would have to "up the ante" and make a more public (and potentially uncomfortable) objection to the smoker's behavior, thereby drawing attention to themselves and risking public rejection or confrontation. These observations seem straightforward, but they draw attention to the highly developed symbolic cultural bases of public behavior and, therefore, their relevance to how legislative reform is experienced and translated into everyday life and the geographic and temporal specificity of their effects (what Kleinman 1991 has called "local moral cultures") in terms of the microsocial contexts in which smoking (and publicly objecting to the smoking of others) is deemed appropriate.

It has been suggested that "threats of shame (self-imposed punishment) and threats of embarrassment (socially imposed punishment) function much like threats of state-imposed legal sanctions to reduce the expected utility of illegal behavior and, thus, to increase the likelihood of compliance with the law" (Grasmick, Bursik, and Kinsey 1991, 233). It has also been suggested that antilittering campaigns such as "Keep America Clean" or antismoking educational programming can bolster social sanctions, increasing threats of shame or embarrassment. The assumption is that the potential for shame, rather than just the belief in the merits of the behavior or its regulation, will be what motivates people to comply. Supporting this hypothesis are public opinion surveys that suggest that 76 percent of smokers in Ontario would comply with more stringent regulations on smoking even though many were not in favor of them (Pederson et al. 1986) although other explanations may also account for these results (e.g., feeling powerless to resist or hoping the new rules would help them kick the habit).

I now return to the primary data collected as narratives during the Brantford study. Despite the stigmatizing effects of tobacco control legislation combined with the inconvenience of restrictions on smoking in public places and in the workplace, almost all of the smokers interviewed were supportive in principle of the existence of restrictions (twenty-nine in favor out of the thirty-one cases in which it was discussed), and nineteen out of twenty-six felt that restrictions help smokers cut down or quit (Poland 1993a). Jessica described how restrictions in her workplace made a difference for her.

> When I could smoke at my desk, especially if it was pressured, or a lot of people would stop and drop in—and a lot of those people were

> smokers—then, yes I smoked a lot more. . . . So . . . although sometimes it annoys me, I think that restricting areas . . . is helpful. You know, it allows you to know that yes, you can do it. You can go without a cigarette and you'll survive and the world won't fall apart; you'll be okay.

Emily said that restrictions preventing her from smoking in certain places really did not bother her much, but added: "What does bother me is if you do smoke and if you're out in a public place like a dance or whatever, people just look at you and, you know, turn up their noses and you know, whatever. That . . . kind of bothers me. If I'm some place and that does happen, I won't smoke after that." Likewise, in discussing the impact of restrictions on smoking Marilyn felt that it had encouraged people to cut down or quit, but added: "I think also though you'll find a lot more closet smokers out there because you do feel shame when you light up a cigarette, so you tend to hide. It may not make everyone quit; it just makes you more self-conscious, so you hide out with the rest of the lepers (laughs) and have your cigarette, you know?" Among those who acknowledged some impact of workplace restrictions on their own smoking behavior, several indicated that although they resented the restrictions, they felt they were, perhaps, being done a favor. Several indicated they would welcome even more stringent regulations, and some of them had devised rules for themselves to limit their smoking at work as part of their own cessation strategies. Bob summarized perhaps better than most what many of the other smokers were thinking in this regard, not just about workplace restrictions but about restrictions in general:

> Oh, yeah, it has to help people cut down. I mean, . . . they're going to resent the hell out of it, but yeah, it'll help people cut down. I think, it's a double-edged sword. As much as I hate the fact that it's being regulated to the point where it's . . . the big brother syndrome. . . . Then again, I like the fact that people can take their children out and not expose them to second-hand smoke. I like the fact that you can go into a restaurant and enjoy your meal without smoke wafting from—because . . . I know when I'm eating I don't like second-hand smoke. But, yeah, the medical costs, the health care costs of people smoking . . . I respect why it's happening. I just resent the way it's being done sometimes. I mean, the end result is good. Anytime you can stop a person from lighting up a cigarette, whether they resent the fact or not, you're doing them a favor and the people around them a favor.

As Bob's testimony illustrated though, support in principle does not always translate into support in practice for how restrictions are devised, phrased, and enforced.

Their predicament is an uncomfortable one for many smokers. Although several admitted that the rising "nuisance factor" was accelerating their readiness to quit, others wondered what good it would do for those who were still too addicted to be able to quit. According to Anne, "[The increasingly negative social evaluation of smoking] makes you feel bad, it makes you feel that you're doing something that's dirty... but what good is that? ... It does get the message across, there's no doubt about it, but then where do you go from there? You carry on smoking and feel bad because you're smoking." In some cases the feelings of diminished worth and stigmatization were voiced very poignantly.

> I mean, everyone makes a smoker feel guilty. I know I felt terribly guilty. When I smoked, I felt like I had the plague. You know, like I'm an unclean, unfit person because I smoked. And that's a terrible feeling. Do you know what that does to you, really? That really makes you feel like hell ... you know, that you're a bad person because you smoke.

Testimonies such as these forced me to reconsider some of the taken-for-granted assumptions I had about the uniquely benevolent nature of tobacco control, including interventions designed to reduce the social acceptability of smoking, whatever my convictions about the physical harms associated with smoking.

Clearly, part of this contextuality relates to the smoker's sense of place and experience of place not just as private and public space but as a series of contingent behavior settings. Several of the quotes above suggest how the regulation of space is experienced by smokers. It appears from this research that one (but not the only) experience of the purification of public space at the level of social interaction is that of stigmatization.

The smokers interviewed in the Brantford study clearly varied in the degree to which they appear to have internalized feelings of guilt and shame associated with the stigmatization of smoking. In fact, several expressed opinions more resembling indignation and resistance although the majority appeared to classify themselves, as might be expected, as "considerate" smokers. Many saw this as the new (and appropriate norm) among smokers: reasonable accommodation of the rights of nonsmokers to smoke-free air. But in many cases deference was more than a sign of courtesy: smokers simply did not feel *comfortable* about lighting up around those who did not smoke. There came a point at which it simply detracted from the enjoyment of smoking. As Jessica put it, "I guess it depends on how comfortable I am with the person that I'm with. . . . It's like smoking in front of my father. No way. I'll just, I'll die with every puff. So . . . if you know the person is accepting of it, and it's not offending them, then you're comfortable to do it. I guess that's true with a lot of the social things." For several respondents the perceived declining social acceptability of smoking has meant an increasing sense of "dis-ease" about their own smoking among strangers or in public. Shauna, for example, indicated that "I try not to smoke as much any more when I am in other company because it is so unacceptable these days, and they want to make you feel so ——, so when I am out in a social situation, I don't smoke nearly as much as I used to, especially at parties and people's homes or meetings." The above quotations indicate that changes in the perceived social acceptability of smoking contribute to the maintenance and enforcement of regulations through self-censorship of public behavior, perhaps because a common experience of the purification of public space at the level of social interaction is that of stigmatization.

To "moral entrepreneurs" (Pfuhl and Henry 1993) and health professionals, the shift in social norms that led smoking to be seen in many quarters as socially inappropriate behavior has been celebrated as a public health victory (Allen and Adler 1989). Yet it is through the sort of interpersonal mechanisms described above (in addition to messages in the print and electronic media) that, in the context of daily lived experience, not just smok*ing* as a behavior but smok*ers* as people have become stigmatized. According to Goffman, stigma is defined as the "deeply discrediting" (1963b, 3) stereotypes about the meaning of a particular social, physical, or behavioral attribute (such as smoking) that reinforce negative judgments about the moral status of persons with those (stigmatizing) attributes (e.g., smokers being stereotyped as weak-willed, dirty, or uncouth). For the socially and economically disadvantaged (former psychiatric patients, the homeless and the unemployed, unskilled manual laborers, welfare recipients, aboriginal peoples, or single mothers) who disproportionately rely on smoking as one of very few coping mechanisms available to them in dealing with the stresses of everyday life, the stigma of being a smoker can be seen as yet another form of social disapproval that may diminish their dignity as worthy human beings struggling to achieve the same basic human goals as the rest of us regarding physical comfort, happiness, and personal growth.

Complicating matters for smokers is the fact that some interactional principles pertaining to behavior in the public realm appear to be in conflict with others and that smoking can be either a social lubricant or stigmatizing, depending on the circumstances. For example, a cigarette or a light offered from, or accepted by, a stranger serves to break the ice and establish reciprocity and friendship by exchange (an extension of hospitality). Smoking has long been a symbol of identification in and of itself (symbolizing status, rebelliousness, or risk taking) (Robbins and Kline 1991). Smoking also contributes to social competence by helping one be more composed through the management of negative emotions, notably anger (Fergusson 1987; Ashton and Stepney 1982), particularly among women, whose gendered socialization prescribes anger management (Jacobsen 1986), and improving vigilance on the job when stress or boredom are high (which can be seen as a form of occupational role adaptation) (Krogh 1991). It also performs an important function in legitimating social disengagement for the purposes of relaxation and regaining one's composure (McCracken 1992). As the title of a recent book by Richard Klein (1993) suggests, cigarettes are sublime for many users as surely as they are addictive and harmful and, therefore, are the source of considerable ambivalence for many smokers.

Furthermore, a state of flux in what rules of public conduct apply to smokers and under what circumstances appears to have created confusion and uncertainty for some smokers about "coming out" in public about their habit. People who smoke, therefore, must often seek supportive environments to engage in the act of smoking. As smokers negotiate the various corridors of public and private space during everyday life, they must continually and reflexively monitor which spaces are permissive and which are spaces of denial vis à vis smoking. In many cases, it would appear that the uncertainty about where and when it is permissible to smoke eventually becomes normalized as "par for the course" of living with social restrictions on one's behavior. In the words of one smoker

> I've found that I've become more and more aware of nonsmoking places now because I'm looking for a place to smoke. You know, you walk into a place and of course, where's the sign? Here or not? So,

> yeah I've become more aware of that, whereas maybe three or four years ago it was not a big deal. Now, I look all the time. I have to know where I can smoke, where I'm going to sit, that type of thing. It becomes second nature.

There is uncertainty in the new moral order; public health discourse is not all-encompassing and may be resisted. Not only the legal status of smoking but the social acceptability of it is highly situational not only across but even within particular behavior settings.

In *Stigma* Goffman (1963b) observes that the stigmatized often seek each other out and congregate in the same places and may become represented by their own organizations that challenge the cultural construction of their stigma (itself the basis for many social movements, e.g., the gay rights movement). The (re)emergence of smoking parlors in parts of the United States and a number of smokers rights groups (such as the Smokers' Freedom Society in Canada) bear witness to similar trends in the realm of smoking.

The social construction of deviance and the politics of social control have resulted in the creation of stigmatizing spaces in which smokers literally feel out of place in designated or informal spaces where smokers congregate to smoke. Given the spaces occupied by the different players, it seems reasonable to conclude that meanings penetrate into these settings to different degrees, depending to some extent on where smokers congregate. This conclusion appears to be consistent with literature on deviance insofar as all forms of deviance have distinctive geographies (Sacco 1988). Several respondents in the Brantford study, including those quoted above, reported feeling uneasy in open public places. When asked where they felt comfortable smoking, many respondents mentioned their own homes, cars, or behavioral settings permissive of smoking (e.g., parties of smoking friends, bars, or some restaurants). It is noteworthy that class divisions in the prevalence of smoking may be reflected in the spatial ordering (and segregation) of spaces in which smoking is most prevalent and socially acceptable, just as class divisions in society are reproduced in—and fundamentally structure—the nature of tobacco control efforts across space and time fueled in part by the dialectic relationship between spatial and social segregation, which is discussed more fully later in the chapter.

The concept of *behavior settings* (Fuhrer 1990) seems particularly appropriate here. Behavior settings are culturally constructed but individually mediated interactional and activity microenvironments with

(1) their own cultural codes of conduct (e.g., one behaves differently in a library than in a bar), (2) situational characteristics (e.g., being in a restaurant with a work acquaintance versus with a lover), and (3) temporal variations (organization of the twenty-four hour day, changes in the nature of a setting over time). This allows one, firstly, to close the gap between psychology, geography, and sociology through careful specification of the parameters and roles of behavior settings in terms of individually apprehended reality and the denotative geography and topography of the setting (Fuhrer 1990) and, thus, secondly, to identify and account for behavior settings in which smoking is socially constructed as more or less permissible (e.g., bars versus maternity wards). One might also investigate how individual biographies (life paths) intersect with particular institutional projects (such as tobacco control) in historically and spatially contingent ways in specific places or locales (c.f. Pred 1986; Giddens 1984). It should also be possible to chronicle and account for changes and spatial/temporal differentiations in the rule structures guiding behavior in public space to which participants must adapt, which signal the contextual embeddedness of lay knowledgeability.

Given the "reasonable" claims of nonsmokers to smoke-free air, many smokers may feel themselves faced with two alternatives. One alternative is to adopt the etiquette of the "considerate" smoker to minimize the effects on others. In much the same way as etiquette books once formalized rules of appropriate public conduct for "women of sophistication" decades ago, smokers themselves have drafted similar "guidelines for the courteous smoker" (Smokers' Freedom Society 1992). Another option open to smokers is to gradually retreat from the public realm altogether. In the Brantford research it was evident that many respondents felt a retreat from the public realm was increasingly being required of them whether they liked it or not. Some foresaw the day when smoking, like sex, would be something that was done in private among consenting adults.

While anticipating further encroachments on their "rights" as smokers, many respondents appeared to "draw the line" at the threshold of private space and the public domain, asserting that what they did in their own home or car was their own business. Given the history of private property rights, individualism, and public responsibilities of citizenship enshrined in North American culture, it is to be expected that one of the primary distinctions governing the categorization of space for smokers is that of public versus private space.

There is an unfortunate irony, however, in the fact that those most heavily exposed to side stream smoke are the family members of heavy smokers and, perhaps, more so as some smokers who retreat from the public realm compensate by increasing their smoking during off-work hours and in private spaces such as the family car and home. Smoking at home is, therefore not just "their own business" but also that of their families, who, it is often expected, voluntarily tolerate greater risks than strangers would be willing to put up with.

Of course, this says little about the organization of space within the home (including the power relations implicated therein) and its relationship to substance abuse (see Lowe, Foxcroft, and Sibley 1993). A recent analysis of 1993 survey data for the province of Ontario indicates that the majority of smokers feel that parents with young children should either limit their smoking to "another part of the house" or not smoke at all (Bondy and Ferrence 1995). Recent small-scale interview and focus group studies with smokers in Ontario suggest that many parents have developed compensatory rules governing where they smoke in the home (e.g., not in the child's room, not in their presence, or not in the house at all) in an attempt to reduce the exposure of their children to second-hand smoke (Bondy et al. 1995; Rhyne 1994) despite research that indicates most of the airborne chemicals other than nicotine associated with smoking are spread relatively evenly throughout the average home even when smoking is restricted to certain rooms (Lofroth 1993).

Another paradox in smokers' claims to personal autonomy in the home and control over private space is that several respondents in the Brantford study also acknowledged not always feeling able to control the smoking of others in their own home. This was particularly true for those who had recently quit and who, as much as they wanted to, were reluctant to ask visiting friends not to smoke for fear of jeopardizing their relationship. A number of respondents in the Brantford study expressed concern that their quitting might come between them and their friends. Interviews conducted with current and former smokers suggested that this could occur in at least three ways: (1) being more edgy as a result of withdrawal symptoms associated with quitting; (2) feeling it is risky to ask friends who visit not to smoke; and (3) reluctance to encourage friends to quit for fear of appearing to "evangelize" to them. The reluctance to alienate smoking friends may create a dilemma for some smokers because the fact that the social network patterns of former smokers more closely approximates that of nonsmokers than of smokers (Ferguson 1987) suggests that former smokers must surround themselves with nonsmokers if they are to maintain abstinence successfully.

If rules and social norms guiding behavior in public and private space seem convoluted, in a state of flux, and even contradictory, then those pertaining to the contested territory of privately owned but publicly used spaces are potentially even more problematic. The law currently gives the private owners of publicly used areas such as shopping malls sweeping legal powers to detain and deport people (such as loitering teenagers, panhandlers, and the homeless) who are perceived to be threatening to the sanitized middle-class atmosphere the owners deem most conducive to profitable business (Hopkins 1993). Assumptions about the inherent rights that should be accorded to the economically advantaged (property owners) are deeply embedded in the collective Western psyche. Survey research suggests that a majority (smokers and nonsmokers) consider the responsibility of designating nonsmoking floor space in restaurants (and stores) to be the appropriate purview of owners/managers and their clientele rather than government (Pederson et al. 1986, 1987). The same polls show that if the impetus were to come from government, respondents preferred that it come from *local* government rather than from provincial or federal authorities. Although no explanation for this was provided, it is noteworthy that the role of local government has been increasing as both an object and an agent of regulation in many areas of public policy, which may have contributed to uneven public policy development between municipalities (Goodwin, Duncan, and Halford 1993) in tobacco control as in other issues.

In light of these considerations I focus in the next section on the more *formal* regulation of public behavior in the form of legislation and examine the nature of restrictions governing where people can smoke as an extension of class-based conflicts over the purification of public space.

The Regulation of Public Behavior: Social Class and the Appropriation of Public Space

Restrictions on smoking are consistent with—and an outgrowth of—a long history of the regulation of public behavior and of the regulation of the body (c.f. Turner 1987), defining and controlling that which is normal or socially acceptable. Legal (and social) sanctions prohibiting such acts as public nudity, loud noise, and the use of skateboards apply to public parks and other spaces. Insofar as public spaces are created and maintained in the interest of public welfare, then restrictions on noxious behaviour that might impede other people's enjoyment of those areas seem logical and consistent with an interest in the public good. Further, insofar as environmental tobacco smoke (ETS) can be shown to be deleterious to the health of nonsmokers (Chilmonczyk et al. 1993; Dayal at al. 1994), such restrictions are consistent with a history of public health legislation governing restaurant food quality and other aspects of commercial and private activity that might compromise public health. At the same time one paradoxical outcome of such legislation is frequently the systematic (if unintentional) exclusion of certain "less socially desirable" groups (groups of teenagers, vagrants, informal retailers, alcoholics, the elderly) from many public spaces, in part because legislation tends to enshrine white adult middle-class etiquette as the yardstick of socially acceptable behavior.

Sibley describes the purification of space as involving the "rejection of difference and securing of boundaries to maintain homogeneity" (1988, 409). He argues that the tendency toward social, economic, and geographic segregation of social groups from one another (particularly acute in large urban centers in North America today) feeds on itself in that "distancing and a narrow range of encounters contribute to the stereotyping of 'others'." Further, "nonconformity is more likely to be recognized in a purified (relatively homogeneous) than in a heterogeneous community" (Sibley 1988, 418–19). Generally, the middle-class and economic/political elites also live in a healthier set of environments in which second-hand smoke becomes an issue of relative importance compared to those who live and work in generally unhealthy or oppressive conditions. Moreover, fewer of the middle and upper classes smoke so that by virtue of being less common, smoking appears less socially acceptable to them and even becomes, in the minds of many, a marker of low social standing (for them, stigmatizing). Each of these factors contributes to the accentuation of "difference" based on class and to efforts to secure this difference in territorial terms as a distancing from the 'other.' A dialectical relationship between spatial and social segregation develops that contributes to the purification of public space.

Although these factors may contribute to the declining social acceptability of smoking and, hence, are applauded by public health advocates, they also raise fundamental questions about who controls public space and to what ends and, therefore, who controls the power relations implicated in (and social control overtones behind) the antismoking movement. Social groups have different degrees of access to power to shape the nature of legal controls over the use of public space. Control in this context may be defined as "the ability of an individual or group to gain access to, utilize, influence, gain ownership over, and attach meaning to a public space" (Francis 1990, 158). The gender and class dimensions of the purification of public space may be profound and should be investigated more thoroughly. What follows are speculations about what may be occurring that require empirical validation. It seems safe to assume that groups of lower socioeconomic status (SES) generally have less access to recreational space than do their higher SES counterparts, are more likely to rent than to own accommodations, and, therefore, rely (perhaps disproportionately) on public space for a variety of functions, including much of their social interaction. For example, they may not have comfortable suburban homes with separate living rooms or private yards in which to entertain friends and instead rely on local coffee shops, malls, and parks as social meeting places. Consider former psychiatric patients (the majority of whom smoke), some of whom must vacate lodging homes during daytime hours and, hence, in winter rely on indoor publicly used spaces available to them. The poor elderly, rooming house occupants, many youths, and others with limited access to private space are other examples of groups who may rely disproportionately on public space for social interaction. Some of those most in "need" of indoor public space may be among those hardest hit by the restrictions. In these cases restrictions on smoking may *in effect,* although probably not by intent, discriminate by socioeconomic status.

Some other (very smokey) indoor areas that have hitherto escaped regulation (with respect to smoking), however, such as bars and bingo halls are less-frequented by middle-class families and are the behavior settings in which smoking is the most permissible socially. In addition, many people in nonprofessional and trade occupations (e.g., painters, construction workers) work in environments that are not regulated or easily regulatable because, in at least some of these cases, they do not occupy on an ongoing basis a shared (indoor) space that can be regulated formally through the legal system.

These discrepancies and variations in the spatial coverage of formal tobacco control legislation, exemplary as they are of the contingent nature of social control pointed to by critical legal geographers (e.g.,

Clark 1989a; Blomley 1994), may, to an extent, be the result of political expediency. Regulations are predictably created first where one has the most support, in other words, where the majority are nonsmokers, in spaces occupied by middle-class professionals (such as office buildings), and so on. It may prove to have been much easier to create nonsmoking environments for nonsmokers than to do so for smokers, many of whom encounter smoking in the home, with peers, and among relatives in ways that nonsmokers typically do not.

It is noteworthy in this regard that different social groups may vary considerably in their norms and expectations about the control of public space. According to research conducted by Lee (1972), the middle class tends to view public space as not for the appropriation of any one group and prefers to rely on formal modes of social control based upon notions of public morality and bolstered by the law and its enforcers. Lower-income groups, however, were reported to view public space as regulated informally rather than through external agents such as the police; in other words it was expected that people would watch out for themselves. Furthermore, in order to be comfortable, it was seen as entirely appropriate (perhaps necessary) that each group have its own space.

Whenever power is exercised by one group over another, the possibility of resistance is created (Eakin et al. 1994; Clark 1994). One might well ask what spaces are appropriated by smokers in light of their retreat from the workplace and many public places. To quote from Warf (1991, 568) "space is pregnant with conflict." Cast out of these spaces, some feel like outcasts. Yet camaraderie develops among some "deviants" thrown together in this process that is described by Goffman (1963b) and by a number of smokers in the Brantford study (e.g., the quote earlier in the chapter about "hanging out with the other lepers"). In fact, recent tobacco industry advertising has begun to use ads that not only empathize with the plight of the "banned" smoker but appear also to portray the camaraderie of "outsidership" as a new "cool" rebellious identity (Mahood 1994).

Given intergroup conflicts over the control of public space, tobacco control may be one example of a wider issue of *territoriality*, which can be defined as "the attempt by an individual or group to affect, influence, or control people, phenomena, and relationships, by delimiting and asserting control over a geographic area" (Sack 1986, 19). Territoriality involves specification of an area, communication of the restrictions (e.g., sign), and enforcement (or threat thereof).

Johnston (1990) has argued that the ability of the state (and its agencies) to control the behaviors of its citizenry resides largely in its sovereign power within bounded territories to enact and enforce legal rules of conduct. Thus, the power of the state is inextricably linked to place. Territorial approaches to social control are relatively ubiquitous in capitalist society as the institutionalization of human relations in space (Sack 1986). In fact, it has been argued that as urban societies become more complex and impersonal, formalized regulations gradually replace informal social sanctions on public behavior and become enshrined in law (Black 1989). Furthermore, it has been suggested that territorial approaches to social control focus attention away from the *exercise* of power to the (spatial) objects of its control (Sack 1986), obscuring the interests vested in social control. The relationship between controller and controlled is depersonalized when territories appear to be doing the controlling ("this is not allowed here," rather than "I say that you cannot") (Johnston 1990).

Of course, this approach to social control via legal control of spaces arises as a strategy to "manage" issues that have been defined as "public problems," which themselves share a number of characteristics (Smith 1988): (1) they are problems that are no longer considered only "private" and are, therefore, the subject of state intervention, (2) they involve some degree of stigma, (3) their definition and interpretation is relative and contextual, (4) they are often persistent over time (despite often massive intervention), wherein the management of public problems has become "a major growth industry," (5) etiological explanations traditionally locate causal factors within the individual, and (6) they are often highly interrelated (concentrated in a few urban locations and population subgroups). Smoking has clearly become one such "public problem."

It is noteworthy that not only are smoking restrictions highly selective but their implementation (interpretation and enforcement) is variable between and within municipalities and across provincial jurisdictions within Canada as well. This variablility is not just in terms of "local legal cultures" but also at a microsocial level, dependent on the interactional context and behavioral setting, as discussed above. It is, therefore, crucial that one understand space as a medium of social interaction and not just as a passive container (cf. Sayer 1984; Thrift 1983). One is led to concur with Kearns (1993) that what is required is a reconstituted geography of health that inserts *place* back into the experience (and production) of health and illness and the time-space "distanciation"

(Giddens 1984) of the activities of public health professionals as "moral entrepreneurs" (Becker 1973; Pfuhl and Henry 1993).

Conclusion

It appears that in an attempt to control smoking behavior public space is manipulated by those with the power selectively to regulate tobacco use in certain places but that despite their apparent success in reducing unwanted exposure to ETS or in reducing smoking itself (1) these measures may not be evenly or consistently distributed with respect to social class and (2) they may contribute to the stigmatization of smoking (and, by extension, of smokers) as a form of social control over tobacco use. It is, therefore, possible that the nature and implementation of tobacco control activities in space and time has contributed, albeit inadvertently, to the intensification of existing inequalities at several levels. These inequalities may also be gendered and ethnically concentrated and pertain, in part, to the clustering of smokers (and of microsocial environments conducive to smoking) in economically and educationally disadvantaged groups. This concentration, in turn, is capitalized upon by the tobacco industry, which plays up the countercultural (somewhat outside the mainstream, but still "hip") connotations of smoking. Furthermore, geosocial irregularities in the application of healthy public policy (not only between but within municipalities and between different types of behavior settings) also contribute to social class differences in the impacts of tobacco control. Goffman's work on stigma can also be employed to consider the nature of the lived experience of tobacco control by smokers in daily life as the production and management of stigma.

My purpose in this chapter has been to explore some of the spatial dimensions of tobacco control in Canada. To determine whether these conclusions can be substantiated it will be necessary to conduct further empirical research to (1) explore in greater detail, from a phenomenological perspective, the daily lived experiences of smokers vis à vis tobacco control and (2) to investigate potential class biases in the sociogeographic distribution of restrictions (and their impacts) within and between municipalities, work sites, and other behavior settings.

12

"Going It Alone"

Place, Identity, and Community Resistance to Health Reforms in Hokianga, New Zealand

ROBIN A. KEARNS

Nau te rourou, naku te rourou, ka ora ai te iwi
(With your basket and my basket we will ensure that the people will live)
—Traditional Maori Proverb

My purpose in this chapter is to examine the relationships between sense of place, communal identity, and health service provision with reference to a specific geographical context (the Hokianga region of northern New Zealand) and a specific historical event (mobilization against the national health reforms). The chapter extends earlier work, examining the relationships between health care services and the meaning of place in this relatively "remote," historically significant, and predominantly Maori area of New Zealand (R. A. Kearns 1991).

Hokianga is but one of many rural communities in New Zealand acutely affected by a range of processes associated with economic and service sector restructuring. Within these "changing places" (Britton, Le Heron, and Pawson 1992) most residents must now travel further for basic service provision as a result of the state and the private sector rationalizing their organization and modes of delivery (Joseph and Chalmers 1995). Whereas most landscapes of opportunity have contracted, in a minority of places rural restructuring has led to enhanced political, economic, or social opportunities for communities that have responded to and reinterpreted new national ideologies of entrepreneurship. The variable effects of restructuring have, therefore, meant that the prevailing senses of place in many communities have themselves been restructured and transformed.

In this chapter I describe Hokianga as an example of a community mobilizing around impending losses in access to and symbolic ownership of local health services. This example of health care in a remote region of New Zealand provides a "lens" through which more general relationships between place, health, and social process can be examined. The central questions addressed in the chapter are (1) How can health services reflect and, in turn, be influenced by the characteristics of place? and (2) What are the preconditions for in-place social action in response to threats to health services?

The information for this chapter was collected during a series of visits to the study area over a six-year period (1988–94). During this time an attempt was made to follow the lead of other geographers who have sought an intimate understanding of people, place, and health (e.g., Cornwell 1984). Given the importance of social scientists constructing narratives *with* rather than simply *about* social groups (Kearns 1994), liaison was established with community leaders and health service providers before an initial month-long period of fieldwork in 1988. Return visits were made over the following years and, as trust was built up, informal interviews and access to minutes of the Hokianga Health Enterprise Trust allowed the retelling of a story[1] that amounts to a singular event in the history of the New Zealand health reforms—a community "going it alone" against the tide of restructuring.

The remainder of the chapter is organized as follows: In section 2 I develop a theoretical context for communities mobilizing in defense of service provision. In section 3 I outline the empirical context for the study: New Zealand and its recent health reforms. In section 4 I turn to the Hokianga case study, examining the sociogeographic character of the area, its health services, and recent community resistance to the health reforms. In the last section I reflect on the study and explore general conclusions that can be drawn from the discussion.

1. According to Rosenau (1994), this process of storytelling is an activity more suited to postmodern social science than to conventional (rational) notions of "research."

Structure, Agency, and Community Change

Victories of human agency against the odds of structure may be uncommon and small-scale, but for health care consumers the struggle to redefine and "own" their health services is both predictable and understandable. For a "central dynamic in life is the innate human tendency to strive for security and status, and to protect those gains that have already been achieved" (Dear and Wolch 1989, 8). With respect to health care "gains" can be appropriate and manageable services, and peoples' identity, according to Dear and Wolch, can be projected onto institutional structures in a community setting so that "people vie for the perpetuation of the institutions as much as for their own self-survival" (Dear and Wolch 1989, 8). In unusual circumstances profound changes to the structure of the social relations of service provision may be won through the autonomous actions of key individuals and social movements. The net result is what Dear and Wolch call *transcendental social action,* a change to the status quo that is sufficient to alter the practices of restructuring by the state and to introduce new ways of structuring local social life.

Dear and Wolch (1989) describe transcendental social action as being precipitated by *crises*-threats to the *economic* wellbeing, *political* legitimacy, or *social* status of groups or communities. For territorially based health "consumers" faced with the impending effects of national health reforms, all three types of threats can be interpreted as converging in the form of a crisis faced by their health services. This convergence might occur given that *local* services potentially have a threefold role: first, they contribute to economic security (for instance, through providing employment and being inexpensive to reach); second, they can embody political identity (for instance, health care can be an outcome of struggle or can have been developed in response to local geography and social needs); and third, services may also address the social deprivations and aspirations of constituent communities of interest.[2]

2. I use the term *community* because this is how Hokianga people describe themselves. I acknowledge, however, following Anderson (1983), that community is an "imagined" construct and there will always be multiple communities of interest, even within an apparently unified geographical and social "community." These communities of interest might be defined by gender (e.g., womens' health centers), class (e.g., trade union health clinics), or ethnicity (e.g., services tailored to the needs of racialized groups).

What might be the preconditions for transcendental social action in the domain of rural health care? First, it is likely that a strong sense of place is a prerequisite to a community challenging political structures in the face of threats to its services. Although most sense of place studies have been based on perception (Ley 1983), I have argued that an exploration of sense of place grounded in experience can provide the basis for research on the relationships between health services and the health of places (Kearns 1991). A strong communal set of shared values and a recognition of the way those values are shaped by and themselves influence the social and physical landscape is likely to provide a basis for defense or even redefinition of *turf*. Defense, however, cannot develop in the abstract. Rather, it requires the insights, strategies, and actions of individuals—people we might call "social entrepreneurs" who can provide leadership through discerning and synthesizing the views of the community and adding a measure of their own political philosophies.

These two preconditions (the presence of strong sense of place and social entrepreneurs) are interdependent as can be illustrated through an extension of Eyles's (1985) thinking. A person's *place-in-the-world* and his experience of an on-the-ground locality are mutually reinforcing aspects of not only a sense of place but also, to a degree, of health itself. Thus, some residents of rural communities gain a measure of their sense of belonging and well-being through proximity to and involvement with health services. Bereft of such key elements of the symbolic landscape and material well-being, the place of a rural settlement within a region or nation will be more tenuous, and its economic and social health will be affected (Joseph and Kearns 1996). As argued elsewhere, this reflexive view of place and health equips one to understand better the contribution of health services to the experience of places themselves (Kearns 1991).

Protests over actual or impending intrusions into community life can represent more than a general defense of turf and a specific defense of services. As Apter and Sawa (1984) conclude, issue-based protests can simultaneously be against local impacts *and* against the state ideology that is driving proposed changes. In other words, events affecting communities can be interpreted as symbolic of larger grievances and political issues. The ensuing community action, thus, becomes a "narrative of struggle" (Feinsilver 1993) in which there is a greater symbolism to (health) politics than to local actions in defence of local services.

Typically, community-based struggles for locally defined health care involve a dispute with quintessentially *modern* ideologies: the authority of medicine, the rationality of planning, and the belief in progress held by capitalist societies that centralize services in the name of efficiency and fiscal austerity. The struggle for and defense of local health services could be regarded as evidence of "postmodern consequences" in the social landscape (Dear 1994). This postmodernism of resistance might entail the opposing of modern ideologies with alternative narratives that involve political activism and the goal of erasing "the distinction between expert and the consumer, the physician and the patient" (Rosenau 1994, 308). Although ideas of communal loyalty and unified collective identity are problematic to a postmodern perspective (Bauman 1987), communal action is not impossible. Rather

> postmodern community may belong to people who have very different points of view. They may, for very different reasons, work together on a specific issue of common concern. They may have conflicting opinions on other issues. They may find themselves on opposite sides of issues in the future. But they agree to work together temporarily until their interest in the common issue wanes, the issue is resolved, or they conclude that further efforts are fruitless. (Rosenau 1994, 312)

For a postmodern social movement rallying around health politics "the local and the personal is . . . superior to the broad, the universal, and the general" (Rosenau 1994, 322). One can speculate that place-specific struggles around health service provision carry many of these postmodern characteristics identified by Rosenau but that they may also differ, retaining goals more often associated with modernism: the sense of mission inherent in the social action of Alinsky (1989) or the social justice concerns that have informed both health planning (Reinken, McLeod, and Murphy 1985) and social science (Smith 1994).

Health Care and Restructuring in New Zealand

At an empirical level in this chapter I trace developments in a focal community set within rural New Zealand. Theoretically, the chapter is embedded within a recognition that relationships between space, place, and health (care) need particularly careful examination given the sociopolitical processes occurring in the 1990s (Kearns and Joseph 1993). In different parts of the Western world over the last two decades there have been variable outcomes in human experience. According to Audrey Kobayashi and Suzanne Mackenzie "a continuous restructuring of economic and social conditions seems to restrict options. . . . We seem to have few choices and less space in which to create them . . . (yet) there appear to be more places, more parts of our lives in which we can deliberately act and exercise control" (1989, 3). This contemporaneous and paradoxical sense of restricted options, yet opening opportunities, speaks to the tension between structural forces and human agency that writers such as Giddens (1984) have grappled with. In this section I sketch the national context for health services in Hokianga. Given the local impacts of national *structures* of health reform, this outline provides a prelude to exploring the potential for human *agency* within this institutional context.

Restructuring involves the capitalist state adjusting to changing international circumstances. The effects of this broad set of processes can be found both tangibly inscribed on the landscape and acutely experienced in the lives of individuals, households, and communities. Restructuring takes place in place (Massey 1991), and, therefore, rather than being merely a container for events, locations, and processes, space is the medium through which the character of places is reproduced both in the visible landscape and in the consciousness of individual residents.

• • •

This chapter represents an extension of an earlier call "to understand the processes by which groups in particular places resist change, or attract or repel resources" (Kearns and Joseph 1993, 715). In general terms the health status of local populations and the status of the local health care systems in remote areas of New Zealand have recently been influenced by national restructuring trends in two ways. First, the needs of certain rural populations have changed. Curtailed urban employment opportunities and nationally reduced levels of social welfare benefits since April 1991 have fueled return migration of (particularly Maori) people with rural connections. This trend has placed a burden on local health and social services at the same time as a second restructuring influence on health care has occured—the reduction, centralization, or even closure of local services.

Since the election of a reform-minded Labour government in 1984, successive administrations have sought to gain optimal performance from the New Zealand health care system (Kearns and Barnett 1992). Since the late 1980s it has been argued that public health care services needed to be targeted increasingly to those groups with both high need and limited ability to pay; that state-financed services should be rationalized to yield improved internal economies of scale; and that the shedding of selected state responsibilities through privatization would reduce overall health costs while providing "consumers" with greater choice (Joseph and Chalmers 1995).

The ongoing debate on the restructuring of the health care system in New Zealand has paid more attention to issues of funding and management than to the desirability of particular services and treatments. There were, however, inevitable consequences for the way in which services could be delivered (Joseph and Kearns 1995). In 1993 elected Area Health Boards were replaced by four appointed Regional Health Authorities (RHAs), which would purchase care from "providers" that included clusters of commercially driven public hospitals (known as Crown Health Enterprises) and a range of private (including voluntary) providers (Blank 1994). With the demise of Area Health Boards there were immediate implications for rural communities such as Hokianga; they lost a sense of representation in the process of health policy and resource allocation. From the time the reforms were announced in 1991 it was apparent that decision making would be more distant and would be based on a more competitive and commercial basis than consumers were accustomed to. For rural communities in the north there would now be three higher-order central places in the hierarchy of health politics to deal with: Whangarei, center of Northland Health Ltd., the Crown Health Enterprise; Auckland, center of North Health (the Regional Health Authority); and Wellington, the national capital and seat of the minister of health.

Since announcements of the health reforms, protests precipitated by the threatened or actual closure of small community-based hospitals have been substantial relative to the size of the communities involved echoing similar protests with respect to closure of other public services such as post offices (Pawson and Scott 1992). These actions have demonstrated that the landscape of health care provision has become a "contested terrain" (Kearns, 1993). The political and academic discourse generated by this disquiet, however, has seldom considered the local meanings ascribed to health care by local users. A necessary prerequisite to interpreting protest is a knowledge of the "stake" that users of health care can feel with respect to their service systems. In rare instances communities have been able to articulate strongly the meaning of their health systems *and* muster sufficient skills and resources to bring about a reversal or transformation of restructuring policy. One such case is that of the Hokianga district of New Zealand.

Place, Health, and Community Mobilization in Hokianga

Hokianga is significant in Maori and *Pakeha* (European) history. It is traditionally recognized as the place at which the Maori explorer Kupe arrived in approximately A.D. 800. Hokianga was also the first place of planned European settlement in Aotearoa,[3] largely through the consent of local *iwi* and *hapu* (tribes and subtribes). Because there has been less land alienation in the Hokianga than elsewhere in New Zealand, local people claim that "there is spirit of one iwi in Maori and Pakeha relationships" (HHET 1994a). The district surrounds the Hokianga harbor and most settlements were at one time reached primarily by water. The isolation of the area is reinforced by the fact that many roads remain unsealed, one in seven households have no car, and public transport is confined to limited schedules on main routes with some communities barely served. It is a very rural area, the largest center being Omapere-Opononi with a population of six hundred. Population density is low, and many people often live far from neighbors and support. Hokianga is also the economically poorest part of the Northland region. Pockets of dairy and beef farming and forestry are profitable, but most work is casual or unwaged (except for state-funded employment in schools and health care) (HHET 1994a). According to the 1991 census, 67 percent of adults were neither employed nor actively seeking work. The per capita income from all sources was $8,035, compared to $12,452 for Northland as a whole.

Despite these indicators of isolation and relative deprivation, Hokianga is the second fastest growing part of Northland. According to the 1991 Census, there was a usually resident population in the Hokianga of 6,147. Although its intercensal growth rate 1976–81 was only 6.3

3. Aotearoa is the generally agreed-upon name given by Maori to what is now known as New Zealand. It has gained some favor as an alternative name for the nation, but as with more localized place names in New Zealand, Aotearoa is a contested term (see Berg and Kearns 1996).

percent, during the period 1981–86, this increased to 20.4 percent and the rate declined only somewhat 1986–91. This population increase is a predominantly youthful one. Young families have returned to their "roots" as a restructured economy has presented fewer opportunities for employment in urban areas (Kearns and Reinken 1994).

Hokianga is also a predominantly Maori area with a majority of the population identifying themselves as Maori. Return migration from urban areas and assisted low-cost housing on collectively owned land through the *papakainga* housing scheme have contributed to a recent increase in population (Davey and Kearns 1994). These changes have strained existing services and highlighted new needs. As return migrants have increased the populations of Hokianga communities, traditional Maori perspectives and practices have remained. The *marae*,[4] for instance, remains the epicenter of both Maori politics and spirituality. This spirituality, which is at once Christian and centered on the physical world, informs local views of health in which tradition adds the spiritual to the familiar World Health Organization (1946) definition ("Health is a 4-sided concept; the spiritual [*taha wairua*], the psychological [*taha hinengaro*], the social [*taha whanau*], and the physical [*taha tinana*]") (HHET 1994a).

Prefiguring assaults on its identity by the health reforms, Hokianga lost its county status in the 1989 local government reforms and is now a ward of the Far North District Council. Health services in the Hokianga have grown to reflect local tradition and identity, dating from Hokianga being the first "special medical area" (SMA) in New Zealand, established in 1947 after an earlier pilot scheme began in 1941. These areas were an initiative of the first Labour government "to encourage doctors to work in areas where private practice is not economically viable" (Health Benefits Review 1986). Generally, they were remote in location and had scattered and often socioeconomically deprived populations. Their introduction was aimed at improving access to health care and as such reflected a remedial response to what has since been identified as the inverse care law: "that the availability of good medical care tends to vary inversely with the needs of the population served" (Hart 1971, 407). Twelve SMAs remained when the health reforms were implemented in July 1993. A key characteristic of SMAs was that, unlike elsewhere in New

4. The *marae* is the sacred house that architecturally and metaphorically embodies tribal ancestors (see Yoon 1986).

Zealand, general practitioners were salaried and health care was provided free of charge to local residents (R. A. Kearns 1991). Although the status of other SMAs is in question, most of the characteristics of the Hokianga SMA remain intact despite Hokianga now "going it alone" with respect to health care provision.

Primary health care is still provided by general practitioners and community health nurses at the health center at Hokianga Hospital (in Rawene) and nine community outpatient clinics. These clinics are located up to fifty kilometers from the hospital, and the distances are exacerbated by poor road conditions and the necessity to cross the Hokianga harbor by vehicular ferry to reach five of the clinics (see fig. 12.1). Despite being distant from higher-order health facilities the

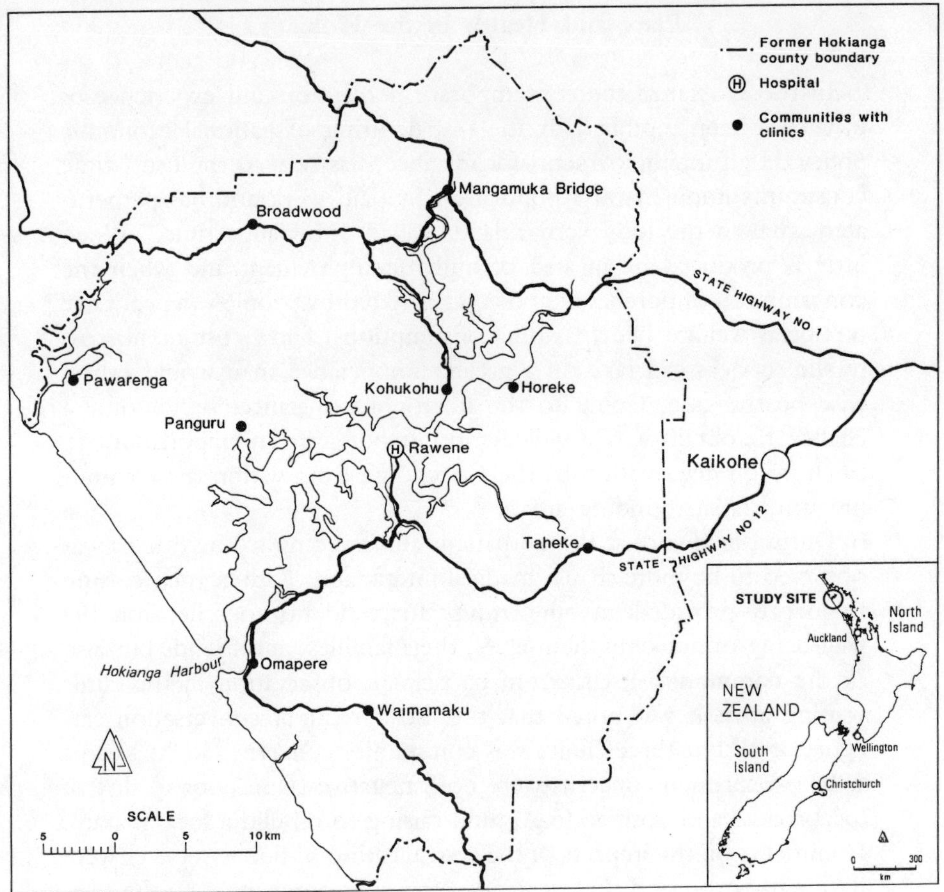

Figure 12.1. Hokianga in its regional context.

Hokianga's health system is appreciated by residents for its informal and available character. People in Hokianga have recognized that appropriate health resources are at their disposal to meet the demands of an isolated rural environment and that their local service system is, to use Antonovsky's (1987) term, highly *manageable*. Indicative of this manageability was the level of protest engendered by 1988 proposals by the Northland Area Health Board (NAHB) to reduce hospital services. The number of individual submissions received by NAHB equaled a total of 17 percent of the entire Hokianga population (NAHB 1988). This high rate of mobilization suggests a recognition by residents that the vitality of their community would be compromised by a reduction of services.

Place and Health in the Hokianga

In the Hokianga the contemporary perception and experience of place has been modified by the restructuring of national economic policy. High unemployment, for instance, has relaxed the usual time constraints imposed on a population by paid work and has perpetuated what in the local vernacular is called "Hokianga time." When little is produced in an area of high unemployment and when the consumption of purchased goods is restricted by people's dependence on social welfare benefits, the consumption of low-cost or no-cost public services can take on a greater importance than would otherwise be the case. Going to the doctor, for instance, is not only a chance to obtain a repeat prescription but also an opportunity to catch up on news with the others attending from within the community and its surrounding area.

During fieldwork at the outpatient clinics going to the doctor was observed to be more than a medical interaction. Rather, the occasion frequently provided an opportunity for residents to reflect on the well-being of not only themselves, their families, and friends but also of the community itself. From participant observation in the clinic waiting areas it was noted that the most frequent conversation category at all but three clinics was community concerns (R. A. Kearns 1991). Expressed concerns were both negative (e.g., poor quality of local roads) and positive (e.g., fund raising to rebuild a local marae). Comments on the impacts of the restructuring of public services were frequently expressed. Conversations focusing on changes to the telephone system, the necessity of inconvenient travel to access banking services, and post office closures represent a frustration with the local impacts of decisions made beyond but affecting daily life within Hokianga communities. Other conversations concerned initiatives arising within the communities themselves and represent attempts to counter the effects of restructuring. These attempts included a local tourism venture, fund raising to send a team to national canoe races, and the building of a garage to house an ambulance. With respect to the last of these concerns, one resident of Mangamuka stated, "It's really pulled the community together after all the layoffs, the post office closure, and losing the bus service." This comment is an example of collective action being interpreted as a palliative to the sense of powerlessness brought about by the experience of restructuring "changing places" (Britton, Le Heron, and Pawson 1992).

The high rate of unemployment in the Hokianga is a factor that facilitates local residents' relaxed approach to clinic attendance and their use of waiting areas as arenas of social interaction. Patients were observed arriving up to forty minutes before their appointment times (sometimes in the company of others who had no intention of consulting the doctor or nurse) and lingering up to twenty minutes afterward, engaging in conversation. The clinics, therefore, function as de facto community centers analogous to the corner pubs or village markets in other countries. The difference, however, is that the place (the clinics) and the time ("clinic day") seemed to prompt a considerable amount of conversation that explicitly centered on health concerns. Two consequences of the decentralized health system in the Hokianga were, therefore, evident: first, the clinics provide public places of interaction and, second, by treating people *in* rather than *away from* places familiar to them the vitality of the place they call home is enhanced (R. A. Kearns 1991).

Community Resistance to Health Reforms

In Hokianga the late 1980s were marked by a relatively unchanged health system embedded within a landscape profoundly changed by economic and service sector restructuring (Kearns and Joseph 1993). The difference to be observed in the 1990s is that national restructuring of the health system has forced local provision of health services to change. Rather than succumbing to national trends such as centralization and managed competition (Malcolm and Barnett 1994), however, and the dissolution of Hokianga as a formal and functional space of health care provision (Moon 1993), a strengthened local ownership of health services has occurred under the impetus of collective action.

The threatened withdrawal of health care services has precipitated a highly spatialized politics of resistance in the area since 1991. As part of the national health reforms, in July 1991 the minister of health issued the "Green and White Paper," which outlined the shift to commercially driven health care provision and the disestablishment of democratically elected Area Health Boards (Upton 1991). These events were anathema to community tradition in Hokianga where residents recognized that the directions of the health reforms would seriously erode the quality of their services and community life. Soon after the minister's paper was issued, a public meeting was called at which about twenty citizens were nominated to form a Community Action Committee (CAC). This group met to read and discuss the document with a view to making a submission with the input of representatives of local Maori political units. As the Hokianga submission was being prepared, an invitation was extended to the minister of health to meet with the committee. It was declined, and instead, the minister's plan to extend pharmacy user charges into SMAs, including Hokianga, became known in November 1991. The Hokianga CAC strenuously opposed this user charge regime, for requiring payment would disrupt the informal system by which medicines were delivered free of charge to isolated settlements under the special area scheme.

It was resolved by the CAC that the "fight should be continued via the media to get support for our case" and that the committee should "show (that) our services are different and cost-effective and that we are not getting more than we are due for." It was also agreed that a case for the exemption of the Hokianga from charges should be made on the basis of "the unique character of the Hokianga special area" and "that pharmaceuticals are a integral part of this" (Community Action Committee 1991). Outlying communities were kept informed by means of local information meetings with interpretation for older Maori who did not speak English. An official response was received through the media from the associate minister of health who encapsulated the government view that "if (the scheme) is that good, then everyone should have it." In other words, whereas local residents argued for retention of special treatment on the basis of precedent and special needs, the state insisted on an equalization of opportunity throughout the nation. In the face of this stalemate a *hikoi tapu* (sacred walk) was planned from Hokianga to Wellington (the capital of New Zealand) with the promised support and participation of the late Dame Whina Cooper, a *kuia* (respected female elder) of national repute. The principal spokesperson for the committee, Father Brian Prendeville, a local Catholic priest, said that the *kaupapa* (purpose) was "the dignity of the person" and an attempt to raise the profile of the Hokianga sufficiently to get the minister to visit the area and meet with the people.[5] New Zealand's highest rated television channel offered to cover the *hikoi* (sacred walk), should it proceed, and in anticipation Pa Brian (Father Brian) appeared on prominent news and talk shows and coverage of the plight of the area's people was provided in a range of national newspapers and magazines. In terms of "symbolic capital" (Feinsilver 1993), the image of a small rural community led by a soft-spoken priest battling an uncaring state rapidly took on David and Goliath proportions in the national consciousness.

Collective Action

As an outcome of its opposition, articulated through a threatened (but ultimately called-off) hikoi, an embarrassed government acquiesced and in December 1991 the CAC successfully negotiated with the minister to institute a pilot program that would involve them holding a budget for Hokianga's total pharmaceutical costs. To undertake budget holding the CAC had to become a charitable trust. The Hokianga Health Enterprise Trust (HHET) was established in January 1992 with two-thirds of its members annually elected to represent clinic areas and an overall goal, "Working Together for Health in the Hokianga." Further avowed priorities echo philosophical influences that range from the World Health Organization, through biculturalism, to community development (table 12.1). Two members were elected from each clinic area and the HHET took on the responsibility to make up any shortfall in pharmaceutical costs from fund raising in the community. In its deed the HHET set itself the

5. This dual purpose (to urge the government to take the needs of the people seriously *and* to have the minister visit the area suggests the duality of protest identified by Apter and Sawa (1984): affront at a local issue (threat to services) *and* toward state ideology (a carefully maintained remoteness from isolated rural areas by politicians).

Table 12.1

Aims of the Hokianga Health Enterprise Trust

Overall goal

Working together for health in the Hokianga

Specific goals

1. Development of the dignity of the person
2. Promotion of good health rather than emphasizing treatment of poor health
3. Continuation of health service preserving integrated service within Hokianga
4. Enhancement and betterment of health services, increasing services in the area
5. No payment at point of need
6. Equity within Hokianga
7. Equity for Hokianga in services both within and outside Hokianga
8. Autonomy and control within Hokianga
9. Putting community first in assessing and providing for peoples' needs

Source: HHET 1992.

goal of preserving the local health care service in the Hokianga and ensuring that no one would be required to pay for their health care at the point of need.

This resolve to maintain free health care was hardened in 1992 when charges for public hospital care were introduced nationally. The HHET took on the responsibility of meeting those charges for the registered patient population. At the minister of health's insistence the HHET enrolled all Hokianga residents, and many offered *koha* (a freely given gift in cash or kind) in return for membership (Kearns and Reinken 1994). A concern raised by the then Department of Health was Should budget holding proceed, what would be appropriate uses of surplus funds? The research manager for the trust responded that such monies, if and when they became available, would be devoted to such community health needs as smoking cessation programs and patient transport. Clearly, the trust viewed health care services as a necessary, but not sufficient, element of community health.

Within the first month 167 individuals were enrolled, and of these 47 gave koha in cash and another 20 gave in kind (e.g., food for the hospital kitchens). These initially low enrollments were supplemented by vigorous publicity in school and community newsletters, radio advertisements, and house-to-house visits by trustees. By the end of February 1992 enrollment had risen to 355 families. Extra koha was raised by means of a charity concert and a Health Festival held at the Rawene school grounds in March 1992. By August a telephone appeal and the placement of forms at local postal agencies for incoming residents to complete had raised enrollment to 7,800.

Late in 1992 the HHET sought guarantees from the Establishment Board of the Northland Crown Health Enterprise (CHE) that existing services would remain in Hokianga, and the absence of charges would continue. No such guarantee was received. The HHET then began to prepare to take over running the health services as an independent organization. This resolve to "go it alone" precipitated a crisis of definition for the trust. In November 1992 a special meeting was held "to investigate and evaluate options for the future role of the HHET." Nine possibilities were identified, including disestablishment of the trust; redefinition as a community trust;[6] and functioning "as a fund holder for the Health Care of the Hokianga people" (HHET 1992). The first option was dismissed as the lowest priority, and the second was seen as irrelevant because Hokianga Health service was not unprofitable. It was, therefore, the third option that captivated the collective imagination in Hokianga.

A quest for self-determination and the continued health of the community lies at the heart of this redefinition phase of the HHET. In opting to "go it alone" the HHET was eschewing being at the mercy of two higher-order centers in the health policy hierarchy: Wellington, the seat of national government and the minister of health; and Whangarei, center of the commercially driven Northland CHE. The disapproval of the former was already evident with the refusal of the minister to visit and the need for a threatened hikoi. The latter

6. The government had identified the role of these entities as taking over the running of unprofitable hospitals.

was also disapproving; representatives of the CHE were vigorous in their opposition to Hokianga's intention to secede from within its region, especially when the CHE would otherwise be inheriting Hokianga's health service assets from the former Northland Area Health Board.

A breakthrough for the trust came in the following months (December and January 1992–93) when visiting policy planners of the Auckland-based Regional Health Authority expressed sympathy for its goals and indicated the possibility of the HHET becoming budget-holder for a wide range of health care functions. Thus, despite the opposition from the subregional state *provider* of health care (Northland Health Limited, the CHE) there was support from the regional *purchaser* of services, North Health (the northern RHA). Hauora Hokianga fostered this enthusiasm, seeing itself as offering the RHA "an opportunity to test one of the options envisaged in the 1991 health reforms" (self-provisioning) (HHET 1994a). A cautious acceptance of this opportunity ensued. The potential for symbolic capital to be made from this support, however, was recognized by the trustees. In the context of widespread opposition to the national health reforms the state (through one of its RHAs) could potentially be seen in a more positive light if it supported the aspirations of a remote, predominantly Maori area. According to the HHET spokesperson, "The RHA wants positive publicity, but we must have the high ground. We must not let the government take the credit" (HHET 1993).

In June 1993 immediately before implementation of the national health reforms that would formally establish CHEs and RHAs meetings were held to formalize separation of Hokianga from the Northland CHE (the provider) and to begin formulation of a contract directly with the Auckland-based RHA (the purchaser). A policy planner with the former Northland Area Health Board who had lived in Hokianga and whose political beliefs had shaped a wide range of involvements in environmental and community groups was appointed as CEO. Her presence in this key position complemented other key agents of change in the Hokianga such as the Catholic priest whose views were steeped in liberation theology, the medical director who had worked in underdeveloped countries, and the research manager whose views on social justice had informed her coauthorship of an influential report to the Department of Health (Reinken, McLeod, and Murphy 1985). Although these articulators of a new vision for health in the Hokianga were all Pakeha, their empathies were very much aligned with the majority Maori population and the trust membership. This lack of Maori/Pakeha distinction epitomized Hauora Hokianga being conceived of as a bicultural health service by and for all people of the Hokianga in both policy and practice.

The culmination of the struggle to "go it alone" occurred 1 July 1993 when the associate minister of health, Maurice Williamson, formally handed over the assets of the Hokianga Health Services (e.g., plant, equipment, hospital, vehicles, clinics, and linen) to the chair of the trust, a local Maori elder, Chris Diamond. The handover was associated with the establishment of an annually renewable contract with the RHA. The contract initiated a uniquely responsive health service in which "policy and future directions are set by the Trust in partnership with the health professionals. Issues are brought back to the communities frequently while community concerns are brought forward to the Trust's monthly meetings" (HHET 1994a, 4). An expansion of the HHET's mandate to recognize that health is larger than health services immediately preoccupied the trust. Three examples indicate the breadth of their deliberations: first, the trust considered a proposal to take over the administration of twenty-eight pensioner housing units within the Hokianga from the Far North District Council to better integrate housing and health services to local elderly; second, the trust considered obtaining a house in Whangarei and/or Auckland for Hokianga people to use when they and their families have to travel to higher-order hospital facilities; third, the HHET entered the field of health promotion, donating monies for local sports groups to bear healthy messages (e.g., caps bearing a "smokefree" message for the Opononi swimming team and jackets for the rugby team). During its monthly meetings, which according to Maori tradition begin and end with *karakia* (prayer), the trust, therefore, continued the tradition of health in the Hokianga by attempting to help Hokianga people access and expand their health service options. The Trust resolved to pay the ferry fares of any residents from the north side of the harbor who needed to visit the hospital. A proposal that a *whare rongo o Hokianga* (house of traditional Maori healing) be established in Hokianga received support from the trust, including the medical director.

In the two years since "going it alone" Hokianga has not been an outlier in the landscape of health care provision in New Zealand. Rather Hauora Hokianga has become central to an emerging network of community-controlled organizations. In 1994 the trust's CEO became chair of an organization (Healthcare Aotearoa), which also includes trade union clinics and Maori initiatives. The trust, therefore, sees itself as an example to other groups who seek to assert difference and autonomy in their health services. According to the research manager, "the people of Hokianga received much support from the public during the period of 'fighting' for our hospital, and we now have an obligation to help other organisations to regain control over their health services" (HHET 1994b). As a budget-holder responsible for sustaining its own resources, the trust has also had to embrace tough decisions based on efficiency. In 1994 an internal review identified an oversupply of domestic staff, and during the subsequent rationalization personnel were redeployed and took voluntary severance. In the immediate term these events indirectly led to the resignation of a trustee and generated a broader feeling of disquiet concerning a mismatch between the practices and the philosophy of the trust. As with other "counter-cultural" health organizations such as hospices, the test of endurance for the HHET will be maintenance of its radical vision within the financial and institutional constraints imposed by its wider operating environment (Field and Johnson 1993).

Health, Place, and the Assertion of Difference

Much medical geography has been and remains fundamentally positivist in approach and based on the assumption that discrete classes of phenomena such as hospitals, regions, or patients can be identified. Under the impetus of humanist and, more recently, feminist and postmodern perspectives space for difference and uniqueness has progressively been made within the subdiscipline. Most of this "making space for difference" (Kearns 1995) has involved a greater recognition of the distinctiveness of the lives, health needs, and health status of individuals. In this chapter I have outlined the recent history of a distinctive locality and event in New Zealand: Hokianga's assertion of "otherness" through its resistance to the centralizing and commercializing implications of the health reforms in New Zealand. To this extent the chapter has been a contribution to a "post-medical geography of health" (Kearns 1994) that connects with wider issues of health and place such as social welfare and the sustainability of communities.

I have outlined the transformation of a community protest at the locally felt implications of the national health reforms in New Zealand into a situation in which a community group now runs its own health service. Whereas the initial protest concerned impending intrusions upon local life and sense of place, a second and more subtle objective of the protest—at least among some activists—was the ideology of the reforms themselves. Public hospitals, for instance, were to become Crown Health *Enterprises* mandated to return a profit, and Hokianga's community hospital and primary health services were in danger of being absorbed into such a structure. The struggle *for* the integrity of a locally defined system became, following Apter and Sawa (1984), an issue-based protest symbolic of a larger grievance, the struggle *against* an ideology of market-based health care.

In the symbolic politics of resistance the struggle to retain public health services in Hokianga has centered on an alternative definition of public to that held by the state. Instead of being fee-paying "consumers" all Hokianga residents would continue to have a stake in service delivery, and any financial returns from the health service would (ideally) be returned to the welfare of the community. These concerns reflect community abhorrence of an encroaching commercial ethos in health services and a preference for guardianship of health, place, and local tradition (Jacobs 1992). The maintenance of the guardian function is possible through the creation of a "commercial envelope" (Allan 1994) comprising the CEO and her financial staff around other trust activities; the medical staff and trustees are, thus, left to be guardians of the people and the health traditions of the place.

The labor of identifying all Hokianga residents and assuring them of the need for and viability of the local health services has made the transformation of Hauora Hokianga a truly community enterprise. Although the process of resistance to health reforms in the Hokianga is not unique, the outcome—a community administered health trust—is. Other community-controlled health organizations exist, but Hokianga remains the only geographically based health trust that serves all the people in its area. The passage from protest group to autonomous service provider is, therefore, a singular event in the history of health service provision in New Zealand in that aspects of this event cannot be accounted for by conclusions or expectations developed elsewhere (Johnston 1989). The cycle of the state reproducing its terms of health service provision in the tangible landscape was broken in Hokianga and an autonomous health service was developed through a subtle combination of preexisting conditions (e.g., holistic Maori health perspectives, Special Medical Area status) and the beliefs and actions of key agents whose commitment to social justice, biculturalism, and the health of the community itself was sufficiently strong to propel them into activism. For these social entrepreneurs "going it alone" in the Hokianga has been a process replete with symbolism and one in which Maori perspectives of health legitimized and extended their own preexisting views. In combination traditional Maori and contemporary Pakeha views were countercultural to the prevailing market ideology of the state.

To what extent do recent events in Hokianga epitomize a process by which "health politics meets postmodernism" (Rosenau 1994)? Certainly those in the district who articulated a new vision of health for the people were following a postmodern trend by questioning authority, "progress," and the imposition of a singular point of view in terms of health services (Rosenau 1994). In common with feminist, environmentalist, and peace movement struggles the philosophy and actions of the HHET embody hope and optimism for the future, which is reflected in Hauora Hokianga being self-designated a "center of excellence" in its literature (HHET 1994a). Further, the commitment of the HHET to increase peoples' capacity to act, to an acceptance of "otherness" (evidenced in biculturalism), and to support for difference in health practices (seen in acceptance of an indigenous healing clinic) are all characteristics that resonate with interpretations of postmodernism.

In important ways, however, the Hokianga experience departs from postmodern tendencies. There is no evidence of the ephemerality of collective action described by Rosenau (1994) as characterizing postmodern social action. Rather the transformation of a Community Action Committee into a trust and its subsequent employment of a CEO indicate the contrary—that this popular movement is committed to the longer term. Nor is there a multiplicity of nonprivileged plans and perspectives that often characterizes postmodern social movements (Rosenau 1994); rather a consensually developed mission statement and strategic plan guides the trust (HHET 1994a). These marks of assuredness and consensus represent traces of modernism that characterize models of community (health) development and social action (Alinsky 1989).

Could it be argued that with the legitimacy bestowed by a contract with the state HHET is sufficiently wedded to the formal health care system to no longer represent a resistance health movement? There is too much space for "difference" in the philosophy of Hauora Hokianga vis à vis the state to sustain such a view. As the only area-based community-owned provider of health care in New Zealand, the HHET has filled a critical role in challenging the rationality and assumptions of the national health reforms. A preferable interpretation is that the future of locality-based health service initiatives lies ultimately between modernism and postmodernism (Berg 1993). Goals of progress and consensus together with a commitment to medicine and dialogue with the state will likely coexist with resistance, the ambiguity of health, and the celebration of difference. To use Feinsilver's (1993) phrase events in the Hokianga constitute a "radical text" in which the symbolic identity of the community has been galvanized through a reassertion of collective values (e.g., prayer before meetings, gift giving, tolerance of diversity) within the health care context.

As advocates of the "new" cultural geography have asserted, places are not static but are actively invented through human creativity within structural constraints (Anderson and Gale 1992). Hokianga has been (at least partially) reinvented as a place as a result of health care having been a contested terrain in the 1990s. The foregoing events represent reactions to the formal space of provision being threatened with redefinition. Under the SMA scheme boundaries equated the domain of health service provision with visible demarcations in the landscape (mountain ridge lines). Soon after the outline of the (former) local government jurisdiction was removed, the area was to be subsumed in a larger region—the domain of the commercially driven Northland CHE. For Hokianga people their district only made sense when the formal space of administration and service provision was equated with the functional space of everyday life (Moon 1990). The fact that community resistance and mobilization has resulted in Hokianga maintaining a congruence of its formal *and* functional space of health care has meant that an already strong sense of place has locally been galvanized and, through media exposure, confirmed in the national consciousness. To this extent Hokianga provides an example of the efficacy of health services and politics in the wider "health" of the place itself (R. A. Kearns 1991).

13

Place, Participation, and Policy

People in and for Health Care Policy

JOHN EYLES AND ANDREÀ LITVA

In this chapter we examine some of the relationships between places and health care policy. In many publicly funded health care systems, there are crises in the delivery of services. In part, these crises are seen as products of the fiscal crisis of the state in which, for health care, the mismatch of revenues and expenditures is being treated by a range of cost containment strategies: user fees, lengthening waiting lists, ward closures and deinsuring services. But there is also a crisis of accountability in that apparently monolithic, expert-driven institutions, such as medical practice and hospital care, are seen as undemocratic and unresponsive, particularly to local needs and preferences. Such care is often seen as ineffective or unnecessary, out of tune with what are seen locally as perceived costs, benefits, and priorities. It is this aspect of the crisis that we address. We explore some aspects of democratization in health care decision making, especially through the ideas of (citizen) *participation*. We also explore potential bases for such localized decision making in *places*. Finally, we examine the possibilities of formalizing places in decision-making structures through, for want of a better term, regions by which the role of people in and for health care policy is discussed. We elaborate first the contexts of the accountability and cost containment crises, especially with respect to Canada.

Context: Decentralization in Decision Making

As Hurley, Birch, and Eyles (1995) note, decentralization is an emerging theme among health care planners, managers, analysts, and policymakers. District-level planning is seen as key in developing and maintaining primary-care-focused health care systems (WHO 1978). Indeed, among others, the Netherlands, New Zealand, the Scandinavian countries, and the United Kingdom have all tried to implement various degrees of decentralization (see Mills et al. 1990; Broegen and Brommels 1990; Malcolm, 1991). Although there are different visions of decentralized health care systems, all visions share the desire to shift the locus of decision making power to local or regional levels, increasing their scope and autonomy for independent action. Decentralization is perceived as an integral part of increasing citizen participation in decision making and increasing the accountability of planners, managers, and providers to the public. In this section we examine these visions of decentralization and relate them to the plans and strategies in different Canadian provinces before turning to participation itself.

Decentralization is the transfer of authority or dispersal of power in public planning, management, and decision making from national to subnational levels or from higher to lower levels of government (Rondinelli 1981; Mills 1993). It is, therefore, explicitly geographical, especially with respect to publicly funded service delivery systems such as health care. Hence we treat places as a key element in determining the nature and scope of decentralization and participation. But decentralization is a fuzzy concept, well-expressed by Furniss (1974, 959) who argued that it

> may mean the transfer of authority over public enterprises from political officials to a relatively autonomous board; the development of regional economic inputs into national planning efforts; the transfer of administrative functions either downwards in the hierarchy, spatially, or by problem; the establishment of legislative units of smaller size; or the transfer of responsibility to subnational legislative bodies, the assumption of control by more people within an economically productive enterprise, the hope of a better world to be achieved by more individual participation.

We return to the hope, but Mills et al. (1990) identify four different visions and types of decentralization (see also Eyles 1993b). Although these visions do not necessarily reflect different degrees of local autonomy (but often do), they do imply different lines of accountability. First is privatization—the transfer of functions to nongovernment bodies that operate the services on a for-profit or not-for-profit basis.

It is intended to give a strong voice to consumers through markets by encouraging competition for clients or contracts. It is an important element in health care reform in many societies (see Scarpaci 1989) but is beyond the scope of this chapter as government cedes much control (except regulatory framework) to the private sector. Second, delegation is the transfer of managerial responsibility for defined functions to organizations largely outside the control of government with the purpose of bypassing much government regulation and bureaucracy to permit efficient, flexible management. Third, deconcentration is the handing over of some administrative authority to the locally based offices of central government ministries (see Regan and Stewart 1982). It is often used as a strategy to reorganize local services but involves the transfer of administrative rather than political authority. Finally, devolution is the creation or maintenance of subnational levels of government to take on a defined set of functions with substantial independence from the central authority (local or municipal government). Tax-raising powers may be granted, and although accountable to higher levels of government through regulations and statutes, devolved authorities are largely responsible to their local electorates or "constituencies." As Perrow (1977) notes, it is/will always be necessary to centralize to be able to decentralize (i.e., setting the standards so that services in different places are provided at comparable levels). It is devolution that has attracted much attention in health care reform in Canada because of its apparent "populist," people-oriented, democratic, accountable nature.

In this attention many different questions remain, pertaining particularly to the scope of activities to be managed by the devolved authority, to the decision-making structure itself (elected or appointed officials, experts, the balance between providers, payers, patients, and the community at large) and the geographical scale of devolution. In this chapter, the last two of these questions is our primary concern, but it should be noted with respect to the first that a whole series of functions can be considered candidates for devolution. Mills et al. (1990) list nine, namely, legislative, making laws on health matters; revenue raising, determining and implementing the mechanisms for raising money to finance the health care system; policy-making, determining the broad and detailed policies that the system should follow; regulation, indirectly controlling the operation of nongovernmental health care services and providers by administrative mechanisms; management, making decisions on the day-to-day operation of the system; intersectoral collaboration, undertaking joint activities or communicating with other sectors; interagency coordination, linking the activities of agencies and providers together; and training, determining and implementing programs for staff. This list coheres around four core activities (see Hurley, Birch, and Eyles 1995): planning, management, delivery, and funding. Indeed, legislative acts are usually the prerogative of the central authority, whereas regulation is the control of delivery through resource availability and practice guidelines (Eyles 1993b). But the core activities are not unproblematic; funding remains in most societies, with the exception of Scandinavia, largely centralized and delivery, especially in fee-for-service systems such as in Canada, appears to be overdevolved with many local providers.

We should not, further, expect agreement across Canada that devolution is the preferred direction for changing health care delivery systems. Of course, different lines of accountability, predicated on democratization, are only one basis for change. It is, in fact, not the major one, which is the financially straitened times in which nearly all publicly funded health care systems find themselves. If cost control and containment are key, the objectives of the reform agenda are complex, including putting medical care in perspective as one of the many determinants of population health, achieving overall improved efficiency, examining the effectiveness of some medical interventions, and incorporating demands for greater patient and citizen participation in decision making. Thus, in a review of provincial commission reports, Hurley et al. (1993) note the remarkably similar language and rationales of reform, differing mainly in emphasis and degree. Consistently, the authors argue that the existing governance and management structures are outmoded. Restructuring health care will ensure better management which

> will not only contain costs, but will produce and deliver services with improved efficiency in ways more flexible and responsive to community needs. It will improve integration and coordination of complementary and substitutive services, ensuring a full continuum of care available, whenever possible, in a community setting and evaluated according to health outcomes. Finally, there is to be a significant increase in community participation in planning decision for health care. (Hurley et al. 1993, 3)

But how? Three organizational models emerge from the six provinces examined: a centralized system (Manitoba), delegated systems

(Quebec, New Brunswick, and Nova Scotia), and devolved systems (British Columbia and Saskatchewan). In the delegated systems the transfer of managerial responsibility will largely remain under central fiat in New Brunswick, whereas in Quebec and Nova Scotia advisory and planning functions are transferred and there is a rhetoric of increased citizen participation. Quebec's use of such rhetoric has a long history, but meaningful participation has proved difficult to achieve (Godbout and Leduc 1987; O'Neill 1992). These problems may lie in the future for British Columbia and Saskatchewan, which Hurley et al. (1993) see as having the greatest potential for change. But will the devolved authorities have power to allocate real resources? Touhy and Evans (1984) provide a salutory tale from previous reforms in Ontario. And will a policy process be put in place that generates sufficient information to make decisions and the ability to use it effectively (Lomas 1990; Hurley, Birch, and Eyles 1995)? Will devolved systems work with centralized control over expenditures and "closed-budget" methods of funding? Although closed regional or sectoral envelopes seem necessary to ensure cost control measures, devolved authorities may be granted the power to allocate resources within broad budgets (e.g., health care and social and community services). With allocation comes the need and basis for strong accountability. In Saskatchewan and British Columbia that accountability is both to the provincial government and to the citizens of districts. And this returns one to the hope of decentralization in the form of devolution—that it will increase accountability of the funding, management, provision, and delivery of health care services by democratizing decision making through increased citizen participation, which, we argue, must be based on appropriate geographical units, or places. We, thus, return to the last two questions raised early in this section: Who is the decision-making authority (the issue of participation)? and To where does devolved authority pertain (the issue of place)?

Participation

It is possible to examine the issue of participation normatively (who should participate) and positively (who does participate). Answers to the question Who participates in elections and other issues of citizen concern (highway construction, neighborhood planning, consultations)? may provide a pointer to the likely success of widespread recruitment for participants in health care decision making. In fact, most of the time a majority of people do not participate in politics. Yet local self-government is seen as desirable if not absolutely necessary to democracy (De Tocqueville 1945; Mill 1958). Normatively, then, everyone should participate. Popular control is the cornerstone of democracy. By sharing in government individuals accept its results and are able to recognize the just needs and demands of others as well as their own (Pateman 1970; Hill 1974). Participation is, thus, educative and community based. But it is well known that if voter turnout is the main indicator of the level of local public participation, then local government is on shaky ground in most democracies (Verba et al. 1978; Barnes, Kaase, and Allerbeck 1979; Higgins 1986; Parry, Moyser, and Day 1992). Yet it is of the greatest importance. Nonelectoral participation is seen as "a potent force: leaders respond to it" (Verba and Nie 1972, 336). It is, of course, not a fault-free democratic ideal, particularly because it is skewed toward the more affluent and the better educated (Smith 1975; Jones and Eyles 1977; Parry, Moyser, and Day 1992). Verba et al. (1993) have shown that different issues attract participation by different socioeconomic groups with the disadvantaged and those relying on state benefits overwhelmingly concerned with basic human needs. In health promotion the young, the better educated, those with high family incomes, and those aware of health risks and possible interventions are more likely to participate (Mettlin et al. 1985; Zakus and Hastings 1988). There is some evidence, however, of a wider demographic spread of participation by age, sex, and race (Bracht and Gleason 1990).

Why is its value of great importance, given this low-turnout and skewed uptake? Part of the answer is already given in the responses of elites to such pressure. If we adopt a broad definition such as that of Verba and Nie (1972, 2) that "participation refers to those activities by private citizens that are more or less directed at influencing the selection of government personnel and/or the actions they take" or Parry, Moyser, and Day (1992, 16) that it involves "taking part in the processes of formulation, passage and implementation of public policies [through] action by citizens which is aimed at influencing decisions which are, in most cases, ultimately taken by public representatives and officials," we again see citizen participation as key for democratic decision making. It provides a check on the power of local elites—the role of influentials (Hunter 1953; Kaplan 1967; Higgins 1986). It also captures concerns in what were perceived to be traditional checks and balances. Thus, Langton (1978) provides three reasons to rationalize the formalization of citizen participation: the decline of traditional mediating institutions between governments and citizens, especially the decline of political parties (one may see this as a crisis in the legitimacy of representation); the rise of bureaucratic decision making as discretion given to bureaucrats and experts by legislators has increased while populist resentment has questioned the competence of such experts (the crisis in accountability and also in trust, see Giddens 1991); and change in public values, especially the desire to control government decisions and to contribute meaningfully to substantive arenas of policy, a crisis in legitimacy (see Habermas 1976).

Participation is, thus, seen as addressing these crises through marshaling what Parry, Moyser, and Day (1992) cogently call "the impulse to participate." Four justifications for citizen participation are presented. First is the instrumentalist argument that it is intended to promote or to defend the goals of participants. Although at first sight this would appear to regard self-interest as sufficient motivation, collective interests and with them community involvement, civic pride, obligation, altruism, and a culture of responsibility may also be implicated. Interesting in this regard is Putnam's (1993) study of regional government in Italy, which shows that its success was largely dependent upon "civicness," a collective and communal sense of obligation found within some but not all subcultures. This points toward the second justification, communitarianism (a concern for the community of which one is a part). Much depends on common courses and on social interaction. But it is argued that mobile societies are characterized by interests that may stimulate participation rather than communities. It is, however, a mistake to dismiss community as place as a basis for interaction and participation. We examine this argument in detail in the next section. Third, participation is seen as an educative experience. Taking part educates people to develop citizen senses of competence and responsibility. It is in some ways at the heart of democratic theory (Verba and Nie 1972), a commitment to which may be strengthened by the fourth justification, an expressive one, which regards participation as an expression of political identity, part of a sense of political belonging. One might ask in what circumstances such belonging can be engendered. Although there are organizational and structural constraints to participation and belonging (Eyles 1993b), we argue that a place-based system may provide a meaningful framework. But before addressing that question, we examine the issue of degree of participation.

If one concurs that citizen participation is justified by its "functions"—those of instrumentality, communitarianism, education, and expressiveness—and in terms of its response to the crises of representation, accountability and legitimacy, one is still left to ponder the degree of participation necessary to ensure accountable local decision making. It is here, too, that one should recognize that participation can involve the political process and also administrative functions. Most attention has been directed at political participation. The degree of citizen involvement in the political process depends on the needs of the decision-making situation and the disposition of those in control of making decisions, local influentials. Arnstein (1969) has developed a ladder of citizen participation, each rung of which corresponds to the degree to which citizens take their places in decision making.

Essentially, the eight rungs may be grouped, the first set, the two bottom rungs, being nonparticipatory. First, manipulation is the organization of participation to educate or to persuade citizens on already-made plans and program decisions so as to gain their support. Some citizen committees have no mandate, even to give advice. They may act as public relation devices for traditional wielders of authority. Second, therapy may be seen as the practice of engaging citizens in diversionary tactics so that attention is deflected from the real issues. Some "workshops" in which citizens learn skills or detail with little connection to the issues of interest may be examples. The second set consists of modest forms of citizen involvement, perhaps accurately described as modest power sharing or participation. Third, informing is providing information to citizens on the nature of tasks, the schedule of likely events, and the role of citizens. At worst, this rung represents one-way communication through media formats and may be combined with user-unfriendly jargon (e.g., the early public meetings to inform citizens of potential health effects of environmental accidents; see Eyles et al. 1990). Fourth, consultation is an explicit attempt to obtain the views of citizens through meetings and surveys. Although citizens may be heard, they may not be fully understood. Nor is their involvement necessarily assured. Consultation is often the legislated level of participation in the land-use planning process. Most planning authorities have a statutory obligation to call such consultation meetings. Fifth, placation is similar to consultation, but there is what amounts to a guarantee that citizens will be heard. They will not necessarily be heeded. Hodge (1991) points out that the citizen policy committees who helped prepare the regional plan for Greater Vancouver were provided with technical assistance. But their reports were only received by government. Further, the planning act of Nova Scotia argues that participation is a requirement of good decision making, but it does not transfer authority from elected representatives to citizens affected by planning schemes (see Grant 1988). A similar advisory position is currently held by the district health councils in Ontario.

The final set indicates degrees of citizen power sharing and high levels of participation. Sixth, partnership is an agreement to share responsibilities for decision making through joint boards and committees. Such partnerships are found for limited activities in neighborhood planning (e.g., Toronto, Winnipeg, Ottawa). Citizens can affect the shape and outcome of a plan through their decisions and votes. Seventh, delegated power is when citizens have the dominant decision-making power over a plan or program. In Richmond, Virginia, citizens were recruited to join municipal decision making and to take responsibility for creating or maintaining viable, vibrant neighborhoods. The neighborhood team process was successful in about eight neighborhoods. Amoury (1990) does not give the reasons for the "lack of interest" in other districts. Finally, citizen control is the governance of a program or project by citizens. Citizens create, plan, and manage the program usually with a budget provided by a central authority. Such control was present in some of the educational initiatives in U.S. cities during the 1960s (Marris and Rein 1967; Morgan 1987). Community control was found to be a rather separatist movement, isolating a program from the rest of the city and society. Although this enabled citizens to focus on their problems, it was eventually self-limiting because any integrative movement was seen as cooptive. Community control appeared to isolate needy groups, whereas the "mobilization of bias" through integration in mainstream organizations isolated the community control movement. Therefore, although community control offered meaningful participation, the route to empowerment, its radical departure from integrative principles, the reasons for citizen participation, doomed it to failure. The experiments did not survive beyond the Great Society years.

Arnstein's ladder is of importance. In fact, Feingold (1977) has modified her work to consist of five rungs: informing, consultation, partnership, delegated power, and citizen control. Charles and DeMaio (1992) go further and reduce it to three: consultation, partnership, and lay domination. Some nuances of meaning are lost with these modifications, especially the distinction between consultation and therapy in Feingold and delegated power and citizen control in Charles and DeMaio. The rungs represent real alternatives in ways of involving citizens in decision making. But if this involvement is to be more than asking publics their views, it is the final three rungs—partnership, delegated power, and citizen control—that are significant. Given the low turnout and skewed uptake in participation, adequate representation is a key element in ensuring citizen involvement in decision making.

Indeed, the question of adequate representation is central to the issue of citizen participation. As Desario (1987) asked about participants in the U.S. health system agencies (HSAs), and as one should ask about the composition of any health decision-making body, Do the mobilized and/or appointed individuals and groups provide society with a "representative" and "accountable" administrative process and are they working on behalf of the "public welfare"? One cannot assume that those who participate are representative of publics. Indeed, mass society renders inoperable the decision mechanisms of classical democracy. Four different types of representation can be identified (see Marmor and Morone 1980; Morone and Marmor 1981; Desario 1987). The most familiar is formal political representation, referring to political officeholders who are entrusted with decision-making power, an elected, institutional view of representation. Quite common, also, is ascriptive representation in which groups delegate decision-making authority to particular individuals because of their social position or knowledge. This representation often takes the form of advocacy in which professionals—planners, lawyers, social workers, consumer counsellors—act for the group to ensure its voice is heard, case put, or claim for resources presented. Advocacy was a common procedure in urban planning in the 1960s and 1970s (see Roweis and Scott 1977). Third, descriptive representation means that individuals become representatives because they reflect the characteristics of the larger group. It assumes that similar characteristics will ensure the pursuit and promotion of common interests. In other words, it is assumed that similarity of outcomes derives from similarity of composition. Descriptive representation determines who the representatives should be, not what they should do.

Two further points should be made. First, what social characteristics should be represented? How far should this process of "demographic mirroring" go (see Morone and Marmor 1981)? The HSA legislation required that the boards should be broadly representative of the social, economic, linguistic, and racial populations of the area served. Second, as any member of a group that merits representation is as qualified as any other to be a representative, there is the possibility of tokenism in that a person may be selected because she is black or he is gay, irrespective of qualities relating to the issue at hand. It has become a way of ensuring that the voices of interest groups are heard. Lastly, substantive representation, refers to the selection of representatives on the basis of a committed personal or professional interest in health issues (see Zakus and Hastings 1988) and a further commitment to work for and espouse the interests of a group. As Marmor and Morone (1980) point out, such people are messengers and guardians although the positioning of these individuals is crucial for the effectiveness of their representation. We have tended to assume that physicians are the guardians of people's interests with respect to medical care, especially technical decisions. The growing importance of a broadly defined "health" and the significance of value decisions in health care (e.g., what resources to what programs) mean that this position is questioned. But the role of physicians as guardians points to a potential problem with substantive representation (its vulnerability to being "captured" by minorities with expertise or strongly held views or highly focused interests). But it is likely that the attempt to build local, accountable, participatory decision-making structures for health care will use the principle of substantive representation.

We turn briefly to administrative participation, the involvement of private citizens in the managing and planning of public enterprises. Thomas (1993) has argued that public managers have in recent years had to respond to demands for citizen involvement not so much in the design but in the operationalization of programs, stimulated by the needs for community acceptance (especially with respect to facility siting) and to improve the fit of public programs to citizen needs. Yet this participation must not be at the expense of program or operational effectiveness. Interestingly, Vroom and Yetton (1973) advocate an effective decision model that emphasizes that the degree of desirable involvement depends on the attributes of the core problem. Thus, more involvement is appropriate when an issue carries a high need for "acceptability" and less when the main requirement is for "quality." Reformulated for public decisions, "greater needs for public legitimacy recommend more involvement; greater needs for managerial efficiency and technical competence recommend less" (Thomas 1993, 446–47). Thomas goes on to demonstrate the utility of this approach in his analysis of some forty public decisions. Luton (1993) adopts a less-pragmatic approach. He notes that there is little attention to the relationships between citizens and public bureaucrats (see also Frederickson 1982) but then goes on to list the points of connection between the two groups in public decision making. Thus, at the lowest level the citizen wants to avoid harm or minimize risk, moving through being a watchdog, personal and community education, and empowerment to (at the highest level) governance. This typology of purposes is similar to Arnstein's ladder and relates, too, to the justifications of participation. But administrators also have purposes: avoiding legal roadblocks to improving their public images, consulting with citizens, obtaining their advice, delegating decisions to interest groups, to, finally, democratizing decision making. Luton, thus, produces a grid of potential connections that is a complex and potent reminder that citizen participation interfaces not only with the political process but also with the machinery of government.

But what are the bases of the connections, for representation, for local, accountable, participatory decision making? One such basis is interest group affiliation. Thus, if individuals are selected to represent interests (as women, as blacks, as consumers, and so on), representativeness and, by implication, accountability are ensured. But can all interests be included? Are all equally important? How are they determined? Do they shift and change? With what effects? Thus, rather than interests, the basis should be citizenship (in terms of equity, commitment, attachment) or, in local terms, residency or geography. But geography is being seen in a particular way as place, representing, articulating a set of core values, pertaining to attachment, identity, and belonging—key features in achieving a local, accountable decision-making structure.

Place

Place, Relph (1985, 26) argues, is qualitatively different from landscape or space. "The latter are part of any immediate encounter with the world, and so long as I can see I cannot help but see them no matter what my purpose. This is not so with places, for they are constructed in our memories and affections through repeated encounters and complex associations." Place is where one is known and knows others.

> Before any choices there is this "place," where the foundations of earthly existence and human condition establish themselves. We can change locations, move, but this is still to look for a place; we need a base to set down our Being and to realize our possibilities, a *here* from which to discover the world, a *there* to which we can return. (Dardel 1952, 56; trans. by Relph 1985, 27)

Such sentiment is also expressed by anthropologists in that consciousness of the world beyond place is the catalyst for the recognition of one's own community as a distinct entity (Cohen 1982). Places are, thus, seen as centers of felt value (Tuan 1977), centers of experience and aspirations of people (Tuan 1976). To be attached to a place is an important human need, perhaps the least-recognized one (Weil 1955). Place is a profound center for human existence (Relph 1976), important for identity of the individual (with the group) (Duncan 1973). It is, of course, not the only basis of identity or attachment but provides a grounding for other dimensions beyond the household.

But place identity remains strong even if the attachment is not positive (Hummon 1992), even if it is disrupted (Brown and Perkins 1992) and at different scales from dwelling to region (Cuba and Hummon 1993). As Cuba and Hummon (1993) note, place identity, as expressed by feeling-at-home, is widespread, rich in its attachment to multiple locales and complex in spatial structures and in its determination. Indeed, in a review of ten definitions of place, Brown and Perkins conclude that place attachments are integral to self-definitions; provide stability and nonthreatening changes; are holistic and multifaceted and multilevel, arguing that

> place attachment involves positively experienced bonds, sometimes occurring without awareness, that are developed over time from the behavioral, affective and cognitive ties between individuals and/or groups and their sociophysical environment. These bonds provide a framework for both individual and communal aspects of identity and have both stabilizing and dynamic features. The environments may include homes or communities, place[s] that are important and directly experienced but which may not have easily specified boundaries. Pre-

> dominately negative connections to place characterize failed attachments, which may be experienced as alienation. Transformations in place attachment occur whenever the people, places, or psychological processes change over time. Disruptions of place attachment are noticeable transformations in place attachment due to noticeable changes in the people, processes, or places. (1992, 284)

Why, then, does place not seem to matter, especially with respect to political decision making? Admittedly, its use is problematic. It is a contestable concept (Gallie 1955–56; Agnew 1993). Much has to do with its scale variability and to it being seen as a physical setting and social activities in that setting (Giddens 1983). Places are also seen as possessing "individuality" in a world of their obvious interdependence and homogenization. They are also seen as synonymous with establishing political boundaries, and, hence, their significance is taken on board by considering those divisions. And they are also taken-for-granted. As Rodman (1992) perceptively puts it, the problem of place arises, paradoxically, because the meaning of place too often seems to go without saying.

The relation between the taken-for-granted nature of place and its homogenization (see Harvey 1982; Smith 1984) and nationalization (Lipset and Rokkan 1967) is well summarized by Foucault (1980, 70):

> A critique could be carried out of this devaluation of space [*sic*] that has prevailed for generations. Space was treated as the dead, the fixed, the undialectical, the immobile. Time, on the other hand, was richness, fecundity, life, dialectic. If one started to talk in terms of space that meant one was hostile to time. It meant, as the fools say, that one "denied history," that one was a "technocrat." They did not understand that to trace the forms of implantation, delimitation and demarcation of objects, the modes of tabulation, the organization of domains meant throwing into relief processes—historical ones, needless to say—of power.

The specific points of argument are taken up by, say, Harvey (1982) in the homogeneous nature of places that are all subject to the logic of the economy. Thrift (1987) and Entrikin (1991) take issue with this approach, arguing that how subjects make themselves and their identities are localized if the "material" is not all local in origin.

Further, the argument that political alignments have crystallized largely around social cleavages to produce national patterns of political mobilization and partisan support has also been challenged. For example, Dunleavy (1979) pointed to the importance of the social and the local in shaping interest perceptions and value formations to charter the growth of "consumption cleavages" on urban political alignment. Agnew (1987) examined the importance of the local—social and historic—in shaping the patterns of support for Scottish nationalism.

From such studies the significance of the local—of places—emerges. But it must be recognized that they have both individuality and interdependence. This dualism is superbly expressed by Entrikin (1991, 134), addressing the apparent divide between places as existence and places in nature:

> The closest that we can come to addressing both sides of this divide is from a point in between, a point that leads us into the vast realm of narrative forms. From this position we gain a view from both sides of the divide. We gain a sense both of being "in a place" and "at a location," of being at the centre and being at a point in a centreless world. To ignore either argument of this dualism is to misunderstand the modern experience of place.

But it is precisely this dualism that may lead to the disregard of place in policy, especially as there is usually no easy coincidence of place as existence and place in nature. Entrikin (1991) does, however, make a spirited defense for the significance of place, seeing it of continued relevance in a mobile world to "place" people (its empirical, theoretical significance), its basis for "community" and significance for democracy (its normative significance), and its utility as a "model" in everyday understandings about the world (its epistemological significance). In some respects, these dimensions have parallels with Agnew's (1987) three dimensions of place: location (the spatial distribution of activities, the impacts of the wider world on place), locale (the setting in which social relations are constituted, akin to "community"), and sense of place (place attachment and the structure of feelings that are used in the everyday). These dimensions must be brought together to be helpful in putting place into health care policy operationally or formally. But before that task is undertaken in the concluding section, we outline two arguments that conspire against place in policy.

Place appears irrelevant to policy because of the usurpation of debate by other discourses that emphasize the patient and the nonplace community. Walter (1988, 97) argues that the dominance of Freud's thought helps unground the self:

> Freud moved theory of the mind away from grounded experience and helped to build the couch as a vehicle abstracting patient from place. Despite his own existential recognition of the inner need that yearns for place, Freud's psychology never integrated personal identity with the sense of belonging, and the real power of place.

We may add that this power of places was further attenuated by the coming of urban places for the mass of people in industrial society. Despite human interdependence, people are individualized, made blasé about interactions, calculating about events, and integrated around the self rather than significant others. Simmel's (1950) description of the mental life of the metropolis and Wirth's (1964) of urbanism as a way of life encapsulate this world of independent, isolated individuals living in densely settled, heterogeneous settlements where only they know their identities. These arguments also have relevance for the "loss of community" and, hence, nonplace communities.

Agnew (1987), in fact, argues that there are two stages to the devaluation of place as a significant social structure. First, it stems from the ambiguity in the language of *community* with the term meaning both physical setting and a morally valued way of life (Nisbet 1966; Calhoun 1980). Tönnies' (1955) ideas of the transition from a place-based community to a placeless or national society link this stage to the second in the devaluation of place, namely the eclipse of community and with it, by implication, places as "history" allows for the evolution of society into associations of interdependent but autonomous workers and consumers. In modern society, individuals become uncoupled from place as social networks and interactions make geography less relevant than in the past. Institutions guide interactions (Stacey 1969) not places, and it is accessibility rather than propinquity that is the important spatial referent (see Webber 1964). Although it is not possible to deny the importance of institutions or accessibility, Tilly expresses our concerns well. He argues that places have persisted in importance but there has been a relative decline in such localized communities as the bases of collective action. "Local ties have diminished little or not at all, extra local ties have increased" (1973, 236). Further, local ties in the past may have been political rather than social as the Lee et al. (1984) study of Seattle demonstrates. And although the influence of national, mass phenomena cannot be doubted (see Pahl 1970), they are just as likely to stimulate dissimilar behavior by individuals in distinct geographical units as similar actions (see Claggett et al. 1984). The irrelevance of place for policy must, too, be doubted.

What is raised, however, implicitly in these debates is the nature of place that is relevant to health care policy and service delivery, specifically its boundaries and size. These factors are important not only for provision of services but also for participation. This point is raised in both the models put forward to explain who participates. Thus, the mobilization model predicts more political activity in urban rather than rural settings:

> Persons close to the center occupy an environmental position which naturally links them into the communications network involved in policy decisions for the society. . . . This central position increases the likelihood that they will develop personality traits, beliefs and attitudes which facilitate participation in politics. . . . One of the most thoroughly substantiated propositions in all of social science is that *persons near the center of the society are more likely to participate in politics than persons near the periphery*. . . . Persons near the center receive more stimuli enticing them to participate, and they receive more support from their peers when they do participate. (emphasis original, Milbrath 1965, 113–14)

The alternative "decline of community" model:

> predicts the decline of participation as one moves from the smallness and intimacy of town or village to the massive impersonality of the city. In the small town, the community is a manageable size. Citizens can know the ropes of politics, know whom to contact, know each other so that they can form political groups. In the larger units, politics is more complicated, impersonal, and distant. In addition, "modernization" shatters political units. What were once relatively independent communities—providing the individual with the social, economic, political, and cultural services that he needs—become small towns in a mass society.
>
> All these changes, according to the decline-of-community model, should reduce the level of participation within the community. For one

> thing, the government of the local community loses its importance. Local participation becomes less and less meaningful. Furthermore, the attention of individuals becomes more diffuse. They no longer concentrate upon their local community. Rather, they are exposed to a wider political realm where meaningful participation is much more difficult because of its larger size and greater complexity. (Verba and Nie 1972, 231)

There is empirical support for both models (Verba et al. 1978). Size certainly matters. Warren (1970) notes the importance of variations in size of unit and scale of activity for both public representation and service implementation. Dahl (1967) argues that smaller units give greater opportunity for participation and accountability than large ones. Even in the range of fifty thousand to two hundred thousand people participation becomes no more than voting. Both functional effectiveness and democracy require small units (Dahl and Tufte 1974; Honey 1976). But this view is rejected empirically by Newton (1982), who challenges the democracy of small units. He argues that large units can be both effective and democratic. Indeed, conceptually Odum (1965) and Mumford (1938) have argued for the importance of the region, seeing in it balance in diversity, strength in interaction, and the positive social and political features of provincialism: to combine the models of participation and mobilization is possible because community-in-places has not been eclipsed. Further, the characteristics of the very local transcend size to some degree. Community attachment is strong in urban as well as rural areas. As Kasarda and Janowitz (1974, 338) note, "Location in communities of increased size and density does not result in a substitution of secondary for primary and informal contacts. . . . [F]ormal ties foster more extensive primary contacts in the local community." As Cuba and Hummon (1993) attest, people call region home.

Conclusion: Formalizing Places

Thus far we have made the case that places are significant in health care policy, especially in the light of reforms to contain costs and democratize health care decision making. Decentralization implies a geographical base, but it could also refer to institutions or sectors. That is not democratic. It could be to interest groups, but as we have argued, places provide a more meaningful and experiential phenomenon. How, though, might such a place-based decentralization occur? How might local participation in health care decision making be facilitated? And how might the local (or the relevant regions) be defined?

Zakus and Hastings (1988) have listed the factors—"preconditions"—for the facilitation of local participation: a political climate supportive of active citizen involvement at all levels of policy and program development, implementation, and evaluation; a political framework in which policy, legislation, and resource allocation take account of local circumstances, aspirations, and needs; a political and administrative structure promoting decentralization and local responsibility and authority for policy and allocative decisions; an acceptable universal level of availability and accessibility of health care services for meeting basic health care needs; a health care system, the institutions and professionals of which are committed to citizen involvement and which are further committed to responding to local needs; intersectoral collaborative possibilities between health care, social services, housing, and others; a public culture supportive of individual and collective awareness, knowledge, and discussion about well-being; a citizenry knowledgeable and skillful concerning health and organizational issues; a community in which health is a priority and in which the broad determinants of health are seen as important; experience in citizen involvement and leadership in responding to community issues through voluntarism, mutual assistance, and advocacy; and responsible, responsive, and efficient media, information communication systems.

Not only preconditions are important but also the process of inclusion, of ensuring representation. In this regard, organizational forms allow voices to be heard in debate and decision making. At the consultation stage, particularly, the citizen panel enables such hearings and the scoping of the issues. This consultation phase is widely practiced in Canadian health care policy. Knowledge based on common sense and personal experience is extremely useful to identify concerns and to establish criteria for change or service provision. Indeed, the priority setting of the Oregon Medicare "experiment" was carried out in such panels or forums. Further, Bryson and Crosby (1993) in their work on planning decisions distinguish between forums (for communication), arenas (for decision making), and courts (for adjudication). This seems a useful distinction for health care decision making too in that boards to make decisions and achieve goals may be seen as arenas. Such coalitions have been used in the Minnesota and Pawtucket

Health programs (Mittelmark 1986; Lefebvre 1990). A "court" or legal framework is necessary for appeal and regulatory oversight.

The move from forum (or panel) to arena (or board) to court does not mean that citizens abdicate the process. Although different forms of knowledge become more or less important at each stage (see Renn et al. 1993), citizen representatives remain important. All health care decisions (perhaps even those involving clinical decisions, although these are beyond the scope of this essay) require the involvement of stakeholders (providers, payers, regulators), experts (epidemiologists, policy analysts, facilitators), and citizens as potential victims or benefactors. Citizens are necessary to transform expert judgments into meaningful group or community preferences and experiences and to evaluate options and recommendations. Citizen members of boards and "courts" then maintain important roles.

But what areas and populations might the boards serve? If our argument has thus far put people in places *into* health care decision making, how might we ensure that such decision making is *for* them too? It is, of course, possible to use existing areal units and boundaries. If this is the case, one must ask which ones—municipal, health, school board, social services, and so on, in Ontario alone—and recognize the importance of historical development with, in Canada, the piecemeal growth of local services grafted onto a more-or-less laissez-faire ideology (see Kingdom 1993). Local governments developed in a piecemeal way and only provided services that citizens could not provide for themselves. There are further few examples of areal units joining together to provide more effectively a larger package of services although the creation of "unicity" centered on Winnipeg would be an example (Brownstone and Plunkett 1983).

There are, as geographers and regional scientists know, a whole range of techniques for dividing space into "regions." Once the lowest tier or community or neighborhood has been derived, it is possible to use grouping techniques to join contiguous areas (see Berry 1967; Ward 1963). This method treats "building regions" as an assignment problem by which units are placed in particular regional classes on criteria of interest. As grouping continues, the similarity between the assigned units declines so that decision criteria must be established. Thus, we argue that the lowest unit is based on meaningful places and that community input is necessary for both this and continued assignment because a local, accountable health-care system is the goal.

But one must, of course, recognize existing health care services. In fact, it is possible to build regions around these through the solution of districting problems, using linear programming techniques. Much work in this regard has been in optimizing school and electoral districts. For example, Yeates (1963) minimized the cost of busing to Wisconsin high schools, given constraints of school capacity. It is possible to change the criteria of optimization to, for example, desired social mix at a school and safe routes to school. In health care resource allocation criteria—efficiency, equity and accessibility—have been built into the models with accessibility often measured by trip distance, given the constraints of facility structure (Mayhew and Leonardi 1982; Taket 1989). Most of this work has examined hospitals, although the market areas of primary health care centers in terms of trip distance, perceived attractiveness and facility characteristics have been investigated (see Martin and Williams, 1992). Indeed, given the nature of health care services, there will be a hierarchy of provision. But just as with the lowest tier in the "region," so too with primary care: they are key for a local, accountable, participatory system. This is, however, the level that is most fraught with problems for "districting" solutions through "gaming." Districting and redistricting can lead to social, economic, and political biases (see Morrill 1981; Johnston 1979) with Webster (1993) recently showing their impact on the political map of Alabama. But places rather than interest groups allow for many agendas and voices in debates and decisions.

It is possible to build a hierarchy of regions using accessibility, facility characteristics and other criteria for drawing boundaries (e.g. Moore and Revelle, 1982). Further, one should not be overly concerned with fragmented jurisdictions so long as relations between the "fragments" in a decentered system are good. Indeed, Warren (1964) refuses to see fragmented government as pathological and Ostrom, Tiebout, and Warren (1955) argue for a polycentric system in which the parts enter into agreements and contracts with one another to obtain the services they and their populations require. The "contracts" can provide an effective means of obtaining higher-order services (for lowest tier participants) and of ensuring demand for services (for higher-order suppliers). Such agreements have been suggested for health service organizations and comprehensive health organization in Canada and provide the basis of purchaser-provider relations in the United Kingdom and of health maintenance organizations in the United States. Although sometimes problematic, they provide a mechanism for effectively linking different parts of the health care delivery hierarchy while retaining degrees of local participation and control.

If the creation of an effective and meaningful hierarchy of services is possible—and helps put into place a health-care system for people—the lowest tier remains key. We have argued that place attachment should be the criterion for determining this tier. We have showed how place matters: a strategy for identifying that place is a political decision that we argue should be based on the notions of participation and representation outlined in this essay. Building on the desire to increase local democracy and on existing local structures such as municipalities, health councils and the like, forums could be used to determine areas of responsibility. It is likely that existing regional sympathies will be confirmed. But the combination of regional identity and effective service or catchment areas nested in a hierarchy of provision makes a powerful basis for local, accountable health care.

14

Place, Space, and Health Service Reform

GRAHAM MOON AND TIM BROWN

This chapter is concerned with the use of geography in health policy. It aims, through a textual analysis of documents and debates, to examine how government constructs and reconstructs place and space in national health policy. In a previous paper, Moon (1990) considered some of the evidence for different concepts of (geographical) space apparent in British health policy in the mid-1980s. He argued that, at the time, there were essentially two such concepts: a formal understanding in which geography was used as jurisdictional partitioning and a functional perspective in which value-laden concepts such as "community" had come to pervade attempts to improve the public face of the contemporary health service. Both concepts were found to be problematic. The 1990 paper saw the shortcomings of formal concepts in terms of their effect on the availability of health information; it could equally have cited the shifting and continuing debate about the redundancy or appropriateness of different partitioning arrangements. Functional concepts were criticized for their inadequate acknowledgement of sociological critiques of community as a romanticized and problem-laden category (Bell and Newby 1971) and for their resonance with new right individualism. It was concluded that Giddens's structuration theory provided a useful basis for understanding the use of space in contemporary health policy. Although we do not wish to depart from parts of the basic analysis presented in the earlier paper, developments in the intervening years have been such that the theme of the unfolding and changing role of space and place as officially constructed in health policy is now ripe for further analysis.

We identify two reasons why our theme is suitable for further consideration. First, there have been significant developments on a worldwide scale with regard to health policy. The dismantling of state welfare systems, advancing privatism, the rising costs of medical technology, and the push to primary care systems are all pressures that have grown and that collectively indicate a need to reappraise the uses of geography in health policy. Second, and more importantly, during a major theoretical turn in geography, questions concerning the nature of "place" have moved to the center of academic inquiry. This academic refocusing has challenged and reformulated more traditional analyses and deconstructed the often mistakenly elided notions of place, community, and space using perspectives drawn from cultural and social theory. These incursions, involving an interlocking constituency consisting of Foucauldian theory, postmodernism, poststructuralism, the sociology of the body, postcolonial and feminist theory, have largely failed to impact on medical geography (Moon 1995; Philo 1995). Yet as this collection and recent debates suggest, this unconnectedness on the part of medical geography with the contemporary thrust of the geographic academy is now showing signs of coming to an end (Kearns 1993, 1994; Dorn and Laws 1994). This chapter is, therefore, intended as both a reaction to the recent and extensive change in the health policy arena and a contribution to the academic reconnection of medical geography.

The chapter is divided into three sections. In the first, we briefly discuss our contention that medical geography is theoretically impoverished and examine the evidence for a developing theoretical renaissance. In the second section we present a detailed discourse analysis of the key official documents and parliamentary debates concerned with the recent reform of the British National Health Service (NHS). The decision to focus on Britain is a largely pragmatic one that reflects the expertise of the authors although the extent of implemented change since the late 1980s is such that Britain provides a peculiarly good basis for the exemplification of the need for a reappraisal of the role of space/place in the construction of health policy. We present a discussion of changing concepts and constructions of space and place, drawing mainly on Foucauldian perspectives concerning capture and surveillance. The chapter concludes with a brief reflection on gaps between official and popular constructions of place/space, mutual awareness, and the difficulty of visioning geographies in dynamic evolving policy settings.

Theory and Medical Geography

Medical geography has been relatively untouched by the contemporary turn of academic geography to particular genres of cultural and social theory. Litva and Eyles (1995) argue that what little theory has penetrated medical geography has tended to link to more distant theoretical traditions. They further suggest that, although these discourses may be implicitly discerned in medical geography, it remains doubtful whether the practitioners of medical geography are always explicitly aware of the theoretical underpinnings of their work. For much of medical geography this judgment is undoubtedly true. There are, however, as Litva and Eyles acknowledge, some clear exceptions. We suggest, nevertheless, that the vast majority of these exceptions do not connect with current directions in social and cultural theory.

To illustrate this point, we consider one of the standard texts on medical geography. Jones and Moon (1987) devoted considerable space in their general text to, first, a rather orthodox Marxist assessment of health inequalities, second, the development of the concept of critical epidemiology, and third, the notion of social construction. Although the Marxist perspective was typical of the period, critical epidemiology was more innovative but it was not, as used at the time, as connected as it perhaps should have been to concerns with cultural meaning and diversity. Similarly, Jones and Moon used the concept of social construction in a relatively untheorized fashion, drawing mainly on secondary sources such as Conrad and Schneider (1980) and Wright and Treacher (1982); there were two passing and, at the time rather innovative, references to Foucault (1965).

Jones and Moon were, of course, writing before geography's cultural turn; their text was largely completed in 1984 and 1985. A few years later the paper by Moon (1990) touched upon issues of community and meaning but essentially concerned the demonstration of the utility of Giddens' structuration theory. That paper, too, resonated with concerns then current in academic geography but did not engage with sociocultural theory. It is only recently that such an engagement has become evident within medical geography. This emergence of a theorized medical geography is closely linked to research seeking to explore the importance of "place" in health (Jones and Moon 1993; Kearns and Joseph 1993).

Of course, this emergence of a theorized perspective on place and health has a past and a contemporary context as well. In both the work of John Eyles carries considerable importance. His projects of the mid-1980s using symbolic interactionism to uncover grass-roots concepts of health in localized settings (e.g., Eyles and Donovan 1986) and his 1985 book, *Sense of Place,* provide the past context, whereas more recently we have already drawn attention to his work with Andreà Litva (Litva and Eyles 1995). With regard to the past we could also cite the voluminous literature on place and placelessness (Relph 1976) and social landscapes (Dear and Wolch 1987). The contemporary context is embodied by the collection of which this chapter forms part, the foundation of the journal *Health and Place,* and the debate in *Professional Geographer* over Robin Kearns's 1993 paper. One of the papers in that debate, Dorn and Laws (1994), is of most interest regarding the rapprochement between medical geography and sociocultural theory. Although they, too, build upon the relatively established project of social constructionism, there are intimations of an extended awareness exemplified most clearly by references to work on postmodernity, the sociology of the body and those icons of contemporary geography: bell hooks (1984) and Julia Kristeva (1982).[1] It is in the areas covered by Dorn and Laws that the size of the dislocation between medical geography and the rest of contemporary (social) geography becomes evident. Of course, *pace* Mayer and Meade (1994), we might wish to debate whether medical geography is, in fact, "social." Our position in such a debate, and we suspect that of Dorn and Laws (and most contributors to this volume as well), would be unequivocally in favor of the social: "diseases," policies, and care systems are socially constructed and socially produced with the interesting questions resting on the nature and underpinning of that construction and production. The limited engagement of medical geography with the theoretical has neglected the possibility that postmodernist and poststructuralist discourses may increase understanding of these almost certainly diverse natures and underpinnings. Although this may well be a logical consequence of medical geography's modernist concern with understanding as explanation and its general reliance on the quantitative, it also means that, despite

1. Cynical readers may wish to note publication dates of these works in relation to their impact on geography.

the signs of a rapprochement with the theoretical, there is, as yet, no medical geographical equivalent of Nick Fox's 1993 text *Postmodernism, Sociology and Health.*

Like many other points we have made in this section, the conclusion reached above could be challenged. There are, of course, geographers who write about health and who draw to various degrees on the perspectives of postmodernism and poststructuralism, for example, Gerry Kearns (1991), Chris Philo (1986, 1989, 1992), and Felix Driver (1985, 1993). These writers tend to focus on the past. That may afford some luxury of commentary, but contemporary medical discourse is no less amenable to such analysis. Perhaps more relevant is their concern with issues of morality and the sociospatial location of "others," for instance, people with mental health problems. These concerns connect with resonating Foucauldian themes of difference and exclusion and, thus, perhaps, direct the theoretical. Do these people, however, consider themselves to be medical geographers? Philo himself addresses this point in a commentary on Litva and Eyles (1995) in which he describes himself as "less a medical geographer and more a social-cultural geographer" (1995, 35). Yet his work and that of the others cited above is of central importance to the geography of health whether or not this is actually synonymous with medical geography.[2] Labels are clearly problematic, artificial, and divisive; the minutiae of academic self-concern (Doel 1993) yet what can be said with some certainty is that there are considerable possibilities for postmodernist and poststructuralist theory in medical geography as the subdiscipline seeks greater awareness (not explanation) of the difference that place makes to health, health care, and health policy.

This brief review of medical geographic discourse has, we trust, indicated something of the nature of contemporary medical geography as it comes belatedly to terms with the challenge of postmodernism (Dear 1988) and other "new" theoretical perspectives. We strongly assert that we are not pessimistic about the position of theory within the subdiscipline, nor would we wish to undervalue the considerable strength that is evidenced in empirical work. We now turn to a con-

2. It is worth noting the recent debates in academic geography over what people who chose to call themselves medical geographers might adopt as an alternative label. "Geographers of health" (and health care) has been favored as indicating a distancing from the medical.

sideration of the ways in which there has been a structuring of space and a constructing of place in recent British health policy. Geographical studies of health policy have tended to forget place in favor of a focus on policy processes and outcomes or a functionalist fascination with jurisdictional partitioning; here we attempt to deconstruct the official use of these concepts through a genealogy of recent health policy.

Structuring Space and Constructing Place in Recent British Health Policy

For the non-British reader we commence this section with a general description of recent British health policy, a highly summarized chronological account of the developments that will form the subject matter of the analysis presented in the following subsections. In brief, Britain's National Health Service (NHS), a creation of the 1945 Labour government and, arguably, one of the major achievements of that government, found itself in 1979 under the control of a Conservative government that was decidedly unenthusiastic about socialism, collectivism, welfare, and public expenditure (Kendall and Moon 1994). The NHS survived the subsequent sixteen years but experienced a regime of continual change that effectively transformed it from a traditional cog of the welfare state to a managed element of a quasi market. In this process important landmarks were the removal of a "redundant layer of administration," the area health authorities, in 1982, the introduction from 1985 of general management in place of reactive administration and medical self-governance, and the implementation through the 1980s of continuing programs of efficiency savings. Most fundamental, however, were a series of four parliamentary White Papers between 1987 and 1992. These, respectively, reshaped primary care (DHSS 1987), introduced an internal market separating purchasers and providers of health care (DOH 1989b) and social care (DOH 1989a), and outlined, for the first time and notwithstanding fifty years of a NHS, a health policy for England (DOH 1992).[3] The primary care (DHSS 1987), internal health care market (DOH 1989b), and health policy papers (DOH 1992) are discussed

3. The distinction here is between a health care policy, which there had been for fifty years, and a health policy. The reference to England is also important; Wales had a policy already in place.

below; interested readers seeking more detail on the historical evolution of the NHS during this period should refer to the review of Kendall and Moon (1994) or, for an excellent fully developed account, to Mohan (1995).

Our analysis examines this terrain through the medium of a detailed discourse analysis of government White Papers and Parliamentary debates. Our approach involves an examination of the language of health policy discourse and an assessment of the extent to which that language employs geographic metaphors—concepts of place, space-based orderings and structurings, notions of separation and ideas of scale—to construct and reconstruct differing forms of negotiated or imposed social order within the policy arena. We examine a language that invests, inscribes, and territorializes space and place to define not the area of its gaze but the "world of objects to be known" (Foucault 1976, x). The negotiations over this (re)definition present a subtle assertion of presence as the discourses seek to claim contested terrain. Our focus is, thus, firmly on the official construction of place and space; the texts that we use portray stylized representations. Nevertheless, they also embody the (carefully?) chosen public expression of government health policy and, as such, offer insight into the exercise of power. In this poststructuralist sense the meanings and nuances of place and space words in their context, of course, reside only in the eyes of the reader and interpreter; they are signifiers and defer meaning. In the following subsections we use these perspectives to examine this slipperiness, this shifting and contextualized meaning.

Primary Care Reform

The White Paper *Promoting Better Health* (DHSS 1987) began the outlining of the government's more conceptual ideas for health. Its approach was embodied in the assertion that "the Government intends to introduce a set of proposals designed to create a family health service, with an emphasis on promotion of good health rather than just on the treatment of illness" (DHSS 1987, 4). Encapsulated in this perspective were two notions central to the neoliberal perspective on health policy. First, there was to be a family *health service;* it was to be about health, and it was to be a service for consumers of care and outward looking. This perspective replaced that of the family practitioner committee; inward looking and concerned with the practitioners rather than with health, a bureaucratic committee rather than a consumer-focused service. Second, concern was to be with health promotion rather than illness treatment. With this notion an agenda that went beyond the biomedical was accepted into official health policy. This had the dual advantage of diffusing official responsibility for health beyond the NHS and, following the hegemonic interpretation of the contested field of health promotion (Macdonald and Bunton 1992), firmly locating practical responsibility for health with the individual. The government's ideological agenda was, therefore, not unsurprisingly, clearly evident in its discourse.

What of space and place in that discourse? *Promoting Better Health* made relatively little use of such devices. The health policy landscape was, however, surprisingly extended to incorporate an acknowledgment of the articulation of health and deprivation; this association had previously been denied by the Conservative government. Thus, "deprived areas such as some inner cities, outlying housing estates and remote rural areas, will benefit from these changes" (DHSS 1987, 5). Space was metamorphosing into place; it was assuming characteristic symbolic attributes that saw the geography in policy as more than a formal partitioning of space. The idea was further extended in the notion of "local need." This idea was to assume increased salience in subsequent years and may be represented as simultaneously a recognition of diversity and a reaction to totalizing concepts of health need. At the same time it also carried resonances of a belief model based on mythic interpretations of the organic community, or demos: "The system should ensure that the fullest possible account is taken of local need; and should encourage Family Practitioner Committees, in collaboration with District Health Authorities, and Health Boards to devise locally agreed strategies" (DHSS 1987, 20). The system was juxtaposed with the local; agreement and collaboration were to be expected within geographically defined areas.

These developments were most clearly articulated in proposals in the White Paper concerning the role of nurses. These proposals extended the use of space and its construction as "community" beyond a vision of cooperating bureaucracies to incorporate a further emerging pillar of the restructured welfare state—the ideologically charged figure of the "consumer." This device inscribed the language of choice, responsiveness, and commodification onto the healthscape through the medium of community and the local. Yet, at the same time, it remained paternalistic in its concept: "The Government accepts that the management and delivery of community nursing services at a level that is closer to consumers and more responsive to their needs is a welcome trend. Community nursing staff, together with other members of the primary health care team, are ideally placed to look after local needs because of their close contact with the community, their local knowledge and range of necessary skills" (DHSS 1987, 41).

Working for Patients

In *Working for Patients* the aim was to complete the restructuring of the NHS. In it a number of key proposals were set out with the central aim "to make the Health Service more responsive to the needs of patients. . . . As much power and responsibility as possible will be delegated to local level" (DOH 1989b, 4). The rhetoric was, thus, one of decentralization with power being shifted to the local. The reality was somewhat different although equally focused on power relations exercised over space.

This paradox is clearly evident in NHS trusts, one of the central instruments of the reforms set out in *Working for Patients.* Trusts were to operate as quasi-autonomous units within the managed health care market; they were to be providers of health care freed of any local control beyond that provided by the market.

> To stimulate a better service to the patient, hospitals will be able to apply for a new self-governing status as NHS hospital trusts. . . . While remaining in the NHS, they will take fuller responsibility for their own affairs. NHS hospital trusts will earn revenue from the services they provide. They will, therefore, have an incentive to attract patients, so they will make sure that the service they offer is what their patients want. . . . In turn they will stimulate other NHS hospitals to respond to what people want locally. (DOH 1989b, 4)

This approach altered the ethos of the hospitals involved. They retained a responsibility to the secretary of state for health but were no longer linked to the regions and districts in which they were located. Although they had to provide core services to their local populations, they were encouraged to improve their services and, therefore, competitiveness by generating a wider market appeal. They were, therefore, concurrently both local, often dependent on a single purchasing agency for the bulk of their business, and supralocal with control and power vested in the broader market and the secretary of state rather than the community and local need determination.

This fragmentation of the spatial locus of health policy was also evident for the other side of the internal market—the health care purchasers. An annihilation of distance and erasure of separation occurred whereby

> to enable hospitals which best meet the needs and wishes of patients to get the money to do so, the money required to treat patients will be able to cross administrative boundaries. All NHS hospitals . . . will be free to offer their services to different health authorities and to the private sector. Consequently, a health authority will be better able to discharge its duty. (DOH 1989b, 5)

The discourse was, thus, market driven; space was subservient to this imperative. Notions of the local and the sanctity of formal space, operating as a barrier to patterns of care use, were transgressed. Money followed contracts, and contracts could be placed according to economic advantage rather than proximity.

This reconceptualization of the role of space in health policy was completed by a furtherance of the linguistic stress upon the idea of community evidenced earlier in *Promoting Better Health* (DHSS 1987). Although container space, the space of bounded power, was weakened, the theme of decentralization and more power to manage at the community level was strengthened: "The Government's main task must be to set a national framework of objectives and priorities. Local management must then be allowed to get on with the task of managing, while remaining accountable to the centre for its delivery of the Government's objectives" (DOH 1989b, 12). This juxtaposition of the national and local is a consistent part of Conservative policy, a decentralization of management responsibility accompanied by a centralization of power relations. The free market ideology of the government and its beliefs in individual rather than state responsibility are central to this paradox. The changes are justified by an appeal to empowerment of the right to choose and responsiveness to local needs.

> Like RHAs, DHAs can then concentrate on ensuring that the health needs of the population for which they are responsible are met; that there are effective services for the prevention and control of diseases

> and the promotion of health; that their population has access to a comprehensive range of high quality, value for money services. (DOH 1989b, 15)

The movement of management and responsibility to the community level was also identified as the main underlying reason for the development of trusts. Ideological preferences became elided with appeals to localism and popular support for health care via adjectival and verbal hyperbole. The language of policy evidenced a belief system in which spatial metaphors provided a crucial underpinning to the quasi-market approach:

> The Government believes that self-government for hospitals will encourage a stronger sense of local ownership and pride, building on the enormous fund of goodwill that exists in local communities. It will stimulate the commitment and harness the skills of those who are directly responsible for providing services. Supported by a funding system in which successful hospitals can flourish, it will encourage local initiative and greater competition. All this in turn will ensure a better deal for the public, improving the choice and quality of the services offered and the efficiency with which those services are delivered. (DOH 1989b, 22)

Our argument so far has been that, where spatialized language was used within *Working for Patients,* it suggested implications for existing concepts of boundaries and belonging; ideas of a local population and community were also blurred. The debates around that White Paper indicated how the government used ideas of community and individual choice to market these changes. When it was presented to Parliament on 31 January 1989 by the secretary of state for health, Kenneth Clarke, notions of localism intermingled with market-speak were clearly evident: "We want all hospitals to have more responsibility for their own affairs, so that they can make the most of *local* commitment, energy and skills, and can get on with what they are best at, which is providing care"[4] and "I believe that this new development will give patients more choice, produce a better quality service, build on the sense of pride in *local* hospitals and encourage other hospitals to do even better in order to compete."[5]

4. Parl. Deb., Official Reports, Commons, 31 Jan. 1989, 146: 168, authors' emphasis.

5. Ibid., 169, authors' emphasis.

The debates surrounding aspects of the White Paper continued until the proposals were translated into policy in the National Health Service and Community Care Act (1990). One later response to the White Paper was tabled by then Labour Shadow Health Secretary Robin Cook and gave a clear indication of how ideas of health and place were perceived by the Opposition:

> What happened to all the talk of greater local decision-making? What happened to the promises of patient choice? If the Secretary of State is serious about choice in local decision-making, why not give local people the choice of whether their hospitals opt out? . . . If the right hon. and learned Gentleman seriously believes opt-out is good, let him put it to the vote of the local community. Let it be decided by the local community which that hospital serves.[6]

For Labour, therefore, the adaptation of space and place to a form of market functionality was unacceptable; crucially, they argued that the invocation of localism and community in policy discourse demanded a participatory element. The Conservative's health geography was unpeopled; it represented the intersection of an ideology and a functional need in which space and place were both used discursively to assist the presentation of the government's goals.

One of the aims of *Working for Patients* was to put in place a framework through which the ideas of *Promoting Better Health* could be developed and operationalized. The NHS was quite clearly being reconstructed into a service whereby the role of the general practitioner (GP), as either a provider or, through fundholding (Glennerster et al. 1994), as a purchaser, would eventually dominate. The GP would become the central figure of his or her locality, choosing hospitals for patients on the basis of waiting times (or possibly mortality rates) with the locality of the chosen hospital also reflecting the distance the patient was willing or able to travel. There was expected to be a clear element of market shaping as a consequence of the spatialized nature of the GP's decision making:

> Whether or not a GP has a practice budget, he will have more contact with and more influence over the developments of the hospital and community services in his area because he will be in contact with his

6. Parl. Deb., Official Reports, Commons, 2 May 1989, 152: 30.

> district health authority. . . . In future how the DHAs use their money to place contracts with hospitals will reflect the referral practices of the local GPs.[7]

Such hopes were, however, not always articulated, even by members of Parliament from the Conservative Party. For Jonathan Aitken, member for a relatively depressed southern England constituency, an appeal to more traditional values in which general practice had an almost organic relationship with its patients was in order.

> They believe with 12 per cent of their patients over 75 and another 33 per cent over 65—that they are serving the kind of community which can best be looked after by the gentler culture of traditional general practice, with all its occasional necessary time-wasting delays and pauses for counselling and sympathy which a caring service involves, rather than the harsher disciplines of competitive, doctor-versus-doctor consumer choice, free market medicine portrayed in the White Paper.[8]

The difference between communities, whether social, geographical or economic, was used to uphold the traditional role of the GP: servant of the health needs of society rather than agent of the market: "The decent, diligent family doctor is part of the culture of Britain, part of the fabric of society, and on the whole general practitioners have served their communities well."[9] Aitken's use of *gemeinschaftliche* concepts was indicative of a wider debate in which the discursive strategy of community as market engine was set alongside arguments that drew on popular support for a reinvented past in which the NHS had always been in harmony with community needs. These arguments cut both ways: "The Tories do not understand that they are up against a profound NHS culture which affects Tory voting doctors in the shires as much as it affects working class communities in inner cities"[10] yet

> I welcome the downward delegation of responsibilities to local level, and the options for hospitals to become self-governing within the NHS.

7. Ibid., 33–34. It would be tempting to interpret the gendered language to indicate an implicit assumption that men are more likely to adapt to the market discipline and to develop brokerage networks.
8. Ibid., Jonathan Aitken, 54.
9. Ibid.
10. Ibid., Harriet Harman, 71.

> That will result in the sort of better organised, more personal hospital service of which local communities were once proud and which many of my constituents feel has been lost in recent years due to excessive bureaucracy and the disappearance of matrons and local hospital boards.[11]

This dual discourse on the use of space and place was particularly evident in debates over local control. For the Opposition, the proposals were deeply antidemocratic; although localist rhetoric might be employed, power would be located elsewhere:

> The Secretary of State has not come up with a system in which the health authorities will be staffed by local people who are respected in local communities, as he put it. He has come up with health authorities that will have no pretence of representing local choices or interpreting local preferences. He has come up with a board of management that will exist to implement central policy—exactly the sort of machinery of the clapped-out centralised state which is being dismantled all over eastern Europe.[12]

For government supporters however, the legislation was seen as a way of returning hospitals to their communities:

> I welcome the opportunity for hospitals to free themselves from bureaucratic health authority control by applying to become self-governing trusts. . . . One of the essential points . . . is that that is voluntary and for local hospitals to decide. . . . I expect that hospitals will return to being much more like the local community hospitals—which they were before nationalisation.[13]

This removal of hospitals from direct control of the NHS was seen by some, however, as a step into another past:

> Hospitals that have opted out will be run as they used to be-on flag days. If they are hospitals in Bournemouth, where there is plenty of local cash and millionaire do-gooders abound they will make money as

11. Parl. Deb., Official Reports, Commons, 11 May 1989, 152: David Atkinson, c. 1064. Compare Jameson (1985) on the use of contested images to recreate selectively a chosen past.
12. Parl. Deb., Official Reports, Commons, 7 Dec. 1989; 163: Cook, c. 509.
13. Ibid., David Atkinson, c. 536–37.

> they did in the 1930s. If they are in places such as Barnsley and Bassetlaw, people will put 20p in the box. . . . The hospitals will have to scratch around, send people where it is cheaper and turn them away.[14]

For other opponents, the structure of community was used to argue against the bill:

> The British people have reacted with such vehemence and distaste to key aspects of the Government's proposals. They regard the Health Service—general practitioners, practices, local hospitals and the long-term care facilities for the chronically sick and infirm—as a keystone in the structure of their communities. . . . They do not want their elderly and very young to be hawked around in search of health care as their young are now being made to hawk themselves.[15]

The Health of the Nation

The language of *Working for Patients* and the associated political debates were redolent of polarized positions regarding the use of spatial metaphors. In some senses space was annihilated: it was secondary to the market; distance and localism were subservient to economic rationality. In other senses space was reconstructed as place, a locus of either control or resistance. These different discourses were extended in the third text, the health policy White Paper *The Health of the Nation* (DOH 1992), through a redefinition of notions of control and responsibility. *The Health of the Nation* used ideas of community and the local to withdraw collectivist power structures and replace them with more central control. At the same time it devolved the responsibility for health issues beyond the Department of Health, envisioning structural changes taking place at a range of spatial levels:

> Health is determined by a whole range of influences—from genetic inheritance, through personal behavior, family and social circumstances, to the physical and social environment—so opportunities and responsibilities for action to improve health are widely spread from individuals to Government as a whole. (DOH 1992, vii)

14. Parl. Deb., Official Reports, Commons, 11 Dec. 1989; 163: Joe Ashton, c. 712–13.

15. Ibid., Kim Howells, c. 724.

Linguistically it, thus, both externalized and internalized risk.

The main instrument proposed in the White Paper was the health target. Targets were set for a number of diseases specified by the Department of Health. These were national targets for disease reduction. There was an expectation that local targets would also be developed. The targets were to be achieved through the familiar recipe of central control of policy and local management of programs:

> In some countries central action stops at the point of setting and agreeing objectives and targets. . . . The Government does not believe this is a sufficient response for England. Although the need for delegation and local discretion has been identified as important in an English health strategy, avoidance of central prescription of how action should be taken does not mean the absence of central oversight and responsibility. . . . Objectives and targets in key areas for health improvements will provide a guide. . . . They will not be a blueprint of the action that the NHS and others will need to take at local level. Action at local level must be determined in the light of local circumstances, and other local priorities. (DOH 1992, 47)

Effectively, what was proposed was a strict limiting of local autonomy tempered by a discourse of discretionary autonomy, a panoptic regulation of the local by the central.

The Parliamentary debates on *The Health of the Nation* centered around this redefinition of health, the NHS, and the government's role. "Clearly a health strategy needs to go wider than the NHS, and wider than my own immediate responsibilities as Secretary of State for Health. . . . If this strategy is to work it cannot be just for Government and the NHS; it must be for the nation as a whole."[16] Health was, thus, reconstructed as a societal rather than a governmental responsibility. Even within government it was to be the concern of more than just one department. Superficially, this might be taken as an overdue recognition of a social model of health and a welcome demedicalization. It also, however, represented governmentality in the Foucauldian sense (Foucault 1988): individualized self-surveillance and an incorporation of "community" through notions of participation. Thus, "there are the vital roles of voluntary groups, community health councils, employers, trade unions and the

16. Parl. Deb., Official Reports, Commons, 4 June 1991, 192: William Waldegrave, c. 156.

media. They can help to get across to people the facts about, for example, how to avoid coronary heart disease and giving them opportunities to put knowledge into practice."[17]

Discussion

Much of what we have said in the preceding paragraphs amounts to fairly straightforward policy analysis. We have, however, occasionally referred to more theorized interpretations. We suggest that the changing views of place and space evident in recent British health policy indicate a fragmentation of the modernist project that was the pre-Thatcherite NHS. The deferral of meaning associated with the employment of the spatial metaphor is such that both space and place emerge as elements in a discursive strategy developed in response to challenges to power interests. We are left with confusing and multifaceted concepts that shift and change with a rapidity reminiscent of Harvey's (1989) analysis of the transforming landscapes of accumulation where the dynamics are so volatile that we have dazzling sequences of deterritorialization and reterritorialization. There are, thus, many narratives embodied in the concept of space and place in health policy from the commodified through the ritualized to the functional. Their meanings signify both the embodiment of power and the challenges to it.

We have already hinted at the utility of a Foucauldian perspective on these discourses. We have seen the annihilation and reconstitution of space through the internal market and note the symbolic manipulation of space to inscribe and reveal structures of power (Philo 1992). The concepts of space and place that we have considered have been characterized by contested constructions of meaning linked with the spatial exercise of power and a discourse driven less by reason and more by ideology. Although the monolith of the NHS has been fragmented, the gaze of the powerful has not (Foucault 1980, 1976). Notions of community and locality have been captured and subsumed within an ideology of self-surveillance and governmentality (Foucault 1988). Thus the notion of the panopticon, "enclosed, segmented space, observed at every point, in which individuals are inserted in a fixed place . . . in which power is exercised . . . according to a continuous hierarchial figure, in which each individual is constantly located, examined and distrib-

17. Ibid.

uted" (Foucault 1977), can be extended to health policy with the "community" as an incorporated and subjugated element.

In considering the spatialized and spatializing exercise of central power we need to reflect briefly on the historical narrative that is embodied in much of the textual material we have considered. The nationalization of the health services in 1948 established a form of control (and, therefore, responsibility and accountability) that was ultimately unacceptable to the Thatcher governments. We can trace three elements to this dissatisfaction. First, the NHS represented nationalization; this position was anathema to the Conservatives but popular with the public. There was, therefore, a conceptual return to an invented and selective past in which it was perceived that local communities played a much greater role in managing their health care. Second, the preexisting mechanisms for the exercise of power had been hierarchical and, at least partially, oriented to local democracy. This suggested a particular conception of the local community that the Conservatives did not share; they argued instead that the market provided a purer and more responsive form of local governance. Third, and as a consequence of the second point, there was a need to reconcile local market freedom and the panoptic gaze of the central state. As a consequence of these diverse pressures, the local was subjugated to the central, but there was a linguistic deferral of meaning in the inscription of notions of control, autonomy, and responsibility. The reinvention of community obscures the new control of the health service achieved by the Conservative government. Although the policies relating to trusts and GP budget imply the ultimate transfer of control to communities, to the local and away from the bureaucrats, the reality may be very different.

Health policy and its use of space and place is clearly inscribed by power and territorialized by discourses of different actors. Following Deleuze and Guattari (1988), we can see this as an attempt to impose order and organization on a "smooth space," in this case, the people's health. The various constructions of community and its use as control provide one element in the wider challenging of the hegemony of the medical gaze. The striation of preexisting assumptions enable government to play out an organizational construction of its own power aspirations in which it creates new realities that are then decoded by local agents and users. The smooth is "structured up" into ideas of what health is and whose responsibility it is; medical discourse is challenged as is the monolith of the NHS.

Conclusion

Geography is a far from simple element in health policy. The official construction of space and place in health policy is replete with contested meanings and emerging and disappearing power relations. We have conveyed something of the fragmented and complex nature of these discourses in contemporary texts on British health policy. Government has a vision of space and place that is multifaceted and polymorphous. Yet it is simultaneously utterly simple: sick people go to their local GPs and, if necessary, are referred to a hospital; care is bought mainly by their local health commission under the watchful eye of the NHS executive. That we have argued that there is more to it than that is, in one sense, merely an artifact of the nature of the academic inquiry that we have presented. It is also, however, an inevitable outcome of the successive unfolding of territorialized and evolving policy subject to negotiated understandings by a range of actors with different goals. In presenting a poststructuralist discourse analysis of health policy informed by the writings of Michel Foucault we have been able to begin a process of disclosure that recognizes policy as performance; a show designed to convey messages that are understood very differently by different people and in which seemingly straightforward concepts may transform and reform in response to the power positions of the interpreter.

Local GPs and local hospitals may be a fixed part of health space, defendable, recognized, even loved, but, we suspect, there is little popular knowledge or even interest in the spatialized governance of British health care. Notions of community and localism do, however, matter. To a considerable extent the material that we have discussed in this chapter indicates that, as a by-product of its annihilation and the fragmentation of the existing architecture of health space, we are witnessing a re-presentation of the local and the community in which popular and official constructions coincide albeit for different reasons. As N. Smith (1993) has argued, scale defines boundaries and contains control, but different people experience and construct this differently.

15

Conclusion

ROBIN A. KEARNS AND WILBERT M. GESLER

The preceding chapters in this volume represent a range of responses to calls for a (re)integration of medical geography within broader social and cultural concerns. Contributors have drawn on a range of theoretical perspectives, including humanism, political economy, and postmodernism to address a key theme of "post-medical geographies of health": the relationships between health and place (Kearns 1993). After a period of intense activity by geographers eager to develop theoretical orientations to health and place, this book represents a collective desire to substantiate theory with case studies grounded in the human experience of health and place. Authors have emphasized the use of social theory in examining the social construction of health and disease, the experience of place, and the consumer orientation of the "new" public health. The key contribution of this volume has, therefore, been the development of these concerns within carefully researched case studies. We have, in other words, added an empirical richness to theoretical orientations that are redefining geographers' interests in health and health care from "the purely spatial to the socio-spatial" (Gesler, Bird, and Oljeski 1997, 30).

We began the substantive chapters with three contributions grouped around the theme of landscape, the traditional focus of cultural geography. The underlying message of chapters by Gesler, Geores, and Frazier and Scarpaci is that landscapes are more than a backdrop to human activity or even determinants of health experience. Rather, contributors showed that the "in-place" experience of either healing or terror are produced by human action and reputation, concretized by symbols in the built environment. The combination of topography, buildings, and explicit signs become layered with the recollection of comfort or violence to create highly localized stratigraphies of collective memory and places that themselves become imbued with hope or fear. The net result is landscapes of consolation or desolation.

Authors in part 1 built upon traditions of humanism and political economy in geography by asking not only what feelings are experienced within particular landscapes and places (in the tradition of Tuan's *Landscapes of Fear*) but also how were these landscapes materially and politically produced (in the tradition of Dear and Wolch's *Landscapes of Despair*). These three chapters demonstrated that with respect to health place is an historically contingent process and in a constant state of becoming (Pred 1984).

Further research directions employing this theme might usefully examine ways in which processes of economic and service sector restructuring are changing both places themselves and the health experience of residents. By focusing on two spa towns and an arena of military dictatorship the authors chose case examples that vividly illustrate the health/landscape connection. The next challenge is to consider the forces shaping a more subtle range of landscapes of ease and dis-ease. Questions are begging to be asked about how the commodification of health (care) within capitalist societies is creating symbolic landscapes that speak of the need to *buy health* rather than *become healthy* (Kearns and Barnett 1997).

In part 2 contributors explored various ways in which identity, difference, and health are produced in and by place. Contributors adopted a range of perspectives that can be summarized as exploring (1) the ways in which the experience of place is shaped by the experience of disability and illness (chapters by Laws and Radford, and Dyck); (2) the ways that geographies of service provision and the subsequent health and welfare of user groups are shaped by perceptions of difference (chapters by Lee, Wolch, and Walsh and Takahashi); and (3) the ways that risk behavior associated with illness is place specific (the chapter by Asthana).

A unifying theme of part 2 has been the idea that "dis-ease," disability, and illness are embodied in the lives, behaviors, and identities of individuals. The common-language expressions "having an illness" or "having a disability" suggest that disease and disablement are add-on features like clothing or prosthetic devices. The authors in part 2 followed in the tradition of Parsons's (1975) discussion of the sick role in demonstrating that one's entire identity is (re)shaped by the experience. Indeed, the authors pointed out that restrictions placed on people by impaired mobility, social stigma, or service deprivation contribute to creating the contours of identity itself.

Further exploration of Dorn and Laws's (1994) call for exploration of the relationship between place and the corporeality of health experience, a theme well established in sociology (Nettleton 1995), might well be part of a larger gendering of geographies of health. As commentators have suggested, medical geographers have written from a largely genderless perspective (Pearson 1989), preferring to conduct research from positions of detachment and apparent objectivity that Rose (1993) names the "unmarked master subject." Part of the challenge to make space for difference in geographies of health and health care (Kearns 1995) involves a symbolic prising of the "medical" from medical geography to allow a greater appreciation of the body in the spatial contexts of lived experience. Through a willingness to "embrace the Other" in research relations and in orientation to illness and disability (Dyck and Kearns 1995; Kearns 1996) there is, we believe, opportunity to move to a position in which health and health care are (re)placed in the contexts of identity formation.

Part 3 comprised contributions investigating the relationship between health, place, and policy. Chapters by Hyndman and Poland considered two determinants of ill health: one, a common element of the built environment (housing), and the second, a chosen behavior (smoking). Whereas in the former Hyndman assessed the (orthodox, scientific) evidence of the ill-health effects of housing, Poland understandably took the ill effects of smoking to be axiomatic and examined the experience of public space that has been "purified" by antismoking policies.

In the final three chapters the way that place is implicated in, and shaped by, policies for the provision of health care services was considered. The provision of services that are appropriately shaped by the character of local places and communities, it has been argued, can in turn enrich the experience of place itself (R. A. Kearns 1991). This observation must be augmented by the fact that across Western nations, people live in times of galvanized localism and diminished political inclination toward collective provision. As Kearns argued in chapter 12, threats to appropriate services can create struggles, which, in turn, may reinvent the community in a celebration of difference. Eyles and Litva followed, assessing the connection between people, place, and policy in health care planning. In sum, in these chapters the authors insist that regardless of whether policy imperatives are aimed at creating "level playing fields" or empowering particular communities through health promotion, health (policy) cannot be displaced from community, and community cannot be displaced from local territory.

Quality of life is produced in and by the places that encircle people whether they be housing environments, residential neighborhoods, or the complex of land, people, and material interventions that make up regions. Within these contexts the health effects of broader socioeconomic policy are mediated by more explicit attempts to intervene in the policy process. Whether this be to promote health or to provide care, all interventions are developed and transmitted by means of language. The closing contribution by Moon and Brown indicated that talk is no idle matter in health policy. On the contrary, place is implicated in various ways by the language of health policy reforms. We suggest that further work in this vein might continue to explore the uses of language in health care environments. A fruitful direction here is suggested by Gesler's (1998) exploration of how "words in wards" define the parameters of such places. Further avenues for research might investigate the way health talk is gendered, racialized, and rarely displaced from local culture.

We close this volume with the observation that in the late 1980s, it was quite reasonable to title a book plainly and definitively *Medical Geography* (Meade, Florin, and Gesler 1988). Now, not only has the "medical" prefix to the subdiscipline been called into question (Kearns 1993) but also, consonant with the diversity of the 1990s, a singular "geography" is problematic. In part the pluralism that now pervades geographies of health, healing, and health care has been a necessary response to the paradigm shift we spoke of in chapter 1. This shift involves seeing location as a necessary but not sufficient element of place. Rather than being reduced to mere location, place is a negotiated and contested reality, part material and part social in character.

Just as place has been seen as excessively reduced to location, so, too, there is a prevalent perception that health and disease have been excessively reduced to physiological processes. Rather, both place and health are sociocultural realities. This recognition is reflected in the foregoing chapters in which it is noticeable that there are few (literal) maps but much mapping of (metaphorical) meaning. Thus, the preceding chapters have been wordier than much traditional medical geography, and this is indicative of an associated shift from the dominance of ***explanation*** as a research goal to ***understanding*** as a more desirable outcome of research. Interpretations are invariably more nuanced than explanations, and although our findings may be less easily appropriated into the public policy process because of this reliance on subtlety of argument, we believe the benefit is a better appreciation of human experience.

As we stressed earlier, this book is reflective of shifts both within the academic perspective of geography and wider academic and health-related debates. We believe that the changing perspectives signaled by this volume auger well for the capacity of geographers to contribute understanding and interpretation to the relationships between society, place, and health.

References

Index

References

Abler, R. F., M. G. Marcus, and J. M. Olson, eds. 1992. *Geography's Inner Worlds: Pervasive Themes in Contemporary American Geography.* New Brunswick, N.J.: Rutgers Univ. Press.

Abrahamson, Alan. 1991. "Been Down So Long Jail Looked Like Up to Him." *Los Angeles Times,* 21 Nov., A1.

Agnew, J. 1987. *Place and Politics.* Boston: Allen and Unwin.

———. 1993. "Representing Space: Space, Scale and Culture in Social Science." In *Place/ Culture/ Representation,* edited by J. Duncan and D. Ley, 251–71. London: Routledge.

Ahrentzen, S. B. 1992. "Home as a Workplace in the Lives of Women." In *Place Attachment,* edited by I. Altman and S. M. Low. New York: Plenum.

Alinsky, S. D. 1989. *Rules for Radicals.* New York: Vintage Books.

Allan, B. 1994. "How Well Are Primary and Secondary Services Being Integrated? A Case Study of Hokianga." Paper presented to Health Sector Summit Conference, 16–17 Mar., Auckland, N.Z.

Allen, S., and B. Adler. 1989. *The Passionate Nonsmoker's Bill of Rights: The First Guide to Enacting Nonsmoking Legislation.* New York: William Morrow.

"Americans Support Smoking Controls in Workplace, Agree That Smokers Should Refrain from Smoking Near Nonsmokers." 1986. *Smoking and Health Reporter* 3:4.

Amoury, A. 1990. "A Neighbourhood Revolution Hits Richmond City Hall." *PM Magazine,* Aug., 2–5.

Anderson, B. 1984. *Imagined Communities.* Verso: London.

Anderson, K., and F. Gale. 1992. *Inventing Places: Studies in Cultural Geography.* Melbourne, Australia: Longman-Cheshire.

Ankrah, M. 1989. "AIDS: Methodological Problems in Studying Its Prevention and Spread." *Social Science and Medicine* 29:265–76.

Antonovsky, A. 1987. *Unraveling the Mystery of Health: How People Manage Stress and Stay Well.* San Francisco, Calif.: Jossey Bass.

Appelbaum, R. P. 1990. "Counting the Homeless." *Homelessness in the United States.* Vol. 2, *Data and Issues,* edited by J. A. Momeni, 219–32. New York: Praeger.

Apter, D. E., and N. Sawa. 1984. *Against the State: Politics and Social Protest in Japan.* Cambridge, Mass.: Harvard Univ. Press.

Argentine National Commission. 1986. *Nunca Más: The Report of the Argentine National Commission on the Disappeared.* New York: Farrar Strauss Giroux.

Arguelles, J., and M. Arguelles. 1972. *Mandala.* Berkeley, Calif.: Shambala Publications.

Arnstein, S. 1969. "A Ladder of Citizen Participation." *Journal of the American Institute of Planners* 25:216–34.

Arundel, A. V., E. M. Sterling, J. H. Biggin, and T. D. Sterling. 1986. "Indirect Health Effects of Relative Humidity in Indoor Environments." *Environmental Health Perspectives* 65:351–61.

Ashley, M. J., S. Bull, and L. L. Pederson. 1994. Restrictive Measures on Smoking in Canada. OTRU working papers series, no. 1. Toronto: Ontario Tobacco Research Unit.

Ashton, H., and R. Stepney. 1982. *Smoking: Psychology and Pharmacology.* London: Tavistock.

Bagley, C. 1974. "The Built Environment as an Influence on Personality and Social Behavior: A Spatial Study." In *Psychology and the Built Environment,* edited by D. Canter and T. Lee, 156–62. New York: John Wiley and Sons.

Ballard, K. 1993. *Disability, Family, Whanau and Society.* Palmerston North, N.Z.: Dunmore Press.

Bamborough, J. B. 1980. *The Little World of Man.* London: Longmans, Green.

Barnes, S., M. Kaase, and K. R. Allerbeck. 1979. *Political Action,* Beverly Hills, Calif.: Sage.

Barrett, F. A. 1986. "Medical Geography: Concept and Definition." In *Medical Geography: Progress and Prospect,* edited by M. Pacione, 1–34. London: Croom Helm.

Bassuk, E. L., and S. Gerson. 1978. "Deinstitutionalization and Mental Health Services." *Scientific American* 238:46–53.

Battle Mountain Sanitarium. 1909. *Annual Report.* Pierre, S.D.: South Dakota State Archives.

Bauman, Z. 1987. *Legislators and Interpreters: Modernity, Post-modernity and Intellectuals.* Ithaca, N.Y.: Cornell Univ. Press.

Baweja, H., and A. Katiyar. 1992. "The Indian Face of AIDS." *India Today,* 30 Nov., 92–97.

Bean, J., et al. 1989. "Methods for the Reduction of AIDS Social Anxiety and Social Stigma." *AIDS Education and Prevention* 1:194–221.

Becker, D. 1990. "Therapy with Victims of Political Repression in Chile: The Challenge of Social Reparation." *Journal of Social Issues* 46:133–49.

Becker, D., and E. Lira, eds. 1989. *Derechos humanos: Todo es según el dolor con que se mira*. Santiago, Chile: Instituto Latinoamericano de Salud Mental y Derechos Humanos (ILAS).

Becker, H. 1963. *Outsiders: Studies in the Sociology of Deviance*. New York: Free Press.

Bell, C., and H. Newby. 1971. *Community Studies: An Introduction to the Sociology of the Local Community*. London: Allen and Unwin.

Berdiansky, H. A., and R. Parker. 1977. "Establishing a Home for the Adult Mentally Retarded in North Carolina." *Mental Retardation* 15:8–11.

Berg, L. D. 1993. "Between Modernism and Postmodernism." *Progress in Human Geography* 9, no. 3:356–78.

Berg, L. D., and Kearns, R. A. 1996. "Naming as Norming? 'Race,' Gender and the Identity Politics of Naming Places in Aotearoa/New Zealand." *Environment and Planning D: Society and Space* 14, no. 1:99–122.

Bernstein, R. J. 1976. *The Restructuring of Social and Political Theory*. Philadelphia: Univ. of Pennsylvania Press.

Berry, B. J. L. 1967. *Grouping and Regionalization*. Studies in Geography, no. 13. Evanston, Ill.: Northwestern Univ.

Bezzant, N. 1980. *Out of the Rock*. London: Heinemann.

Bhaba, H. K. 1990. "The Other Question: Difference, Discrimination and the Discourse of Colonialism." In *Out There: Marginalization and Contemporary Culture,* edited by R. Fergenson et al. New York: New Museum of Contemporary Art.

Bhaskar, R. 1975. *A Realist Theory of Science*. Leeds: Leeds Books.

Bickenbach, J. E. 1993. *Physical Disability and Social Policy*. Toronto: Univ. of Toronto Press.

Birenbaum, A., and M. A. Re. 1979. "Resettling Mentally Retarded Adults in the Community—Almost Four Years Later." *American Journal of Mental Deficiency* 83:323–29.

Black, D. 1989. *Sociological Justice*. New York: Oxford Univ. Press.

Blackford, K. A. 1993. "Images of Mothers with Multiple Sclerosis and Their Children: A Discourse Analysis of MS Society Newsletters (1957–1992)." *The Operational Geographer* 11:18–21.

Blacksell, M., C. Watkins, and K. Economides. 1986. "Human Geography and Law: A Case of Separate Development in Social Science." *Progress in Human Geography* 10:371–96.

Blank, R. H. 1994. *New Zealand Health Policy: A Comparative Study*. Auckland, N.Z.: Oxford Univ. Press.

Blau, Joel. 1992. *The Visible Poor: Homelessness in the United States.* New York: Oxford Univ. Press.

Bleasdale, M. 1994. "Deconstructing Social Role Valorization." *Interaction* 4:16–22.

Blendon, R. J., and K. Donelan. 1989. "AIDS, the Public and the NIMBY Syndrome." In *Public and Professional Attitudes Towards AIDS Patients,* edited by D. E. Rogers and E. Ginszberg, 19–30. Boulder, Colo.: Westview Press.

Blissland, J. H., and R. Manger. 1983. "A Qualitative Study of Attitudes Toward Mental Illness: Implications for Public Education." Paper presented at the Annual Convention of the American Psychological Association. Aug., Anaheim, Calif.

Blomley, N. K. 1989. "Text and Context: Rethinking the Law-Space Nexus." *Progress In Human Geography* 13:512–34.

———. 1992." Spacing Out: Towards a Critical Geography of Law." *Osgoode Hall Law Review* 30:661–90.

———. 1994. *Law, Space, and the Geographies Of Power.* New York: Guilford Press.

Blomley, N. K., and G. L. Clark. 1990. "Law, Theory and Geography." *Urban Geography* 11:433–46.

Bondi, L. 1990. "Feminism, Postmodernism, and Geography: Space for Women?" *Antipode* 22:156–67.

———. 1993. "Gender and Geography: Crossing Boundaries." *Progress in Human Geography* 17:244–56.

Bondi, L., and M. Domosh. 1992. "Other Figures in Other Places: On Feminism, Postmodernism and Geography" *Environment and Planning D: Society and Space* 10:199–213.

Bondy, S., et al. 1995. *Promoting Smoke-free Families.* Toronto: Ontario Tobacco Research Unit.

Bondy, S., and R. Ferrence. 1995. *Smoking Behaviour and Attitudes in Ontario, 1993.* Toronto: Ontario Tobacco Research Unit.

Bone, R. 1992. *The Geography of the Canadian North.* Toronto: Oxford Univ. Press.

Bordo, S. 1992. "Postmodern Subjects, Postmodern Bodies." *Feminist Studies* 18:159–75.

Boyarin, J., ed. 1994. *Remapping Memory: The Politics of TimeSpace.* Minneapolis: Univ. of Minnesota Press.

Bracht, N., and J. Gleason. 1990. "Strategies and Structures for Citizen Participation." In *Health Promotion at the Community Level,* edited by N. Bracht. Newbury Park: Sage.

Brennan, M., and R. Lancashire. 1978. "Association of Childhood Mortality with Housing Status and Unemployment." *Journal of Epidemiology and Community Health* 32:28–33.

Britten, R. H. 1942. "New Light on the Relation of Housing to Health." *American Journal of Public Health* 32:193.

Britton. S. G., R. Le Heron, and E. P. Pawson. 1992. *Changing Places in New Zealand: A Geography of Restructuring*. Christchurch: New Zealand Geographical Society.

Broegen, P. O., and M. Brommels. 1990. "Central and Local Control in Nordic Health Care." *International Journal of Health Planning and Management* 5:27–40.

Brooner, R. K., et al. 1993. "Antisocial Personality Disorder and HIV Infection among Intravenous Drug Abusers." *American Journal of Psychiatry* 150:53–58.

Brown, B. B., and D. D. Perkins. 1992. "Disruptions in Place Attachment." In *Place Attachment,* edited by I. Altman and S. M. Low. New York: Plenum.

Brown, M. 1995. "Ironies of Distance: An Ongoing Critique of the Geographies of AIDS." *Environment and Planning D: Society and Space* 13:159–83.

Browne, M. W. 1992. "Forensic Scientists and Computers Help Chilean Dead Tell Their Tales" *New York Times,* 14 Jan.

Brownstone, J., and T. J. Plunkett. 1983. *Metropolitan Winnipeg*. Berkeley and Los Angeles: Univ. of California Press.

Bruininks, R. H., et al., eds. 1981. *Deinstitutionalization and Community Adjustment of Mentally Retarded People*. Washington, D.C.: American Association on Mental Deficiency.

Brunner, J., A. Barríos, and C. Catalan. 1989. *Chile: Transformaciones culturales y modernidad*. Santiago: Facultad Latinoamericana de Creencias Sociales (FLACSO).

Bryson, J., and B. C. Crosby. 1993. "Policy Planning and the Design and Use of Forums, Arenas and Courts." *Environment and Planning B* 20:175–94.

Burawoy, M., A. Burton, and A. A. Ferguson. 1991. *Ethnography Unbound: Power and Resistance in the Modern Metropolis*. Berkeley and Los Angeles: Univ. of California Press.

Bureau of Publicity. 1895. *The Carlsbad of America*. Hot Springs, S.D.: Chamber of Commerce.

Burr, M. L., A. S. St. Leger, and J. W. G. Yarnell. 1981. "Wheezing, Dampness and Coal Fires." *Community Medicine* 3:205–9.

Burrow, J. 1966. *Evolution and Society: A Study in Victorian Social Theory*. Cambridge: Cambridge Univ. Press.

Burt, W. O. 1945. "Poverty, Housing and Health." *Medical Journal of Australia* 2:167–73.

Butler, J. 1990. *Gender Trouble: Feminism and the Subversion of Identity*. New York: Routledge.

Buttimer, A. 1974. *Values in Geography.* Commission on College Geography Research Report no. 24. Washington, D.C.: Commission on College Geography.

———. 1976. "Grasping the Dynamics of the Lifeworld." *Annals of the Association of American Geographers* 66:77–292.

Calhoun, C. J. 1980. "Community." *Social History* 5:105–29.

Canada. Secretary of State. 1986. *Profile of Disabled Persons in Canada.* Ottawa.

Canter, D. 1986. "Putting Situations in Their Place." In *Social Behavior in Context,* edited by A. Furnham, 208–39. Boston: Allyn and Bacon.

Canter, D., and S. Canter, eds. 1979. *Designing for Environment: A Review of Research.* New York: John Wiley.

Castellani, P. J. 1987. *The Political Economy of Developmental Disabilities.* Baltimore: Paul H. Brookes Publishing.

Chaney, D. 1994. *The Cultural Turn: Scene-Setting Essays on Contemporary Cultural History.* New York: Routledge.

Charles, C., and S. DeMaio. 1992. "Lay Participation in Health-care Decision-making." McMaster Univ., Centre for Health Economics and Policy Analysis, working paper 92, no. 16.

Chicago and Northwestern Railway. 1916. *The Black Hills, South Dakota: The Richest Hundred Mile Square in the World.* Chicago: Chicago and Northwestern Railway.

Chile Information Project (CHIP) News. 1991. Internet News Service. 9, 10, 11 Feb.

———. 1994. Internet News Service. 6 Aug.

Chilmonczyk, B., et al. 1993. "Association Between Exposure to Environmental Tobacco Smoke and Exacerbations of Asthma in Children. *New England Journal Of Medicine* 328:1665–69.

Claggett, W. W., et al. 1984. "Nationalization of the American Electorate." *American Political Science Review* 78:77–91.

Clark, Badger. 1927. *When Hot Springs Was a Pup.* Hot Springs, S.D.: Star Printing.

Clark, C. 1994. "Managing Righteousness: Smokers' Strategies in Problematic Public Encounters." Indianapolis: Indiana Univ. Manuscript.

Clark, G. L. 1989a. "The Geography of Law." In *New Models in Geography: The Political Economy Perspective,* edited by R. Peet and N. Thrift, 310–37. London: Unwin Hyman.

———. 1989b. "Law and the Interpretive Turn in the Social Sciences." *Urban Geography* 10:209–28.

Cloke, P., C. Philo, and D. Sadler. 1991. *Approaching Human Geography: An Introduction to Contemporary Theoretical Debates.* New York: Guilford Press.

Coates, Robert B. 1981. "Deinstitutionalization and the Serious Juvenile Offender: Some Policy Considerations." *Crime and Delinquency* 27:477–86.

Cohen, A. 1982. *Belonging.* Manchester, Eng.: Univ. of Manchester Press.

Cohen, I. J. 1989, *Structuration Theory: Anthony Giddens and the Constitution of Social Life.* London: Macmillan.

Colectivo Latinoamericano (COLAT) (J. Barudy et al.). 1982. *Psicología de la Tortura y el Exilio.* Madrid: Editorial Fundamentos.

Coley, N. G. 1982. "Physicians and the Chemical Analysis of Mineral Waters in Eighteenth-century England." *Medical History* 26:123–44.

———. 1990. "Physicians, Chemists and the Analysis of Mineral Waters: The Most Difficult Part of Chemistry." *Medical History,* suppl., no. 10:56–66.

Collins, J. 1992. *When Eagles Fly: A Report on Resettlement of People with Learning Disabilities from Long-Stay Institutions.* London: Values into Action.

Collins, K. J. 1986. "Low Indoor Temperatures and Morbidity in the Elderly." *Age and Ageing* 15:212–20.

———. 1987. "Effects of Cold on Old People." *British Journal of Hospital Medicine* (Dec.): 506–13.

Collins, P. H. 1990. *Black Feminist Thought: Knowledge, Consciousness and the Politics of Empowerment.* London: Harper Collins.

Comisión Nacional de Verdad y Reconciliación. 1991. *Informe Rettig: Informe de la Comision Nacional de Verdad y Reconciliacion.* Vol. 2. Santiago, Chile: Gobierno.

Community Action Committee. 1991. *Minutes.* Rawene, N.Z.: Community Action Committee.

Conrad, P., and J. Schneider. 1980. *Deviance and Medicalization.* St Louis, Mo.: Mosby.

Constable, P., and A. Valenzuela. 1991. *A Nation of Enemies: Chile under Pinochet.* New York: Norton.

Cook, S. D. 1888. *The Hot Springs of South Dakota.* Sioux City, Iowa: Exchange Printing

Cornwell, J. 1984. *Hard-earned Lives: Accounts of Health and Illness from East London.* London: Tavistock.

Cosgrove, D. 1984. "Landscape and Social Formation: Theoretical Considerations." In *Social Formation and Symbolic Landscape.* Totowa, N.J.: Barnes and Noble.

———. 1985. *Social Formation and Symbolic Landscape.* Totowa, N.J.: Barnes and Noble Books.

———. 1986. "Sense of Place". In *The Dictionary of Human Geography,* edited by R. Johnston, 425. London: Blackwell.

———. 1987. "New Directions in Cultural Geography." *Area* 19:95–101.

Cuba, L., and D. M. Hummon. 1993. "A Place to Call Home". *Sociological Quarterly* 34:111–31.

Cunliffe, B. 1969. *Roman Bath.* Oxford: Oxford Univ. Press.

———. 1986. *The City of Bath.* Gloucester, Eng.: Alan Sutton.

Dahl, R. A. 1967. "The City in the Future of Democracy". *American Political Science Review* 61, no. 4: 953–70.

Dahl, R. A., and E. R. Tufte. 1974. *Size and Democracy,* London: Oxford Univ. Press.

Dakota Hot Springs Company. 1888. Advertisement in *Daily Hot Springs Star.*

Dales, R. E., R. Burnett, and H. Zwanenbug. 1991. "Adverse Health Effects among Adults Exposed to Home Dampness and Molds." *American Review of Respiratory Disease* 143:505–9.

Daniel Yankelovich Group. 1990. *Public Attitudes Toward People with Chronic Mental Illness: Executive Summary.* Princeton, N.J.: Robert Wood Johnson Foundation.

Daniels, S., and D. Cosgrove. 1988. "The Iconography of Landscape". In *The Iconography of Landscape,* edited by D. Cosgrove and S. Daniels, 1–10. Cambridge: Cambridge Univ. Press.

Dardel, E. 1952. *L'homme et la terre.* Paris: Presses Universitaires de France.

Dassin, J., ed. 1986. *Torture in Brazil: A Report by the Archdiocese of Sao Paulo.* New York: Vintage Books.

Davey, J. A., and R. A. Kearns. 1994. "Special Needs Versus the 'Level Playing-field': Recent Developments in Housing Policy for Indigenous People in New Zealand." *Journal of Rural Studies* 10:73–82.

Dayal, H. H., et al. 1994. "Passive Smoking and Obstructive Respiratory Diseases in an Industrialized Urban Population." *Environmental Research* 65:161–71.

de Certeau, M. 1984. *The Practice of Everyday Life.* Berkeley and Los Angeles: Univ. of California.

de Lauretis, T. 1990. "Eccentric Subjects: Feminist Theory and Historical Consciousness." *Feminist Studies* 16:115–50.

De Tocqueville, A. 1945. *Democracy in America.* New York: Phillips Bradley.

Deal, E. C., Jr., et al. 1979. "Role of Respiratory Heat Exchange in Production of Exercise-induced Asthma." *Journal of Applied Physiology* 46:467–75.

Dear, M. 1988. "The Postmodern Challenge: Reconstructing Human Geography." *Transactions, Institute of British Geographers* 13:262–74.

———. 1994. "Postmodern Human Geography: A Preliminary Assessment." *Erdkunde* 48:2–13.

Dear, M., et al. 1980. *Coping in the Community: The Needs of Ex-Psychiatric Patients.* Hamilton, Ont.: Mental Health, Hamilton.

Dear, M., and B. Gleeson. 1991. "Community Attitudes Toward the Homeless." *Urban Geography* 12:155–76.

Dear, M., and L. Takahashi. 1992. Health and Homelessness. In *Community, Environment and Health: Geographic Perspectives,* edited by M. V. Hayes, L. Foster, and H. D. Foster, 185–212. Victoria, British Columbia: Univ. of Victoria.

Dear, M., and S. M. Taylor. 1982. *Not on Our Street: Community Attitudes Toward Mental Health Care.* London: Pion.

Dear, M., and G. Wasmandorf. 1993. "Postmodern Consequences". *Geographical Review* 83:321–29.

Dear, M., and J. R. Wolch. 1987. *Landscapes of Despair: From Deinstitutionalization to Homelessness.* Princeton, N.J.: Princeton Univ. Press.

———. 1989. "How Territory Shapes Everyday Life." In *The Power of Geography: How Territory Shapes Everyday Life,* edited by J. Wolch and M. Dear, 134–51. Boston: Unwin Hyman.

Dear, M., J. Wolch, and R. Wilton. 1994. The Service Hub Concept in Human Services Planning. *Progress in Planning* 42: 173–271.

Deleuze, G., and F. Guattari. 1988. *A Thousand Plateaus: Capitalism and Schizophrenia.* London: Athlone.

Department of Health (DOH). 1989a. *Caring for People.* London: Her Majesty's Stationery Office.

———. 1989b. *Working for Patients.* London: Her Majesty's Stationery Office.

———. 1992. *The Health of the Nation.* London: Her Majesty's Stationery Office.

Department of Health and Social Services (DHSS). 1987. *Promoting Better Health.* London: Her Majesty's Stationery Office.

Desario, J. 1987. "Consumers and Health Planning." In *Citizen Participation in Public Decision-making,* edited by J. Desario and S. Langton. New York: Greenwood Press.

de Shazo, P. 1983. *Urban Workers and Labor Unions in Chile.* Madison: Univ. of Wisconsin Press.

Dijkstra, L., et al. 1990. "Respiratory Health Effects of the Indoor Environment in a Population of Dutch Children." *American Review of Respiratory Disease* 142:1172–78.

Doel, M. 1993. "Proverbs for Paranoia: Writing Geography on Hallowed Ground." *Transactions, Institute of British Geographers* 18:377–94.

Domínguez V., Rosario, et al. 1994. *Salud y derechos humanos: Una experiencia desde el sistema público Chileno 1991–1993.* Santiago, Chile: Programa de Reparación y Atención Integral de Salud y Derechos Humanos, Ministerio de Salud (PRAIS).

Donovan, J. 1986. *We Don't Buy Sickness, It Just Comes: Health, Illness and Health Care in the Lives of Black People in London.* London: Tavistock.

Dorn, M. 1993. "Physical Disability as Spatial Dissidence: A Cultural Geography of the Stigmatized Body." Master's thesis, Department of Geography, Pennsylvania State Univ.

Dorn, M., and G. Laws. 1994. "Social Theory, Medical Geography and Body Politics: Extending Kearns' Invitation" *Professional Geographer* 46:106–10.

Drake, P. W., and I. Jaksić, eds. 1991. *The Struggle for Democracy in Chile 1982–1990.* Lincoln: Univ. of Nebraska Press.

Drake, R. E., G. J. McHugo, and D. L. Noordsy. 1993. "Treatment of Alcoholism among Schizophrenic Outpatients: 4-Year Outcomes." *American Journal of Psychiatry* 150:328–29.

Driver, F. 1985. "Power, Space and the Body: A Critical Assessment of Foucault's 'Discipline and Punish.'" *Environment and Planning D: Society and Space* 3:425–46.

———. 1993. *Power and Pauperism: The Workhouse System 1834–1884.* Cambridge: Cambridge Univ. Press.

Dudley, J. R. 1983. *Living with Stigma.* Springfield Ill.: Charles C. Thomas.

Duncan, J. 1973. "Landscape Taste as a Symbol of Group Identity." *Geographical Review* 63:334–55.

Duncan, J., and N. Duncan. 1988. "(Re) reading the Landscape." *Environment and Planning D: Society and Space* 6:117–26.

Dunleavy, P. 1979. "The Urban Basis of Political Alignment." *British Journal of Political Science* 9:409–43.

Dyck, I. 1989. "Integrating Home and Wage Workplace: Women's Daily Lives in a Canadian Suburb." *The Canadian Geographer* 33:329–41.

———. 1990. "Space, Time, and Renegotiating Motherhood: An Exploration of the Domestic Workplace." *Environment and Plannning D: Society and Space* 8:459–83.

———. 1992. "Health and Health Care Experiences of the Immigrant Woman: Questions of Culture, Context and Gender." In *Community, Environment and Health: Geographical Perspectives,* edited by M. Hayes, L. T. Foster, and H. D. Foster, 231–50. Victoria, B.C.: Univ. of Victoria Press.

———. 1995. "Hidden Geographies: The Changing Lifeworlds of Women with Multiple Sclerosis." *Social Science and Medicine* 40:307–20.

Dyck, I., and R. A. Kearns. 1995. "Transforming the Relations of Research: Towards a Culturally Safe Medical Geography." *Health and Place* 1:137–47.

Eakin, J., et al. 1994. "Framework for a Critical Social Science Perspective: Implications for Health Promotion Research". Paper presented at the Third National Conference on Health Promotion Research, 16–18 June, Calgary, Canada.

Earle, C. V. 1992. *Geographical Inquiry and American Historical Problems.* Stanford: Stanford Univ. Press.

Edgerton, R. B. 1967. *The Cloak of Competence: Stigma in the Lives of the Mentally Retarded.* Berkeley and Los Angeles: Univ. of California Press.

Edgerton, R. B., and S. M. Bercovici. 1976. "The Cloak of Competence—Years Later." *American Journal of Mental Deficiency* 80:485–97.

Eliade, M. 1959. *The Sacred and the Profane: The Nature of Religion.* New York: Harcourt, Brace.

Elias, P. 1988. *The Dakota of the Canadian Northwest: Lessons for Survival.* Winnipeg: Manitoba Univ. Press.

Empfield, M., et al. 1993. "HIV Seroprevalence among Homeless Patients Admitted to a Psychiatric Inpatient Unit." *American Journal of Psychiatry* 150:47–52.

Engels, F. 1969. *The Condition of the Working Class in England in 1844.* Frogmore, Eng.: Panther Books.

Entrikin, J. N. 1991. *The Betweenness of Place: Towards a Geography of Modernity.* Baltimore, Md.: Johns Hopkins Univ. Press.

Epp, J. 1986. *Achieving Health For All: A Framework for Health Promotion.* Ottawa: Ministry of Supply and Services.

Equipo de Denuncia, Investigación y Tratamiento al Torturado y su Núcleo Familia (DITT). 1989. *Persona, estado, poder: Estudios sobre salud mental en Chile 1973–1989.* Santiago, Chile: Comité de Defensa de los Derechos del Pueblo (CODEPU).

Erickson, P. G. 1993. "The Law, Social Control, and Drug Policy: Models, Factors, and Processes." *International Journal of Addictions* 28:1155–76.

Erickson, P. G., and C. A. Ottaway. 1993. "Policy: Alcohol and Other Drugs." *Annual Review Of Addictions Research and Treatment* 3:331–41.

Evans, R., M. Barer, and T. Marmor. 1994. *Why Are Some People Healthy and Others Not?: The Determinants of Health of Populations.* New York: Aldine de Gruyter.

Eyles, J. 1985. *Senses of Place.* Warrington, Eng.: Silverbrook Press.

———. 1993a. "From Disease Ecology and Spatial Analysis to . . . ? The Challenges of Medical Geography in Canada." *Health and Canadian Society* 1:113–45.

———. 1993b. "The Role of the Citizen in Health-care Decision-making." Policy Commentary C93-1, Centre for Health Economics and Policy Analysis, McMaster Univ., Hamilton, Ont.

Eyles, J., et al. 1990. "The Impacts and Effects of the Hagersville Tire Fire." In *The Challenges of a New Decade,* vol. 2, 818–29. Toronto: Environment Ontario.

Eyles, J., and J. Donovan. 1986. "Making Sense of Sickness and Care: An Ethnography of Health in a West Midlands Town." *Transactions, Institute of British Geographers* 11:415–27.

Eyles, J., and D. M. Smith. 1988. *Qualitative Methods in Geography.* London: Polity Press.

Eyles, J., and K. Woods. 1983. *The Social Geography of Health and Health Care.* London: Croom Helm.

Fain, A., B. Guerin, and B. J. Hart. 1990. *Mites and Allergic Disease.* Varennes en Argonne, France: ALLERBIO.

Feingold, E. 1977. "Citizen Participation." In *The Consumer and the Health-care System,* edited by H. M. Rosen et al. New York: Spectrum.

Feinsilver, J. M. 1993. *Healing the Masses: Cuban Health Politics at Home and Abroad.* Berkeley and Los Angeles: Univ. of California Press.

Ferguson, K. 1993. *The Man Question: Visions of Subjectivity in Feminist Theory.* Berkeley and Los Angeles: Univ. of California Press.

Ferguson, T. 1987. *The No-Nag, No-Guilt, Do-It-Your-Own-Way Guide To Quitting Smoking.* New York: Ballantine.

Ferrence, R. 1990. *Deadly Fashion: The Rise and Fall of Cigarette Smoking in North America.* New York: Garland.

Field, D., and I. Johnson. 1993. "Volunteers in the British Hospice Movement." In *The Sociology of Death,* edited by D. Clark, 198–220. Oxford: Blackwell.

Fine, M., and A. Asch. 1988. "Disability Beyond Stigma: Social Interaction, Discrimination, and Activism." *Journal of Social Issues* 44:3–21.

Fischer, P. J. 1988. "Criminal Activity among the Homeless: A Study of Arrests in Baltimore." *Hospital and Community Psychiatry* 39:46–51.

Fisher, R. 1977. *Contact and Conflict: Indian-European Relations in British Columbia, 1774–1890.* Vancouver: British Columbia Univ. Press.

Fiske, J. 1989. *Reading the Popular.* Boston: Unwin Hyman.

Flax, Jane. 1993. *Disputed Subjects: Essays on Psychoanalysis, Politics and Philosophy.* New York: Routledge.

Flynn, M. C. 1986. "Adults Who Are Mentally Handicapped as Consumers: Issues and Guidelines for Interviewing." *Journal of Mental Deficiency Research* 30:369–77.

Ford, N., and S. Koetsawang, S. 1991. "The Socio-cultural Context of the Transmission of HIV in Thailand." *Social Science and Medicine* 33:405–14.

Foucault, M. 1965. *Madness and Civilization: A History of Madness in the Age of Reason.* New York: Random House.

———. 1973. *The Birth of the Clinic: An Archaeology of Medical Perception.* Translated by A. M. Sheridan Smith. New York: Pantheon.

———. 1976. *The Birth of a Clinic: An Archaeology of the Human Sciences.* London: Tavistock.

———. 1977. *Discipline and Punish: The Birth of the Prison.* New York: Pantheon.

———. 1978. *The History of Sexuality.* Vol. 1, *An Introduction.* Translated by R. Hurley. London: Allen Lane.

———. 1980. *Power/Knowledge.* New York: Pantheon.

———. 1988. "Technologies of the Self." In *Technologies of the Self,* edited by L. H. Martin et al., 16–49. London: Tavistock.

Fox, A. J., and P. O. Goldblatt. 1982. *Longitudinal Study. Socio-demographic Mortality Differentials.* Ser. L.S., no. 1. London: Her Majesty's Stationery Office.

Fox, N. J. 1993. *Postmodernism, Sociology and Health.* Milton Keynes, Eng.: Open Univ. Press.

Fox, R. H., et al. 1973. "Body Temperatures in the Elderly: A National Survey of Physiological, Social and Environmental Conditions." *British Medical Journal* 1:200–206.

Francis, M. 1990. "Control as a Dimension of Public-Space Quality." In *Public Places and Spaces,* edited by R. Altman and E. Zube, 147–72. New York: Plenum.

Frederickson, H. G. 1982. "The Recovery of Civism in Public Administration." *Public Administration Review* 42:501–8.

Fuhrer, U. 1990 "Bridging the Ecological-Psychological Gap: Behavior Settings as Interfaces." *Environment and Behavior* 22:518–37.

Furniss, M. 1974. "The Practical Significance of Decentralization." *Journal of Politics* 36:958–82.

Gadd, D. 1971. *Georgian Summer: Bath in the Eighteenth Century.* Bath: Adams and Dart.

Gale, C., C. F. Ng, and L. Rosenblood. 1988. "Neighborhood Attitudes Toward Group Homes for Persons with Mental Handicaps." *Mental Retardation and Learning Disability Bulletin* 16:7–26.

Gallie, W. B. 1955–56. "Essentially Contested Concepts." *Proceedings of the Aristoleian Society* 56:167–98.

Garcia Villegas, J. R. 1990. *Pisagua! Cain: ¿Qué has hecho con tu hermano?* Santiago, Chile: Editora Periodística Emision S.A..

Gardner, L. I., et al. 1989. "Spatial Diffusion of the Human Immunodeficiency Virus Infection Epidemic in the United States 1985–1987." *Annals of the Association of American Geographers* 79:25–43.

Gatens, M. 1992. "Power, Bodies and Difference." In *Destabilizing Theory: Contemporary Feminist Debates,* edited by M. Barrett and A. Phillips, 120–37. Cambridge: Polity.

Gesler, W. M. 1991. *The Cultural Geography of Health Care.* Pittsburgh: Univ. of Pittsburgh Press.

———. 1992. "Therapeutic Landscapes: Medical Issues in Light of the New Cultural Geography." *Social Science and Medicine* 34:735–46.

———. 1993. "Therapeutic Landscapes: Theory and Case Study of Epidauros, Greece." *Environment and Planning D: Society and Space* 11:171–89.

———. 1996. "Lourdes: Healing in a Place of Pilgrimage." *Health and Place* 2:95–106.

———. Forthcoming. "Words in Wards: Language, Place and Medical Geography." *Health and Place.*

Gesler, W. M., S. Bird, and S. Oljeski. 1997. "Disease Ecology and a Reformist Alternative: The Case of Infant Mortality." *Social Science and Medicine* 44:65–71.

Gibbons, F. X. 1986. "Stigma and Interpersonal Relations." In *the Dilemma of Difference: A Multidisciplinary View of Stigma,* edited by S. C. Ainlay, G. Becker, and L. M. Coleman, 123–44. New York: Plenum.

Giddens, A. 1984a. "Comments on the Theory of Structuration." *Journal for Theory of Social Behavior* 13:75–80.

———. 1984b. *The Constitution of Society.* Berkeley and Los Angeles: Univ. of California Press.

———. 1991. *Consequences of Modernity.* Cambridge: Polity.

Gilman, S. L. 1988. *Disease and Representation: Images of Illness from Madness to AIDS.* Ithaca, N.Y.: Cornell Univ. Press.

Girimaji, P. 1992. "Professional Blood Donors Protest." *World AIDS* (July): 9–10.

Giroux, H. A. 1993. *Living Dangerously: Multiculturalism and the Politics of Difference.* New York: Peter Lang.

———. 1994. *Disturbing Pleasures: Learning Popular Culture.* New York: Routledge.

Glennerster, H., et al. 1994. *Implementing GP Fundholding.* Milton Keynes, Eng.: Open Univ. Press.

Godbout, J., and M. Leduc. 1987. *Une vision de l'exterieur du reaseau des affairs sociales.* Montreal: Institute for Urban and Regional Research.

Goffman, E. 1959. *The Presentation of Self in Everyday Life.* London: Penguin.

———. 1963a. *Behavior in Public Places.* New York: Macmillan.

———. 1963b. *Stigma: Notes on the Management of Spoiled Identity.* Englewood Cliffs, N.J.: Prentice-Hall.

———. 1971. *Relations in Public: Microstudies of the Public Order.* New York: Basic Books.

Gold, J. R. 1994. "Locating the Message: Place Promotion as Image Communication." In *Place Promotion: The Use of Publicity and Marketing to Sell Towns and Regions,* edited by J. R. Gold and S. V. Ward. New York: John Wiley and Sons.

Gollay, E., R. Freedman, M. Wyngaarden, and N. R. Kurtz. 1978. *Coming Back: The Community Experiences of Deinstitutionalized Mentally Retarded People.* Cambridge, Mass.: Abt Books.

Golledge, R. 1993. "Geography and the Disabled: A Survey with Special Reference to Vision Impaired and Blind Populations". *Transactions, Institute of British Geographers* 18:63–85.

Gómez, L. 1990. *Tras La huelga de los desaparacidos.* Santiago, Chile: Ediciones Caleuche.

Goodin, R. E. 1989. *No Smoking: The Ethical Issues.* Chicago: Univ. of Chicago Press.

Goodwin, M., S. Duncan, and S. Halford. 1993. "Regulation Theory, the Local State, and the Transition of Urban Politics." *Environment and Planning D: Society and Space* 11:67–88.

Gould, P. 1993. *The Slow Plague: A Geography of the AIDS Pandemic.* Oxford: Blackwell.

Graham, L., and R. Logan. 1990. "Social Class and Tactics: Neighborhood Opposition to Group Homes." *Sociological Quarterly* 31:513–29.

Grant, J. 1988. "They Say 'You Can't Legislate Public Participation.'" *Plan Canada* 27:260–67.

Grasmick, H. G., R. J. Bursik, and K. A. Kinsey. 1991. "Shame and Embarassment as Deterrents to Noncompliance with the Law: The Case of an Antilittering Campaign." *Environment and Behavior* 23:233–51.

Gravesen, S. 1989. "Fungi as a Cause of Allergic Diseases." *Allergy* 34:135–54.

Green, D. E., I. A. McCormick, and F. H. Walkey. 1987. "Community Attitudes to Mental Illness in New Zealand Twenty-two Years On." *Social Science and Medicine* 24:417–22.

Green, G. H. 1975. "The Effect of Indoor Relative Humidity on Absenteeism and Colds in Schools." *ASHRAE Journal* (Jan.): 57–62.

———. "Field Studies of the Effect of Air Humidity on Respiratory Disease." In *Indoor Climate: Effects on Human Comfort, Performance and Health in Residential, Commercial and Light-industry Buildings,* edited by P. O. Fanger and O. Valbjorn, 207–15. Copenhagen: Danish Building Research Institute.

Gregory, D., R. Martin, and G. Smith. 1994. *Human Geography: Society, Space, and Social Science.* Minneapolis: Univ. of Minnesota Press.

Griffin, E., and L. Ford. 1980. "A Model of the Latin American City." *Geographical Review* 37:397–422.

Grosz, E. 1994. *Volatile Bodies: Toward a Corporeal Feminism.* Bloomington: Indiana Univ. Press.

Groth, P. 1994. *Living Downtown: The History of Residential Hotels in the United States.* Berkeley and Los Angeles: Univ. of California Press.

Guerrero, B., ed. 1990. *Vida, pasión y muere en Pisagua.* Iquique, Chile: Centro de Investigación de la Realidad del Norte (CREAR).

Gusfield, J. R. 1989. "Constructing The Ownership of Social Problems: Fun and Profit in the Welfare State." *Social Problems* 36:431–41.

Habermas, J. 1976. *Legitimation Crisis.* London: Heinemann.

Haddon, J. 1973. *Bath.* London: B. T. Batsford.

Hagey, R. 1984. "The Phenomenon, the Explanations and the Responses: Metaphors Surrounding Diabetes in Urban Canadian Indians." *Social Science and Medicine* 18, no. 3:265–72.

Halifax, J. 1982. *Shaman, the Wounded Healer.* London: Thames and Hudson.

Hamlin, C. 1990. "Chemistry, Medicine, and the Legitimization of English Spas, 1740–1840." *Medical History,* suppl., no. 10:67–81.

Hanson, S., and G. Pratt. 1988. "Reconceptualising the Links Between the Home and Work in Urban Geography." *Economic Geography* 64:299–321.

Haraway, D. 1990. "A Manifesto for Cyborgs: Science, Technology, and Socialist Feminism in the 1980s." In *Feminism/Postmodernism,* edited by L. J. Nicholson, 190–233. New York: Routledge.

Harley, D. 1990. "A Sword in a Madman's Hand: Professional Opposition to Popular Consumption in the Waters Literature of Southern England and the Midlands, 1570–1870." *Medical History,* suppl. no. 10:48–55.

Harris, C. 1978. "The Historical Mind and the Practice of Geography." In *Humanistic Geography: Prospects and Problems,* edited by D. Ley and M. S. Samuels. London: Croom Helm.

Harrison, B., and B. Bluestone. 1988. *The Great U-Turn: Corporate Restructuring and the Polarizing of America.* New York: Basic Books.

Hart, J. F. 1991. *The Land That Feeds Us.* New York: Norton.

Hart, J. T. 1971. "The Inverse Care Law." *Lancet* 1:405–12.

Harvey, D. 1969. *Explanation in Geography.* New York: St. Martin's Press.

———. 1982. *The Limits to Capital.* London: Arnold.

———. 1989. *The Condition of Postmodernity.* Oxford: Blackwell.

Hayes, M. V. 1994. "Evidence, Determinants of Health and Population Epidemiology: Humming the Tune, Learning the Lyric." In *The Determinants of Population Health: A Critical Assessment,* edited by M. V. Hayes, L. T. Foster, and H. D. Foster, 121–33. Victoria, B.C.: Univ. of Victoria.

———. 1995. "Missing People in Depthless Spaces: Health, Place and Social Epidemiology." Paper presented at annual meeting, Association of American Geographers, 15 Apr., Chicago.

Heal, L. W., and G. T. Fujiura. 1984. "Methodological Considerations in Research on Residential Alternatives for Developmentally Delayed Persons." *International Review of Research in Mental Retardation* 12:205–44.

Healey, P. 1986. "Interpretive Policy Inquiry: A Response to the Limitations of the Received View." *Policy Sciences* 19:381–96.

Health Benefits Review Committee. 1986. *Choices for Health Care: Report of the Health Benefits Review Committee.* Wellington, N.Z.: Government Printer.

Heginbotham, C. 1985. "Health and Housing." *Hospitals and Health Services Review* (Sept.): 218–20.

Herbert, D. T. 1983. "Crime and Delinquency." In *Progress in Urban Geography,* edited by M. Pacione. London: Croom Helm.

Herek, G. M., and E. K. Glunt. 1988. "An Epidemic of Stigma: Public Reaction to AIDS." *American Psychologist* 43, no. 11:886–91.

Hertzberg, E. L. 1992. "The Homeless in the United States: Conditions, Typology and Interventions." *International Social Work* 35:149–61.

Heywood, A. 1990. "A Trial of the Bath Waters: The Treatment of Lead Poisoning." *Medical History,* suppl., no. 10:82–101.

Higgins, D. J. H. 1986. *Local and Urban Politics in Canada.* Toronto: Gage.

Hill, D. M. 1974. *Democratic Theory and Local Government.* London: Allen and Unwin.

Hill, M. K. 1989. *Bath and the Eighteenth Century Novel.* Bath: Bath Univ. Press.

Hoch, C., and R. A. Slayton. 1989. *New Homeless and Old: Community and the Skid Row Hotel.* Philadelphia: Temple Univ. Press.

Hodge, G. 1991. *Planning Canadian Communities.* Scarborough, Can.: Nelson.

Hokianga Health Enterprise Trust (HHET). 1992. *Minutes.* Rawene, N.Z.: Hokianga Health Enterprise Trust.

———. 1993. *Minutes.* Rawene, N.Z.: Hokianga Health Enterprise Trust.

———. 1994a. "Hauora Hokianga Business Plan for Year Ending June 1995" Rawene, N.Z.: Hokianga Health Enterprise Trust.

———. 1994b. *Minutes.* Rawene, N.Z.: Hokianga Health Enterprise Trust.

Holstein, J. A., and G. Miller, eds. 1993. *Reconsidering Social Constructionism: Debates in Social Problems Theory.* New York: Aldine de Gruyter.

Honey, R. 1976. "Conflicting Problems in the Political Organization of Space." *Annals of Regional Science* 10:45–60.

hooks, b. 1984. *Feminist Theory: From Margin to Center.* Boston: South End.

———. 1991. *Yearning: Race, Gender and Cultural Politics.* London: Turnaround Press.

Hopkins, J. S. P. 1993. "A Balancing Act? Trespass Amendments for Public/Private Places." *Urban Geography* 14:114–18.

Horvath, R. J. 1992. "Between Political Economy and Postmodernism. Review Essay." *Antipode* 24:157–62.

Hot Springs Chamber of Commerce. Ca. 1893. *Resolution of 50 Illinois Physicians.* Hot Springs, S.D.: Chamber of Commerce.

———. 1932. *Hot Springs, South Dakota.* Hot Springs, S.D.: Chamber of Commerce.

———. 1961. *Community Industrial Inventory Report for Hot Springs, South Dakota.* Hot Springs: S.D.: Chamber of Commerce.

———. 1986. *Our History Can Be Your Future.* Pamphlet. Hot Springs, S.D.: Chamber of Commerce

Hot Springs Commercial Club. Ca. 1909. *The National Health Resort, Hot Springs, South Dakota.* Pamphlet. Pierre, S.D.: South Dakota State Archives.

———. 1924. *Black Hills Health Resort Hot Springs, South Dakota. Fascinating Climate All the Year Round, Endorsed by the United States Government as a National Health Resort.* Pamphlet. Pierre, S.D.: South Dakota State Archives.

———. 1928. *Hot Springs on the Health Trail.* Sioux Falls, S.D.: Will A. Beach Printing.

"Hot Springs Offers Cure for Disillusionment." 1975. *Aberdeen (S.D.) American News,* May 7.

Human Rights Watch/Americas. 1994. "Chile, Unsettled Business: Human Rights in Chile at the Start of the Frei Presidency." New York: *Human Rights Watch/Americas* 4.

Hummon, D. M. 1992. "Community Attachment". In *Place Attachment,* edited by I. Altman and S. M. Low, 253–78. New York: Plenum.

Hunt, S. M., C. J. Martin, and S. D. Platt. 1986. "Housing and Health in a Deprived Area of Edinburgh." Institute of Environmental Health Officers Legal Research Institute Conference, *Unhealthy Housing: A Diagnosis.* 14–16 Dec. Univ. of Warwick, Warwick, Eng.

Hunter, F. 1953. *Community Power Structure.* Chapel Hill: Univ. of North Carolina Press.

Hurley, J., et al. 1993. "Is the Wolf Finally at the Door?" McMaster Univ., Centre for Health Economics and Policy Analysis, working paper, ser. 93, no. 12.

Hurley, J., S. Birch, and J. Eyles. 1995. "Information and Efficiency in Geographically Decentralized Health-care Systems." *Social Science and Medicine* 41:3–11.

Hyndman, S. J. 1990a. "Housing Dampness and Health Amongst British Bengalis in East London." *Social Science and Medicine* 30:131–41.

———. 1990b. *Housing Dampness and Health Amongst British Bengalis in Tower Hamlets.* Queen Mary and Westfield College, Department of Geography, research paper no. 3.

The Improved Bath Guide 1825. 1825. London: S. Simms.

Indian Council of Medical Research (ICMR). 1991. "HIV Infection: Current Status and Future Research Plans". *ICMR Bulletin* 21:125–44.

———. 1992. "HIV Infection: Current Dimensions and Future Implications." *ICMR Bulletin* 22:113–26.

Institute of Environmental Health Officers (IEHO). 1985. "Mould Fungal Spores: Their Effects on Health, and the Control, Prevention and Treatment of Mould Growth in Dwellings." In vol. 1 of *Environmental Health Professional Practice,* 1–16.

Institute of Medicine. 1988. *Homelessness, Health, and Human Needs.* Washington, D.C.: National Academy Press.

Illich, I. 1977. *Disabling Professions.* London: Marion Boyers Publishing.

Jackson, P. A. 1989. *Maps of Meaning.* London: Unwin Hyman.

———. 1993."Changing Ourselves: A Geography of Position." In *The Challenge for Geography,* edited by R. J. Johnston, 198–214. London: Blackwell.

Jackson, R. 1990. "Waters and Spas in the Classical World." *Medical History,* Supp. 10:1–13.

Jacobs, J. 1992. *Systems of Survival.* London: Hodder and Stoughton.

Jacobs, M., and G. Stevenson. 1981. "Health and Housing: A Historical Examination of Alternative Perspectives." *International Journal of Health Services* 1:105–22.

Jacobsen, B. 1986. *Beating the Ladykillers: Women and Smoking.* London: Pluto Press.

Jakle, J. A. 1987. *The Visual Elements of Landscape.* Amherst: Univ. of Massachusetts Press.

James, F. J. 1991. "Counting Homeless Persons with Surveys of Users of Services for the Homeless." *Housing Policy Debate* 2, no.3:133–56.

Jameson, F. 1985. "Postmodernism and the Consumer Society." In *Postmodern Culture,* edited by H. Foster. London: Pluto.

Jayaraman, K. S. 1992. "Injecting Drug Users in India: 'Little Manipurs All Over.'" *WorldAIDS* (May): 7.

Jenness, D. 1932. *The Indians of Canada.* Ottawa: National Museum of Canada.

Jennings, B. 1983. "Interpretive Social Science and Policy Analysis." In *Ethics, the Social Sciences, and Policy Analysis,* edited by D. Callahan and B. Jennings, 3–35. New York: Plenum.

Johnston, R. J. 1979. *Political, Electoral and Spatial Systems,* London: Oxford Univ. Press.

———. 1989. "Philosophy, Ideology and Geography". In *Horizons in Human Geography,* edited by D. Gregory and R. Walford, 48–66. London: Macmillan.

———. 1990. "The Territoriality of Law: An Exploration." *Urban Geography* 11:548–65.

———. 1991. *A Question of Place: Exploring the Practice of Human Geography.* London: Blackwell.

Jones, C. 1992. "Listening to Hidden Voices: Power, Domination, Resistance and Pleasure Within Huronia Regional Centre." *Disability, Handicap and Society* 7:339–48.

Jones, E., and J. Eyles. 1977. *An Introduction to Social Geography.* Oxford: Oxford Univ. Press.

Jones, E. E., et al. 1984. *Social Stigma: The Psychology of Marked Relationships.* New York: Freeman.

Jones, K., and G. Moon. 1987. *Health, Disease and Society.* London: Routledge and Kegan Paul.

———. 1993. "Medical Geography: Taking Space Seriously." *Progress in Human Geography* 17:515–24.

Joseph, A. E., and A. I. Chalmers. 1995. "Growing Old in Place: A View from Rural New Zealand." *Health and Place* 1:79–90.

Joseph, A. E., and R. A. Kearns. 1996. Deinstitutionalization Meets Restructuring: The Closure of a Psychiatric Hospital in New Zealand." *Health and Place* 2, no. 3:179–89.

Julin, S. 1982. "South Dakota Spa: A History of the Hot Springs Health Resort, 1882–1915." *Historical Collections South Dakota* 41:193–272.

Kaplan, H. 1967. *Urban Political Systems.* New York: Columbia Univ. Press.

Kasarda, J. D., and M. Janowitz. 1974. "Community Attachment in Mass Society." *American Sociological Review* 39:328–29.

Katz, I. 1981. *Stigma: A Social-Psychological Analysis.* Hillsdale, New Jersey: Erlbaum.

Kearns, G. 1991. "Biology, Class and the Urban Penalty." *Social History of Medicine* 4:391–92.

Kearns, R. A. 1991. "The Place of Health in the Health of Place: The Case of the Hokianga Special Medical Area." *Social Science and Medicine* 33, no. 4:519–30.

———. 1993. "Place and Health: Toward a Reformed Medical Geography." *The Professional Geographer* 45:139–47.

———. 1994. "Putting Health and Health Care into Place: An Invitation Accepted and Declined." *The Professional Geographer* 46:111–15.

———. 1995. "Medical Geography: Making Space for Difference." *Progress in Human Geography* 19:144–52.

———. 1996. "AIDS and Medical Geography: Embracing the Other?" *Progress in Human Geography* 20:123–31.

———. 1997. "Narrative and Metaphor in Geographies of Health." *Progress in Human Geography* 21:269–77.

Kearns, R. A., and J. R. Barnett. 1992. "Enter the Supermarket: Entrepreneurial Medical Practice in New Zealand." *Environment and Planning C: Government and Policy* 10:267–81.

———. 1997. "Consumerist Ideology and the Symbolic Landscapes of Private Medicine." *Health and Place* 3:171–80.

Kearns, R., and A. Joseph. 1993. "Space in Its Place: Developing the Link in Medical Geography." *Social Science and Medicine* 37:711–17.

Kearns, R. A., and J. A. Reinken. 1994. "Out for the Count? Questions Concerning the Population of the Hokianga." *New Zealand Population Review* 20:19–30.

Keatinge, W. R., et al. 1984. "Increases in Platelet and Red Cell Counts, Blood Viscosity and Arterial Pressure During Mild Surface Cooling: Factors in Mortality from Coronary and Cerebral Thrombosis in Winter." *British Medical Journal* 289:1405–8.

Keithley, J., et al. 1984a. "Health and Housing Conditions in Public Sector Housing Estates." *Public Health* 98:344–53.

———. 1984b. "Health Hazards of Bad Housing." *Primary Health Care* 2:8–9.

Kelly, M. P., J. K. Davies, and B. G. Charlton. 1993. "Healthy Cities: A Modern Problem or a Postmodern Solution?" In *Healthy Cities: Research and Practice* edited by M. P. Kelly and J. K. Davies, 159–68. London: Routledge.

Kendall, I., and G. Moon. 1994. "Health Policy and the Conservatives." In *Public Policy in Britain,* edited by S. Savage et al., 162–81. London: Macmillan.

Kingdom, J. 1993. "Canada." In *Local Government in Liberal Democracies,* edited by J. A. Chandler. London: Routledge.

Kirby, T. 1925. "The Royal Mineral Water Hospital: A National Hospital for Rheumatic Diseases." In *The Book of Bath,* 123–29. Bath: Ballantyne Press.

Kleck, R. 1969. "Physical Stigma and Task-oriented Interactions." *Human Relations* 22:53–59.

Klein, R. 1993. *Cigarettes Are Sublime.* Durham, N.C.: Duke Univ. Press.

Kleinman, A. M. 1973. "Medicine's Symbolic Reality: On a Central Problem in the Philosophy of Medicine." *Inquiry* 16:206–13.

Kleinman, I. 1991. "Towards an Ethnography of Suffering: A Qualitative Approach to the Study of the Illness Experience." Paper presented at the Qualitative Health Research Conference, 22–23 Feb., Edmonton, Can.

Kobayashi, A., and S. Mackenzie, eds. 1989. *Remaking Human Geography.* Boston: Unwin Hyman.

Kondratas, A. 1991. "Estimates and Public Policy: The Politics of Numbers." *Housing Policy Debate* 2, no. 3:631–48.

Korsgaard, J. 1983. "Mite Asthma and Residency." *American Review of Respiratory Disease* 128:231–35.

Kristeva, J. 1982. *Powers of Horror: An Essay on Abjection* New York: Columbia Univ. Press.

Krogh, D. 1991. *Smoking: The Artificial Passion.* New York: W. H. Freeman.

Landesman-Dwyer, S., J. G. Stein, and G. P. Sackett. 1978. "A Behavioral and Ecological Study of Group Homes." In *Observing Behavior.* Vol. 1, *Theory and Applications in Mental Retardation,* edited by G. P. Sackett, 349–77. Baltimore, Md.: Univ. Park Press.

Langness, L. L., and H. G. Levine. 1986. *Culture and Retardation: Life Histories of Mildly Mentally Retarded Persons in American Society.* Dordrecht: Reidel Publishing.

Langton, S. 1978. *Citizen Participation in America,* Lexington, Mass.: Lexington Books.

Larousse Encyclopedia of Mythology. 1988. London: Hamlyn Publishing Group.

Lau, S., et al. 1989. "High Mite-allergen Exposure Increases the Risk of Sensitisation in Atopic Children and Young Adults." *Journal of Allergy and Clinical Immunology* 84:18–25.

Lawrence, J. S. 1977. *Rheumatism in Populations.* London: Heinemann Medical.

Laws, G. 1994a. "Oppression, Knowledge and the Environment." *Political Geography* 13:7–32.

———. 1994b. "Theorising Ageism: Lessons from Postmodernism and Feminism." *The Gerontologist* 35:112–18

———. 1995. "Embodiment and Emplacement: Identities, Representation and Landscape in Sun City Retirement Communities." *International Journal of Aging and Human Development* 40:253–80.

Lazarus, E. 1991. *Black Hills White Justice.* New York: Harper Collins.

Learmonth, A. 1975. "Ecological Medical Geography." *Progress in Geography* 7:201–26.

Lee, B. A., et al. 1984. "Testing the Decline of Community Thesis." *American Journal of Sociology* 89:1116–88.

Lee, J. 1993. "Creating Effective Human Service Delivery Systems for the Homeless." Ph.D. diss., Univ. of Southern California.

Lee, R. G. 1972. "The Social Definition Of Outdoor Recreation Places." In *Social Behavior, Natural Resources and the Environment,* edited by W. Burch, 68–84. New York: Harper and Row.

Lees-Milne, J., and D. Ford. 1982. *Images of Bath.* Richmond-upon-Thames: Saint Helena Press.

Lefebvre, R. C. 1990. "Strategies to Maintain and Institutionalize Successful Programs." *Health Promotion at the Community Level,* edited by N. Bracht. Newbury Park, Calif.: Sage.

Leffingwell, W. B. 1894. *The Vale of Minnekahta.* Hot Springs, S.D.: Hot Springs Herald.

Leichter, H. M. 1991. *Free to Be Foolish: Politics and Health Promotion in the United States and Great Britain.* Princeton, N.J.: Princeton Univ. Press.

Lescarbot, M. 1609. *Histoire de la nouvelle France.* Rev. ed., 1617. Paris: n.p.

Lewis, N. D., and E. Kieffer. 1994. "The Health of Women: Beyond Maternal and Child Health." In *Health and Development,* edited by D. R. Phillips and Y. Verhasselt, 122–37. London: Routledge.

Ley, D. 1977. "Social Geography and the Taken-for-Granted World." *Transactions of the Institute of British Geographers,* n.s. 2:498–512.

———. 1983. *A Social Geography of the City.* New York: Harper and Row.

Lilienfeld, A. M., and D. E. Lilienfeld. 1980. *Foundations of Epidemiology.* 2d ed. Oxford: Oxford Univ. Press.

Lineberry, R. 1977. *Equality and Urban Policy: The Distribution of Municipal Public Services.* Beverly Hills, Calif.: Sage.

Lipset, S. M., and S. Rokkan. 1967. "Cleavage Structures, Party Systems and Voter Alignments." In *Party Systems and Voter Alignments,* edited by S. M. Lipset and S. Rokkan. New York: Free Press.

Lira, E., and M. I. Castillo, eds. 1991. *Psicología de la amenaza política y del miedo* Santiago, Chile: Institute of Latin American Studies.

Litva, A., and J. Eyles. 1995. "Coming Out: Exposing Social Theory in Medical Geography." *Health and Place* 1:5–14.

Lofland, L. H. 1989. "Social Life in the Public Realm: A Review." *Journal Of Contemporary Ethnography* 17:453–82.

Lofroth, G. 1993. "Environmental Tobacco Smoke: Multicomponent Analysis and Room-to-Room Distribution in Homes." *Tobacco Control* 2:222–25.

Lomas, J. 1990. "Finding Audiences, Changing Beliefs." *Journal of Health Politics Policy and Law* 15:525–42.

Longhurst, R. 1994. "The Geography Closest In: The Body and the Politics of Pregnability." *Australian Geographical Studies* 32:214–23.

Lovell, G. W. 1978. *Conquest and Survival in Colonial Guatemala: A Historical Geography of the Cuchumatan Highlands, 1500–1821.* Kingston, Ont.: McGill-Queen's Univ. Press.

Loveman, B. 1988. Chile: *The Legacy of Hispanic Capitalism.* New York: Oxford.

Lowe, G., D. Foxcroft, and D. Sibley. 1993. *Adolescent Drinking and Family Life.* Chur, Switzerland: Harwood Academic Press.

Lowenthal, David. 1976. "Social Geography and the Taken-for-Granted World." In *Geographies of the Mind,* edited by D. Lowenthal and M. Bowden. New York: Oxford Univ. Press.

Lowry, S. 1991. *Housing and Health.* London: British Medical Journal Publications.

Loytonen, M. 1991. "The Spatial Diffusion of Human Immunodeficiency Virus Type I in Finland, 1982–1997." *Annals of the Association of American Geographers* 81:127–51.

———. 1994. "Growth Models and the HIV Epidemic in Finland." *Social Science and Medicine* 38:179–85.

Luba, J. 1986. *Tenants' Rights.* London: Legal Action Group.

Luton, L. S. 1993. "Citizen-Administrator Connections." *Administration and Society* 25:114–34.

Lykes, M., and R. Liem. 1990. "Human Rights and Mental Health in the United States: Lessons from Latin America." *Journal of Social Issues* 46:151–65.

Macdonald, G., and R. Bunton. 1992. "Health Promotion: Discipline or Disciplines." In *Health Promotion: Disciplines and Diversity,* edited by R. Bunton and G. Macdonald, 6–22. London: Routledge.

Mackenzie, S. 1989. "Restructuring the Relations of Work and Life: Women as Environmental Actors, Feminism as Geographical Analysis." In *Remaking Human Geography,* edited by A. Kobayashi and S. Mackenzie, 40–61. London: Unwin Hyman.

Mahood, G. 1994. "The Empathy Advertising Campaign: Preparing Smokers for the Inevitable Social Isolation." *Tobacco Control* 3:270–72.

Malcolm, L. A. 1991. "Service Management." *International Journal of Health Planning and Management* 6:23–36.

Malcolm, L. A., and P. A. Barnett. 1994. "New Zealand's Health Providers in an Emerging Market." *Health Policy* 29:85–100.

Mammoth Springs. 1909. *Mammoth Springs Publicity Pamphlet.* Pierre, S.D.: South Dakota State Archives.

Mann, J., D. J. M. Tarantola, and T. W. Netter, eds. *AIDS in the World.* Cambridge, Mass.: Harvard Univ. Press.

Markle, G. E., and R. J. Troyer. 1979. "Smoke Gets in Your Eyes: Cigarette Smoking as Deviant Behavior." *Social Problems* 21:611–25.

Marmor, T. R., and J. A. Morone. 1980. "Representing Consumer Interests." *Milbank Memorial Fund Quarterly* 58:126–65.

Marris, P., and M. Rein. 1967. *Dilemmas of Social Reform,* Harmondsworth, Eng.: Penguin.

Martin, A. E., F. Kaloyanova, and S. Maziarka. 1976. *Housing, the Housing Environment and Health: An Annotated Bibliography.* World Health Organization Offset Publication no. 27.

Martin, C. J., S. D. Platt, and S. M. Hunt. 1987. "Housing Conditions and Ill-health." *British Medical Journal* 294:1125–27.

Martin, D., and H. C. Williams. 1992. "Market-area Analysis and Accessibility to Primary Health-care Centres." *Environment and Planning A* 24:1009–19.

Massey, D. 1991. "The Political Place of Locality Studies." *Environment and Planning A* 23:267–81.

———. 1994. *Space, Place, and Gender.* Oxford: Polity Press.

May, J. J., et al. 1986. "Organic Dust Toxicity (Pulmonary Mycotoxicosis) Associated with Silo Unloading." *Thorax* 41:919–23.

Mayer, J. D. 1982. "Relations Between Two Traditions of Medical Geography: Health Systems Planning and Geographical Epidemiology. *Progress in Human Geography* 6:216–30.

Mayer, J. D., and M. S. Meade. 1994. "A Reformed Medical Geography Reconsidered." *Professional Geographer* 46:103–5.

Mayhew, L. D., and G. Leonardi, 1982. "Equity, Efficiency and Accessibility in Urban and Rural Health-care Systems." *Environment and Planning A* 14:1479–1509.

Maynard, D. 1989. "On the Ethnography and Analysis of Discourse in Institutional Settings." *Social Problems* 1:127–46.

Mccracken, G. 1992. *"Got a Smoke?" A Cultural Account of Tobacco in the Lives of Contemporary Teens.* Toronto: Ontario Ministry Of Health.

McCuaig, M., and G. Frank. 1990. "The Able Self: Adaptive Patterns and Choices in Independent Living for a Person with Cerebral Palsy." *The American Journal of Occupational Therapy* 45:224–34.

McDowell, L. 1991. "The Baby and the Bathwater: Difference and Diversity in Feminist Geography." *Geoforum* 22:123–33.

———. 1992. "Doing Gender: Feminism, Feminists and Research Methods in Human Geography." *Transactions, Institute of British Geographers* 17:399–416.

———. 1993a. "Space, Place and Gender Relations: Part 1. Feminist Empiricism and the Geography of Social Relations." *Progress in Human Geography* 17:157–79.

———. 1993b. "Space, Place and Gender Relations: Part 2. Identity, Difference, Feminist Geometries and Geographies." *Progress in Human Geography* 17:305–18.

———. 1994. "The Transformation of Cultural Geography." In *Human Geography: Society, Space and Social Science,* edited by D. Gregory, R. Martin, and G. Smith, 146–73. Minneapolis: Univ. of Minnesota Press

McGregor, A. 1963. "Housing and Health." *Public Health* 77:72–81.

McIntyre, S. 1981. "Bath: The Rise of a Resort Town, 1660–1800." In *County towns in Pre-industrial England,* edited by P. Clark, 198–247. New York: St. Martin's Press.

McKnight, J. 1977. "Professionalized Service and Disabling Help." In *Disabling Professions,* edited by I. Illich, I. K. Zola, and J. Mcknight. London: Marion Boyers Publishing.

McLafferty, S. 1989. "The Politics of Privatization: State and Local Politics and the Restructuring of Hospitals in New York City." In *Health Services Privatization in Industrial Societies,* edited by J. L. Scarpaci, 130–54. New Brunswick, N.J.: Rutgers Univ. Press.

Meade, M., J. Florin, and W. Gesler. 1988. *Medical Geography.* New York: Guildford.

Melia, R. J. W., et al. 1982a. "Childhood Respiratory Illness and the Home Environment 1. Relations Between Nitrogen Dioxide, Temperature and Relative Humidity." *International Journal of Epidemiology* 11:155–63.

Melia, R. J. W., et al. 1982b. "Childhood Respiratory Illness and the Home Environment 2. Association Between Respiratory Illness and Nitrogen Dioxide, Temperature and Relative Humidity." *International Journal of Epidemiology* 11:164–69.

Mettlin, L. K., et al. 1985. "Risk Factors and Behavioural Correlates of Willingness to Participate in Cancer Prevention Trials." *Nutrition and Cancer* 7:189–98.

Meyer, W. B., D. Gregory, B. L. Turner II, and P. F. McDowell. 1992. "The Local-Global Continuum." In *Geography's Inner Worlds: Pervasive Themes in Contemporary American Geography* edited by R. F. Abler, M. G. Marcus, and J. M. Olson, 255–79. New Brunswick, N.J.: Rutgers Univ. Press.

Milbrath, L. W. 1965. *Political Participation.* Chicago: Rand McNally.

Mill, J. S. 1958. *Considerations on Representative Government.* New York: Liberal Arts Press.

Milloy, J. 1983. "The Early Indian Acts: Development Strategy and Constitutional Change." In *As Long as the Sun Shines and the Water Flows: A Reader in Canadian Native Studies,* edited by I. A. Getty and A. Lussier, 56–64. Vancouver: Univ. of British Columbia Press.

Mills, A. 1993. "Decentralization and Accountability from an International Perspective." Paper presented at the Sixth Annual Health Policy Conference, Centre for Health Economics and Policy Analysis, 20 May, Hamilton, Ont.

Mills, A., et al., 1990. *Health System Decentralization.* Geneva: World Health Organization.

Mills, W. J. 1982. "Metaphorical Vision: Changes in Western Attitudes to the Environment." *Annals of the Association of American Geographers* 72:237–53.

Miranda, E., J. L. Scarpaci, and I. Irarrázaval. 1995. "A Decade of HMOs in Chile: Market, Consumption, and the Role of the State." *Health and Place* 1:51–59.

Miranda, P. N. 1989. *Terrorismo de estado: Testimonio del horror en Chile y Argentina,* Colección Expidiente Negro. Madrid: Editorial Sextante.

Mitchell, B. 1986. "English Spas." In *Bath History,* 1:189–204. Oxford: Alan Sutton.

Mitchell, B., and H. Penrose. 1983. "Introduction." In *Letters from Bath 1766–1767 by the Rev. John Penrose,* 1–17. Gloucester, Eng.: Alan Sutton.

Mittelmark, M. 1986. "Community-wide Prevention of Cardiovascular Disease." *Preventive Medicine* 15:1–17.

Mohan, J. 1989. "Rolling Back the State? Privatization of Health Services under the Thatcher Governments." In *Health Services Privatization in Industrial Societies,* edited by J. L. Scarpaci, 112–29. New Brunswick, N.J.: Rutgers Univ. Press.

———. 1995. *A National Health Service?* London: Macmillan.

Moon, G. 1990. "Conceptions of Space and Community in British Health Policy." *Social Science and Medicine* 30, no. 1:165–71.

———. 1995. "(Re)placing Research on Health and Health Care." *Health and Place* 1:1–4.

Moore, G. C., and C. Revelle. 1982. "The Hierarchical Service Location Problem." *Management Science* 28:775–80.

Morgan, E. P. 1987. "Technocratic versus Democratic Options for Educational Policy." In *Citizen Participation in Public Decision-making,* edited by J. Desario and S. Langton. New York: Greenwood Press.

Morgan, L. M. 1993. *Community Participation in Health: The Politics of Primary Care in Costa Rica.* Cambridge: Cambridge Univ. Press.

Morone, J. A., and T. R. Marmor. 1988. "Representing Consumer Interests." In *Citizens and Health Care,* edited by B. Checkoway. New York: Pergamon.

Morrill, R. L. 1981. *Political Redistricting and Geographic Theory.* Washington: Association of American Geographers.

Morris, J. 1992. "Personal and Political: A Feminist Perspective on Researching Physical Disability." *Disability, Handicap and Society* 7:157–66

Moss, P., and I. Dyck. 1996. "Inquiry into Environment and the Body: Women, Work, and Chronic Illness." *Environment and Planning D: Society and Space* 14:737–53.

Mowbray, C. T., E. Cohen, S. Harris, S. Trosch, S. Johnson, and B. Duncan. 1992. "Serving the Homeless Mentally Ill: Mental Health Linkage." *Journal of Community Psychology* 20:215–27.

Mueller, D., and N. Petty. 1983. *Early Hot Springs.* Hot Springs: A Star Publication.

Mumford, L. 1938. *The Culture of Cities,* New York: Free Press.

Naik, T. N., et al. 1991. Intravenous Drug Users: A New High-risk Group for HIV Infection in India. *AIDS* 5:117–18.

Nataraj, S. 1990. "Women Freed from Illegal Detention. *World AIDS* 3:3.

National Academy of Sciences (NAS). 1981 *Indoor Pollutants.* Washington D.C.: Academy Press.

National AIDS Control Organization (NACO). 1993. *National AIDS Control Programme India. Country Scenario: An Update.* National AIDS Control Organization, Ministry of Health and Family Welfare, Government of India. Apr. 1993, New Delhi.

———. 1994. Unpublished data. National AIDS Control Organization, Ministry of Health and Family Welfare, Government of India, New Delhi.

Neale, R. 1973a. "Society, Belief, and the Building of Bath, 1700–1793." In *Landscape and Society,* edited by C. W. Chalklin and M. Havinden, 253–80. London: Longman.

———. 1973b. "Bath: Ideology and Utopia, 1700–1760." *Studies in the 18th Century* 3: 37–54.

Nettleton, S. 1995. *The Sociology of Health and Illness.* Cambridge: Polity.

Neve, M. R. 1984. "Natural Philosophy, Medicine and the Culture of Science in Provincial England: The Cases of Bristol, 1790–1850, and Bath, 1750–1820." Ph.D. diss., Univ. College, London.

Newton, K. 1982. "Is Small Really So Beautiful?" *Political Studies* 30:190–206.

Nirje, B. 1969. "The Normalization Principle and Its Human Management Implications". In *Changing Patterns in Residential Services for the Mentally Retarded,* edited by R. Kugel and W. Wolfensberger, 179–95. Washington, D.C.: President's Committee on Mental Retardation.

Nisbet, R. 1966. *The Sociological Tradition.* London: Heinemann.

Northland Area Health Board (NAHB). 1989. *Strategic Plan: Towards 2000.* Whangarei, N.Z.: Northland Area Health Board.

———. 1988. *Summary of the Submissions on the Draft Strategic Plan.* Whangarei, N.Z.: Northland Area Health Board.

———. 1989. *Strategic Plan: Towards 2000.* Whangarei, N.Z.: Northland Area Health Board.

NorthWestern Line. 1910. *South Dakota Hot Springs Endorsed by the U.S. Government Through the Construction of the Battle Mountain Sanitarium.* Pamphlet. Pierre, S.D.: South Dakota State Archives.

Oberhauser, A. 1995. "Gender and Household Economic Strategies in Rural Appalachia." *Gender, Place and Culture* 2:51–70.

Odette, F. 1994. "Body Beautiful/Body Perfect: Challenging the Status Quo. Where Do Women with Disabilities Fit In?" *Canadian Women's Studies* 14:41–43.

Odum, H. W. 1965. "The Promise of Regionalism." In *Regionalism in America*, edited by M. Jensen. Madison: Univ. of Wisconsin Press.

Oliver, M. 1990. *The Politics of Disablement*. Basingstoke, Eng.: Macmillan.

O'Neill, J. 1992. "Community Participation in Quebec's Health System." *International Journal of Health Services* 22:287–301.

Ontario Ministry of Community and Social Services. 1987. *Challenges and Opportunities: Community Living for People with Developmental Handicaps*. Toronto: Ontario Ministry of Community and Social Services.

Oostvogels, R. 1992. *Sex Workers, Clients, Brokers and Brothels in the City of Madras: Assessment Study*. Unpublished report to World Health Organization Global Program on AIDS, Dec. 1992, New Delhi.

Ostrom, V., et al. 1955. "The Organization of Government in Metropolitan Areas." *American Political Science Review* 55:831–42.

Our Lady of Lourdes Hospital. 1910–11. *Annual Report*. Pierre, S.D.: South Dakota State Archives.

Packard, R. M., and P. Epstein. 1991."Epidemiologists, Social Scientists and the Structures of Medical Research on AIDS in Africa." *Social Science and Medicine* 33:771–94.

Páez, D., and N. Basabe. 1993. "Trauma político y memoria colectiva: Freud, Halbwachs y la psicología política contemporánea." *Psicología Política* 6:7–34.

Pahl, R. 1970. *Patterns of Urban Life*. London: Longman.

Parker, W. 1966. *Gold in the Black Hills*. Lincoln, Nebr.: Univ. of Nebraska Press.

Parry, G., G. Moyser, and N. Day. 1992. *Political Participation and Democracy in Britain*. Cambridge: Cambridge Univ. Press.

Parsons, T. 1975. "The Sick Role and the Role of the Physician Reconsidered." *Health and Society* 53:257–78.

Passenger Department, Chicago and Northwestern Railway. 1916. *Black Hills, the South Dakota Hot Springs Endorsed by the U.S. Government as a National Sanitarium*. Pamphlet. Pierre, S.D.: South Dakota State Archives.

Pateman, C. 1970. *Participation and Democratic Theory*. Cambridge: Cambridge Univ. Press.

Pawson, E., and Scott, G. 1992. "The Regional Consequences of Economic Restructuring: The West Coast, New Zealand (1984–1991)." *Journal of Rural Studies* 8:373–86.

Pearson, M. 1989. "Medical Geography: Genderless and Colorblind." *Contemporary Issues in Geography and Education* 3:9–17.

Pederson, L., et al. 1986. "A Population Survey on Legislative Measures to Restrict Smoking in Ontario. 2. Knowledge, Attitudes, and Predicted Behaviour." *American Journal Of Preventive Medicine* 2:316–23.

———. 1987. A Population Survey in Ontario Regarding Restrictive Measures on Smoking: Relationship of Smoking Status to Knowledge, Attitudes and Predicted Behaviour. *International Journal Of Epidemiology* 16:383–91.

———. 1989. "A Population Survey on Legislative Measures to Restrict Smoking in Ontario. 3. Variables Related to Attitudes of Smokers and Nonsmokers." *American Journal Of Preventive Medicine* 5:313–22.

Perrow, C. 1977. "The Bureaucratic Paradox." *Organizational Dynamics* 5:3–14.

Pfuhl, E. H., and S. Henry. 1993. *The Deviance Process.* 3d ed. New York: Aldine De Gruyter.

Phillips, D. R., and Y. Verhasselt, eds. 1994. *Health and Development.* London: Routledge.

Philo, C. 1986. "*'The Same and the Other': On Geographies, Madness and Outsiders.* Occasional Paper 11, Loughborough Univ., Department of Geography, Loughborough, Eng.

———. 1989. " 'Enough To Drive One Mad': The Organisation of Space in Nineteenth-century Lunatic Asylums." In *The Power of Geography: How Territory Shapes Social Life,* edited by J. Wolch and M. Dear, 258–90. London: Unwin Hyman.

———. 1992. "Foucault's Geography." *Environment and Planning D: Society and Space* 10:137–61.

———. 1995. "Staying In: Invited Comments on 'Coming Out': Exposing Social Theory in Medical Geography." *Health and Place* 2:35–40.

Pinch, S. 1979. "Territorial Justice in the City: A Case Study of the Social Services for the Elderly in Greater London." *Social Problems and the City: Geographical Perspectives,* edited by D. T. Herbert and D. M. Smith, 201–23. Oxford: Oxford Univ. Press.

Pioneer. 1994. 12 Aug.

Platt, S. D., et al. 1989. "Damp Housing, Mould Growth, and Symptomatic Health State." *British Medical Journal* 298:1673–78.

Platts-Mills, T. A. E., and M. D. Chapman. 1987. "Dust Mites: Immunology, Allergic Disease, and Environmental Control." *Journal of Allergy and Clinical Immunology* 80:755–75.

Plotnick, Hermine D. 1986. "De-institutionalization: The Queens Experience." Paper presented at the annual meeting of the American Public Health Association. 28 Sept.–2 Oct. 1986, Las Vegas, Nev.

Pocock, D. C. D. 1994. "Place and the Novelist." In *Re-reading Cultural Geography,* edited by K. E. Foote, P. J. Hugill, K. Mathewson, and J. M. Smith, 363–73. Austin: Univ. of Texas Press.

Poland, B. 1992. "Learning to 'Walk Our Talk': The Implications of Sociological Theory for Research Methodologies in Health Promotion." *Canadian Journal of Public Health* 83:S31–46.

———. 1993a. *From Concept to Practice in Community Mobilization for Health: A Qualitative Evaluation of the Brantford COMMIT Intervention for Smoking Cessation.* Ph.D. diss., McMaster Univ., Hamilton Ont.

———. 1993b. "Some Promises and Pitfalls of Lay Perception Research in the Social and Health Sciences." *The Operational Geographer.* 11:23–27.

Poland, B., et al. 1995. "Qualitative Evaluation of the Brantford COMMIT Intervention Trial: The Smokers' Perspective." *Health and Canadian Society* 2, no. 2:269–316.

Politzer, P. 1989. *Fear in Chile: Lives Under Pinochet,* New York: Pantheon Books.

Porteus, J. D. 1985. "Smellscape." *Progress in Human Geography* 9, no. 3:356–78.

Poser, C. M., et al. 1984. *The Diagnosis of Multiple Sclerosis.* New York: Theime-Stratton.

Powell, M. 1992. "Hospital Provision before the NHS: Territorial Justice or Inverse Care Law?" *Journal of Social Policy,* 21:145–63.

Pratt, G. 1993. "Reflections on Poststructuralism and Feminist Empirics, Theory and Practice." *Antipode* 25:51–63.

Pratt, G., and Hanson, S. 1991. "On the Links Between Home and Work: Family-household Strategies in a Buoyant Labour Market." *International Journal of Urban and Regional Research* 15:55–74.

Pred, A. 1984. "Place as Historically Contingent Process: Structuration and the Time-geography of Becoming Places." *Annals of the Association of American Geographers.* 74:279–97.

———. 1986. *Place, Practice and Structure.* Cambridge: Polity.

Proctor, R. 1988. *Racial Hygiene: Medicine under the Nazis* Harvard, Mass.: Cambridge Univ. Press.

Publicity Bureau of Hot Springs, 1896. "The Carlsbad of America: Hot Springs South Dakota in the Famous Black Hills."

Pue, W. W. 1990. "Wrestling With Law: (Geographical) Specificity vs. (Legal) Abstraction." *Urban Geography* 11:566–85.

Putnam, R. D. 1993. *Making Democracy Work.* Princeton: Princeton Univ. Press.

Pyle, G. F., and B. M. Lauer. 1975. "Comparing Spatial Configurations: Hospital Service Areas and Disease Rates." *Economic Geography* 51:50–68.

Radford, J. P. 1994. "Intellectual Disability and the Heritage of Modernity." In *Disability Is Not Measles: New Research Paradigms in Disability,* edited by M. H. Rioux and M. Bach, 9–27. Toronto: Roeher Institute.

Ramasubban, R. 1990. "Sexual Behaviour and Conditions of Health Care: Potential Risks of HIV Transmission in India." Paper presented at the seminar Anthropological Studies Relevant to the Sexual Transmission of HIV. International Union for the Scientific Study of Population in collaboration with the Department of International Development Cooperation. 19–22 Nov., Sønderborg, Denmark.

Ray, A. 1976. "Diffusion of Diseases in the Western Interior of Canada 1830–1850." *Geographical Review* 66, no. 2:139–57.

———. 1984. "Periodic Shortages, Native Welfare and the Hudson's Bay Company, 1670–1930." In *The Subarctic Fur Trade: Native Social and Economic Adaptations,* edited by S. Krech, 1–20. Vancouver: Univ. of British Columbia Press.

Rees, K. 1985. "Medicine as a Commodity: Hydrotherapy in Matlock." *The Society for the Social History of Medicine Bulletin* 36:24–27.

Regan, D. E., and J. Stewart. 1982. "An Essay in the Government of Health." *Social Policy and Administration* 23:252–68.

Reinken, J., J. W. McLeod, and T. I. D. Murphy. 1985. *Health and Equity.* Wellington, N.Z.: Department of Health.

Relph, E. 1976. *Place and Placelessness.* London: Pion.

———. 1981. "Phenomenology." In *Themes in Geographic Thought,* edited by D. E. Harvey and B. P. Holly, 99–114. New York: St. Martin's.

———. 1985. "Geographical Experiences as Being-in-the-World." *Dwelling, Place and Environment,* edited by D. Seamon and R. Mugerauer. New York: Columbia Univ. Press.

———. 1987. "Modernity and the Reclamation of Place". In *Dwelling, Seeing and Designing: Toward a Phenomenological Ecology,* edited by D. Seamon, 25–40. Albany: State Univ. of New York Press.

Renn, O., et al. 1993. "Public Participation in Decision-making" *Policy Sciences* 26:189–214.

Report of the Bath Society for the Suppression of Vagrants. 1810. Bath: Richard Cruttwell.

Rezatto, H. 1989. *Tales of the Black Hills.* Rapid City, S.D.: Renwyn.

Rhyne, I. 1994. *ETS in the Home: A Study of Knowledge, Attitudes, and Receptiveness to Change among Parents Who Smoke.* North York, Ont.: Institute for Social Research.

Richardson, S. A. 1981. "Living Environments: An Ecological Perspective." In *Living Environments for Developmentally Retarded Persons,* edited by H. C. Haywood, and J. R. Newbrough 15–30. Baltimore, Md.: Univ. Park Press.

Rioux, M. H. 1994. "Introduction." In *Disability Is Not Measles: New Research Paradigms in Disability.* edited by M. H. Rioux and M. Bach, 1–7. Toronto: Roeher Institute.

Rioux, M. H., and C. Crawford. 1990. "Poverty and Disability." *Canadian Journal of Community Mental Health* 9:97–109.

Robbins, M. C., and A. Kline. 1991. To Smoke or Not to Smoke: A Decision Theory Perspective. *Social Science and Medicine* 33:1343–47.

Robinson, D. 1955. "Slum Clearance Pays Off." *National Municipal Review* 14:461–65.

Rodman, M. C. 1992. "Empowering Place." *American Anthropologist* 94:640–56.

Rollinson, P. 1990. "The Story of Edward: The Everyday Geography of Single Room Occupancy (SRO) Hotel Tenants." *Journal of Contemporary Ethnography* 19:188–206.

Rolls, R. 1978. "In Pursuit of the Cure." In *Bath—Museum City?* edited by G. Hanes, 47–50. Bath: Bath Univ. Press.

———. 1984. "The Rise and Fall of the Bath Waters." *Society for the Social History of Medicine Bulletin* 35:17–20.

———. 1988a. "Bath Cases: Care and Treatment of Patients at the Bath General Hospital During the Mid-Eighteenth Century." In *Bath History,* 2:139–62. Oxford: Alan Sutton.

———. 1988b. *The Hospital of the Nation.* Bath: Bird Publications.

Rondinelli, D. 1981. "Government Decentralization in Comparative Theory and Practice in Developing Countries." *International Review of Administrative Sciences* 47:133–45.

Rose, G. 1993. *Feminism and Geography.* Minneapolis: Univ. of Minnesota Press.

Rosenau, P. V. 1994. "Health Politics Meets Post-modernism: its Meaning and Implications for Community Health Organising." *Journal of Health Politics, Policy and Law* 19:303–33.

Rosenfield, S. 1991. "Homelessness and Rehospitalization: The Importance of Housing for the Chronic Mentally Ill." *Journal of Community Psychology* 19:60–69.

Rosenheck, R., and C. Leda. 1991. "Who Is Served by Programs for the Homeless? Admission to a Domiciliary Care Program for Homeless Veterans." *Hospital and Community Psychiatry* 42:176–81.

Ross, A., M. Collins, and C. Sanders. 1990. "Upper Respiratory Tract Infection in Children, Domestic Temperatures, and Humidity." *Journal of Epidemiology and Community Health* 44:142–46.

Rossi, P. H. 1989. *Down and Out in America: The Origins of Homelessness.* Chicago: Univ. of Chicago Press.

Rowe, S., and J. Wolch. 1990. "Social Networks in Time and Space: Homeless Women in Skid Row, Los Angeles." *Annals of the Association of American Geographers* 80:184–205.

Roweis, S. T., and A. J. Scott, 1977. "Urban Planning in Theory and Practice." *Environment and Planning A* 9: 1097–119.

Rowntree, L. B., and M. W. Conkey. 1980. "Symbolism and the Cultural Landscape." *Annals of the Association of American Geographers* 70:459–74.

Rozario, H. R., 1988. *Trafficking in Women and Children in India.* New Delhi: Uppal Publishing House.

Rubington, E., and M. S. Weinberg. 1981. *Deviance: The Interactionist Perspective.* 4th ed. New York: Macmillan.

Sacco, V. F. 1988. *Deviance: Conformity and Control in Canadian Society.* Scarborough, Ont.: Prentice-Hall.

Sack, R. D. 1986. *Human Territoriality: Its Theory and History.* Cambridge: Cambridge Univ. Press.

———. 1988. "The Consumer's World: Place as Context," *Annals of the Association of American Geographers* 78, no. 4:642–64.

Salisbury, B., J. Dickey, and C. Crawford. 1987. *Service Brokerage: Individual Empowerment and Social Service Accountability.* North York, Ont.: Roeher Institute.

Salter, R. 1972. "Bath and Its Entertainments." In *Bath in the Age of Reform (1830–1841),* edited by J. Wroughton, 58–66. Bath: Morgan Books.

Salvaggio, J., and L. Aukrust. 1981. "Mold-induced Asthma." *Journal of Allergy and Clinical Immunology* 68:327–46.

Sayer, A. 1984. *Method in Social Science: A Realist Approach.* London: Hutchinson.

Scarpaci, J. L. 1988. *Medical Care in Chile: Accessibility under Military Rule.* Pittsburgh: Univ. of Pittsburgh Press.

———., ed. 1989. *Health Services Privatization in Industrial Societies.* New Brunswick: Rutgers Univ. Press.

———. 1990. "Medical Care, Welfare State and Deindustrialization in the Southern Cone." *Environment and Planning D: Society and Space* 8:191–209.

———. 1991. "Primary Care Decentralization in the Southern Cone: Shantytown Health Care as Urban Social Movement." *Annals of the Association of American Geographers* 81:103–26.

———. 1993. "On the Validity of Language: Speaking, Knowing and Understanding in Medical Geography." *Social Science and Medicine* 37:719–24.

———. 1994. "Chile." In *International Handbook of Latin American Urbanization,* edited by G. Greenfield, 37–69. Westport, Conn.: Greenwood Press.

Scarpaci, J. L., and L. Frazier. 1993. "State Terror: Ideology, Protest, and the Gendering of Landscapes." *Progress in Human Geography* 17:1–21.

Scarpaci, J. L., A. Gaete, and R. Infante. 1988. "Planning Residential Segregation: The Case of Chile." *Urban Geography* 9:19–36.

Scheper-Hughes, N., and M. M. Lock. 1987. "The Mindful Body: A Prolegomenon to Future Work in Medical Anthropology." *Medical Anthropology Quarterly* 1:6–41.

Schnorrenberg, B. B. 1984. "Medical Men of Bath." *Studies in Eighteenth Century Culture* 13:189–203.

Schoef, B. G. 1991. "Ethical, Methodological and Political Issues of AIDS Research in Central Africa." *Social Science and Medicine* 33:749–63.

Schwier, K. M. 1990. *Speakeasy: People with Mental Handicaps Talk about Their Lives in Institutions and the Community.* Austin, Tex.: PRO-ED.

Scott, C. J., and S. G. Gerberich. 1989. "Analysis of a Smoking Policy in the Workplace." *American Association of Occupational Health Nurses Journal* 37:265–73.

Segal, E. A. 1989. "Homelessness in a Small Community: A Demographic Profile." *Social Work* 25:27–30.

Segal, S. P., and U. Aviram. 1978. *The Mentally Ill in Community-Based Sheltered Care: A Study of Community Care and Social Integration.* New York: Wiley.

Segal, S. P., J. Baumohl, and E. W. Moyles. 1980. "Neighborhood Types and Community Reaction to the Mentally Ill: A Paradox of Intensity." *Journal of Health and Social Behavior* 21:345–59.

Seidel, G. 1993. "The Competing Discourses of HIV/AIDS in Sub-Saharan Africa: Discourses of Rights and Empowerment vs. Discourses of Control and Exclusion." *Social Science and Medicine* 36:175–94.

Seley, J. E. 1983. *The Politics of Public-Facility Planning.* Lexington, Mass.: Lexington Books.

Selik, R. M., et al. 1989. "Birthplace and the Risk of AIDS among Hispanics in the United States." *American Journal of Public Health* 79:836–39.

Selik, R. M., K. G. Castro, and M. Pappaioanou. 1988. "Racial/Ethnic Differences in the Risk of AIDS in the United States." *American Journal of Public Health* 78:1539–45.

Selik, R. M., S. Y. Chu, and J. W. Buehler. 1993. "HIV Infection as Leading Cause of Death among Young Adults in U.S. Cities and States." *Journal of the American Medical Association* 269:2991–94.

Shannon, G. W., and G. E. A. Dever. 1974. *Health Care Delivery: Spatial Perspectives.* New York: McGraw-Hill.

Shannon, G. W., and G. F. Pyle. 1989. "The Origin and Diffusion of AIDS: A View from Medical Geography." *Annals of the Association of American Geographers* 79:1–24.

Shinn, M. 1992. "Homelessness: What is a Psychologist to Do?" *American Journal of Community Psychology* 20:1–24.

Sibley, D. 1988. "Survey 13: Purification of Space." *Environment and Planning D: Society and Space* 6:409–21.

Sigelman, C. K., et al. 1980. "Surveying Mentally Retarded Persons: Responsiveness, and Response Validity in Three Samples." *American Journal of Mental Deficiency* 84:479–86.

———. 1982. "Evaluating Techniques of Questioning Mentally Retarded Persons." *American Journal of Mental Deficiency* 86:511–18.

Simmel, G. 1950. *The Sociology of George Simmel.* New York: Free Press.

Simmons, H. G. 1982. *From Asylum to Welfare.* Toronto: National Institute on Mental Retardation.

Sinson, J. C., and C. L. S. Stainton. 1990. "An Investigation into Attitudes (and Attitude Change) Towards Mental Handicap." *British Journal of Mental Subnormality* 36:53–63.

Sitwell, E. 1987. *Bath.* London: Faber and Faber.

Skelcher, B. 1992. "Historic Preservation Arrives in the Black Hills: Hot Springs South Dakota, Starts the Main Street Pilot Program." *Small Town,* July–Aug. 1992.

Smallman-Raynor, M., A. Cliff, and P. Haggett. 1992. *Atlas of AIDS.* Oxford: Blackwell.

Smith, C. J. 1988. *Public Problems: The Management of Urban Distress.* New York: Guilford Press.

Smith, C. J., and J. A. Giggs, eds. 1988. *Location and Stigma: Contemporary Perspectives on Mental Health and Mental Health Care.* Boston: Unwin Hyman.

———. 1989. *Location and Stigma: Emerging Trends in the Study of Mental Health and Mental Illness.* London: Allen and Unwin.

Smith, C. J., and R. Q. Hanham. 1981. "Any Place but Here! Mental Health Facilities as Noxious Neighbors." *Professional Geographer* 33:326–34.

Smith, D. E. 1993. "What Welfare Theory Hides" In *New Approaches to Welfare Theory,* edited by G. Drover and P. Kerans. Brookfield, Vt.: Edward Elgar.

Smith, D. 1994. *Social Justice and Geography.* London: Blackwell.

Smith, D. H. 1975. "Voluntary Action and Voluntary Groups." *Annual Review of Sociology.* 1:247–70.

Smith, J. D. 1995. *Pieces of Purgatory: Mental Retardation In and Out of Institutions.* Pacific Grove, Calif.: Brooks/Cole Publishing.

Smith, N. 1984. *Uneven Development,* Oxford: Blackwell.

———. 1993. "Homeless/Global: Scaling Places." In *Mapping the Futures: Local Cultures, Global Change,* edited by J. Bird et al. London: Routledge.

Smith, S. J., R. Knill-Jones, and A. McGuckin. 1991. *Housing for Health.* Longman: Harlow.

Smokers' Freedom Society. 1992. Guidelines for the Courteous Smoker. *Today's Smoker* (spring–summer): 5.

Solomon, P. 1983. "Analyzing Opposition to Community Residential Facilities for Troubled Adolescents." *Child Welfare* 62:361–66.

Solomon, Suniti. N.d. AIDS Cell, Madras Medical College, Madras, Tamil Nadu. Personal communication.

Special Committee on Indian Self-Government in Canada. 1983. *Report.* Ottawa: Queen's Printer.

Speck, D. C. 1987. *An Error in Judgement: The Politics of Medical Care in an Indian/White Community.* Vancouver: Talonbooks.

Spector, M., and J. I. Kitsuse. 1977. *Constructing Social Problems.* New York: Benjamin/Cummings Publishing.

Spengler, J., et al. 1994. "Respiratory Symptoms and Housing Characteristics." *Indoor Air* 4:72–82.

Spivey, G. H., and E. P. Radford. 1979. "Inner-city Housing and Respiratory Disease in Children: A Pilot Study." *Archives of Environmental Health* 34:23–29.

Sporik, R., et al. 1990. "Exposure to House-dust Mite Allergen and the Development of Asthma in Childhood." *New England Journal of Medicine* 323:502–7

St. Lawrence, J. S., et al. 1990. "The Stigma of AIDS: Fear of Disease and Prejudice Toward Gay Men." *Journal of Homosexuality* 19, no. 3:85–101.

Stacey, M. 1969. "The Myth of Community Studies." *British Journal of Sociology* 20:134–47.

Standing, H. 1992. "AIDS: Conceptual and Methodological Issues in Researching Sexual Behaviour in Sub-Saharan Africa." *Social Science and Medicine* 34:475–83.

Stave, G. M., and G. W. Jackson. 1991. "Effect of a Total Work-site Smoking Ban on Employee Smoking and Attitudes." *Journal of Occupational Medicine* 33:884–90.

Stein, L. 1952. "T.B. and the 'Social Complex' in Glasgow." *British Journal of Social Medicine* 6:1–48.

Stewart, B. 1981. *The Waters of the Gap: The Mythology of Aquae Sulis.* Bath: Bath City Council.

Stones, R. 1991. *Strategic Context Analysis: A New Research Strategy For Structuration Theory. Sociology,* 25:673–95.

Strachan, D. P. 1988. "Damp Housing and Childhood Asthma: Validation of Reporting of Symptoms." *British Medical Journal* 297:1223–26.

Strachan, D. P., and R. A. Elton. 1986. "Relationship Between Respiratory Morbidity in Children and the Home Environment." *Family Practice* 3:137–42.

Strachan, D. P., and C. H. Sanders. 1989. "Damp Housing and Childhood Asthma: Respiratory Effects of Indoor Temperature and Relative Humidity." *Journal of Epidemiology and Community Health* 43:7–14.

Sundeen, R. A., and S. Fiske. 1982. "Local Resistance to Community-based Care Facilities." *Journal of Offender Counseling, Services and Rehabilitation* 6:29–42.

Surber, R. W., et al. 1988. "Medical and Psychiatric Needs of the Homeless: A Preliminary Response." *Social Work* 33:116–19.

Takahashi, L. 1992. "National Attitudes Towards Controversial Human Services." Ph.D. diss., Univ. of Southern California.

———. 1994. "AIDS, Race, and Community: Minority Attitudes Towards Facilities for People with AIDS." Paper presented at the Annual Conference of the American Collegiate Schools of Planning.

Taket, A. R. 1989. "Equity and Access." *Journal of the Operations Research Society* 40:1001–10.

Taylor, S. M., M. J. Dear, and G. B. Hall. 1979. "Attitudes Toward the Mentally Ill and Reactions to Mental Health Facilities." *Social Science and Medicine* 13D:281–90.

Thomas, J. 1993. "Public Involvement and Government Effectiveness." *Administrative and Society* 24:444–69.

Thomson, W. A. R. 1979. *Black's Medical Dictionary.* London: A. and C. Black.

Thrift, N. J. 1983. "On the Determination of Social Action in Space and Time." *Environment and Planning D: Society and Space* 1, no. 1:23–56.

———. 1987. "No Perfect Symmetry." *Environment and Planning D: Society and Space* 5:400–407.

Tilley, C. 1973. "Do Communities Act?" *Social Inquiry* 43:209–40.

Tobias, J. 1988. "Canada's Subjegation of the Plains Cree 1879–1885." In *Out of the Background: Readings on Canadian Native History,* edited by R. Fisher and K. Coates, 190–219. Toronto: Cop Clark Pitman.

Tönnes, F. 1955. *Community and Society.* New York: Harper and Row.

Torgerson, D. 1986. "Interpretive Policy Inquiry: A Response to Its Limitations." *Policy Sciences* 19:397–405.

Torjman, S. 1988. *Income Insecurity: The Disability Income System in Canada.* North York, Ont.: Roeher Institute.

Touhy, C., and R. Evans. 1984. "Pushing a String." In *The Costs of Federalism,* edited by R. T. Gotembiewski and A. Wildavsky. New Brunswick, N.J.: Transaction Press.

Townsend, P., and N. Davidson, eds. 1982. "Inequalities in Health." In *The Black Report,* edited by P. Townsend and N. Davidson. London: Penguin.

Trigger, B. 1985. *Natives and Newcomers: Canada's Heroic Age Reconsidered.* Montreal: McGill-Queen's Univ. Press.

Tringo, J. L. 1970. "The Hierarchy of Preference Toward Disability Groups." *Journal of Special Education* 4:295–306.

Trute, S. P., and S. P. Segal. 1976. "Census Tract Predictors and the Social Integration of Sheltered Care Residents." *Social Psychiatry* 11:153–59.

Tuan, Y-f. 1974a. "Space and Place: Humanistic Perspective." *Progress in Geography* 6:211–52.

———. 1974b. *Topophilia: A Study of Environmental Perception, Attitudes and Values.* Englewood Cliffs, N.J.: Prentice-Hall.

———. 1976. "Humanistic Geography." *Annals of the Association of American Geographers* 66:206–76.

———. 1977. *Space and Place.* London: Arnold

———. 1979. *Landscapes of Fear.* Oxford: Blackwell.

———. 1991. "Language and the Making of Place: A Narrative-Descriptive Approach." *Annals of the Association of American Geographers* 81, no. 4:684–96.

Turner, B. S. 1987. *Medical Power and Social Knowledge.* Newbury Park, Calif.: Sage.

U.S. Bureau of the Census. 1990. *Census of Population and Housing.* Washington, D.C.

Upton, S. 1991. *Your Health and the Public Health: A Statement of Government Health Policy.* Wellington, N.Z.: Government Print.

Valenzuela, A., and Valenzuela, S., eds. 1986. *Military Rule in Chile.* Baltimore, Md.: Johns Hopkins Univ. Press.

Verba, S., et al. 1993. "Citizen Activity." *American Political Science Review* 87:303–18.

Verba, S., and N. H. Nie. 1972. *Participation in America.* New York: Harper and Row.

Verba, S., K. L. Schlozman, and H. Brady. 1978. *Participation and Political Equality,* Cambridge: Cambridge Univ. Press.

Verdugo, P. 1990. *Tiempo de días claros: Los desaparacidos.* Santiago, Chile: Centros de Estudios Sociales (CESOC).

Vroom, V., and P. Yetton, 1973. *Leadership and Decision-making.* Pittsburgh: Univ. of Pittsburgh Press.

Waegemaekers, M., et al. 1989. "Respiratory Symptoms in Damp Homes." *Allergy* 44:192–98.

Wakesman, B. H., S. C. Reingold, and W. E. Reynolds. 1987. *Research on Multiple Sclerosis.* 3d ed. New York: Demos.

Wallace, R. 1990. "Urban Desertification, Public Health and Public Order: Planned Shrinkage, Violent Death, Substance Abuse and AIDS in the Bronx." *Social Science and Medicine* 31:801–13.

Walter, E. V. 1988. *Placeways* Chapel Hill: Univ. of North Carolina Press.

Ward, J. H. 1963. "Hierarchical Grouping to Optimize an Objective Function." *Journal of the American Statistical Association* 57:572–78.

Warf, B. 1991. "Power, Politics, and Locality." *Urban Geography* 12:563–69.

Warren, R. 1964. "Municipal Services Market Model of Metropolitan Organization." *Journal of the American Institute of Planners* 30:193–204.

———. 1970. "Federal-Local Development Planning." *Public Administration Review* 30:584–95.

Webber, M. M. 1964. "Urban Places and the Non-place Urban Realm." In *Explorations into Urban Structure,* edited by M. M. Webber et al. Philadelphia: Univ. of Pennsylvania Press.

Webster, G. R. 1993. "Congressional Redistricting and African-American Representation in the 1990s." *Political Geography* 12:549–64.

Weil, S. 1955. *The Need for Roots.* Boston: Beacon.

Weinreb, L. F., and E. L. Bassuk. 1990. "Health Problems for Homeless Families." In *Community Care for Homeless Families: A Program Design Manual,* edited by E. L. Bassuk, R. W. Carman, and L. F. Weinreb, 67–82. Newton Center, Mass.: Better Homes Foundation.

Weitzel, R. 1991. *Tumbas de cristal: Libro testimonio de la vicaría de la solidaridad del arzobispado de Santiago.* Santiago, Chile: Ediciones Chile América, CESOC.

Weschler, L. 1990. *A Miracle, a Universe: Settling Accounts with Torturers.* New York: Pantheon Books.

White, P. 1991. "Enemies of the People: The Tobacco Pushers." In *Health Through Public Policy,* edited by P. Draper. London: Merlin Press.

Whitehead, M. 1987. *The Health Divide: Inequalities in Health in the 1980s.* London: Health Education Council.

Whittacker, A., S. Gardner, and J. Kershaw. 1991. *Service Evaluation by People with Learning Difficulties.* London: King's Fund Centre.

Willer, B., and J. Intagliata. 1984. "An Overview of the Social Polity of Deinstitutionalization." In *International Review of Research in Mental Retardation,* edited by N. R. Ellis and N. W. Bray, 1–23. Orlando, Fla.: Academic Press.

Wilner, D. M., et al. 1962. *The Housing Environment and Family Life. A Longitudinal Study of the Effects of Housing on Morbidity and Mental Health.* Baltimore: Johns Hopkins Medical School.

Wilson, E. O. 1984. *Biophilia: The Human Bond with Other Species.* Cambridge, Mass.: Harvard Univ. Press.

Winsor, D. 1980. *The Dream of Bath.* Bath: Travel and Trade Publications.

Wirth, L. 1964. *On Cities and Social Life.* Chicago: Univ. of Chicago Press.

Wolch, J. R. 1990. *The Shadow State: Government and Voluntary Sector in Transition.* New York: Foundation Center

———. 1992. "Skid Row, U.S.A.: Place and Community." In *Geographical Snapshots of North America,* edited by D. G. Janelle, 108–13. New York: Guilford Press.

Wolch, J. R., and M. J. Dear. 1993. *Malign Neglect: Homelessness in an American City.* San Francisco: Jossey-Bass.

Wolch, J. R., M. J. Dear, and A. Akita. 1988. "Explaining Homelessness." *Journal of American Planners Association* (autumn): 443–53.

Wolch, J. R., and R. Geiger. 1983. "The Distribution of Urban Voluntary Resources: An Exploratory Analysis." *Environment and Planning A* 15:1067–82.

Wolch, J. R., A. Rahimian, and P. Kroegal. 1993. "Daily and Periodic Mobility Patterns of the Urban Homeless." *Professional Geographer* 45:159–70.

Wolfensberger, W. 1972. *Normalization: The Normalization Principle in Human Services.* Toronto: National Institute on Mental Retardation.

Wolpert, J. 1976. "Regressive Siting of Public Facilities." *Natural Resources Journal* 16:103–15.

Wood, W. B. 1988. "AIDS North and South: Diffusion Patterns of a Global Epidemic and a Research Agenda for Geographers." *Professional Geographer* 40:266–79.

Woodhouse, P. R., K-T Khaw, and M. Plummer. 1993. "Seasonal Variation of Blood Pressure and Its Relationship to Ambient Temperature in an Elderly Population." *Journal of Hypertension* 11:1267–74.

Workers of the South Dakota Writers' Project, Works Progress Administration. 1941. *Legends of the Mighty Sioux.* Interior, S.D.: Badlands Natural History Press.

World Health Organization (WHO). 1946. *Constitution.* New York: World Health Organization.

———. 1961. *Public Health Aspects of Housing.* World Health Organization Technical Report, ser. no. 225. Geneva, Switzerland.

———. 1978. *Primary Health Care.* Geneva, Switzerland: World Health Organization.

———. 1985. *Research in Health Promotion: Priorities, Strategies, Barriers.* Copenhagen, Denmark: World Health Organization Europe.

———. 1987. *Health Impact of Low Indoor Temperatures.* Copenhagen, Denmark: World Health Organization.

Wright, B. 1972. "Public Health and Housing in Bath." In *Bath in the Age of Reform (1830–1841),* edited by J. Wroughton. Bath: Morgan Books.

Wright, J. D. 1989. *Address Unknown: The Homeless in America.* New York: Aldine de Gruyter.

Wright, P., and A. Treacher. 1982. *The Problem of Medical Knowledge: Examining the Social Construction of Medicine.* Edinburgh: Edinburgh Univ. Press.

Wriston, B. 1978. *Rare Doings at Bath.* Chicago: Art Institute of Chicago.

Wrong, D. 1979. *Power: Its Form, Bases and Uses.* New York: Harper and Row.

Wroughton, J. 1973. *The Civil War in Bath and North Somerset (1642–1650).* Bath: Morgan Books.

Yeates, M. H. 1963. "Hinterland Delimitation." *Professional Geographer* 15:7–10.

Yoon, H-k. (1986). *Maori Mind, Maori Land.* Zurich: Peter Berne.

Young, I. M. 1990. *Justice and the Politics of Difference.* Princeton N. J.: Princeton Univ. Press.

Zakus, J. D., and J. E. Hastings. 1988. "Public Involvement in Health Promotion and Disease Prevention." Health and Welfare Canada, Health Services and Promotion Branch, working paper 88–10. Ottawa.

Zwi, A. 1993. "Reassessing Priorities: Identifying the Determinants of HIV Transmission." *Social Science and Medicine* 36:iii–viii.

Zwi, A., and J. Cabral. 1991. "Identifying 'High Risk Situations' for Preventing AIDS." *British Medical Journal* 303:1527–28.

Index

Agency and structure, 3, 231
Agnew, John, 263
Architecture, 34

Behavior settings, 217–18
Black Hills, 38–39
Bodies, 4, 81, 103, 105–8, 118–19, 221

Canada, 210–11, 250–52, 256, 268
Celts, 18–19
Commercial sex industry, 176–77; condom use in, 177; knowledge of AIDS in, 185; in Madras, 181–87
Community, 270, 279, 282, 285; activism, 229–30, 238–39; attachment, 265; opposition, 139–40, 143–44; reinvention of, 287
Consumers, 250, 277–78
Cultural construction, 17; in geography, 5; of landscape, 7–8

Decentralization, 248–49, 265–66, 278, 280
Deinstitutionalization, 78–79, 81, 95, 161–62
Deprivation, 193, 277
Disability, 78, 115–16; and identity, 113; intellectual, 77–79, 101; services, 115
Discourse analysis, 276, 288
Disease, 6; ecology, 4

Entrikin, Nicholas, 262
Ethnography, 87
Everyday life, 77
Eyles, John, 9, 272–73

Feminist geography, 105–6
Foucault, Michel, 105, 210, 261, 286

Gesler, Wilbert, 292
Goffman, Erving, 210–11, 217, 223
Governmentality, 285–86
Great Chain of Being, 25

Harris, Cole, 37
Healing, 17
Health, 1, 35; care purchasers, 279; commodification of, 36–37; definition of 2, 10–11, 192, 234; geography of, 1–2, 4; link to nature, 46; medical model of, 104–5, 117; policy (British), 275–87;

Health *(continued)*
promotion, 277, targets, 285; trusts, 278, 280
Hierarchies of acceptance, 147–49, 152–54
HIV/AIDS, 162, 165–66, 169; attitudes to facilities for, 153–57, 160; geographical study of, 168, 171–72; in India, 172–75, 178–81; infected blood and, 178–80; prevention of, 169–70; surveillance of, 171–73
Home, 109–14, 116–17, 118–19, 218–19
Hospitals, 8, 31–32, 48, 281, 283
Housing, 193–94; coldness in, 205–6; dampness in, 196, 200–01; deprivation, 194–95; and health relationships, 197–207
Hygiene, 29

Identity, 8–10, 81, 291
India, 172–75, 176–81
Interviewing, 82–84

Jackson, Peter, 7

Kearns, Robin, 3–4, 77, 103, 273

Landscape, 7–8, 289; of terror, 62, 73; therapeutic, 8
Language, 276; of policy, 280
Los Angeles, 127–31, 135–36, 138–39

Madras, 181–87
Maori, 11, 233–39
Marginalization, 100, 146
Medical geography, 1–2, 168, 244, 271–75, 291; and sociocultural theory, 273
Medicine, 11
Mental health, 64–65; and human rights, 70; patients, 222; and torture, 67;
Metaphor, 2, 36–38, 51–52, 60, 291
Method, 3
Multiple sclerosis, 102, 107–8

Nash, Richard, 20, 33, 35
National Health Service (British), 275–76, 278–79, 281
Nettleton, Sarah, 11
New Zealand, 230–31, 232–47, 249
NIMBY syndrome, 139–40, 159–60
Normalization, 78
Nursing, 278

Ontario, 101

Panopticon, 286
Participation, 252–59, 266
Patients, 278
Physicians, 29–30, 48, 258, 281
Pisagua (Chile), 61, 64, 71–72
Place, 2, 143, 259–65, 271–73, 277; and health, 5–6, 81–82; and identity, 82, 260; meaning of, 37, 100, 261; and mental health, 56; naming of, 1, 43, 60; perceptions of, 17; in policy, 262–63; reputation of, 17; sense of, 229; space and, 281, 283, 286, 288
Postmodernism, 9–10, 144; and difference, 144–45; of resistance, 230, 246–47
Power, 146
Primary care, 276–77

Regions, 267
Relph, Edward, 259–60
Representation, 145–46
Respiratory problems, 200–201
Restructuring, 226, 231; health care, 251

Romans, 19
Rose, Gillian, 7

Service hubs, 137
Sioux Nation, 40–42
Skid rows, 138–39
Social entrepreneurs, 229
Social support, 98
Space, 208–9, 218–20; formal and functional, 247, 279; in health policy, 270, 284; public, 208–9, 220; purification of, 221; relational view of, 104
Spas, 20
Special Medical Areas, 234–35
State violence, 91–95
Stigma, 215–17
Symbols, 18, 21

Tarapacá (Chile), 62–64, 67
Territoriality, 223–24
Theory, 2–4
Tobacco, 208; industry, 225
Torture, 58–59
Transcendental social action, 228–29

Voluntary sector, 141

Water, 27–28, 46–47
Well-being, 10–11
Wirth, Louis, 263
Wood, John, 20, 22–26

Zone of dependence, 129–30